Lyrical Satirical
Harold Rome

ALSO BY TIGHE E. ZIMMERS

*Tin Pan Alley Girl: A Biography of Ann Ronell*
(McFarland, 2009)

# Lyrical Satirical Harold Rome

*A Biography of the Broadway Composer-Lyricist*

Tighe E. Zimmers

McFarland & Company, Inc., Publishers
*Jefferson, North Carolina, and London*

LIBRARY OF CONGRESS CATALOGUING-IN-PUBLICATION DATA

Zimmers, Tighe E., 1949–
    Lyrical satirical Harold Rome : a biography of the Broadway composer-lyricist / Tighe E. Zimmers.
        p.    cm.
    Includes bibliographical references and index.

    **ISBN 978-0-7864-7026-6**
    softcover : acid free paper ∞

    1. Rome, Harold, 1908–1993.    2. Composers—United States—Biography.    3. Lyricists—United States—Biography. I. Title.

ML410.R63298Z56 2014
782.1'4092—dc23
[B]                                                            2013032596

BRITISH LIBRARY CATALOGUING DATA ARE AVAILABLE

© 2014 Tighe E. Zimmers. All rights reserved

*No part of this book may be reproduced or transmitted in any form or by any means, electronic or mechanical, including photocopying or recording, or by any information storage and retrieval system, without permission in writing from the publisher.*

Manufactured in the United States of America

*McFarland & Company, Inc., Publishers*
  *Box 611, Jefferson, North Carolina 28640*
    *www.mcfarlandpub.com*

To Molly Elizabeth Fontana and Maggie Clare Zimmers.
We are so glad you're here.
I can't wait for you to hear all the old songs.

# Acknowledgments

*Special thanks to the following*: Joshua Rome, son of Harold Rome, who was most helpful in a personal interview and shared family photographs with me; Emily Ferrigno, public services assistant, and other members of the staff of the Irving S. Gilmore Library of Yale University who gave much assistance with the Harold Rome Papers.

*Thanks to the personnel of libraries, collections, and various institutions*: Morgen Stevens-Garmon, theater collections archivist, and staff members of the Museum of the City of New York; Mark Horowitz, senior music specialist, and staff members of the Music Division of the Library of Congress; Maryann Chach, director, the Shubert Archive, New York; Bryna Freyer, curator, National Museum of African Art, Smithsonian Institution, Washington, D.C.; New York Public Library for the Performing Arts: Performing Arts Research Collections, Special Collections, and Billy Rose Theatre Collection; New York Public Library, Schomburg Center for Research in Black Culture and Dorot Jewish Division; the Paley Center for Media; New York; the Park Ridge Public Library and Oakton Public Library, Illinois; the Hartford Public Library, Connecticut.

*Thanks to family, friends and others who helped out in various ways*: readers and critics of my various drafts of the book: my wife Noreen, my sister Malilee Elis; my computer wizards, Kathy and Patrick Donahue; the friendly staffs at the Starbucks Coffee shops where I did much of my work; Jerry Rome, nephew of Harold Rome, Hartford; proofreaders Joan Dahlquist, Ellen Davidson, Gail Mandell, and the Donahues.

*Thanks to others interested in the world of music*: cabaret singers Joan Curto and Justin Hayford, both of whom read early chapters; author John Bush Jones; composer-director Barry Kleinbort; musical theatre scholar-writer Bruce F. Wiener.

# Table of Contents

*Acknowledgments* vi
*Preface* 1

1. Early Life and Career 5
2. Harold Rome and the ILGWU 10
3. *Pins and Needles* on Broadway 17
4. Kaufman and Hart and *Sing Out the News* 26
5. Political Endeavors and *The Little Dog Laughed* 34
6. Wartime Efforts 42
7. Vernon Duke and Other Work 54
8. *Call Me Mister* and the Revue 57
9. The 1950 Shows 70
10. Liberal Politics and the Right Wing 82
11. *Wish You Were Here* 85
12. Movie Work and Shows Gone Awry 94
13. *Fanny* 99
14. *Destry Rides Again* 117
15. *I Can Get It for You Wholesale* 127
16. *Harold Rome's Gallery* and Artistic Endeavors 142
17. The 1965 Shows and African Art 149
18. *Scarlett* in Japan 162
19. *Gone with the Wind* in London and America 174
20. Later Years 187

*Appendices*
   A. Chronology   199
   B. Songs   202
   C. Song Recordings and Artists   215
   D. Discography   216
   E. Cast Recordings of Harold Rome's Musicals   217
   F. Chronology of Produced Shows   217
   G. Chronology of Unproduced Shows   218
   H. Movie Work   219
   I. Political Endeavors   220

*Chapter Notes*   222
*Bibliography*   245
*Index*   253

# Preface

"His interests and enthusiasms are considerably broader than those of the average songwriter." — Theodore Goldsmith

Years ago, by serendipity, I bought a used album of Bobby Short doing the songs of Cole Porter. Here were great songs — hits and others that were never done outside of Porter shows — performed and put into context by a master of cabaret. It hooked me on the American Popular Songbook. Over the years, Short worked his way through the American popular composers in his shows and albums. I first saw him at the Café Carlyle doing the songs of Henderson, DeSylva, and Brown, whom I had barely heard of, and was amazed at what they had written, when, and in what context. Through the years, other cabaret performers have been doing the same including Julie Wilson, Andrea Marcovici, Barbara Cook, K.T. Sullivan, Karen Mason, Joan Curto, Justin Hayford, and Philip Officer, among many others.

Without any singing talent, my involvement with these songs has been confined to amateur piano playing and collecting autographs of the composers and performers of their songs. Thirteen years ago, I bought a 25-box collection of the papers of Ann Ronell, the composer of "Willow Weep for Me." In the boxes were letters, notes, and other information, and it dawned on me that there was a book in those papers of Ms. Ronell and her eclectic talents. It eventually became *Tin Pan Alley Girl: A Biography of Ann Ronell*, published in 2009 by McFarland. I soon began looking for another composer about whom to write.

Irving Berlin, Jerome Kern, George and Ira Gershwin, Cole Porter, Richard Rodgers and Lorenz Hart and Oscar Hammerstein II, Duke Ellington, Frank Loesser, Alan Jay Lerner, Frederic Loewe, Harold Arlen, E.Y. Harburg, Sigmund Romberg, Kurt Weill, Stephen Sondheim, Jule Styne, Harry Warren, and Hoagy Carmichael have all had two or more works devoted to them. I found there were several important composers who had been overlooked, most notably Burton Lane, Arthur Schwartz, and Harold Rome.

Rome caught my eye. I knew him from the title songs of his shows *Fanny* and *Wish You Were Here* as Eddie Fisher had had a hit with each. I also knew through autographs that he had studied law but that music and art were his interests. As happened with Ann Ronell, the deeper I got into his body of work, the more interesting it became. He began his musical career playing piano for dance bands and started doing regular composing at an adult summer camp in the Catskills. His songs attracted the attention of the producers of a revue for the International Ladies' Garment Workers' Union. The show became *Pins and Needles*, ran for 1,108 performances, and launched Rome's Broadway career.

Harold Rome is important because of his contributions to the American Popular Songbook and his catalogue of Broadway musicals. Although it may be folly to judge the best of the best, one way to view these composers is to look at their best five shows. Except for Ellington and Carmichael, the aforementioned gentlemen all had five successful Broadway shows or more. From 1938 through 1959, Rome, as both composer and lyricist, wrote a series of shows that withstand the test of time. These include *Pins and Needles, Call Me Mister, Wish You Were Here, Fanny,* and *Destry Rides Again.* They each ran over 400 performances and toured outside of New York, and songs from each became part of the American Popular Songbook.

Rome was different from many of the prominent composers. By the time he began composing, Tin Pan Alley was mostly gone or had moved uptown. But then he might not have done well there as he would not have been a great song plugger like George Gershwin or Jimmy McHugh. Rome was not much of a self-promoter.

The era of operetta would not have been to his liking because those shows required marches and beautiful waltzes written to stand by themselves in a setting of nostalgic continental life. He left that to Sigmund Romberg and Rudolph Friml. Rome needed an idea and purpose for his songs, often touched with a bit of satire.

Hollywood held no draw for him. He left movies and the money to Frank Loesser, Harry Warren, and others. When he wrote his songs, he wanted them performed as written and did not want a studio producer or music department head dictating how and when a song would be used. By his own admission, California seldom called. And besides, Rome was a confirmed New Yorker.

Rome began his career writing songs for musical revues — *Pins and Needles* and *Sing Out the News* — music and lyrics with satire and "social significance." As Broadway musicals evolved, so did Rome's work. Under the influence of Rodgers and Hammerstein and Lerner and Loewe, the book musical began to dominate the Great White Way. Rome tried his hand at this art form and had great success with *Wish You Were Here* and *Fanny*. Not to be forgotten is that Rome wrote both words and music, a talent limited to but a few on Broadway.

Beyond his music, Rome was a painter, African art collector, and a supporter of liberal, often controversial causes. Although he was never called before the House Un-American Activities Committee, several of his pursuits drew the interest of right wing organizations and the Federal Bureau of Investigation. As late as 1965, he was writing songs of social concern with *The Zulu and the Zayda,* a play with music. A journalist said of Rome: "His interests and enthusiasms are considerably broader than those of the average songwriter."[1]

A few comments about writing this biography. There was a large collection of information at several institutions, most importantly the Gilmore Music Library at Yale University, to which Rome had donated his papers. From these collections, I relied on newspaper articles of the day, reviews, interviews, and critical commentary. These sources were accurate, written during the period of his work, in the language and context of that time. There were also numerous pages of notes by Rome himself — typed or handwritten — which were on point. Helpful for Chapters 18 and 19 were the comments of Rome's wife, Florence, in *Scarlett Letters,* her memoir of their trip to work on his show *Scarlett* in Japan. Her book was completed within a year of that show.

There are few interviews of people with whom Rome worked, as they were his age and had passed on. Those younger — mostly the singers and dancers — I did not speak with. Efforts to contact the stars of his shows who are still alive were unproductive. When I wrote *Tin Pan Alley Girl: A Biography of Ann Ronell,* I found interviews to be inaccurate. The interviews I have included were done by musical director Lehman Engel and are part of the Lehman Engel Collection, also at the Gilmore Music Library. Engel's interview with Rome himself has several inaccuracies. There were also several taped interviews of Rome in various collections at the New York Public Library.

There was one interview I did do that was an exception to all this. Harold Rome's son, Joshua, was extremely helpful in giving me a sense of the personality of his father. He also filled in some dates and places but admitted freely when he was unaware of something. Our interview at his home in Wells, Vermont, was one of my best experiences in doing this biography.

With the information available, I have put together *Lyrical and Satirical: A Biography of Harold Rome.* I hope it will educate the reader of a songwriter who has been overlooked and deserves a high place in the history of Broadway and popular song.

*Chapter 1*

# Early Life and Career

"I was fancy at the piano. I had a 'sound.'" — Harold Rome

Harold Rome said he began piano at age seven because "[i]t was what was done in middle class Jewish families at that time."[1] Born May 27, 1908, he was the first child of Louis Rome and Ida Aronson; born in Vilna, Russia, they had come to America in their teens.[2] Louis was the president of the Connecticut Coal and Charcoal Company in Hartford, and Ida raised Harold and his siblings Sidney, Milton, Ruth, and Betty. Louis and Ida acclimated to their new country and seldom was anything spoken besides English. Although the children attended synagogue and participated in Jewish rites and rituals, neither parent was religious nor was Judaism of importance in the household. Rome carried this into his adult life.[3]

What also carried over to the Rome offspring was an appreciation of the arts which were burgeoning in the country: modern art, jazz, musical theater, and America's own classical composers. All five Rome children took piano, and Harold, showing talent early on, was soon enrolled in an experimental program in Hartford where children learned to read music as they were learning reading.[4] Presaging his career, Rome won a songwriting contest at age ten, urging citizens to buy bonds: "If you want to help Uncle Sam, buy a bond, buy a bond, buy a bond!" he sang cheerily to an interviewer sixty years later.[5] His musical training began in earnest at the Arsenal School which he attended prior to Hartford High School. One of his first songs was about his former teachers at Arsenal, and another featured the drug store in his neighborhood at the corner of Sigourney and Ashley streets.[6] By his teen years, he was a member of the local musicians' union in Hartford.[7]

It was the twenties and jazz and dance bands were flourishing, each one needing a pianist. Jazz had drifted to the East Coast from New Orleans, Chicago, and Kansas City. Big bands had formed all over the country as people not only wanted to hear jazz, but they also wanted to dance: the fox

Harold "Hecky" Rome at piano with big band at the Roger Sherman Theatre in New Haven, Connecticut, in 1928 (courtesy Gilmore Music Library, Yale University).

trot, the Charleston, and a dozen other dances of the era. Composers of the day were providing plenty of songs for Tin Pan Alley, Broadway, and the growing medium of radio. The bands would take these songs and create jazz or dance arrangements for their audiences. Rome liked the music and the work — and the money. The Harold Rome Papers at the Gilmore Music Library of Yale University contain a marvelous picture of a big band at Hartford, Connecticut's, Roger Sherman Theatre. Seated at the piano on the left side is a 19-year-old Harold Rome, hair parted in the middle in the style of the day. The nineteen band members are in tuxedoes and project a feeling of youth and professionalism. There are numerous wind instruments and a rhythm section that includes a banjo.

Rome's talent flourished and his skills were in demand. Years later, he explained his success: "I was fancy at the piano. I had a 'sound.' The sound was, to those listening: 'This kid sounds as though he could do much better things if people would give him a chance.'"[8] The young pianist was to get that chance when he went to college and played in dance bands.

Rome started at Trinity College in Hartford, but felt too much like a "townie" and transferred to Yale.[9] Soon after, he became pianist for Eddie Wittstein's band, accompanying dances at Smith, Dartmouth, and Yale as well as the New Haven Lawn and Country Clubs. At the time, there was anti–Semitism at the New Haven school, and Rome became a member of a Jewish fraternity, Tau Epsilon Phi. The bigotry on campus did not bother him because, as he explained almost fifty years later, "That's the way things were. There was no way to fight against it." In the same interview, he admitted he "loved Yale."[10] Years later he was to work on *Pins and Needles*, a show for the International Ladies' Garment Workers' Union, and said of that experience: "It was the first time for me that I'd seen real democracy in action because in that union there was no prejudice of any kind, color, or ethnic origin or anything else. Everybody was treated alike. For a boy fresh from Yale where Jews were frowned on, it was quite an experience."[11]

After earning his Bachelor of Arts in 1929, Rome began at Yale Law School. Within two years, he decided he did not want to become a lawyer, which probably would have meant joining his uncle's firm back in Hartford. Rome was not the only songwriter of his era to reject the law. Those who studied but practiced little or none included Cole Porter, Hoagy Carmichael, Oscar Hammerstein II, Kim Gannon, Arthur Schwartz, and Ralph Rainger.[12] Porter's study of the law was particularly brief.

Quitting law school did not mean leaving Yale for Rome soon enrolled in the School of Architecture, graduating with a Bachelor of Fine Arts in 1934.[13] Eight years was a long time to be earning bachelor degrees, and Rome kidded a symposium audience years later that he "[s]pent ten years in college and came out a bum."[14] He was quick to point out that he had an annual net "twice what any professor there was earning and it seemed silly to let go of a good thing."[15] During these years, Rome was making a living accompanying dance classes, teaching piano, writing band arrangements, vocal coaching, and playing in college dance bands including the Yale Collegians.[16] He was also a member the Yale Orchestra which made four trips to Europe during his tenure in New Haven. The summer after Yale, he toured the South in a band with Miss America.[17]

Rome went to find work as an architect in the midst of the Depression, when nobody was "building anything but apple stands."[18] His first job was in the Works Progress Administration (W.P.A.) surveying the Holland Tunnel and old buildings in Greenwich Village.[19] He was then hired by the New York firm of William Lescaze[20] but his architectural career floundered within a year as he tried to perform and compose in his off hours, sometimes in conflict with his job.[21] Rome described the end of it all:

> I was a hired architect at $10 a week. Although this was $8.15 a week more than most bank presidents were earning at the time, I took a haughty stance for $15 and was forthwith thrown, not ushered, out into the bleak streets. By then, I knew what I had to do: I had to play piano and not design houses.[22]

By this time, he had found work at Green Mansions, an adult camp in the Catskill Mountains. Green Mansions afforded him the opportunity to be composer, lyricist, and sketch writer for the entertainment presented every weekend that used employees and sometimes willing visitors in the casts: "Green Mansions was a great experience because in a place like that, at least in those days, they had a resident cast. [You would] write the show, see the audience reaction, and rewrite the show."[23] It trained Rome to be open to anything, an absolute necessity for his future on Broadway. He was to learn that Broadway shows evolved as they were being created. What seemed like genius one day might be thrown out a week later and have to be rewritten, usually on short notice. Musical theater history is filled with stories of major revisions during late night sessions in hotel rooms with the director, book writer, and composers — and a producer on edge. George S. Kaufman, one of the theater's true geniuses, told Rome early on: "A musical isn't written; it's rewritten."[24]

Rome was also able to hone his satirical talent, writing lyrics of the foibles of the day and having fun with camp visitors. He remembered: "I was in with a couple of left-wing writers. We did social significance. We did what we thought were numbers having political significance or satirical political significance."[25] These shows were free and allowed Rome the liberty to experiment with "an audience that dared to be entertained."[26] He told an interviewer years later of the Green Mansions audiences: "They would accept a kind of social comment which at the time Broadway wouldn't take."[27] Twenty years later, he and Arthur Kober would collaborate on a story and songs for *Wish You Were Here* based on Green Mansions and similar camps from that era (see Chapter 11).

During his three-summer stint in the Catskills, Rome wrote nine revues with 100 songs which he began to peddle to producers and song publishers, with little success.[28] He managed to sell a song to Gypsy Rose Lee, "For Charity, Sweet Charity," for $80 and another one, "Horror Boys of Hollywood," for the 1936 Sonja Henie movie *One in a Million*. The latter song, co-written with Lester Lee, was sung by the Ritz Brothers — Al, Harry, and Jimmy — as they roller-skated on an ice rink while imitating Charles Laughton, Boris Karloff, and Peter Lorre.[29]

Part of the problem of not being able to sell his songs was one which would plague Rome for years, that his writing had too much "social significance." He was politically involved throughout his professional life and that carried over to his songwriting. He was never afraid to engage an audience in the issues and ideas of the day, usually left-wing, if not radical. By his admission, "[H]idden in my subconscious mind there was always a tune and a catch-line of social significance."[30] Publishers, producers, Broadway, and Tin

Pan Alley shied away from this: "[A]lmost unanimous in their reactions: nobody, they chorused, wanted to hear songs about the nation's current problems while the economic situation was still so serious [1935–36]."[31] A few years later, critic Richard Watts "rejoiced that [Cole Porter's] *Leave It to Me* had no social significance."[32] The same could be said of Hollywood.[33] Rome, of course, disagreed with them all: "People enjoy facing their problems in the theater. Being aware of issues of the day is important, and it's good theater to couple such problems with the technique of writing. Audiences don't go to the theater to forget. They go to be moved or entertained, and the trick is to do both jobs with a song."[34]

With no more architecture in his life and few song sales, Rome had to rely on his piano skills. Then he met Louis Schaffer of the International Ladies' Garment Workers' Union.

*Chapter 2*

# Harold Rome and the ILGWU

"Rome's only political agenda was satire, satire of everyone and everything in his contemporary society."—Amanda Ameer

It started as trade union propaganda, the brainchild of David Dubinsky, president of the International Ladies' Garment Workers' Union (ILGWU).[1] It ended as the longest running Broadway musical up to that time, a masterful revue that tried to "draw blood as well as laughter,"[2] with words and music by Harold Rome, a budding songwriter.

In the mid-thirties, America's labor movement had public relations problems, and membership in unions had dropped severely. The ILGWU had bucked this pattern to some degree, mostly because of Dubinsky's leadership. The union had been formed in 1900; by winning organizing battles across the country, its membership rose to 100,000 around 1920. In 1926, its image and influence were adversely affected when a communist faction within the union attempted to gain control.[3] Through Dubinsky's efforts, the takeover was averted but enrollment continued to drop, plummeting as low as 24,000 in 1931 because of the Depression. A year later, Dubinsky was elected president of the ILGWU and came to prominence in the national labor movement as well. By 1935, helped by the improved image of the union under Dubinsky's leadership and pro-labor measures of Franklin Roosevelt's New Deal, membership had risen to 217,000.[4]

Dubinsky had appointed Louis Schaffer head of the union's Cultural Division of the Educational and Recreational Department. This was the creation of Dubinsky, who wanted his members to have opportunities for further education, physical activities, and exposure to the arts, "to create a better-working environment for union members."[5] The courses offered included tap dancing, mandolin, acting, choral groups, and elocution.[6] Dubinsky felt this "social education" had a twofold purpose for the union: "[F]irst, the union members became better-rounded, educated and contributing citizens. Second, the union made the best possible contact with the non-union public."[7] Other projects of the Cultural Division included participation in Labor Stage, Inc., a collaboration of several of the needle trade unions, designed to become a labor-based professional theater. However, as union enrollment declined during the Depression, the other unions pulled out, so with Dubinsky's support, Labor Stage became the amateur theater solely of the ILGWU.[8]

Labor Stage was not the first theater ensemble to mix entertainment and politics. Groups including the Workers' Theatre, Yiddish Theatre, Workers' Laboratory Theatre, Theatre Union, and the Federal Theatre Project had pioneered this.[9] Although these theater groups usually performed dramas to further social or political agendas, musicals had also been attempted. In 1935, Paul Peters, George Sklar, and Jerome Moross had collaborated on a musical revue, *Parade*, whose skits included satires of radio demagogues, society matrons, a Hearst reporter, and tabloid accounts of bomb-throwing Reds. *Parade* achieved minimal success with only forty performances as its songs and sketches lacked "sparkle ... bite ... and good humor."[10]

One of the first theatrical attempts by Labor Stage was *Steel*, a drama labeled by its author John Wexler "a proletarian document." Focusing on a steel workers' strike, the play was too somber to be a success, although it was staged over fifty times between New York and steel town Pittsburgh. Schaffer had produced *Steel* and realized that he, the union, and Labor Stage had to take a different tack: "What people wanted," Schaffer claimed, "was amusement and not class consciousness."[11] Art historian Amanda Ameer further explained:

> Schaffer recognized 1. the need to attract a wider audience, and 2. that the only way to do that would be to create a highly entertaining product. Schaffer had the idea of creating an amateur labor revue that was funny and witty. This idea was in complete contrast to the solemn, far left-wing proletarian dramas so popular at the time.[12]

Schaffer and Dubinsky envisioned a show poking fun at current issues of the day (including both sides of the union issue) that they hoped would improve the ILGWU image. To merge entertainment and politics and improve the union's image, Schaffer was the perfect man:

> Schaffer is a veteran newspaperman and labor editor with a long background in the socialist movement and in business. He is the typical New Yorker — breezy, sophisticated and extremely likable. His sense of publicity is far more Broadway than "proletarian." He is a sort of link between the theatrical world and the New York labor movement.[13]

Schaffer aimed to deliver the union's message, disguised in skits and songs, witty and thoughtful. Not a creative artist himself, Schaffer needed to engage a bona fide songwriter, but the problem was this: "It seemed that the regular revue contributors didn't know labor, and left-wing writers and composers didn't know revue technique."[14] Enter Harold Rome, a little-known composer of words and music who had achieved success writing skits and songs for Green Mansions, an adult camp in the Borscht Belt.

Upstate New York's Catskill Mountains encompassed numerous resorts, predominantly Jewish, designed for one- or two-week getaways for adults featuring plenty of planned activities and frequent musical entertainment. Other theatrical "graduates" of the Catskills included Moss Hart, Allen Boretz, Charles Friedman, Jack Murray, and Arthur Kober.[15] Kober and Rome would use their upstate experience in creating the successful 1952 musical *Wish You Were Here*, based on Kober's play *Having Wonderful Time*. Similar camps in the Poconos also served as starting points for theater careers, including Unity House, run by the ILGWU, and Camp Tamiment, established by the socialist Rand Institute in the twenties. In the late thirties, the staff at the latter included Imogene Coca, Jerome Robbins, Jules Munshin, Danny Kaye, Sylvia Fine, and dancers Dorothy Bird and Anita Alvarez.[16]

At the time Labor Stage began developing its musical show, to be called *Pins and Needles* (*P & N*), Rome was employed part-time in a WPA Theater Project but had little else pending. He stopped by Schaffer's office to offer several lyrics, and when Schaffer showed interest, Rome played him the accompanying melodies. In an interview with Rome years later, *Chicago Tribune* critic Cecil Smith concluded: "At precisely that psychological moment, Mr. Schaffer was shaping up his idea for the first edition of *P & N*, and Harold Rome's vivacious songs, shot thru and thru with 'social significance,' looked like the right bet."[17]

Rome was a decade or more removed from the initial wave of writers of American Popular Song who had composed numerous hits for Tin Pan Alley, Broadway and early Hollywood. These included Irving Berlin, Jerome Kern, George and Ira Gershwin, Cole Porter, Harry Warren, Richard Rodgers, Lorenz Hart, E.Y. Harburg, and Oscar Hammerstein. Rome began as a dance band pianist in high school and college but had done little composing prior to his Green Mansions assignment. Weekend entertainments at the camp required a large outpouring from Rome, and over his three summers there he penned more than ninety songs.

Unlike his famous predecessors, he had never worked as a song plugger on the Alley, never been involved in a Broadway production, and had never been invited to Hollywood for the easy money the prominent composers were earning there at the time. The song publishers were not interested in Rome's work, as Richard Carlin explained in the *American National Biography*:

> Most of his songs had topical content, commenting on the plight of the worker during the depression years, an unusual topic for popular songs of the day, so he met with little success in selling his music to the standard popular publishers.... While writing in a typical pop style of the day, the topical content of his lyrics was daring, mirroring the work of left-leaning folk song writers like Woody Guthrie.[18]

From another compendium, *The Encyclopedia of Popular Music*:

> Much of the music Rome was writing at this time was socially conscious and was thus of little interest to Tin Pan Alley.... More than any other American composer in the field of mainstream popular music, Rome's work consistently demonstrated an awareness of social issues, often to the extent that it kept him from the massive successes enjoyed by many of his contemporaries.[19]

But Rome had a facile mind, was extremely attuned to current affairs, and was constantly improving his artistic skills. Over the years, he studied piano with Arthur Lloyd and Loma Roberts and composition and orchestration with Reuven Kosakoff, Tim Timothy, Meyer Kupferman, Lehman Engel and Joseph Schillinger.[20] Engel had been music director for Kurt Weill's *Johnny Johnson* in 1936 and would serve in that capacity for most of Rome's future shows. Kupferman would later do orchestrations for Rome's *Scarlett/Gone with the Wind* in the seventies. Studying with the Russian-born Schillinger was important to Rome's career. Schillinger had come from a strict musical education system as well as a strong mathematics background. He was committed to turning out professional musicians — performers, popular and classical composers, and arrangers. Among those he taught and advised were Henry Cowell, Tommy Dorsey, George Gershwin, Benny Goodman, Oscar Levant, Glenn Miller, Gerry Mulligan, John Lewis, and Vernon Duke.[21]

Under the influences of his several music teachers, Rome's composing abilities developed well. His lyric writing was more developed as he had a wonderful sense of humor and satire, both of which Schaffer and Dubinsky needed to promote their union and yet entertain. Despite his lack of experience, Rome was an excellent choice:

> Perhaps it was his lack of political bias that allowed Rome to freely criticize both the radical left and right and everyone who wavered in between. Unlike many of his contemporary proletarian dramatists and writers, Rome's only political agenda was satire, satire of everyone and everything in his contemporary society.[22]

Rome's attitude toward his lack of bias was expressed well in *The New Yorker*, several weeks after *P & N* opened, in "Talk of the Town":

> Young Harold Rome (words and music) was patiently giving out the piano accompaniment. We crept up behind him and whispered, "Are you a Leftist?"

He didn't miss a note. "It's not a question of being a Leftist," he whispered back. "It's a question of keeping your eyes open."[23]

Another advantage for the Labor Stage producers was that Rome wrote both words and music, saving them the cost of another creator. One critic said of Rome's words and music skills, "[I]n nearly all of his songs the tune and the text give a happy impression of having been conceived together."[24] Beyond this, the composer was also to serve as rehearsal pianist for the show. Rome later admitted that while he was excited to write songs for the show, he was more enthused to have a steady job as the rehearsal pianist for $25 a week.[25]

Initially, the amateur performers of the ILGWU balked at the idea of a musical revue. Sure it could not deliver their message, they wanted a more serious work. To sell them on it, Schaffer cobbled together professional entertainers and put on a shortened version of *P & N* for the union members at the Belmont Theatre on Broadway with Rome and Earl Robinson at the pianos. Several producers saw this one-time presentation in June of 1936, and more than a few thought it might be Broadway material, with one, the owner of the Belmont, making a preliminary offer to keep the show right there and continue on. But Schaffer held firm and convinced the amateurs that the show was substantial and that "humor and song were better weapons with which to fight the Union cause than any grim drama."[26] He felt it was worth doing at their own theater, Labor Stage, and that they need not go to Broadway. Rome later said of Schaffer's resolve: "I couldn't believe it, here was a chance to go to Broadway and Schaffer, that lunatic, stood pat!"[27]

Dubinsky and Schaffer felt that the use of these theater amateurs—union professionals on their own stage better presented their message. "In press releases, Schaffer stressed that his new group did not intend to pose as professional, noting that no one performing in an ILGWU production was a trained actor, actress or musician; they all literally came from behind the sewing machines."[28] To *The New Yorker*, Schaffer averred: "There are absolutely no ringers—everybody's a paid-up member of the ILGWU."[29] Rome's position as rehearsal pianist was a real commitment, as he explained: "[T]hese were untrained kids for the most part and at times it was pretty slow going."[30] The performers were all union members—cutters, pressers, dressmakers, operators, pinkers, finishers and a Bonnaz embroiderer (operator of the Bonnaz embroidery machine)—working their jobs on the manufacturing line during the week, attending rehearsals on offtime.[31] Typically, they rehearsed three hours after work, three nights a week, and often on weekends.[32] One of the lead singers, Ruth Rubinstein, said, "While at work, I would keep peeping into my machine drawer where I kept the lines of the new skit or song, memorizing as the brassieres flowed out of the machine."[33]

All were amateurs, a few having received a bit of theatrical training at the artistic workshops run by the ILGWU's Cultural Division, and all required instructions in the skills needed for a musical — singing, dancing, and acting. Rome, who had done his share of vocal coaching at Green Mansions, said, "I remember having to take Ruth Rubinstein, who had two solos, into Central Park to make her yell at the top of her voice so that she could learn how to project in the theater."[34] A small group of men — members of cutters and knitwear locals — became a harmonizing quartet under Rome's tutelage.[35]

Upon recommendations by Rome and director Charles Friedman, Schaffer called upon a number of young, professional writers of the time to contribute skits and ideas. Arnold B. Horwitt would go on to write sketches and lyrics for *Make Mine Manhattan*, a successful 1948 revue, and lyrics for another, *Plain and Fancy*, which focused on Pennsylvania Amish life and featured the song "Young and Foolish."[36] Horwitt would also write sketches with Arnold M. Auerbach for Rome's successful postwar review *Call Me Mister*. John Latouche, in his late teens at the time, also created sketches. He was to write lyrics for three musicals with Vernon Duke including *Cabin in the Sky*. Most importantly, Latouche was lyricist for the critically and popularly successful *The Golden Apple* with Jerome Moross, composer of the aforementioned *Parade*. Latouche died twenty years after *P & N*, while working on Leonard Bernstein's *Candide*.[37]

Schaffer's third wunderkind was Marc Blitzstein, recently famous for *The Cradle Will Rock* with John Houseman as producer and Orson Welles as director. The idea behind *Cradle* had been given to Blitzstein by German dramatist Bertolt Brecht, who suggested a musical play featuring all members of the establishment as prostitutes. It was written under the aegis of the Federal Theatre Project and then cancelled by that same organization when it deemed the subject too politically sensitive. A dramatic last-minute change of venue so that the show could go on is a part of theater lore. One of Blitzstein's skits for *P & N* poked direct fun at the Federal Theatre Project, "FTP Plowed Under."[38] He was a proponent of new music and forms and his works, socially and politically sensitive, met with limited commercial success. He often wrote incidental music for plays, but his most successful venture was a translation and adaptation of Kurt Weill's *The Threepenny Opera*.[39]

Besides Horwitt, Latouche, Blitzstein, and Rome, other sketch writers included Arthur Arent, David Gregory, Joseph Schrank, Friedman, and the press agent of the ILGWU, Emmanuel Eisenberg.[40] Although they were mostly liberal and pro-union, the show attempted to remain good-humored as it satirized bigots, big business, communists, Daughters of the American Revolution, Fascists, Nazis, reactionaries and warmongers — in no particular order — as well as labor unions and the labor movement.[41] Commenting on the show's give-

and-take, Stanley Green wrote: "Perhaps [its] most winning trait was the ability to laugh at the labor movement itself while also, of course, taking jabs at the foibles of those on the other side of the bargaining table."[42]

*P & N* and its creators were not alone in their satire of the American scene as other Broadway shows of the period were also heavily political. Music historian Laurence Maslon elaborated in *Broadway: The American Musical*:

> The style of the shows ranged from the sublime to the ridiculous — but they each caught a different facet of the American consciousness. By the fall of 1937, it looked as if the depression would be forever clouding the skies. A whopping budget deficit, a series of explosive struggles between management and labor, the progressive unionization of America — these events filled the headlines and made their appearance, one way or another, on the Broadway musical stage.[43]

Stanley Green wrote specifically about these shows:

> The season of 1937–1938 provided theatergoers with four political musicals containing viewpoints ranging from mildly liberal to radical: *I'd Rather Be Right* (President Roosevelt and his administration); Marc Blitzstein's *The Cradle Will Rock* (the evils of capitalism and the virtues of the working class); *Hooray for What!* (the need for international disarmament); and *Pins and Needles*.
> Of them all, it was *Pins and Needles* that won the largest following.[44]

To present their amateur musical, Labor Stage had at its disposal the historic Princess Theatre, famous for the eponymous shows created by Jerome Kern, Guy Bolton, and P.G. Wodehouse from 1915 through 1918. The 299-seat theater, renamed Labor Stage, was a good size for a show with few expectations and a planned short run, and it was by chance the union had acquired it. Ethan Mordden, in his review of 1930s Broadway musical *Sing for Your Supper*, explained:

> This is the fluke: The International Ladies' Garment Workers' Union took over the Princess building as a recreation center, possibly only because it stood mere blocks from the garment center where the union members worked. But for the fact that there was a perfectly utilizable auditorium downstairs, it seems unlikely that the union ever would have considered mounting a show....[45]

It was all about to happen.

*Chapter 3*

# *Pins and Needles* on Broadway

"But when it came to portraying the working class man or woman, Harold Rome was about the best in the business." — Thomas S. Hischak

After eighteen months of rehearsals with their willing amateurs, *Pins and Needles* was brought into Labor Stage by Harold Rome, director Charles Friedman, Louis Schaffer et al., opening on November 27, 1937. Its opening was unlike that of any previous Broadway musicals:

> One of the show's virtues was the rapport established between performers and audience. In place of an orchestra, two pianists (one of them Harold Rome himself) strolled down the aisle and took their places. When the curtain went up, cast members described their work, and then broke into the witty "Sing Me a Song with Social Significance."[1]

For the first several weeks, Rome and Baldwin Bergersen were the "orchestra," each playing a Steinway. The original cast members, listed with each one's local, were as follows[2]:

Lydia Annucci 62, Whitegoods
Sol Babchin 10, Cutters
Sadie Bershadsky 22, Dressmakers
Anne Brown 155, Knitgoods
Rose Czitron 22, Dressmakers
Vincent Dazieri 10, Cutters
Sam Dratch 60, Pressers
Zitta Edinburgh 22, Dressmakers
Al Eben 117, Cloakmakers
Anthony Fazio 145, Dressmakers
Tillie Feldman 22, Dressmakers

Irene Fox 22, Dressmakers

Rose Kaufman 22, Dressmakers
Bella Kinburn 22, Dressmakers
Al Levy 22, Dressmakers
Elias Levine 10, Cutters
May Martin 91, Children's Dressmakers
Murray Modick 60, Pressers
Bettie Morrison 22, Dressmakers
Miriam Morrison 22, Dressmakers
Rose Newmark 22, Dressmakers
Jean Newman 22, Dressmakers
Olive Pearman 91, Children's Dressmakers
Joseph Roth 10, Cutters

Julius Frankel 10, Cutters
Sandra Gelman 22, Dressmakers
Eugene Goldstein 22, Dressmakers
Hyman Goldstein 10, Cutters
Enzo Grassi 89, Dressmakers
Nettie Harary 22, Dressmakers
Hattie Hausdorf 22, Dressmakers
Lynne Jaffee 22, Dressmakers
Harry Kadison 142, Ladies' Neckwear
Hyman Kaplan 10, Cutters
Ruth Rubinstein 32, Underwear
Emanuel Scheintoub 10, Cutters
Fred Schmidt 22, Dressmakers
Moe Schreier 10, Cutters
Paul Seymour 66, Bonnaz embroiderers
Isaac Sides 155, Knitgoods
Sidney Sklar 10, Cutters
Mae Spiegel 22, Dressmakers
Millie Weitz 22, Dressmakers
Beatty Uretsky 22, Dressmakers

Cast members without locals listed:

Harry Clark
Grace Quatropani
Tony Heath

*P & N* had an initial production cost of $12,000 with the entire weekly salary just over $1,000; no one in the cast was paid over $40 per week.[3] As a comparison, the initial costs of various *Ziegfeld Follies* productions were $13,000 (1907), $110,000 (1918), and $250,000 (1921). Ziegfeld's biggest stars were making nearly $1,000 per week. Two years before, Billy Rose's production of the extravaganza *Jumbo* had cost $200,000.[4] Generally, bringing a musical production to opening night in 1937 cost 50,000 to 75,000 dollars.

On opening night at Labor Stage, the song list of *P & N* included the following, most of them accompanying a skit[5]:

"Sing Me a Song with Social Significance"
"Chain Store Daisy"
"I've Got the Nerve to Be in Love"
"Bertha the Sewing Machine Girl"
"Back to Work"
"When I Grow Up" ("The G-Man Song")
"Cream of Mush Song"
"Doing the Reactionary"
"Four Little Angels of Peace"
"Not Cricket to Picket"
"One Big Union for Two"
"What Good is Love?"
"Sunday in the Park"
"Status Quo"
"Nobody Make a Pass at Me"

Director Friedman had been part of the radical Shock Troupe of the Workers Laboratory Theatre and had also directed at the Theatre Union, considered at the time to be *the* most professional of the radical theaters. With this artistic background, he was responsible for the "unique fusion of proletarian drama and vaudeville revue"[6] for which *P & N* was acclaimed. Other principals on the creative team were choreographer Benjamin Zemach, dance director Gluck Sandor, and set designer Sointu Syrjala, another member of Theatre Union.

Friedman was also credited for his patience with the newcomers, going out of his way to teach theatrical techniques, and he and Rome were the impetus behind the original production. But Louis Schaffer was strongly anti-communist, and eventually Friedman and one of the stars, Millie Weitz, were edged out of the production because of strong communist ties. Friedman was bitter about this toward both Schaffer and Rome. He had written the lyrics to two of the songs, "First Impression" and "We've Just Begun," and felt that as soon as he was gone from the show, his songs were eliminated so that he would receive no further royalties. Friedman sued the two but eventually settled out of court, saying, "It was heartbreaking to hear Schaffer and Rome lie on the witness stand."[7] The two directors who succeeded Friedman, Robert Gordon and Howard Da Silva, were part of the radical Popular Front, as was Rome, but their lack of communist connections made all the difference with Schaffer.[8] Gordon had collaborated with Rome on revues at Green Mansions and over twenty-five years later, Da Silva would write the book for Rome's *The Zulu and the Zayda*.

Ultimately, it was Rome who was credited with giving *P & N* its "special flavor and appeal."[9] In a review of the 1978 revival, *Time* critic T.E. Kalem said: "Rome's lyrics achieve something that is perhaps rarer than wit, a good humor that arises from compassionate fellow feeling."[10] Longtime musical director and orchestrator for several of Rome's later shows, Lehman Engel, explained that despite the intention of *P & N* to propagandize the union, "Rome succeeded in making something of it so ebullient, witty, and engaging that without departing from its original purpose it moved far beyond 'public relations' and became a genuinely pungent, inspired, and serious-minded piece of hilarious entertainment."[11]

If one song represented Rome, his songs, and the show, it was "Sing Me a Song with Social Significance." This was an ensemble number that opened the show, telling the audience "where the hearts of these young workers lay."[12] Rather than the usual lyrics of love and romance, the cast asked for songs about "wars and ... breadlines ... strikes and last-minute headlines."[13] It was not the usual Broadway opening number, and it caught the attention of the audience. The opening crowd had few critics as it was just an amateur show with limited hope, and the first-night habitués were off elsewhere. The audience was mostly union members, and it was as if Rome was giving them a voice, expressing what they felt in music and lyrics, something they had never imagined. As Stanley Green summed it up in *The World of Musical Comedy*: "The ability to express in songs the honest emotions of those who are least articulate has been one of his most distinguishing characteristics. For Rome is, essentially, a people's composer and lyricist, one who, without being sentimental or patronizing, provides the common man with uncommon musical expressions."[14] Thomas S. Hischak echoed this in his book on Broadway lyricists, *Word Crazy*: "But when it came to portraying the working class man or woman, Harold Rome was about the best in the business."[15]

After the "Social Significance" opening, the Rome songs were based on several headline stories with generous doses of satire and humor. The song-skit "Four Little Angels of Peace" focused on four bellicose state leaders of the day: Hitler, Mussolini, Anthony Eden of England, and an unnamed Japanese general. In a "merry waltz," they sang about "their ability to unleash devastation on other nations" while "insisting on their desire for peace."[16] Like several of Rome's tunes for the show, "Four Little Angels" underwent several lyric revisions as the political climate changed. When England went to war against Germany and Italy, Eden's character in the skit was eliminated.

Several songs were offensive to one group or another. The communist paper *Daily Worker* had initially applauded the show, but when satire of Stalin was done in a later edition of "Four Little Angels of Peace" and then "Mene, Mene, Tekel," they withdrew support.[17] The Archdiocese of New York, through its Catholic Theatre Movement list, found *P & N* "wholly objectionable," and the Daughters of the American Revolution said it was "so profane, so communistic and so broad in its implication [as to make it unfit] for any child." Various towns on the show's road tour demanded that specific songs be eliminated.[18]

"One Big Union for Two" was a lovers' song laying down the terms of their upcoming marriage. Smart and clever as a romantic duet, the song had a subtext evident to most of the audience, the ongoing battle between the American Federation of Labor (AFL) and the Congress of Industrial Organization (CIO). The AFL was the largest labor organization in the country, representing mostly the trades, coal miners, and railroad craftsmen. In 1935, it refused to incorporate the semi-skilled and unskilled laborers in the mass production industries (steel, auto, rubber, clothing, and textiles). When this occurred, several of these industrial unions, including the ILGWU, broke off from the AFL and formed the CIO under John L. Lewis. But in 1938, David Dubinsky pulled the ILGWU out of the CIO and went back to the AFL. It was during this upheaval of union leadership that *P & N* was produced. Twenty years later, the two union organizations finally became "one big union for two," the AFL-CIO under George Meany.[19]

"Chain Store Daisy" and "Not Cricket to Picket" also had the worker in mind. Rome claimed to have written it for Fanny Brice before *P & N* and that the Ziegfeld star had rejected it. After she heard it in the show, Rome said she offered him $50,000 for it, but he stubbornly refused. Both claims seem a bit preposterous, but Rome stuck to his story with an interviewer years later.[20] English musical comedy star Beatrice Lillie also asked to sing "Chain

Store Daisy" as well as "Not Cricket to Picket" and met with greater success with Rome.[21] *P & N* not only recounted plights of union workers and other downtrodden members of society, but several songs showed interest in their personal lives, something seldom found in a musical revue. The singers and their songs with personal touches included:

| Singer | Song | Topic |
| --- | --- | --- |
| Millie Weitz | "Nobody Makes a Pass at Me" | Cosmetics and other aids to romance |
| Ruth Rubinstein | "Chain Store Daisy" | Sales clerk with nasty customers |
| Bernie Gould | "When I Grow Up" | Wishing to become a G-Man |

In a musical filled with topical satire, the aforementioned songs were to be expected. But "Sunday in the Park," described by one critic as "a musical idyll to the garment workers' one day off,"[22] was set apart from the others. It was an easygoing, hummable melody with lyrics having no obvious agenda. From Rome's viewpoint, the song was "revolutionary" for a Broadway show, as there was no love interest in the song and its topic was about a lower class family spending a day in the park. Hardly material for a Broadway showstopper.[23]

"Sunday in the Park" was Rome's first hit on the strength of a recording by the Hudson-DeLange Orchestra with vocalist Mary McHugh on Brunswick Records. It was recorded by several other artists and made *Your Hit Parade* of April 1938.[24] Rome remembered taking a ride in the car with his wife Florence when they both heard it on the radio for the first time on that show.[25] Of the song, Chicago critic Claudia Cassidy remarked: "Almost everyone knows 'Sunday in the Park,' the 'Easter Parade' of its day, but about quite different people. It is an easy charmer of a song and dance piece, utterly relaxed in the sense that someone very tired can sigh with relief and let go."[26] Another Chicago critic, Cecil Smith, felt even stronger about Rome's song:

> He accepts, as I have said, the stereotyped repetition of four measure phrases as a basis for his rhythmic form, but within each four measure unit he achieves enviably smooth continuity and complete naturalness. Think of "Sunday in the Park" in *New Pins and Needles*. How graciously and spontaneously the music flows along to the end of the fourth measure, and how easily and simply the content of the whole chorus seems to grow out of the opening musical idea![27]

Because of the controversial nature of Rome's other songs, most of them were banned from the radio. One of these was the "Cream of Mush Song" which accompanied a skit satirizing censorship in radio. Other banned songs included "Doing the Reactionary," "Not Cricket to Picket," "Mene, Mene, Tekel," and "Sing Me a Song with Social Significance."[28] Rome had to persuade John Royal, head of NBC programming, that "Sunday in the Park" was merely a romantic lyric and contained nothing critical of the current economic system. Another controversial song was "One Big Union for Two." To please the NBC censors, Rome had to omit such terms as "court injunction," "closed shop," "scab," "lockout," as well as one entire line.[29]

The initial plan for *P & N* was to perform it on a few consecutive weekends, as an entertainment for union members, their families, and a few outsiders. But word spread fast that this was no small-time musical and could hold its own with the best of Broadway. Rome's words and music were infectious. After a few months, the audience changed. Not only union members but the Broadway crowd and out-of-towners were lining up. *Variety* explained: "The very people it mocked — the carriage trade — came in droves."[30]

The performance schedule followed the usual Broadway format of six days a week with matinees. This became draining on most of the cast and of concern in an industry dependent on heavy machinery. As one performer noted: "I work at a cutting machine all day. If I don't get my sleep, I'm liable to lose a finger tomorrow morning."[31] So the amateur performers took leaves of absence from their jobs and were paid their hourly rate for performances and rehearsal time. *The New Yorker* detailed:

> The ILGWU will pay them strictly according to garment union scales. This being a slack season in the garment industry, the girls are receiving $23 a week, the men $45. If the run extends to February, when business always picks up, the pay will be raised to $45 and $80 respectively.[32]

Beyond this, when the show was clearly a success, Actors' Equity insisted that the *P & N* cast join their union — something that Schaffer was strongly against. After much negotiating, Schaffer relented. Cast principals joined Actors Equity and the rest of the cast joined Chorus Equity as extras.[33]

Within a year, the small Labor Stage could no longer meet the ticket demand for *P & N*, so in 1939, several changes occurred. In April, the title was changed to *Pins and Needles 1939* with the second edition directed by Robert Gordon and new choreography added by Felicia Sorel.[34] Two months later, *P & N* was moved to the much larger, Broadway-sized Windsor Theater. In November, the show was renamed *New Pins and Needles*. With each new edition, Schaffer would call in the critics for a re-evaluation. This drove the theater regulars to distraction, especially Rome:

> We said: "You're crazy. You got great reviews before... Why take chances?"
> But he did; he called in the critics to see the *new* edition. And we got even better reviews than the first time.... All the judgments he made, which were against sound theatrical policy, all worked out fine for him and us.[35]

Because of the show's long run and its commitment to topicality, songs and skits were introduced every few months, another of Schaffer's practices

*Left to right*, front row: David Dubinsky (ILGWU president), cast member Rose Newmark, President Franklin D. Roosevelt; back row: cast members Ruth Rubinstein, Lynn Jaffee, Adele Diamond, Anne Brown, Nettie Harary. The cast was backstage at a command performance of *Pins and Needles* for President and Mrs. Roosevelt at the White House in 1938 (courtesy of the Museum of the City of New York).

that Rome disliked. But again, Schaffer was right, and Rome admitted: "So we had a running political cabaret."[36] There were nearly fifty songs used during the run, and only four lasted the entire time: "Sing Me a Song with Social Significance," "Sunday in the Park," "Four Little Angels of Peace," and "Nobody Makes a Pass at Me." The last of these had been written by Rome originally for a show at Green Mansions and had been one of his audition numbers for Schaffer.[37] One of the biggest hits of the show, "Mene, Mene, Tekel," was not added until July 1939.

On June 22, 1940, after a run of 1,108 performances, the record for a musical at the time, *P & N* closed. Scenic designer Sointu Syrjala observed, "*Pins and Needles* opened as an amateur show and closed as near a professional show as you can get."³⁸ Though many of these early performances were in the small Labor Stage, the show was eventually seen by over one million theatergoers. The New York cast did a command performance for President and Mrs. Roosevelt at the White House in early 1938 at the latter's insistence. That performance was cloaked in secrecy until the last minute not only for obvious security reasons, but also because Schaffer and Dubinsky did not want to unnerve their amateur cast.³⁹

There were also two road companies that played the United States and Canada in eighty-five cities, and another troupe which did union lunchtime matinees and welcomed Albert Einstein backstage. The road shows closed by May of 1941.⁴⁰

*P & N* and the union were to be re-linked nearly thirty years later, through the efforts of Manhattan's Roundabout Theater. The underfinanced Roundabout had opened in 1965 beneath the Chelsea Consumers Co-op Supermarket, using a 132-seat basement theater leased to them by the ILGWU under generous terms.⁴¹ As a tribute to the union, Roundabout produced a successful revival of *P & N* during its 1966–67 season, directed by Gene Feist.⁴² One of the reviews pinpointed the reason for the success of that show: "By picking the best numbers from the three editions of the revue that were seen in New York between 1937 and 1940, Mr. Feist has been able to eliminate material that the years have not treated kindly without sacrificing the period flavor."⁴³

In 1978, a well-financed and matured Roundabout team again revived it, this time in a larger theater with Philip Campanella as musical director. Reviews were mixed.⁴⁴ The stars were Corliss Taylor-Dunn and Elaine Petricoff.⁴⁵ Walter Kerr said of them and Rome's score:

> [They] take their time, style their phrasings and make it cheerfully clear that the ebullient melodies and sassy lyrics Mr. Rome wrote 40 years ago are more than viable today. For the most part (a few are inevitably dated), they're impertinent, funny and urgently hummable, a reminder of the stored-up energy that was just waiting to be unleashed in late–Depression days.⁴⁶

Despite these successful revivals, *P & N* was not the kind of show to be included in professional or amateur repertoire. No show that topical or political ever made it into that category, and it was not meant as a high school spring musical or summer stock presentation. Nonetheless, *P & N* achieved success beyond any other political-satirical musical of that period or any other. As mentioned previously, the Depression and the years following prompted numerous shows: *Parade* (1935), *Johnny Johnson* (1936), *The Cradle Will Rock* (1937), *I'd Rather Be Right* (1937), *Hooray for What!* (1937), and *Sing for Your Supper* (1939). But *P & N* enjoyed a run that totaled more than all of these put together.

Ethan Mordden attributed its success to the "good humor in which it cloaked its commentary," and said it was "amusing rather than preachy."[47] Leading critic George Jean Nathan, in a belated review, thought *P & N* to be "welcome evidence that labor cannot only laugh at itself now and then but that it doesn't always regard a piano as a musical soapbox," a jibe at *The Cradle Will Rock*.[48] Perhaps it was just that *P & N* played no favorites. Everyone and everything took it on the chin. Rome and the other sketch writers used their satire to cut across all boundaries. If you were in the audience, you didn't care if you were a target, because you knew that the people in the next row, whoever they were, might get it in the next scene. Few left the theater early or in a huff.

*P & N* has a solid place in theatrical history:

> A half a century later, *Pins and Needles* lives on in both union and Broadway lore. In the labor movement, it remains an emblem of a time when union-sponsored theater could be a popular success; on Broadway, it stands as a curious anomaly, its amateur cast and atypical audience peculiar products of the "socially conscious" 1930's.[49]

David Dubinsky, the man who had started all this back in the early thirties, wrote a brief commentary for the 1962 recording of *Pins and Needles*; in it he wrote, "They stirred the Great White Way with the new note of social significance."[50]

*Chapter 4*

# Kaufman and Hart and *Sing Out the News*

"The young composer ... felt that Kaufman and Hart lacked firm political convictions."—Malcolm Goldstein

Rome said of the success of *Pins and Needles* that it made "a big difference." Not only in his career, but it allowed him to buy a car and put him in a different income bracket. Best of all, it made things comfortable enough that he could marry Florence Miles on February 3, 1939. She had moved to New York from her hometown of Chicago after graduating from the University of Illinois. She had been hired by Young and Rubicam to work as a radio advertising writer.[1]

Success on the order of *Pins and Needles* not only got you a wife and a car, but it drew much attention from the movers and shakers of Broadway. During its run, a prominent Broadway triumvirate—Max Gordon, George S. Kaufman, and Moss Hart—asked Rome and director Charles Friedman to create another revue, not unlike *Pins and Needles*. This was heady stuff for the two Broadway newcomers. Gordon was to produce in association with Kaufman and Hart, and the three had invested a total of $100,000, the show's original budget.[2]

Max Gordon had been much impressed by the most non-satirical song in *Pins and Needles*, "Sunday in the Park." As Rome remembered it:

> Max Gordon came to see *Pins and Needles* and he rushed up to me and said, "That number 'Sunday in the Park' is the story of my life! Why don't you do a show for me?" So I said, "All right."[3]

Gordon had success in the early thirties with two of Jerome Kern's biggest shows, *The Cat and the Fiddle* (1931) and *Roberta* (1933), although in 1939 a Kern show, *Very Warm for May*, had fizzled despite the presence of "All the

## 4. Kaufman and Hart and Sing Out the News

Things You Are." At the same time, Gordon had produced shows for two masters of the revue, Arthur Schwartz and Howard Dietz: *Three's a Crowd* (1930) and *The Band Wagon* (1931).[4]

George S. Kaufman and Moss Hart had over twenty years experience at the time of their collaboration with Gordon, Rome, and Friedman. By 1938, their accomplishments on Broadway included[5]:

| G.S.K / M.H. | Contribution | Show | Composer(s) | Year |
|---|---|---|---|---|
| G.S.K. | Sketches | *Music Box Review* (3rd) | Irving Berlin | 1923 |
| G.S.K. | Book | *The Cocoanuts* | Irving Berlin | 1925 |
| G.S.K. | Book[A] | *Strike Up the Band* | George & Ira Gershwin | 1927; 1930 |
| G.S.K. | Sketches | *The Little Show* | Arthur Schwartz & Howard Dietz | 1929 |
| G.S.K. | Sketches | *Nine-Fifteen Revue* | Harold Arlen & Ted Koehler | 1930 |
| G.S.K. | Sketches | *The Band Wagon* | Arthur Schwartz & Howard Dietz | 1931 |
| G.S.K. | Book[B] | *Of Thee I Sing* | George & Ira Gershwin | 1931 |
| G.S.K. | Director | *Face the Music* | Irving Berlin | 1932 |
| M.H. | Book | *Face the Music* | Irving Berlin | 1932 |
| M.H. | Sketches | *As Thousands Cheer* | Irving Berlin | 1933 |
| G.S.K. | Book[C] | *Let 'Em Eat Cake* | George & Ira Gershwin | 1933 |
| M.H. | Book | *Jubilee* | Cole Porter | 1935 |
| M.H. | Sketches[D] | *The Show Is On* | George & Ira Gershwin | 1936 |
| G.S.K.–M.H. | Book | *I'd Rather Be Right* | Richard Rodgers & Lorenz Hart | 1937 |

Notes:
A — G.S.K. wrote the original book for the 1927 version which closed during tryouts; Morrie Ryskind rewrote it for the more successful 1930 show.
B — G.S.K. won the Pulitzer Prize for Drama in 1931 with book co-writer Morrie Ryskind and lyricist Ira Gershwin.
C — Book co-written with Morrie Ryskind.
D — The majority of sketches were written by M.H. and David Freedman with other minor collaborators.

Like most Broadway musical theater creators, Kaufman and Hart had been involved in several revues, usually satirical. In the early thirties, Kaufman had co-written three shows with Morrie Ryskind, all with songs by George and Ira Gershwin, their first being *Strike Up the Band*, so anti-war that it was not well-received. Their next effort, however, *Of Thee I Sing*, not only ran 441 performances and won a Pulitzer Prize but was considered to be a new form of musical satire with integrated songs and a plot.[6] While the fully integrated book musical was yet to clearly emerge with the shows of Rodgers and Hammerstein in the early forties, *Of Thee I Sing* progressed towards that end, especially uncommon in a satire. *Let 'Em Eat Cake*, the follow-up effort of Kaufman, Ryskind and the Gershwins, with many of the same characters, failed.

While all four creators of *Sing Out the News* were New York, Jewish liberals, Rome and Friedman were in a different league. They had both been committed not only to the success of *Pins and Needles* and their amateur union cast, but they believed much in its messages. Their association during that show with left-wing talents such as Marc Blitzstein and John Latouche was not by chance. Rome and Friedman wanted to continue in a similar vein and be "morally uncorrupted,"[7] although they realized they were doing a show uptown in a deluxe version, not in the garment district at Labor Stage. The initial production budget for this show was $100,000, while that of *P & N* had been $12,000, all financed through the ILGWU and Labor Stage. They hoped that the new show would have "the structural format ... of Big Broadway while the philosophy was that of an ILGWU theater night."[8]

However, in early creative conferences, Rome was put off by Kaufman and Hart's politics and overall concept for the show. As Hart biographer Jared Brown put it:

> [Rome] was distressed to find that Kaufman and Hart's plan was to combine social commentary with satirical humor, some of which would be aimed at left-wing targets. Rome particularly resented Kaufman, who, he felt, paid no heed to his objections.
>
> Rome and Friedman were motivated at least as much by social conviction as by the desire to produce entertaining material, while the primary goal of Kaufman and Hart was to write the funniest comic sketches of which they were capable.[9]

Kaufman biographer Malcolm Goldstein echoed these thoughts:

> The young composer ... felt that Kaufman and Hart lacked firm political convictions. Their hearts were in the right place but they were in the distressing habit of firing off jokes at virtually everything, left, right, and center....[10]

At times, it was as if the two teams were working in parallel, never meshing. This was not Kaufman and Hart's only project as they were hard at work finishing a new play, *The Fabulous Invalid*. Although Friedman was the principal writer, it was their practice to pop in and out of rehearsals and creative meetings for *Sing Out the News* and make quick changes and sweeping cuts. Despite their sometimes unwanted participation, they were not credited for their writing efforts. In his review, *New York Post* critic John Mason Brown thanked them "for not having tampered with the social convictions of their authors."[11]

As sole composer, Rome was less affected by Kaufman and Hart and was busy writing more songs than were needed, as was his wont. His score had the usual satires, a few closely akin to songs from *Pins and Needles*. The latter's most biting political number had been "Four Little Angels of Peace," aimed at the megalomania of prominent world leaders. In *Sing Out the News*, a sketch entitled "International Mountain Climbers" involved three leaders of free Europe — Benes of Czechoslovakia, Edouard Daladier of France, and Neville Chamberlain of England — roped together with Hitler, Mussolini, and Stalin to ascend a mountain. The outcome is not good.[12] In another parallel, the female lead Mary Jane Walsh sang "My Heart Is Unemployed," juxtaposing her love life and the economic situation.[13] This was much like the love duet from *Pins and Needles*, "One Big Union for Two," in which a couple couches their relationship in terms of the union struggle of the day between the AFL and CIO.

What stopped the show on opening night[14] was a rousing number with Rex Ingram and the chorus, which included cabaret star and bandleader Hazel Scott.[15] This was Rome at his tuneful, liberal best, celebrating the birth of a black baby while paying homage to Franklin D. Roosevelt.[16] The song, initially entitled "Man of the Year," was staged at a Harlem block party and became known simply as "F.D.R. Jones." It sold over 70,000 sheet music copies[17] and was recorded by Cab Calloway, Ella Fitzgerald, Judy Garland, Glenn Miller, and Chick Webb, among others.[18] The song had a patriotic bent to it and was featured in the climactic scene from *Babes on Broadway*, a show within a show film, with Judy Garland singing it in blackface. Rome was especially fond of the song and related a brief story told to him by a friend: "At Dunkirk, in that heroic evacuation, the soldiers kept singing while waiting for the boats to pick them up, singing at the top of their voices to keep up their spirits. And the song they kept repeating was one of mine — 'Franklin D. Roosevelt Jones.'"[19]

*Sing Out the News* premiered in Philadelphia on August 27, 1938, and played there two weeks. The principal creative staff included[20]:

| | |
|---|---|
| Max Meth — musical director | Will Irwin — ballet music |
| Jo Mielziner — set design | Charles Friedman — director and sketches |
| Hans Spialek — orchestrations | Ned Wayburn & Dave Gould — dances |
| John Hambleton — costumes | |

Mielziner and Spialek would work on several of Rome's shows over the years.

George Ross of the *Inquirer* was quite favorable to the show's satire, saying that "Messrs. Rome and Friedman have a little list that takes a pretty full evening."[21] The *Philadelphia Record* tabbed it "a large, handsome, and witty revue, with sophisticated leftist tendencies," and cited Rome's lyrics as "smart and engaging."[22] Most prominently, Brooks Atkinson of the *New York Times* said of their satire and politics: "Although Mr. Rome and Mr. Friedman work for the bourgeoisie with somewhat more restraint than for the working class, they still have a fancy way with the forces of reaction and compassion for the submerged nine-tenths of our population."[23]

The *New York World-Telegram* critic exclaimed, "[T]he music ... has more fire than Mr. Rome's previous work."[24] *Post* critic John Mason Brown concurred, calling Rome's lyrics "pungent and witty," and his score "rhythmic and pleasing."[25] Richard Watts, Jr., of the *Tribune* liked the show overall, declaring it "the first musical hit of the season."[26]

Among the performers singled out in the various reviews were singer Mary Jane Walsh, comic Philip Loeb, dancers Dorothy Fox and Burton Pierce, and especially "F.D.R. Jones" performer Rex Ingram. By the time of *Sing Out the News*, he had starred as De Lawd in the 1936 movie of *Green Pastures* and in the Negro Theatre's 1938 production *Haiti*.[27] Ingram would go on to starring roles in Vernon Duke's *Cabin in the Sky* (1940) and Harold Arlen's *St. Louis Woman* (1946).[28]

In both Philadelphia and New York, critics devoted several paragraphs comparing the show to *Pins and Needles*. John Mason Brown wrote:

> It may resemble a *Pins and Needles* which has struck it rich [producer Gordon et al.] and moved uptown [Broadway] into a fashionable apartment [Music Box Theatre] done by an expert interior decorator [Jo Mielziner]. It may seem to be a *Pins and Needles* which has opened a charge account at Cartier's, taken dancing lessons at Arthur Murray's, patronized Valentina or Bergdorf-Goodman, and been to Elizabeth Arden's for countless beauty treatments.[29]

Despite this setup, he ultimately thought it stood on its own merits as an entertaining revue.

But others did not. *Pins and Needles* ran over 1,100 performances, *Sing Out the News* only 105. Why the disparity? Despite a professional cast and production staff, *Sing Out* did not capture the audience with the same intensity, and if theatergoers were looking for one satirical revue to see, *Pins and Needles* was still the preferred one, Messrs. Kaufman and Hart notwithstanding. No less than Sigmund Romberg had suffered a similar fate with his 1925 operetta *Prince Flavia* which faltered at the box office because people preferred to see his megahit, *The Student Prince*.[30]

As for *Sing Out the News*, besides competition from *Pins and Needles*, another revue down the street was attracting a crowd: *Hellzapoppin'* had opened two days earlier at the 46th Street Theatre. This show was written by the comedy team of Ole Olsen and Chic Johnson with a score mostly by

Sammy Fain and Charles Tobias. Though its songs were inferior to Rome's revues, the lighthearted, slapstick, sometimes topical *Hellzapoppin'* had a wide audience appeal and ran a total of 1,404 performances, breaking the Broadway record of *Pins and Needles*.[31]

Rome knew that *Pins and Needles* had succeeded and beat the odds because it was done by the very people it was about: the garment workers. The audience recognized this, which created a synergy for success. Rome would say the same thing of his *Call Me Mister* in 1946. With *Sing Out the News*, the songs and satire were there, but it was all done by a professional cast, just a cast, not a group of people who actually worked with "pins and needles." It lacked the same emotional appeal of the earlier show.

Rome thought that another deterrent to attendance was that *Sing Out the News* had opened only a month before the Munich Agreement,[32] the pact signed by England, France, Italy, and Germany ceding Sudetenland, an area of Czechoslovakia inhabited mostly by Germans, over to Nazi Germany and Adolf Hitler.[33] The pact was executed without the approval of the Czechs and their leader Eduard Benes and caused tensions on the Continent. Rome felt such unrest left potential audiences hesitant to carry on life as usual, rendering the "romp of merry radicals" ill-timed and out of place, particularly in light of their "International Mountain Climbers" sketch.[34]

Ultimately though, competition and world politics notwithstanding, critical consensus was that *Sing Out the News* was merely derivative of *Pins and Needles* and lacked the punch of the earlier show. Richard Lockridge in the *Sun*:

> [F]or some reason, the evening still seems a little thin; satire without feathers is, perhaps, rather meager fare for a full-dress revue.... [T]he authors have this time a little pulled their punches, tempering the wind of their crusade to the Persian lamb of their audience.[35]

John Anderson in the *Journal-American* was in agreement, but made the unfavorable comparison more to the "point":

> [I]nstead of the bright and friendly, if semi-amateur informality, of the labor stage show they have a slicked up Broadway revue, weakened by an evasive viewpoint, a tedious and rather dull echo of a clever original, celebrating, I suspect, nothing sharper than safety pins and knitting needles.[36]

Whatever it was, *Sing Out the News* closed within a few months and returned little money to its backers.

* * *

Around this time, Rome became peripherally involved in a project for the WPA Federal Theatre, *Sing for Your Supper*, a musical revue in two acts with twenty scenes. The title was a takeoff on the Rodgers and Hart song of the same name from *The Boys of Syracuse* (1938). Most of the music was written by Ned Lehac and Lee Wainer with lyrics by Robert Sour. Two of Rome's former collaborators from *Pins and Needles*, Earl Robinson and John Latouche, were also involved.[37]

With music by Sour, Rome was asked "to come up with a lyric in the 'F.D.R. Jones' vein."[38] His "Papa's Got a Job" featured the celebration for a man about to be evicted for non-payment of rent, the neighbors showing enthusiasm over his employment in the moving sketch.[39] Rome took credit for the song under the name of Hector Troy as he did not want to be presented with lyrics-only offers at this point in his career.[40] His nickname for years had been Hecky so he just formalized it for the program. No matter, as neither the song nor *Sing for Your Supper* fared well, not uncommon for the WPA Federal Theatre which was about to be disbanded.

Rome was also asked to add a few songs to a Shubert musical revue, *Streets of Paris*, with a score by Jimmy McHugh and Al Dubin. Final contracts were signed by spring of 1939.[41] The show's revue roots were deep with the producers Ole Olsen and Chic Johnson of *Hellzapoppin'* fame and stars Louella Gear and Bobby Clark, vaudeville and Broadway veterans.[42] Featured were newcomers Gower Champion, Hugh Martin, Bud Abbott and Lou Costello, and a French import, Yvonne Bouvier. Born in Paris, she had made her reputation as a singer in New York clubs then returned to her native city to star in the 1937 *Folies Bergere*.[43] She was the only French performer among the principals and sang Rome's "History Is Made at Night," a seductive ballad.

From Brazil came singer-dancer Carmen Miranda, a discovery of Lee Shubert, who "heard her perform in Rio and signed her for stardom."[44] So proud and sure of his find was Shubert that Miranda was kept under wraps, away from press, spectators, and even other cast members until opening night. She had come north with her own Brazilian musicians so her rehearsals were done separately, and she only walked through the dress rehearsal.[45] Hugh Martin had been hired as a dancer but became more important to *Streets of Paris* as a vocal arranger.[46] Years later, he would perform that role for Judy Garland, accompany her in her solo career, and write the songs for *Meet Me in St. Louis*.

Martin had seen Carmen Miranda in Brazil and was sure she would be a hit, an opinion not shared by everyone involved with the show. What happened on opening night was detailed by him in his autobiography, *Hugh Martin: The Boy Next Door*:

> Upon her head was a turban, flaming with vivid colors, sporting a variety of fruits and flowers. She wore it like a crown.
> At the end of the first song the roof of the Broadhurst [Theatre] almost

*4. Kaufman and Hart and* **Sing** Out the News    33

came off. She sang three more song in Portuguese, then concluded with "The 'Souse' American Way." The curtain fell and she walked to her dressing room with the show neatly wrapped up in her pocket.[47]

Within a few weeks, her photograph graced the cover of the show's *Playbill*.[48]

Luckily for Rome, one of the two songs he wrote for the show, "The French Have a Word for It," was sung by Miranda in the finale. Although it was never a hit outside of the show, its performance by the Brazilian star every night for 274 performances could not but help the career of the budding songwriter, keeping his name in front of audiences and producers.[49]

*Chapter 5*

# Political Endeavors and *The Little Dog Laughed*

> "However left-of-center his points of view, Rome's good sense, judgment, and taste made his songs attractive to general audiences...."
> —John Bush Jones

Joshua Rome, the composer's son, felt he had had a very liberal upbringing as both of his parents, especially his father, "had no borders toward people."[1] Harold Rome was involved in liberal and left-wing causes much of his life, but the mid-thirties through the war years were particularly active. Exemplary of this, circa 1936–37, was his organization and music for the *Spring Frolic* of the Federal Arts Council of the Workers Alliance along with entertainment notables including choreographer Martha Graham, actor Sam Jaffe, and music impresario John Hammond, Jr.[2] Also occupying him at this time was Cabaret TAC, a political cabaret developed by the Theatre Arts Council (TAC). TAC had originated in 1937 from the Theatre Committee to Aid Spanish Democracy, and its ultra-liberal members published a monthly magazine, made recordings, and aired a radio show. These spawned a weekly cabaret:

> Cabaret TAC made its debut on 5 May 1938 and continued for almost two years with a series of shows—"Radio Show," "Hollywood Show," "Chinese Cabaret"—made up of skits, dances, and topical songs. They featured exiled cabaret artists like the mime Lotte Goslar; radical dancers like Si-Lan Chen; satires of the federal theater ("One Third of a Mitten"), Hollywood film ("Gone with the Movie Rights"), and Tin Pan Alley (Marc Blitzstein's "What's Left?")....[3]

Rome contributed several songs to Cabaret TAC including "One Big Union for Two," a light-hearted love duet that also satirized the battle between the A.F.L. and C.I.O. Soon after its Cabaret TAC premier, it was added to

*Pins and Needles*.⁴ Two other Rome songs from Cabaret TAC which caught critics' ears were "Good Little Girls" and "Let Freedom Swing."⁵

At the time, another liberal entertainment site was flourishing, Café Society, "New York's only truly integrated nightclub, a place catering to types with open minds."⁶ Opening in the late thirties, it was designed as a democratic venue to "take the stuffing out of stuffed shirts."⁷ The audiences were politically open, which attracted entertainers like singers Billie Holiday and Hazel Scott and pianist Teddy Wilson, artists who often performed racially or politically sensitive material. Most notable among these was "Strange Fruit," written in 1939 by Abel Meeropol, a.k.a. Lewis Allan. Holiday's version of the song, about a lynching in the South, was a frequent highlight at Café Society. After a year there, Holiday moved to West 52nd Street jazz clubs where the politics were less progressive but the drugs were more liberal.⁸

\* \* \*

During all this, Rome was an ardent pacifist and felt that America should stay out of the war, which at the time was confined mostly to Europe. "The Yanks Aren't Coming" was a straightforward expression of his feelings, written in 1940 for *Pins and Needles*. Both Holiday and Scott sang the song frequently, and Scott recorded it for the TAC along with "Mene, Mene, Tekel," Rome's musical send-up of bellicose dictators, also from *Pins and Needles*.⁹

Such criticism of dictatorships had been made for years by artists in one form or another. From Pablo Picasso's *Guernica*, Charles Chaplin's *The Great Dictator*, and Jean-Paul Sartre's short story "Le Mur" ("The Wall") to E.Y. Harburg and Harold Arlen's *Hooray for What?*, creative people had taken aim at the likes of Hitler, Stalin, and Franco. Rome wrote "Death in the Afternoon!," on which he made the notation "Dedicated to *Guernica*" in 1937.

The advancement of Hitler and Nazism across Europe by 1940 made musical lampooning of dictators problematic, but producer-director Eddie Dowling knew two men he thought could still pull it off. Dowling had started out as a performer in vaudeville in 1911, then graduated to Broadway in *Ziegfeld Follies of 1919*, *Sidewalks of New York* (1927) and *Thumbs Up* (1935). He also worked as a director, composer, and movie star, finding his true niche in the arts after the war as a producer of Broadway plays, including *The Glass Menagerie* and *The Iceman Cometh*.¹⁰ To create his show, "part social satire, part fantasy, part vaudeville, and part boy-meets-girl,"¹¹ Dowling predicated it on a phrase from a nursery rhyme:

> The little dog laughed to see such sport,
> And the dish ran away with the spoon.

The pair he hired were composer Harold Rome and librettist Joseph Schrank. They were friends, associates, and liberal birds of a feather who had worked together on the highly successful *Pins and Needles*, a twosome who "felt that there were a few more heads to be lopped off."[12] Schrank had written "The Red Mikado" for that show, a lampoon of the refusal of the Daughters of the American Revolution to allow black soprano Marian Anderson to perform at Constitution Hall.[13]

Rather than the real dictators of the day, Schrank's libretto for *The Little Dog Laughed* focused on the "dictatorship" of a young boy who banished redheads and frightened dissidents with a toy dragon. *Variety* referred to the libretto as "a fantasy patterned after *The Connecticut Yankee*,"[14] the 1927 hit by Richard Rodgers and Lorenz Hart which transported a modern-day man to King Arthur's court. Another review found it to be "rather reminiscent of *The Wizard of Oz* in its prankish fairyland characters and doings."[15] Rather than a tornado, Schrank and set designer Jo Mielziner employed a blackout technique to transform the set to a dictatorship run by a pre-adolescent. From there, the satire began, interspersed with a love story involving a princess — from Brooklyn.

Boston critic Helen Eager summarized *The Little Dog Laughed* as "Social Significance ... set to music,"[16] and *The Christian Science Monitor* called it an "ambitious effort to unite fantasy and satire.[17] Rome and Schrank, the veterans of social significance from *Pins and Needles*, had emphasized the dictatorship and forgotten the musical, causing one opening night critic to suggest, "Maybe it isn't good theater, especially in the realm of musical comedy, to make an audience think when it came to be entertained."[18]

Social significance had been a two-edged sword for Rome. It had given him great success with *Pins and Needles*, although ironically, his lasting hit from that show was "Sunday in the Park," a song with no political agenda. He always claimed that the socially significant tag was "an accident," and a Boston critic concluded after interviewing Rome that "he is really doing his level best to get away from the burden of the world's troubles to avoid putting out words and music which have no mission but to entertain."[19] Rome added in that same interview, "[T]here's a headache and a handicap trying to write music with a message."[20] Whatever problems he may have had composing such songs, Rome was among the few who could do it, as song historian John Bush Jones explained:

> That the tone of his songs was never extremist helped Harold Rome's success as one of the most committed Depression-era, left-wing composer-lyricists. However left-of-center his points of view, Rome's good sense, judgment, and taste made his songs attractive to general audiences by couching pro-union (sometimes almost pro–Communist), anti-establishment, and anti–Fascist sentiments in clever, topical lyrics set to catchy tunes.[21]

## 5. Political Endeavors and The Little Dog Laughed

The plot of *The Little Dog Laughed* was considered too thin to support a legitimate Broadway musical, although several performers were highly praised, mostly the dancers — Paul Draper, Melissa Mason, Louis Hightower, and Marjorie Bell — working with the strongly ballet-influenced choreography of Chester Hale.[22] Bell would go on to great success, teaming with her future husband as Marge and Gower Champion. Receiving less praise was European chanteuse Mili Monti, whose voice was felt to be too limited for the musical stage.[23] The show's musical director, Lehman Engel, referred to her as "a nightclub singer of infinitesimal talent."[24]

Although *The Little Dog Laughed* was considered more political than musical, Rome managed to write "some grand tunes and set them with telling lyrics,"[25] although another critic felt the show "lacks voices" to carry off the songs — Miss Monti again. Singled out favorably by several critics were "I Want Romance" and "Happily Ever After," although none of his tunes had any life outside of the show, and hardly any within it.[26] Pre-Broadway tryouts started in Atlantic City on August 13, 1940, and the show closed in Boston eleven days later.[27] Despite a lavish production, large cast and two choruses, *The Little Dog Laughed* was "an experimental [but] impractical musical" that went nowhere.[28] Orchestrator Hans Spialek put it bluntly:

> The show was ... revoltingly bad.... Although the first showing met with a very lenient audience, the show was still bad, and all the concerted efforts of the talented Paul Draper, Lehman Engel, Philip Loeb, Harold Rome, etc., failed to transform this childishly symbolic monstrosity into a modicum of entertainment.[29]

More so than the failure of *Sing Out the News*, the failure of this show bothered Rome, as he had worked on two other shows around this time that also went nowhere, *Caleb Calum's America* and *Give a Viva!* He told oral historian Martin Bookspan in an interview four decades later, "A show that doesn't go on is something, somehow that you put away and don't want to look at again. It represents so many hours of anguish and writing."[30] Bookspan took the idea of failure a bit farther, asking Rome if he felt these shows had been "mistreated." Rome was philosophical: "Sometimes they don't work out. That's show business for you."[31]

Rome seldom felt his work underrated or ignored. When he hit his stride on Broadway, he felt that there were producers willing to do his shows, often saving him from shopping a show around and the ordeal of "angel" auditions. These were the intimate presentations of the songs of a show to potential investors (angels). They were usually presented by the composer at the piano with the lyricist singing, often at the home of one of the potential backers. The duo of composer-lyricist could be compelling. A reluctant Moss Hart was convinced to direct *My Fair Lady* by a presentation by Frederick Loewe and Alan Jay Lerner.[32] Many composers—Harold Arlen, Johnny Mercer, Rome—had more than passable voices and could pull off a mini-show. In other cases, a singer might be brought in, although the artistic intensity of a songwriting duo performing their works could be quite compelling. Angel auditions were usually dreaded by the creative team, especially if they were trying to sell a new concept. Innumerable angel auditions had to be done for *Oklahoma!* as Richard Rodgers, Oscar Hammerstein II, and Theresa Helburn from the struggling Theater Guild tried to raise money for their new kind of book show.

During attempts to get *The Little Dog Laughed* to Broadway, Rome continued writing songs for causes. Two from this period are especially noteworthy. "We Sing America" was a patriotic anthem written for and dedicated to the Council Against Intolerance in America. As political conflict spread through Europe, Americans became more patriotic and appreciative of their way of life, bringing Rome to write the song and its dedication which read as follows:

> WE SING AMERICA is dedicated to the Independence Day Ceremony of the Council Against Intolerance in America, in which thousands of American communities have joined to make July Fourth, 1939, a stirring reaffirmation of those basic principles of liberty and equality set forth in the Declaration of Independence upon which our nation is founded.[33]

In the same vein and year, Rome wrote a satire aimed at the recent incursions on the rights of citizens. Although McCarthyism and the House Un-American Activities Committee had not yet come into existence, suspicions were rising within the government regarding various political persuasions and nationalities. A rally against such intrusions was staged at Madison Square Garden and Rome's song, "Who's Gonna Investigate the Man Who Investigates Me?," was performed by Zero Mostel.[34] Representative of the tenor of the song was the Interlude:

> Maybe they won't like the clothes he's wearing—
> Maybe he has too much class.
> Maybe he's a guy who's fond of herring,
> Maybe he drinks tea from a glass.
> Believe me, brother, that won' pass.[35]

Rome had written a similar song in 1937 for *Pins and Needles* entitled "When I Grow Up" ("The G-Man Song") which was a satire on J. Edgar Hoover. Hoover had been director of the precursor of the FBI, the Bureau of Investigation, since 1924 and had gained much power in the halls of government. He would lead the Bureau through 1972, into the era of the FBI. Rome explained years later that when "G-Man" was sung during *Pins and Needles*, local FBI agents, often four or five at a time, would slip in to hear the song and get a laugh at their boss's expense. Rome claimed that by the end of the run, every agent in New York had heard that song performed.[36]

Throughout the thirties, Rome had been supportive of the Soviet Union and the communist way of life, though he never became a member of the Communist Party. He told an interviewer in 1982 that he had been approached to join. Though always open to liberal causes, he said of communism: "It never appealed to me.... It was too un–American somehow. It was too alien to me..."[37] On the lighter side of this topic, his obituary in the *New York Times* noted: "He once recalled that he used to slip into his [piano] repertory a swing version of the 'Internationale,' the communist anthem."[38]

Never a Communist but very much a liberal Democrat, Rome wrote special lyrics for the 1940 re-election campaign of Franklin Roosevelt, to the tune of—what else?—"Franklin D. Roosevelt Jones"[39]:

> I hear tell that there's good news for the whole country
> Yessiree! Yessiree!
> Franklin D.
> I hear tell Franklin D. is gonna stay in D.C.
> Yessiree! Yessiree! Washington, D.C.
> Won't the nation dance about, cheer and shout, when they find out.
> Yessiree! Yessiree! Yessiree!
> It's a big holiday everywhere
> There is one man that our country cannot spare!
> We'll keep him to the fore
> For we're voting once more
> For the Franklin D. Roosevelt Way!

Roosevelt ran successfully and would lead the country into the growing war in Europe and Asia.

By 1939, defending Joseph Stalin and other Soviet leaders became problematic as they had signed a non-aggression pact with Germany; but by 1941, Hitler reneged and invaded Russia. This action spawned numerous pro–Soviet songs by several noted composers of the day including Irving Berlin, Clarence Gaskill, Woody Guthrie, Andy Razaf, and Meredith Willson. Jerome Kern and the always politically active E.Y. Harburg wrote "And Russia Is Her Name," combining a love song with support of Russia.[40]

Of course, leading the barrage of songs was Harold Rome. In *The Songs That Fought the War*, John Bush Jones expands on this:

> It's not at all surprising that composer-lyricist Harold Rome had a hand in one-fourth of the sixteen songs written after the United States entered the war that dealt in whole or in part with the Soviet Union.... [O]nce Germany violated the pact and invaded the Soviet Union on June 22, 1941, numbering Russia now among the Allies, pro–Russian sympathy returned

to left-leaning songwriters once again, with Harold Rome very much in the forefront.[41]

Rome's five songs from the period were[42]:

| Song | Publisher | Year | Lyrics | Music |
|---|---|---|---|---|
| "United Nations on the March" ("United Nations March") | Am-Rus Music | 1942 | Harold Rome | Dmitri Shostakovich |
| "Franklin D.—Winston C.—Joseph V. Victory March" | Leeds Music | 1942 | Harold Rome | Harold Rome |
| "Meadowland" ("Cavalry of the Steppes") | Leeds Music | 1943 | Harold Rome | Lev Knipper |
| "Forward" ("Song of the Red Army Tank Parade") | Unpublished | 1943 | Harold Rome | Dan Pokrass and Dimitri Pokrass |
| "Anthem of the Union of Soviet Socialist Republics" | Am-Rus Music | 1944 | Sergei Mihalkov and El-Registan (Russian), Harold Rome (English) | A.V. Alexandrov |

For his "Franklin D.—Winston C.—Joseph V. Victory March," Rome commingled two earlier songs, "F.D.R. Jones" from *Sing Out the News* and "Little Miss Liberty Jones" from *Let Freedom Sing*.

Rome's best known Soviet-related song was "United Nations on the March," adapted from the film music of Dmitri Shostakovich. He was the brilliant Russian composer, born in St. Petersburg in 1906, who wrote his first of fifteen symphonies at age eighteen. His most famous was his 7th, subtitled *The Leningrad Symphony* and written during the Nazi siege of Russia, symbolical of that struggle.[43] Despite his talent and fame, Shostakovich was ordered to work within the Soviet system and had begun doing film work in 1931 with *Alone*, which included the song "How Beautiful Life Will Be," which became a minor hit for him. A year later, he was assigned to do music for *The Counterplan*, a.k.a. *The Passer-by*, whose plot involved efforts to catch "wreckers" (anti–Soviet saboteurs) within a Soviet factory.[44] Strongly opposed to the story, he chose to compose music only for the lighter, happier scenes. As described in the *All Music Guide*:

> [O]ne piece became his best-known music, "The Song of Meeting." This theme, which Shostakovich used in other film scores, where it never failed to bring down the house, so penetrated Russian consciousness that it is as ubiquitous there as "Happy Birthday to You," and, similarly, it surprises people (even in Russia) that it not only has a composer, but that the composer is Shostakovich.[45]

Whether Rome and Shostakovich ever met is unclear, but Rome took "The Song of Meeting" and wrote lyrics to create "United Nations on the

March," a song of hope, looking ahead to "a new day for mankind."[46] At the time, "United Nations" was synonymous with the Allied forces and because of patriotic fervor during the war, the march achieved some popularity. In 1943, it was played at a program entitled *Music at Work*, the first installment of a series of benefits held at Carnegie Hall for Russia War Relief that included composer Marc Blitzstein and pianist Teddy Wilson.[47] The song was heard with different lyrics in the 1943 MGM film *Thousands Cheer*, and was used at War Bond drives and political rallies. As late as 1946, "United Nations on the March" was sung at an anti–Dewey rally by a CIO chorus with new lyrics by Rome.[48] An intelligent, liberal composer could always find a way to get the word out.

*Chapter 6*

# Wartime Efforts

"In the vanguard and doing a very patriotic turnaround was prewar leftist and isolationist Harold Rome...."— John Bush Jones

In the early forties, America was at war and Broadway was in transition. The smart musicals of the previous decade had faded, and revivals of Viennese operettas were doing poorly, closing after less than fifty performances.[1] Vaudeville had likewise suffered. With the country's eyes and efforts focused on Europe, 1942 looked like a bleak year for Broadway. It was as if all those employed on the Great White Way were waiting for Richard Rodgers and his new collaborator, Oscar Hammerstein II, to wake them up. Into this atmosphere, showman Michael Todd brought *Star and Garter*, a burlesque revue, opening on June 24, 1942.[2] Burlesque had been an extremely popular entertainment, featuring lots of girls in elaborate costumes and various stages of undress, coupled with satirical skits or burlesques, poking fun at topics of the day or classical theater, Shakespeare, and opera.[3]

In addition to the recreation of burlesque, Todd and director Hassard Short used another practice of old musical theater, the employment of several composers and lyricists to supply the songs. Many of the great songwriters got their start contributing songs to revues or other musical theater. Often, there would be a main composing team, but then several songs would be interpolated into the score. In other shows, no main songwriting team would be used, but several songwriters would be asked to contribute a song or two. Once in awhile, a song contributed to a show in such a fashion would stand out and put the songwriter on the map. Some of the more outstanding examples of this include[4]:

| Songwriters | Song | Show | Year |
|---|---|---|---|
| Jerome Kern–<br>    Edward Laska | "How'd You Like to Spoon with Me" | *The Earl and the Girl* | 1905 |
| Irving Berlin | "Alexander's Ragtime Band" | *Friar's Frolic of 1911* | 1911 |

| Songwriters | Song | Show | Year |
|---|---|---|---|
| Richard Rodgers–Lorenz Hart | "Manhattan" | *Garrick Gaieties* | 1926 |
| Harold Arlen–Ted Koehler | "Get Happy" | *Nine-Fifteen Revue* | 1930 |

To score *Star and Garter*, several well-known songwriters were employed, each contributing a song or two, many from their trunks, that collection of songs previously written but never used; for a few, even tunes used previously were employed. The composers and their songs for *Star and Garter* included[5]:

| Song | Lyrics | Music |
|---|---|---|
| "Star and Garter Girls; For a Quarter" | Jerry Seelen | Lester Lee |
| "Les Sylphides Avec la Bumpe" "Don't Take on More Than You Can Do" | Jerome Brainin, Irving Gordon, and Alan Roberts | |
| "The Bunny" | Harold Rome | Harold Rome |
| "The Girl on the Police Gazette"[A] | Irving Berlin | Irving Berlin |
| "I Can't Strip to Brahms" | Gypsy Rose Lee | Gypsy Rose Lee |
| "Blues in the Night"[B] | Johnny Mercer | Harold Arlen |
| "Robert the Roue"[C] | Al Dubin | Jimmy McHugh |
| "I Don't Get It" | Sis Wilner | Doris Tauber |
| "Brazilian Nuts" | Al Stillman | Dorival Caymmi |

A — from the film *On the Avenue*
B — from the film *Blues in the Night*
C — from the Broadway show *Streets of Paris*, 1939

Names like Berlin, Arlen, Mercer, Dubin and McHugh often showed up on the roster of composers for a revue, but the name of Gypsy Rose Lee never had. Not known as a songwriter, the "doyenne of the burlesque wheel" was 31 years old at the time and had made quite a bit of money in her field.[6] This allowed her to be one of the main investors in *Star and Garter*.[7] She also starred in the show along with Georgia Sothern and dozens of younger girls, performing her own song, "I Can't Strip to Brahms." Another veteran performer was Bobby Clark, who did a burlesque of Shakespeare entitled "That Merry Wife of Windsor" as well as a repeat performance of "Robert the Roué" from *Streets of Paris*.[8]

Rome's contribution to the revue was "The Bunny," a song with a story that he told to an interviewer, circa 1987:

> [T]he girls came out holding a small bunny against their midriffs... The girls just sang that you couldn't get their bunny, bunny, bunny for no amount of money, money, money. After a year, we received a complaint from the City. So "Bunny, Bunny, Bunny" became "Money, Money, Money." Regardless of the City's attitude, I got a letter from Cole Porter asking for a copy of the song, which was not published.[9]

This may seem like thin fare, but it was the type of entertainment that wartime theatergoers in New York were looking for. Much to producer Todd's advantage, Mayor Fiorello La Guardia had closed New York's burlesque houses in April of 1942, two months before *Star and Garter* opened. Not only were there ready customers for the show, but the city's best comics and showgirls were available to bolster the cast. It ran 609 performances, impressive for any show, especially a revue heavy with burlesque.[10] Apparently, *Star and Garter* allowed them to take their minds off the war for a few hours because otherwise, nearly everyone was becoming engaged in one aspect or another.

Until the Japanese bombed Pearl Harbor on December 7, 1941, America had been reluctant to enter World War II. After that "date that will live in infamy," the country convincingly joined the war with personnel, equipment, and funding. Like most men of the era, the artistic crowd from Broadway, Hollywood, and Tin Pan Alley joined up in whatever capacity was appropriate. Entertainers were soon performing in all the theaters of war. At the behest of President Roosevelt and General George C. Marshall, the United States Service Organization (USO) had been created; the private, non-profit organization worked in conjunction with the Department of Defense.[11] From 1941 through 1945, the numbers for USO performances and entertainers are astounding[12]:

| | |
|---|---|
| Performances: 293,738 | Visits: 208,178 |
| Service people entertained: over 160,000,000 | Troupes: 702 |
| Hospitals visited: 192 | Wounded entertained: over 3,000,000 |

The roster of stars involved in USO tours was a who's who of American entertainment. In addition, the Army had a Special Services division devoted to entertainment, a unit where Harold Rome worked during most of his time in the service.

There was also entertainment stateside under the auspices of the American Theatre Wing (ATW), Broadway's wartime service organization. ATW was well-known for its successful War Bond drives as well as the Stage Door Canteens it sponsored and manned, entertaining military personnel across the country.[13] Wanting to increase their wartime efforts, ATW decided to organize shows to entertain defense workers and was led by director Moss Hart, actress Aline MacMahon, producer Kermit Bloomgarden, actor and executive secretary of the American Federation of Radio Artists George Heller, and composer Kurt Weill.[14] Their initial efforts were modeled on Britain's Entertainment National Service Association (ENSA):

> This assembly of performing artists, entertainment industry trade unions, and managerial associations was formed as part of England's home front campaign.... Among the many programs administered by ENSA was a

series of mealtime entertainments presented to defense plant workers, and operated under the coined name of ENSAtainment.[15]

British manufacturers were of the belief that such entertainment improved productivity by five percent or more; as one shipyard worker said: "You bring the shows, we'll build the ships!"[16] Like ENSA, ATW developed shows that included songs, sketches, and comedy, presented in an atmosphere of relaxation and escapism as, after all, this was break time. In addition to its primary purpose of providing a brief change of pace and a morale boost for defense workers, ATW also hoped to engender an interest among blue collar workers in music and theater that could translate to larger postwar audiences.[17] Living in New York and socializing with the theater crowd, Rome became involved with ATW soon after Moss Hart, his *Sing Out the News* collaborator. Rome's grasp of popular culture and politics and his sense of humor made him ideal for the project.

The first performance of *Lunchtime Follies* was given at the Wheeler Shipyard complex just outside of New York City on June 8, 1942.[18] Within a year, the various units had performed in fifty-five factories for over 250,000 workers.[19] Stages for the shows included factory floors and parking lots; what little scenery there was might be hung from beams and ceilings. The shows' formats were developed along the lines of early Broadway revues with sketches and songs presented in no particular order and with little plot. Time was of the essence in order to fit the shows within the parameters of the particular factory's breaks or lunch hours, which varied from fifteen to fifty minutes.

Typically, since many plants were working 24-hour days, shows were presented at noon, 4 P.M., 8 P.M., and 4 A.M.[20] Among the larger East Coast companies participating in the *Follies* were Sperry Gyroscope Company, RCA-Victor, Revere Copper and Brass, Gould & Eberhard War Plant, Maryland Drydock Company, Rustless Ironworks, Wheeler Shipyard, and Curtiss-Wright, a propeller factory.[21] Factories paid fees to the American Theatre Wing, usually around $200, mostly to defray costs of transportation and the supporting cast, as any stars involved would usually contribute their time.[22]

*Follies* topics were world-wide and ranged from World War II down to local politics or even the foibles of a particular factory and its management. The director usually met with the plant operators and got the lowdown on anything local. Of course, the primary focus was the Axis enemies and especially Hitler, about whom numerous skits were performed. Hart and George S. Kaufman wrote one entitled "The Man Who Went to Moscow."[23]

Once in a while, a more substantive topic was presented, as detailed by Aline MacMahon, one of the originators of the *Follies*: "The war production board had a tasty list of troubles — tardiness, absenteeism, accidents, lack of war consciousness, and we converted the problems into entertainment."[24] Tardiness was most common, and at his comic best, Rome addressed the problem with "On Time," combining war and romance, sung by the show's star."[25] Harold Arlen and Frank Loesser had written on the same subject in "On the Swing Shift" for *Star Spangled Rhythm*, a 1942 Paramount production. Because Rome was writing for a private production not to be aired, his lyrics were more risqué and made the point with greater humor.

Safety was a topic addressed by Rome in two songs, "Flippy, Floppy, Mopey, Dopey, Sloppy Joe" and "That's My Pop," as mishandling of the heavy machinery, materials, and explosives could mean death or disability. The first song tells "the mock mournful tale of a worker who disregarded safety regulations," while the latter lauds a safe and conscientious worker from the eyes of his child.[26] Again, Rome was not alone among popular songwriters in dealing with the subject, as Irving Caesar and Gerald Marks wrote "Father in the Factory," advice from a child to his two war-worker parents.

Always sensitive to the opposite sex, especially their adjustment to life in wartime, Rome wrote several songs focusing on women on the assembly line: "The Lady's On the Job," "Solid, Solid, Suzabelle," and "She Rolled Up Her Sleeves — She Hitched Up Her Hose."[27] Also focused on the distaff side was "On That Old Production Line," acknowledging the contributions of housewives to the war effort. Rome's other songs used frequently for the *Follies* were "Gee, But It's Cold in Russia," and "Victory Symphony Eight to the Bar."[28]

East Coast *Lunchtime Follies* included other well-known theater personnel: producers Max Liebman and John Murray, writers Kaufman, Maxwell Anderson, J.P. McEvoy, and Kenneth White, comedians Milton Berle and George Jessel, and Broadway performers Arlene Francis, Anne Franchine, Josh White, Arthur Elmer, Vivienne Segal, Ella Logan, and Betty Garrett, who was to star in Rome's postwar success *Call Me Mister*.[29] In all, the ATW talent committee kept 150 performers on tap to fill the demand of various factories of different sizes, time schedules, and locales.[30]

Similar efforts were made on the West Coast with Hollywood creators and stars chipping in generously. Among the contributors were Joseph Field, Ira Gershwin, Jerome Kern, and Groucho Marx. The Writers' Mobilization organization in Hollywood worked closely with ATW, and for much of the war there were ten West Coast and eight Hollywood units touring plants in California and the Far West.[31] The overall effort of ATW to entertain American workers was a great success.

Despite his extensive work on *Lunchtime Follies*, Rome found time to get involved in a more commercial though no less patriotic show, *Let Freedom Sing*. This was to be pure revue, conceived by Youth Theatre, Joseph Pevney, and Sam Locke, who wrote the book, a term used lightly in the genre. Originally known as the Flatbush Art Theater and presenting amateur productions, Youth Theatre had evolved enough that its principals felt it was time to take on a bigger show and go professional.[32] Their success with *Of V We Sing* the previous year had encouraged them.[33] They felt that the patriotic fervor of the day would carry the show.

Rome was asked to write the majority of the score, but as often occurred with revues, other songwriters were enlisted to add one or two. These included a few of the well-known composers of the day including Marc Blitzstein, Lou Cooper, Edward Eliscu, Jay Gorney, Roslyn Harvey, Walter Kent, Earl Robinson, and Hy Zaret. Morton Gould and Phil Lang did the musical arrangements with Lou Cooper as musical director.[34] Rome wrote ten songs, most with a patriotic or militaristic theme[35]:

| | |
|---|---|
| "Run Up the Curtain" | "It's Fun to Be Free" |
| "The Lady Is a WAAC" | "I Did It for Defense" |
| "History Eight to the Bar" | "Little Miss Victory Jones" |
| "Johnny Is a Hoarder" | "Of the People Stomp" |
| "Give a Viva!" | "Be Calm" |

Rome's songs, as with many from *Lunchtime Follies*, were dictated by the times. In *Lunchtime Follies*, he had focused on other unpatriotic actions such as tardiness at work with "On Time" and carelessness and unsafe work practices with "Flippy, Floppy, Mopey, Dopey, Sloppy Joe." With "Johnny Is a Hoarder" in this new show, he took a shot at those on the home front who were keeping "assets" to themselves in the face of shortages and rumors of rationing of consumer goods such as sugar, coffee, canned goods, and rubber.[36]

Hoarding was a particularly sensitive topic on the home front, leading songwriters Mickey Gillette and Dick McCaffrey to write "The Bad Little Piggie" and Gene Carroll and Glenn Rowell to create "You're Out of Order, Mrs. Hoarder."[37] In *Let Freedom Sing*, Rome's anti-hoarding song was done by Betty Garrett, who had attracted attention in *Of V We Sing*, performing striptease and political satire in "You've Got to Appease with a Striptease."[38] With Rome's "Johnny Is a Hoarder," she wrote in her autobiography *Betty Garrett and Other Songs* that the emphasis of one particular line was "Your sister is a HOAR-der."[39] She also distinguished herself with a Latin song, "Give a Viva!," presaging her big hit "South America, Take It Away" in Rome's *Call Me Mister*.[40]

Another topical theme was getting stateside girlfriends to be appreciative of their soldiers. Sung by star Mitzi Green, Rome's "I Did It for Defense" was written in a comic vein, paralleling other songs of the day[41]:

| Song | Songwriters | From |
|---|---|---|
| "On Leave for Love" | Ann Ronell | *Count Me In* (Broadway show) |
| "You Can't Say No to a Soldier" | Mack Gordon–Harry Warren | *Iceland* (movie) |
| "Something for the Boys" | Cole Porter | *Something for the Boys* (Broadway show) |
| "I'm Doing It for Defense" | Johnny Mercer–Harold Arlen | *Star Spangled Rhythm* (movie) |

Green and Garrett were singled out for their performances,[42] though both were considered too inexperienced to carry a show. Ultimately, it was Rome's songs that were found wanting, considered across the board to be not up to the standards of *Pins and Needles* or *Sing Out the News*.[43] A more specific comment found the composer to be "merely repeating himself."[44] Whatever it lacked, *Let Freedom Song* ran only eight performances.

During this time, Rome had also been working on a musical of larger scope, described by Joshua Logan, the man later to direct two of Rome's biggest shows, *Wish You Were Here* and *Fanny*: "Years later, before I got into the Army, Harold Rome played me a score he had written for a musical show based on a current novel about the history of America. It was teeming with imagination and had great variety but it was early '42 and I had a prior commitment with the Army."[45] Less than a year later, Rome would have a similar commitment and the historical musical was never done.

Shortly after *Let Freedom Sing*, Rome was asked to contribute songs to another *Follies*, this one the *Ziegfeld Follies of 1943*, the twenty-fourth in the long-running series of revues. Florenz Ziegfeld had passed away by this time, so by special arrangement with his widow Billie Burke Ziegfeld, Lee and J.J. Shubert produced the new edition.[46] They had the show devised and staged by John Murray Anderson, who had produced his own revue series, *Greenwich Village Follies*, from 1919 through 1928.

This *Follies* was mostly a vehicle for Milton Berle, a veteran comedian of vaudeville and revues and a future fixture in early television. According to Ethan Mordden, "The star vehicle was the easiest musical to produce, because this extraordinarily central figure could walk onto the stage — even, into the first day of rehearsals — with an evening's worth of material all built-in."[47] Principal writers of the unremarkable score were Ray Henderson and Jack Yellen. Also contributing was Baldwin Bergersen, who had played one of the twin Steinways along with Rome for the opening weeks of *Pins and Needles*. Rome's only contribution that made it into the show was "The Micromaniac," a comedic piece for Berle. Rome also wrote "The Advertising Song" which was to earn him the usual songwriting royalties as well as additional income anticipated "from advertising or other commercial tieups as a result of this song."[48] It was cut.

Although "The Micromaniac" and the other songs had little life outside the show, it ran for 553 performances, the longest-running of the entire *Follies* series.[49] At this time on Broadway, there were few long-running shows. A comparison of *Playbills* from 1943 and 1944 demonstrates that only three shows had lasted a year at that time — *Ziegfeld Follies of 1943*, *Angel Street*, and *Oklahoma!*[50] This was elite company and somewhat ironic as the book musical that would redefine Broadway — *Oklahoma!* — was competing against a simple revue of a soon-to-be-bygone era. By the time *Follies* closed in July of 1944, Rome was deeply involved in efforts for World War II.

When war broke out in Europe, Rome had been a confirmed pacifist. Like many Americans, the deaths and injuries of World War I made the thought of another war abhorrent, especially one sacrificing young Americans. Into the early forties, Rome had remained against intervention in the European conflict, clearly stated in two of his songs in his mostly satirical *Pins and Needles*:

> Two songs Rome added late in the show's run were explicitly anti-interventionist, although dramatically different in their statements. When the third edition of *Pins and Needles* premiered on November 29, 1939, the new song, "Stay Out, Sammy!" (Mills, 1940), had a mother trying to keep her kid out of a brawl on the other side of the street, Rome's metaphor for Uncle Sam not scrapping with the European belligerents. But the number ends aggressively.... "The Yanks Aren't Coming" repeats the idea that America should have learned from the last war and not to get suckered into another one....[51]

But as Hitler marched through Europe and the Japanese bombed Hawaii, satirical songs were not enough and seemed almost out of place to audiences. Rome abandoned his isolationism and pacifism even before he entered the service. As explained by John Bush Jones: "In the vanguard and doing a very patriotic turnaround was prewar leftist and isolationist songwriter Harold Rome with "This Is Our War!"[52] Rome's song urged unity and participation in the war effort by the citizens of the United States. Thirty-five at the time, he was inducted on March 15, 1943, had six weeks of basic training, and was assigned to a Special Services unit, first to the New York Port of Embarkation, then to Fort Hamilton in Brooklyn. He was not alone, as several Tin Pan Alley and theater composers had joined up. The services recognized that many of these men were not front line material but that their capacities to entertain would be invaluable. Rome's description of his service position was delineated by him on his discharge papers:

> ENTERTAINMENT SPECIALIST: Wrote and staged soldier shows and entertainments. Also worked with units travelling to camps throughout the States.[53]

Rome's first large-scale effort in the service was *Stars and Gripes* which opened in July. This show was assembled by the entertainment talent assigned

Corporal Harold Rome works on songs for Army entertainments (probably at Fort Hamilton in Brooklyn) in 1943 (courtesy of Joshua Rome).

to Fort Hamilton, which was considerable, as illustrated by this roster of creators[54]:

| Personnel | For Stars and Gripes | Pre-war position |
|---|---|---|
| Pvt. Charles Mackenburg | Orchestrator | Arranger for Russ Morgan and Sigmund Romberg |
| Sgt. Murray Karpilovsky | Conductor | Musician for NBC |

| | | |
|---|---|---|
| Cpl. Ziggy Lane | Singer | Featured star at New York's Paramount Theater; toured with Chico Marx; radio |
| Sgt. Ace Goodrich | Comic-songwriter | Appeared in Broadway's *Panama Hattie* (1940) and *Nice Goin'* (1939) |
| Cpl. Dave Sugarman | Performer | Chicago night club; radio performer on NBC's *Breakfast Club* |
| Pvt. Glenn Jordan | Director | Assistant to Otto Preminger |
| Pvt. Martin Gabel | Director-actor | Theatrical producing firm of Wharton & Gabel |

Wartime productions always hoped to be entertaining, but most importantly they had to be "flexible ... to play under any conditions of posts, camps, and stations," some of them quite remote.[55] This was part of what became known as "blueprint specials — variety shows in kit form, for troops to present for themselves, with ready-made scripts, song sheets, and even do-it-yourself sets and costume designs."[56] For this flexibility, *Stars and Gripes* was created for a small cast (fourteen), with simplified sets and lighting, all presentable on any makeshift stage, which is what would be used at the various embarkation points and hospitals where it was to play.[57] In its three-week tryout tour, one performance was given on an old skating rink with an "ancient player piano,"[58] but when *Stars and Gripes*— "the revue for the soldier, by the soldier and of the soldier"[59]— premiered officially at Fort Hamilton, it was done up lavishly for the 650-seat theater. After all, the cachet of its experienced Broadway creators was drawing critics from Manhattan along with generals and other brass from the Eastern seaboard all the way to Brooklyn.

What they saw was a show of sixteen acts, ranging from sentimental to hilarious, designed to spoof the service with a healthy dose of sentiment for the boys leaving for and returning from the war, done with a "broad humor ... definitely patterned for the G.I. audiences for which it was intended."[60] Rome said of it:

> This show was designed strictly for soldiers, and is full of G.I. gags that might be incomprehensible to the layman. Our intention was to poke fun at the seamy side of Army life, such as goldbricking, saluting of officers, and the tongue-in-cheek camaraderie, with all your pals trying to do you dirt....
>
> [Audience of soldiers are] enthusiastic, they get the gags very quickly, and they laugh as no other audience I've ever seen before.[61]

High praise for comic talent was given to Ace Goodrich, to Ziggy Lane for his singing, and to the transportable sets and lighting. Besides the broad military humor, the other audience and critic pleaser was the music of Private Harold Rome who wrote seven original songs and modified a few old ones to fit his military agenda. In the latter category was his parody of "Begin the

Beguine," focusing much on the rhyming of beguine and latrine, etc.[62] Also singled out on the lighter side was "The Little Brown Suit My Uncle Gave Me," a song which compared "the positives of army life with the negatives of being a civilian."[63] The benevolent uncle is, of course, Uncle Sam.

Despite the overall comical tenor of the evening, two of Rome's original songs were of a more serious nature, "My Pinup Girl" and "Love Sometimes Has to Wait." The latter stood out and had some legs after the run of the show. This song paralleled many of the hits that came from and before World War II, sentimental ballads for the girl back home or the boy sent abroad. Some of these were wildly successful and were performed by numerous artists of the time. These same songs were featured decades later on albums by singers such as Rosemary Clooney and Andrea Marcovici.[64] Among the biggest of the World War II hits were[65]:

| *Song* | *Composers* | *Popularized by* |
| --- | --- | --- |
| "I Don't Want to Walk Without You" | Jule Styne–Frank Loesser | Helen Forrest with Harry James and Orchestra |
| "The Last Time I Saw Paris" | Jerome Kern–Oscar Hammerstein II | Kate Smith |
| "I'll Be Seeing You" | Irving Kahal–Sammy Fain | Bing Crosby |
| "I'll Walk Alone" | Jule Styne–Sammy Cahn | Dinah Shore |
| "It's Been a Long, Long Time" | Jule Styne–Sammy Cahn | Kitty Kallen with Harry James and Orchestra |
| "For All We Know" | J. Fred Coots–Sam Lewis | Morton Downey |
| "Sentimental Journey" | Bud Green–Lester Brown–Ben Homer | Doris Day with Les Brown and His Orchestra |

*Stars and Gripes* was a phenomenal success, playing all over the East and several times overseas, especially in the Pacific theater of war. Though critics made mention of the production as Broadway quality, the predominance of military topicality made the songs and sketches unfit for a general audience. What did work out for the show was conversion to a movie of the same name. The stars and several other members of the stage cast appeared in the movie, which was made at the Army's own Signal Corps Astoria studios, the first musical filmed there. Broadway veteran Captain Sheppard Traube directed, and the script was modified for the screen by Private William Saroyan.[66] The film was released in the fall of 1943 and shown to service personnel throughout the world; it was never given a general release.

Rome's *Stars and Gripes* songs were also included in *Skirts!*, a wartime production presented in England in 1944. It was a joint production in a few ways — English and Americans, Army and Air Force, stars and amateurs — and borrowed generously from numerous sources. Billed as "An All American Musical Adventure," *Skirts!*, like any show worthy of the troops, was designed to be mobile and flexible. It played all over England, including shows at the

Cambridge Theater in London and a command performance for Lt. General Jimmy Doolittle of the 8th Air Force and the Dowager Queen Mary at her country estate in Gloucestershire.[67]

Eighth Air Force Captain Arthur G. Brest conceived and produced it, tapping British comedienne Wendy Toye to star and choreograph and Major Tom Lee for costumes and scenery, a job he had performed for Irving Berlin's *Louisiana Purchase* in 1940.[68] Available for composing was Private Frank Loesser, who had been drafted and shipped back from California to serve in a Special Services unit like Rome. Just before coming east, he had written lyrics to "They're Either Too Young or Too Old" for Bette Davis in Warner Brothers' *Thank Your Lucky Stars*. After this song, he began writing music as well as lyrics and never looked back, forging one of Broadway's most successful careers.[69] Loesser stayed busy during the war, writing two legitimate hits based on true war stories, "Praise the Lord and Pass the Ammunition" and "The Ballad of Rodger Young." In between all this, he found time to help Captain Brest with *Skirts!*, writing the title song as well as much incidental music.

The creators of *Skirts!* borrowed bits and pieces from *Stars and Gripes*, including three of Rome's songs: "The Little Brown Suit My Uncle Gave Me," "My Pin-Up Girl," and "Jumping to the Juke Box."[70] Rome also wrote extra music for the show. His and Loesser's talents, each as composer-lyricist, combined to make it a musical success.[71] But the two of them were not finished, as they were both members of Special Services, the morale-boosting arm of Army Service Forces (ASF), that section of the military which handles non-combat functions. To honor their own unit, each man penned a song in 1944, Loesser's entitled "Salute to the Army Service Forces" and Rome's "The Army Service Forces."[72] It is not known if either one stood out, but neither made *Your Hit Parade*.

*Chapter 7*

# Vernon Duke and Other Work

"I can't get any emotion into Sanka Coffee."—Harold Rome

When Army Corporal Harold Rome was stationed in Brooklyn, he joined forces with Coast Guard Lieutenant Vernon Duke. Duke had come to America as Vladimir Dukelsky, Russian-born and -trained. He wrote both classical and show music, having had success by this time with *Walk a Little Faster* (1932) and *Ziegfeld Follies of 1934*, the latter including "What Is There to Say?" and "I Like the Likes of You."[1]

Rome and Duke became interested in a 19th century story centered on Nantucket, Rhode Island, a whaling town. It was a community that included the Religious Society of Friends — Quakers — and several of the plot elements emerged through that sect's view of the outside world. As always, Rome immersed himself in the cultures — whaling and Quaker — working along with book writers Samuel Hoffenstein and Gottfried Reinhardt. Typed notes by Rome in the Gilmore Music Library at Yale elucidate some of the idioms he used in the story and lyrics[2]:

| *Idiom* | *Meaning* |
| --- | --- |
| It isn't worth a hannacock | worthless |
| pooqua | quahugh (quahaug) chowder; clam chowder |
| flip | brandy concoction |
| sail loft frolic | impromptu dance in room where sails were made and mended, with music played on an accordion by a local sailor |
| I don't give a hooter | I don't give a damn. |

Rome also made notes regarding sea chanties (songs designed to get the sailors to work as a team when hauling ropes) and wrote comments on a capstan chanty, sung when sailors would use this mechanical device to move heavy weights such as an anchor.[3]

## 7. Vernon Duke and Other Work

*Nantucket* was never produced, but much work was done on it, including music by Duke and lyrics by Rome for at least nine songs[4]:

| | | |
|---|---|---|
| "The Devil Played the Fiddle" | "I Knew You Well" | "Je T'aime — I Love You" |
| "My Heart Decided" | "Song of Our Love" | "There You Are Again" |
| "You After All These Years" | "They Never Told Me" | "When It's Love" |

These songs and the book for the show were written mostly in 1943.[5] There was talk about doing it in 1946 with the same songs but a different book, but again to no avail.[6] "Song of Our Love" was used in the 1948 movie *The Angry God*.[7] In the fall of 1960, Rome and Duke corresponded about a possible production, bringing up the names of New York theatrical lawyer-agent Arnold Weissberger or Edwin Lester of the Los Angeles and San Francisco Light Civic Operas as possible producers.[8] Rome mentions a "new version" of "When It's Love"[9] as well as scenery sketches that Duke's brother had done, apparently on spec, as Rome declares, "Until we have a production set we can't even talk about scenery."[10] None of their efforts was fruitful, and *Nantucket* never sailed.

\* \* \*

In postwar America, the economy was booming, the advertising industry was flourishing on Madison Avenue, and songs and jingles were a big part of ad campaigns. Hard-working songwriters were always willing to lend their skills to works other than shows or movies. In some cases, composers would permit companies to use their melodies, as Cole Porter leased "It's De-Lovely" to the Desoto Car Company.[11] For most other products, new melodies and lyrics were written for a particular company or ad campaign.

Commercial work became so lucrative that Frank Loesser, seldom missing a business opportunity, used his Frank Music Corporation to organize songwriting talent under the aegis of Frank Productions, Inc., and hired such talents as Rome, Richard Adler, Hoagy Carmichael, Ogden Nash, and the songwriting teams of Charles Strouse / Lee Adams and Cy Coleman / Carolyn Leigh.[12] Raymond Scott formed The Jingle Workshop to create musical plugs.[13] Examples of specific commercial work by well-known songwriters over the years include[14]:

| Songwriter(s) | Product(Song) |
|---|---|
| Charles Abbott | Wesson cooking oil |
| Richard Adler | Kent and Newport cigarettes |
| Jerry Bock–Sheldon Harnick | Ford Motor Company tractors and implements ("More Power to You"; "Any Speed for Any Need") Ballantine beer ("Riddle Song") |
| Woody Herman–Neal Hefti | Wildroot Cream Oil ("Wildroot") |
| Woody Herman–Tad Dameron | Wildroot Cream Oil ("Cream Oil Charlie") |
| Frank Loesser | Piels beer |
| John Kander–Fred Ebb | *Go Fly a Kite* (General Electric industrial show); *Action '68* (Ford Motor Company industrial show); Citizens Committee to Keep NYC Clean ("Hey Litterbug") |
| Barry Manilow | State Farm Insurance ("Like a Good Neighbor") |
| Randy Newman | Dr. Pepper ("Most Original Soft Drink Ever") |
| Raymond Scott | Lucky Strike ("Be Happy, Go Lucky") |

This was not for art's sake but rather an economic decision. In most cases, ad writers would share their fees with the publishers and as with a song, would get ASCAP or BMI royalties with each performance. Richard Adler confessed to a *Time* reporter: "They kept asking me, and I finally decided, 'Why the hell not?' Rock 'n' roll was eating up all the air time anyway, and I was offered a good piece of money..."[15]

Even before his affiliation with Frank Music, Rome had tried his hand at jingle writing and achieved some success in 1943 with the Lever Brothers Company for which he wrote the "Rinso White Song."[16] He also wrote lines for the Sanka Coffee Company extolling the attributes of the decaffeinated brand:

> Take a sniff.
>     Smell the difference.
>         AROMA ROAST INSTANT SANKA COFFEE!
> Drink your fill
>     When you will, 'cause it's
>         AROMA ROAST INSTANT SANKA COFFEE!
>             Only Sanka gives all three
>             Aroma, flavor, caffeine free.
> It's terrif!
>     Smell the difference.
>         AROMA ROAST INSTANT SANKA COFFEE![17]

These lyrics were probably never used and are obviously not Rome at his best. As he admitted years later: "I can't get any emotion into Sanka coffee."[18]

*Chapter 8*

# *Call Me Mister* and the Revue

"We spoofed the Army ... but we had all fought in it, so that we were talking about something that we were part of." — Harold Rome

Harold Rome understood the revue. He had cut his teeth writing songs and sketches for evening entertainments at Green Mansions in the Catskills, and a few years later he had great success with *Pins and Needles*, a labor-based revue for the International Ladies' Garment Workers' Union. After this, Rome and other theater professionals helped the war effort by entertaining troops and factory workers with music and skits with *Lunchtime Follies*. As an enlisted man, he had written shows and other entertainments for the armed services. This experience would help him write the show he was planning while in the service in the late months of World War II, a musical revue to celebrate victory and freedom for the returning servicemen and women. To do this, he enlisted another soldier, Arnold Auerbach.

Like Rome, Auerbach had entertained troops, writing shows including *Hi, Yank!*, *About Face*, and *PFC Mary Brown* with songs mostly by Private Frank Loesser.[1] Before the war, Auerbach had co-authored scripts with Fred Allen for his radio show. Corporal Rome and Sergeant Auerbach became acquainted late in the war when both worked in Brooklyn at the Entertainment Branch of the Army's Special Services Division, Auerbach as a radio script writer.[2] The productions of the Special Services Division were utilized overseas wherever American troops were engaged, the shows being presented on temporary stages or on radio. Auerbach was to have more success writing sketches with Moss Hart and Arnold Horwitt for the successful 1948 revue *Inside U.S.A.*, with music by Arthur Schwartz and Howard Dietz. A year after that, Auerbach and Rome would collaborate on *Bless You All*, a revue starring Pearl Bailey which met with little success.[3] To get their demobilization revue staged, Rome and Auerbach needed producers. They turned to Melvyn Douglas and Herman Levin.

In the China-Burma-India theater of war, producer-actor Melvyn Douglas had been a major with Army Special Services and director of the Entertainment Production Unit which was responsible for theatrical entertainment of troops. During the war, the unit staged some 1,300 performances, entertaining close to one million audience members.[4] In his position, Douglas saw a wide variety of performances and artists. He wrote, "I began to notice a lot of fine material that could stand up with the best that Broadway offered... I took particular notice of the songs by Corp. Harold J. Rome and the sketches by Sgt. Arnold Auerbach."[5]

Rome and Auerbach's other producer, Herman Levin, had not been in the war. A lawyer since 1935, he had always been more interested in the theater than law. He gravitated toward the creative crowd that constantly fascinated him, serving as a personal manager and legal counselor for several artists including dancer Sono Osato. Rome had met Levin in the thirties through mutual acquaintances, and when the war ended, Rome became one of Levin's clients. When approached by Rome regarding the show, Levin tried to get several different producers but, when this failed, decided to produce the show along with Douglas. As co-producers, Levin and Douglas were able to raise the $150,000 needed with only three backers' auditions.[6]

All four men — Rome, Auerbach, Douglas, and Levin — envisioned a show focusing on G.I.s returning to civilian life, a show mostly on the light side that would not ignore the grim realities of the war and adjustment back home.[7] They all believed the best format for their views about demobilization and reconversion was a musical revue.

The musical revue was one of the main forms of entertainment that had developed in America. Musical entertainments evolved from the mid–19th century, starting out with minstrelsy shows, pantomimes, and extravaganzas, on through burlesque, vaudeville (variety), operettas, revues, and book musicals.[8] As each form evolved, with much overlap and intermingling, there were periods of discovery, popularity, and decline. As an example, up until World War I, the European operetta had been an extremely popular form on Broadway, featuring imaginary royal settings, elegant costumes, waltzes, and prominent sopranos and tenors. Anti-German sentiment of the time and the realization that a unique American culture had evolved, eventually pushed the operetta off center stage. As historian Lehman Engel phrased it: "One of the things necessary for the growth of the new musical theater was the liberation of its practitioners from the old romantic musical form. One of the primary instruments of this liberation was the revue."[9]

*The Passing Show* produced by George W. Lederer in 1894 is considered to be the first revue,[10] but the rise of the American revue, emerging mostly from minstrelsy, burlesque, and vaudeville,[11] began around 1906 with Florenz

Ziegfeld and his wife Anna Held, a French entertainer. They both admired the revues in Paris that included "contemporary skits, dances, songs, and vaudeville turns, all presented in rapid succession."[12] Moreover, Ziegfeld had the financial and promotional skills to follow through with the concept. Presented initially on theater rooftops, revues featured singers, musicians, and plenty of costumed girls, and as success came, they were presented in increasingly larger theaters. Ziegfeld's revues became a franchise — *Ziegfeld Follies* — as he presented over twenty editions from 1907 until his death in 1932. But as the *Follies* popularity grew, so did that of the revue form, and Ziegfeld had to share audiences with many producers who also serialized their revues, including[13]:

| Revue | Years | Producers-Creators |
|---|---|---|
| Ziegfeld Follies | 1907–1925\*; 1927; 1931; 1933; 1936; 1943; 1956; 1957 | Florenz Ziegfeld |
| The Passing Show | 1912–1919; 1921–1924 | J.J. and Lee Shubert |
| Artists and Models | 1923–25; 1925; 1927; 1943 | J.J. and Lee Shubert |
| Greenwich Village Follies | 1919–1925; 1928 | John Murray Anderson |
| George White's Scandals | 1919–1926; 1928–1929; 1931; 1936; 1939 | George White |
| Music Box Revues | 1921–1924 | Irving Berlin and Hassard Short |
| Earl Carroll's Vanities | 1923–1928; 1930–1932 | Earl Carroll |
| Lew Leslie's Blackbirds | 1926; 1928; 1933–1934; 1936; 1939 | Lew Leslie |
| New Faces | 1934; 1936; 1943; 1952; 1956; 1962; 1968 | Leonard Sillman |

Over the years of peak popularity of the revue, perhaps 1915 to 1930, the talent drawn to these productions — performers and writers — steadily improved. Nearly every star in Broadway or early Hollywood musicals had performed in revues, although few of them made it a full-time career. Revues were likewise a great impetus to the careers of the composers and lyricists of the era. Producers and directors would hire a primary composer who would, in turn, draw from many sources. This included interpolating songs of other composers into a show. From historian William A. Everett: "A song could be inserted either because the principal composer recognized its merits or because a star insisted upon its inclusion. It was also common practice for the principal composer, usually a staff composer for the producing body, to share credit on songs he chose to include."[14]

Almost all of the well-known composers achieved fame with a song that had been interpolated into a show and became a hit. Lehman Engel summarized: "As impressive as is the list of young performers supported and nurtured by the revue, it played an even more significant part in providing a useful showcase for composers and lyricists. Because of the musical hodgepodge and absence of stylistic unity, it was possible for a new young composer to write in his own individual style."[15]

To wit, two of the songs from Rome's first show, *Pins and Needles*, had become popular and brought him to the attention of Broadway producers. "Sing Me a Song with Social Significance" and "Sunday in the Park" had lives well beyond that ILGWU–inspired show, especially the latter one, which had caught the ear of producer Max Gordon, landing Rome a job as composer for *Sing Out the News*. For Rome, "Sunday in the Park" was a watershed and changed the image he had earned as "a sort of socially significant newsreel in the flesh; a Noël Coward with a conscience."[16] A more sweeping opinion of Rome's work prior to *Call Me Mister* is provided in *American National Biography*:

> Most of his songs had topical content, commenting on the plight of the worker during the depression years, an unusual topic for popular songs of the day, so he met with little success in selling his music to the standard popular publishers. While writing in a typical pop style of the day, the topical content of his lyrics was daring, mirroring the work of left-leaning folk song writers like Woody Guthrie.[17]

Rome's reputation as "socially conscious ... and of little interest to Tin Pan Alley"[18] had stayed with him well into the post–Depression years. He explained in an ASCAP symposium years later that in the late thirties, he had been hired to do *Pins and Needles* by Louis Schaffer of the Labor Stage because "he was looking for social significance, which I couldn't sell to anybody else on Broadway at all."[19] But as World War II ended and the economy was beginning to boom, he was able to adapt, and producers like Melvyn Douglas and Herman Levin took a new look at him and the revue.

The revue as a form had ebbed in popularity, causing critic George Jean Nathan to claim that "the average revue is indistinguishable from a second-rate, old-time vaudeville show."[20] When the successful revue producers passed away or retired, the revue foundered, as "audiences were indifferent to the format, which already belonged to another age,"[21] and "the disconnected, thrown-together patchwork revue of the old days [had] gone for good," the last spoken by Rome himself.[22] He also felt that from a composer's standpoint, the revue had become too difficult to do and still maintain the interest of the audience: "A revue is much harder ... you don't have the story and the characters going for you.... You've got to start again with every number. That's one reason revues had died out."[23]

But the early revue form had served its purpose and held its own against other forms of entertainment: "[W]hen revue, per se, flourished as an American art form and mass entertainment, it matched and more than fulfilled the entertainment requirements of a less demanding standard."[24]

To survive, the revue had to become more topical, focusing on a given subject — patriotism, society's excesses, politics — allowing songwriters to focus on ideas and themes. During the thirties, several revues centered on a topic and became big hits. Stand-out representative of these include[25]:

| Year | Title | Words–Music | Performances |
|---|---|---|---|
| 1930 | Three's a Crowd | Arthur Schwartz–Howard Dietz | 271 |
| 1931 | The Band Wagon | Arthur Schwartz–Howard Dietz | 260 |
| 1933 | As Thousands Cheer | Irving Berlin | 400 |
| 1938 | Hellzapoppin! | Sammy Fain–Charles Tobias | 1,404 |

These shows did well, musical director-historian Lehman Engel explained, because they fulfilled the desire of audience members who wanted these entertainments "to deal with literate ideas which would give a show some intelligent, audience-identifiable and sustained interest."[26]

Literate, intelligent shows had started to develop in the form of book musicals, shows that would tell a story much as would a play, but use not only dialogue but well-integrated songs and dances to advance the plot. Several productions over the years had moved toward this form, most prominent among them the Princess Theatre shows of Jerome Kern, P.G. Wodehouse, and Guy Bolton, then Kern and Oscar Hammerstein II's *Showboat*, and the later shows of Richard Rodgers and Lorenz Hart, especially *Pal Joey*. Lehman Engel declared: "From then [*Pal Joey*, 1940] on, in the best shows, drama and characters were to be believable; music, lyrics, and dancing were to become integrated and an inevitable part of the whole."[27] The final blow was Rodgers and Oscar Hammerstein II's *Oklahoma!* Numerous other writers and shows were also part of this evolution, and the creators welcomed the change — especially the composers. Gerald Bordman, composer Vincent Youmans' biographer, explained: "[L]ike most of the other better composers, Youmans preferred book shows. A story helped to suggest songs, while the formlessness of a revue gave composers little assistance."[28]

The book musical notwithstanding, Rome and his co-creators felt they had a workable subject to return to the revue form: young soldiers coming back from World War II into civilian life, leaving the military world which had been not only replete with danger but also with bureaucracy, logistical problems, and colorful characters. Post–World War I, Cole Porter had addressed the topic with "When I Had a Uniform On," also called "The Demobilization Song," from *Hitchy-Koo of 1919*.[29] There had been wartime revues: Porter's *Something for the Boys* and, more notably, Irving Berlin's *This Is the Army*, a hit on Broadway and all over the military world. That revue usually featured the master himself singing "Oh, How I Hate to Get Up in the Morning" which he had written for his World War I show *Yip-Yip-Yaphank*. Rome's revue was to be the logical successor to *This Is the Army* as these young people were now demobilizing from the military.[30]

Since Auerbach, Douglas, and Rome had served (in entertainment capacities), they wanted to tell their story. Rome put it succinctly for all of them: "No one who hadn't been in the Army could know why I had to write that show. I enjoyed it enormously and when it was produced I felt a great weight had fallen from my shoulders."[31] They were sure the revue would resonate with the ex–G.I.s. They also wanted to get across to their non-military audience the experiences, hopes, fears, and dreams that were part of the lives of the young men and women returning from Europe, Africa, and Asia. Rome would say of the show during its tryouts in Philadelphia: "And it's an optimistic show, because we believe this is a time for optimism. Through it all — and through my songs, I hope — there's a feeling that we had gone through a lot in the war, but somehow it wasn't for nothing."[32]

To capture all of this, Douglas and Levin insisted upon an all-military cast, young talents who had not only served in one way or another but also had the chops to pull off a Broadway show:

> [W]hen the time came for the legal formalities the men were lined up before a table where they first were required to show their honorable discharge papers before signing the Equity contract. The distaff side got by without troubles — besides a couple of Wacs and Waves, everyone had done some work for the veterans in hospital shows, USO-Camp-Show tours or in the canteen.[33]

The show's star, Betty Garrett, had performed in numerous *G.I. Jane* shows on military bases and hospitals as well as *Lunchtime Follies*.[34] Not just the cast of *Call Me Mister* had served during the war, but most of the creative staff had been in uniform as well, including the composer, director, sketch writer, dance director, music director, set designer, and costume designer. The *Playbill* of cast and creators included military records along with the usual litany of theatrical credits.[35]

The necessary closeness and hard work of the theater promotes a camaraderie that is well-known. As in any work place, solving problems, long hours, and dislike of a tyrannical boss (choreographer or director) bring a cast and crew together. With *Call Me Mister*, this phenomenon was especially true, as they had all been in the service. Rome said:

> There was a spirit in that show that was wonderful.... Everybody was so happy to be out and to be working; that was a happy show. We spoofed the Army, we spoofed some of the restrictions of the Army, but we had all fought in it, so that we were talking about something that we were part of.... I think we all felt it had to be fought, and we were all part of it — and we were all glad to be civilians again too.[36]

With demobilization their topic, the creators could focus on what the servicemen and women were demobilizing from and where it would take them. The sketches conformed well to this premise, Auerbach and his team coming up with the following scenes[37]:

- living the Hollywood-Noël Coward life in an Air Corps bar;
- Paul Revere fighting military red tape to get a horse for his midnight ride;
- a cafeteria waitress missing her boys after they leave for home;
- a trainload of G.I.s heading home, jubilant and hopeful;
- an anxious family, worried their ex–G.I. might have psychological problems;
- employment lines and the racial discrimination that existed in hiring;
- the guy who nobody liked, before, during, or after the war;
- the sailor home from the sea, seeing his newborn son for the first time;
- a barber describing troop movements on a customer's face;
- the act and thrill of finally purchasing "civvies."

Sketches have been called "the Achilles' heel of most revues,"[38] but Auerbach came through in spades. Critical compliments on his work included "a high level of hilarity,"[39] "sketches ... have pith and point,"[40] and "sly good humor."[41] Credited along with Auerbach was sketch writer Arnold B. Horwitt, who went on to write lyrics for the music of Albert Hague for their successful 1955 musical *Plain and Fancy*, set in 19th-century Pennsylvania Dutch country.[42]

What distinguished a good revue for a composer was maintaining a coherent theme and doing it with a balance of ballads, duets, chorus songs, dances, and the like. The military theme — during and after war — was right in Rome's wheelhouse. He believed a show required an idea,[43] and whatever he hadn't lived during the war, he had learned from the thousands of men and women he had entertained: "You've got to start with an idea that means something to people. Tie the song in with 'em."[44] The Rome songs were lively, sad, heartwarming, satirical, jubilant, witty, patriotic, and intelligent, in various combinations, but they all made their point about what these young people had faced or were about to face on returning home.

One of Rome's showstoppers was representative of this and it was singled out in several reviews: "Goin' Home Train."[45] This was an especially hopeful song, described by one critic as "a good, semi-spiritual chant"[46] and by another as "nicely contrived to establish the mood of the evening."[47] This song featured a solo by baritone Lawrence Winters but also encompassed five or six melodies sung separately, then in unison, a form Rome would use in later shows.[48] The set was a train car, one side opened to the audience and rocked from behind by four stage hands as the sounds of a chuffing train accompany the music.[49] Rome said of "Goin' Home Train": "If I succeeded getting into that song one-

The cast of *Call Me Mister* (1946) in the scene for the song "Goin' Home Train." Star Lawrence Winters is seated in center. The train car set was rocked by several stagehands behind the car to simulate the motion of a train (collection of the author).

hundredth of the mixture of joy, sorrow, nostalgia, impatience and emotional excitement of ex–GIs in the homeward bound coach, I think I've done all right."[50]

Another song popular with audiences, especially with servicemen, was "The Jerk Song." Rome told interviewer Roland Winters of the song's origin:

> I told George Kaufman I had an idea: "He was a jerk before he got into the army, and he's still a jerk."
> Kaufman replied: "What the hell more do you want? There's nothing better than a good one-joke song."[51]

The showstopper of all was Betty Garrett, the most veteran of the *Call Me Mister* cast and the only one to receive featured billing. Before Broadway, she had danced with the Martha Graham troupe and had a night club act. She had played supporting roles in *Jackpot*, *Laffing Room Only*, and *Something for the Boy*, understudying Ethel Merman in that Cole Porter hit.[52] Garrett's first song in *Call Me Mister* was "Surplus Blues," also singled out in several reviews.[53] It is sung by a cafeteria waitress lamenting her life, "wasted and lonely now that the soldiers and sailors no longer make passes at her."[54] The song captures the essence of her character's role in the war, working at a military eatery, putting up with the young soldiers, yet in the same song, worrying what the future held.[55] It is Rome at his best, capturing the plight of the everyday person, yet staying on target with the theme of demobilization. As he told *Times* critic Theodore Goldsmith: "Once I had the picture of the girl pleading with the president to bring back her uniformed boyfriends, the rest was merely a matter of variations on the original thesis."[56] Betty Garrett wrote:

> I sang "South America, Take It Away," as a worn-out hostess in a canteen where everybody is doing the latest Latin dances, while all I want to do is sit down and rest my aching back.... Four guys in Army uniforms keep sweeping me out onto the floor to dance the samba, the conga, or the rumba while I keep complaining about it.[57]

It was written as a satire on the dance crazes that had struck the States—conga, rumba, cha-cha, meringue, etc.—brought on by the popularity of things South American, spurred on by President Franklin Roosevelt's Good Neighbor Policy. Ironically, the least topical song of the show was the only hit to emerge. It was recorded by Bing Crosby and the Andrews Sisters for Decca Records, selling over one million copies and making *Your Hit Parade*.[58] It was also recorded by Bobby Clark, Xavier Cugat, Mel Torme, and Ted Heath, all to the favor of Rome's bank account.[59] Garrett's recording of the song was banned on the radio because a censor had determined that a line was "dirty"! The Andrews Sisters recorded their version with a more modest phrase and avoided censorship.[60]

As to "South America, Take It Away" and its hit status, when Rome was asked in a 1971 interview in *ASCAP Today* if he could tell if a song was going to be a hit he said:

> You may have a general idea about the whole thing, but about any particular song, I would say "no." And anybody who tells you he does is whistling up the wrong road because it's hard to tell the ultimate effect of a song.... The producer wanted to put ["South America, Take It Away"] in the show. We needed another number for Betty Garrett who was the star, and I said, "Well, I wrote it a couple of years ago and it may be out of date—and I don't especially like it." He said, "Let's try it." We tried it, and I still had no confidence in it. We opened the show and that became one of the big hits of the show.[61]

"South America, Take It Away" was not the only trunk song to become the hit of a show. A few years earlier, during tryouts for *Cabin in the Sky*, songwriters Vernon Duke and John Latouche felt a song was needed to lift the image of Petunia, the starring role played by Ethel Waters. Composer Duke remembered a song he had abandoned a few years before, "Fooling Around with Love," written with lyricist Ted Fetter. Historian Ethan Mordden tells the rest of the story: "Waters herself suggested reblending it as 'Taking a Chance on Love,' and Latouche reworked Fetter's lyrics. It proved to be Waters' great moment.... [T]he insertion of this one number utterly rebalanced the show.... Put simply, *Cabin in the Sky* took the critics' breath away."[62]

*Call Me Mister* was put through its paces in pre–Broadway tryouts in New Haven and Philadelphia. The out-of-town critics generally loved it, singling out Garrett, comic Jules Munshin, Lawrence Winters and various songs and sketches. All agreed it needed to be shortened. During the Philadelphia run, Vernon Duke took in the show and sent Rome a letter detailing problems with certain songs and scenes, prefaced by the following paragraph:

> Since I am a sincere and affectionate friend of yours, I cannot refrain from giving you some uncalled for but, believe me, well-meant advice. Your show, as you know yourself, stands an excellent chance of clicking in New York, as it is likable, engaging and bright, and the G.I. angle is all to the good. There are some rather serious flaws in it, however, that might cause some critics to become unduly patronizing or even abusive. You are a pretty determined guy and may not be swayed by any of the following, but here it is for what it's worth[63]:

Duke closed the letter, "Love and kisses, Spermin Puke." Duke critiqued four songs and/or scenes; it is unclear how much they were changed, but all stayed in the show.

In March of 1946, Rome received the U.S. Treasury's Silver Medal award for his artistic contributions, mostly on radio, to war bond drives. The letter from Lt. David Levy, chief of the Radio Section of the United States Naval reserve, stated that the award was being given "to a handful of persons in radio who have made substantial contributions."[64] One month later, Rome's demobilization revue *Call Me Mister* opened on Broadway at the National Theatre to extremely favorable reviews. The annual critics' poll in *Variety* awarded Rome Best Lyric Writer for the 1945–46 season, although the Best Composer prize went to Irving Berlin for *Annie Get Your Gun*.[65]

Perhaps the best compliment was from John Chapman of the *New York Daily News* who said that one of the songs, "The Red Ball Express," "stamps Rome as a composer and lyricist whom the war has taken far from Tin Pan Alley — praise be!"[66] Chapman was referencing the song and its scene featuring a black serviceman who applies for a job with three white ex-soldiers; of the four, only he is turned down. Such a racial topic for a Broadway musical was well ahead of its time in a country where the civil rights movement would not gain momentum for another fifteen years. This was vintage Rome, prompting his conservative friend Irving Berlin to ask, "Why do you do something like that?"[67]

Only a few weeks before *Call Me Mister*, the Ray Bolger–starring revue *Three to Make Ready* had opened and ran for 327 performances.[68] Despite these two promising shows, critics realized that the revue as a musical entertainment was all but gone with the advent of the well-defined book musicals of Rodgers and Hammerstein and others. Several commented how difficult revues were to assemble, and at the same time, lamented their passing.[69] Veteran columnist Elinor Hughes of the *Boston Herald* expressed the view of the majority of the aisle-sitters regarding *Call Me Mister*: "[S]o long has it been since a topnotch revue came along that I, for one, was beginning to fear lest this particular type of show ... had gone with the wind or to join the dodo."[70] Another critic wrote: "One Broadway musical production took cognizance of peace with one of the last of the distinguished socio-political revues."[71]

Within one year, this simple military revue with the initial investment of $150,000 had grossed over two million dollars,[72] and the initial investors, who had been recruited in less than a week by Douglas and Levin, had quadrupled their money.[73] *Call Me Mister*, having played in three different theaters, ended up with a Broadway run of ninety-one weeks and 734 performances,[74] the last American revue to enjoy a long run.[75] The national tour (which began before the Broadway closing) included New Haven, Philadelphia, Pittsburgh, Cleveland, Buffalo, Boston and Chicago, including a record four-and-a-half-month run in Boston and twenty weeks in Chicago.[76]

In Philadelphia, Betty Kean and William Warfield took the Garrett and Winters roles for the road tour.[77] Warfield would go on to great success as a baritone in recitals and night clubs. He played Joe in the 1951 film version and the 1966 Broadway revival of *Showboat*, putting his stamp on "Ol' Man River." *Call Me Mister* was a good show for a baritone, required on "Goin' Home Train," "The Red Ball Express," and "The Face on the Dime."[78] Also in this road cast were two emerging talents, dancer Bob Fosse and comedian Carl Reiner.[79] Betty Kean's sister Jane replaced Betty Garrett in the New York cast during the Broadway run.

In the fall of 1947, 20th Century–Fox bought the movie rights for $250,000.[80] Rome said years later, "They made a complete mess of *Call Me Mister*, putting other numbers in it, even other songs not mine."[81] Songs were added by Frances Ash as well as the teams of Mack Gordon and Sammy Fain and Jerry Seelen and Earl K. Brent. Fortunately, Rome's "Goin' Home Train" was kept and sung with great emotion by Bobby Short in his raspy tenor as he walked through train cars of G.I.s. The title song was done in ensemble led by stars Betty Grable and Dan Dailey. The only other Rome tune retained was "Military Life," but the lyrics were revised by Jerry Seelen.

Of the many successful Broadway skits, the Air Corps bar scene was the lone holdover.[82]

Unlike so many of the notable songwriters who had taken a liking to the money and sunshine of Hollywood, Rome did almost nothing out there. He felt he was doing well in the New York theater at the time, did not like Tinseltown's atmosphere, and never put much effort into getting work there. He did, however, confess to an interviewer years later, "I didn't get many offers."[83] Rome said of the whole *Call Me Mister* project and the movie world:

> I hated Hollywood because you weren't your own boss. You were completely at their mercy and whim. Broadway is the only place where the author is still nominally his own boss.
>
> I sold Hollywood *Call Me Mister*, took the money and ran. I knew they were going to kill it and I didn't want to watch.
>
> It may have been a terrible mistake, a failing, on my part, because I would have had a tremendous catalog of songs now if I had come here. I would have been richer. Maybe I was a little scared that I could only work in my own métier.[84]

Even those songwriters with more success there than Rome held Hollywood in contempt, as explained by Dorothy Fields' biographer Charlotte Greenspan: "[I]t was not in the hands of the songwriters to decide which — if any — of the songs he or she wrote for a film would be used. Not even the most highly esteemed songwriters — Irving Berlin, Cole Porter, Richard Rodgers, George Gershwin — escaped the humiliation of having their songs discarded from a film."[85] Many of them sounded off on the topic. When asked to compose for the movie musical *State Fair*, Rodgers agreed, so long as he and Oscar Hammerstein II did not have to come out to Hollywood. He and Lorenz Hart had had their difficulties there; Rodgers would say later: "[Larry and I] were enormously unhappy there. They didn't understand us, and we didn't understand them. There was no meeting of minds at all."[86]

Jimmy McHugh lost more than a few songs to the Hollywood cutting floor: "Such perfunctory decisions, often after weeks of ... work, were not exactly morale-boosting, but they came to be a commonplace experience for all composers and lyricists who worked in Hollywood."[87] Jerome Kern, the dean himself, did not like the way its producers and directors handled his songs, admitting that "he had all but given up fighting Hollywood's strange ideas and ways. He missed the authority Broadway granted him to impose his taste on his material."[88] Composer Hugh Martin, who along with Ralph Blaine became well-respected in Hollywood with *Meet Me In St. Louis*, put it more sarcastically: "All artistic choices were presented to us as *faits accomplis*. If we were pleased, 'That's nice, boys.' If not, 'Oh, really? I thought you'd like that, too bad.'"[89]

## 8. Call Me Mister *and the Revue*

The plot of *Call Me Mister*, conforming to Hollywood musicals of the day, was more boy-meets-girl than the musical, the screen duo of Betty Grable and Dan Dailey fulfilling their roles well — especially Dailey who could hoof with the best of them. The supporting cast was a who's who of television stars-to-be: Danny Thomas (*Make Room for Daddy*), Richard Boone (*Have Gun, Will Travel*), Dale Robertson (*Tales of Wells Fargo*), and Harry Von Zell (*The Burns and Allen Show*).[90] Unfortunately, the movie did not come out until 1951, and the World War II demobilization theme was stale by then.

Rome pointed out that both this show and *Pins and Needles* were truly done by people whom the show was about.[91] He elaborated on this to an interviewer years later, discussing his shows as well as later ones by other writers: "That's what gave their roles validity, because they were from the jobs they were singing about. The way I used all ex-servicemen in *Call Me Mister*. It's what made *A Chorus Line* work, that these were real gypsies talking to the audience. That was what *Hair* had at the beginning."[92] Of *A Chorus Line*, and implicitly *Pins and Needles* and *Call Me Mister*, he said that this "gave the audience a sense of identification with the people."[93]

He felt that in *Call Me Mister*, focusing on these particular people — servicemen and women — had made possible the re-emergence of the revue, arguably Rome's best genre. He also felt that these two revues of his were successful for another reason: "I think I did two outstanding revues, and they were outstanding because they had great ideas behind them. One was *Pins and Needles*, and the other was *Call Me Mister*."[94] He would go on to embrace the book musical, as would most of Broadway, but he always held these two revues in high esteem.

So true were the creators of *Call Me Mister* to their military men and women that the *Saturday Review* compared the focus of the show to the work of Bill Mauldin, the two-time Pulitzer Prize–winning cartoonist who struck a chord with the soldiers in the trenches with his infantrymen, Willie and Joe:

> [*Call Me Mister*] serves as a ventilator for gripes, both familiar and new. It blows the lid with something of Bill Mauldin's steam. It is far too removed from the feeling and atmosphere of combat to produce a Willie and Joe. Yet its spirit is as young as Mauldin's; its sanity as marked; and its thrust can often claim his accuracy.[95]

The most touching example of this was the show's ending. For the entire show, all sketches and songs had been done with the cast in military uniforms. Then in a spirited closing, the entire ensemble enters wearing civilian clothes to sing the finale "Call Me Mister," an effect that brought down the house as well as the curtain.

*Chapter 9*

# The 1950 Shows

"More shows have been killed by good reviews out of town than by bad reviews on Broadway." — Jerome Chodorov

Type — Musical Revue  Cast — Prodigal with talent
Credit — Superlative peaks  Debit — Ordinary valleys
Dances — Sensational  I find it — Fresh and winning[1]

These comments boded well for *Bless You All*, a musical revue with songs by Rome and sketches by Arnold Auerbach. The revue as an entertainment form had been waning on Broadway as book musicals came to the forefront. Producer Herman Levin had reassembled several members of the team from his and Melvyn Douglas's highly successful postwar revue *Call Me Mister*, banking on them to produce another hit. Levin was to co-produce with set designer Oliver Smith, the duo already having had successes with Jean Paul Sartre's *No Exit* in 1946 and *Gentlemen Prefer Blondes* which had opened in 1949 and was still running. Their initial investment in *Bless You All* was approximately $230,000.[2]

From *Call Me Mister*, Levin had tapped Rome, Auerbach, musical director Lehman Engel, comedian Jules Munshin, and general manager Philip Adler. Rome had emerged as a premier revue songwriter and was more than willing to keep the form alive. He was as topical as Cole Porter or Lorenz Hart and, along with E.Y. Harburg, was more in touch with the world of the common man, having demonstrated so with *Pins and Needles* in 1937 and with *Call Me Mister* in 1946. As encyclopedist Colin Larkin surmised: "More than any other American composer in the field of mainstream popular music, Rome's work consistently demonstrated an awareness of social issues, often to the extent that it kept him from the massive successes enjoyed by many of his contemporaries."[3] This impediment was the "social significance" label that had been placed on Rome during his early career and which he was slowly losing. Not until the mid-fifties with his book shows *Wish You Were Here* and *Fanny* would he be free of it.

The creators went to work in the spring of 1950. While *Call Me Mister* had had a strong, unifying theme — demobilization of G.I.s after the war — Rome and Auerbach thought they could revert to an older style, the revue, using a variety of topical material with little in common. This, despite Rome's assertion to a New York writer soon after the opening of *Call Me Mister*: "A revue needs a unifying idea. The disconnected, thrown-together patchwork revue of the old days has gone for good."[4]

With no previous book, play, movie, or other source, Auerbach and Rome were starting from scratch, inventing their sketches and musical accompaniments. Not working with a plot-driven book required more imagination and creativity for sketch writers and composers. Book shows often dictated where a song belonged, its tempo, feeling, and even some of the lyrics; for Rome, this was important. He preferred an idea for a song, finding it more and more difficult to write from scratch as his career progressed. In an extensive 1971 article in *ASCAP Today*, he explained: "Usually what comes to me first is the necessity for doing the song. The first thing you do is go over the book and find the high emotional points.... You find out what the situation or the scene has to say. You figure out the characters that are going to do it, and then you think of a song that will convey that — in music and lyric."[5]

Oscar Hammerstein II pointed out that his songwriting partner, Richard Rodgers, worked similarly: "He writes music only for a specific purpose. Ideas for tunes seldom come to him while he is walking down the street or riding in taxicabs, and he doesn't rush to his piano very often to write a tune just for the sake of writing a tune."[6] Their collaborator on *Oklahoma!*, choreographer Agnes de Mille, concurred: "To make up a dance, I still need, as I needed then, a pot of tea, walking space, privacy and an idea."[7]

In early American musical theater, this process of songwriting was reversed. It required songwriters to work from scratch, trying to get their songs interpolated into a show, usually a vaudeville or a revue. If a song were accepted for interpolation, it would then have a scene or skit created to accompany it; the idea followed the song. The producer would usually hire a songwriting team to anchor a show, but interpolations were frequent, competitive, and could make or break a show or songwriter. The dancing, costumes, and show girls were big draws, but were much the same from show to show. Beyond this, there were no interesting plots or characterizations to catch the audience. A revue needed songs and that is when the interpolations became crucial. Robert Baral said that the Shuberts' *Passing Shows*, presented at their Winter Garden Theatre, were "a melting pot for interpolated songs that quite frequently carried a show."[8]

As a result, the songs of these shows were eclectic, rendering it uncommon to see one composer and lyricist do an entire show. This held for shows from 1900 and even before, on through the twenties. Any accomplished Broadway composer could claim numerous interpolations — Irving Berlin, George and Ira Gershwin, et al. Jerome Kern, only a few years before his successful run of Princess Theatre Shows with Otto Harbach and P. G. Wodehouse, had a hit in the *Ziegfeld Follies of 1916* with "Have a Heart."[9] Lehman Engel in his *The American Musical Theater: A Consideration* broadened the importance of interpolations:

> As impressive as is the list of young performers supported and nurtured by the revue, it played an even more significant part in providing a useful showcase for composers and lyricists. Because of the musical hodgepodge and absence of stylistic unity, it was possible for a new young composer to write in his own individual style.
>
> All of the principal composer-lyricist personnel in our contemporary musical theater came to their larger Broadway assignments via one or two song contributions in revue....[10]

Prior to *Bless You All*, 1950 found Rome involved in two other revues, both reliant on these older revue practices and opening only a few months apart[11]:

| Title | Alive and Kicking | Michael Todd's Peep Show |
| --- | --- | --- |
| Opened | January 17 | June 28 |
| Rome songs | "Cry, Baby"; "Love It Hurts So Good"; "French with Tears" | "I Hate a Parade"; "Pocketful of Dreams"; "Gimme the Shimmy!" |
| Other Songwriters | Hal Borne; Hoagy Carmichael; Sammy Fain; Ray Golden; Irma Jurist; Paul Francis Webster | Sammy Fain; Bob Hilliard; Herb Magidson; Walter Mourrant; Raymond Scott; Dan Shapiro; Sammy Stept; Jule Styne |
| Foibles of the Day | newspaper offices; armed services brass; Edith Piaf imitators; psychiatrists | revivals of dances from the twenties; parade-goers; superiority of nature over science |
| Attractions | Jack Cole (dancer-choreographer) Lenore Lonergan (comedienne-singer) | "beautiful, bare showgirls and low, rowdy comedians"[12] |
| Weaknesses | no outstanding songs; disorganized | one good song, "Stay with the Happy People" by Jule Styne and Bob Hilliard |
| Performances | 46 | 278 |

Both shows were revue, reaching even farther back to burlesque, where skits were more far-fetched and costumes and scenery lavish. Fortunately, the composers and sketch writers of the shows had been well-exposed to and had written for both burlesque and revue. *Alive and Kicking* had comic songs for comedienne Lenore Lonergan and dances by Jack Cole. While Cole and his dancers — including Gwen Verdon — were artistic and effective and won a Donaldson award for choreography,[13] the show merely "attested to the waning interest in that genre [revue]."[14] Thirty years later, when Rome was interviewed by his friend and music director Lehman Engel, the two of them had another view of the failure:

> ROME: Now a lot of those numbers were used in a show called *Alive and Kicking*.
>
> ENGEL: I was just going to say we should talk about that show because that show is an example of people producing a musical show when they don't know how to do it and they attempt to control it.
>
> ROME: Oh Lord that was awful, it was a terrible experience.[15]

Rome's two best songs in *Alive and Kicking*— both sung by Lonergan — were "Cry, Baby," "a spoof of cheer-up tunes"[16] of the Depression era, and "French with Tears," a burlesque of "all those terribly sad and sexy French numbers which Edith Piaf sings to glassy-eyed sentimentalists who frequent night clubs."[17] But these ditties were pure revue with little to appeal melodically and no life outside of the theater. *Cue* magazine called the score "a scrabble of mournful numbers, songs in search of a supper club."[18] Not one to steal from his previous shows or his trunk, Rome did so for at least two songs of these 1950 shows, reusing "French with Tears" and "Pocketful of Dreams" from the previous summer's *Pretty Penny*.

*Pretty Penny* had been an attempt by Rome, director George S. Kaufman, and writer Jerome Chodorov to create a revue that would tour the summer theater circuit, beginning with the highly regarded Bucks County Playhouse in Pennsylvania, then Atlantic City, all the while being groomed for Broadway. Because of the limited budget and size restrictions in summer venues, Rome's score called for an "orchestra" of only two pianos, a device he had used with success in the initial version of *Pins and Needles* a decade earlier.

Opening in June of 1949, *Pretty Penny* ran up against sketch problems, inadequate rehearsal time, and Actors' Equity rules that made book changes difficult to do in summer productions. Beyond this, Kaufman quit after a tirade of abuse from one of the show's stars, comedian David Burns. Kaufman wrote Rome regarding the incident:

> I left Jerry to extend my apologies to you — I feel very bad that you and he and Lennie have to bear the brunt of Davy's behavior. His attack was so violent that I was deeply shaken by it, and it was just impossible to stay.
>
> You are not to feel that you should let Burns go on my account. He is more important to you at this stage than I am. However, I am filing [Equity] charges against him and I doubt if he will be allowed to work.[19]

Kaufman filed a grievance which resulted in Burns receiving a reprimand from the Actors' Equity Association.[20] The setback was a small one for Burns as he went on to a career that spanned over forty years, collapsing on stage during pre–Broadway tryouts for John Kander and Fred Ebb's *70, Girls, 70* in 1971.[21] Despite efforts of several talented people and favorable comments by Kaufman, *Pretty Penny* never saw a Broadway stage.

After using it in *Pretty Penny* and then *Alive and Kicking*, Rome moved "Pocketful of Dreams" to *Michael Todd's Peep Show* several months later. However, music was in no way the main attraction of *Peep Show*. Producer Michael Todd wanted to bring an old-fashioned entertainment to Broadway *a la* Ziegfeld, creating a "burlesque revue" featuring the Ladies of the Ensemble.[22] As John Chapman of the *New York Daily News* put it: "Dames, Prince Mike has been heard to say — people want dames... And [Todd] seems so fond of navels that he would go quite off his rocker in an orange grove."[23]

Todd, of course, was not the first to recognize the drawing power of "dames." Though Ziegfeld had taken the idea and classed it up, other producers of the day advanced the concept. In response to Ziegfeld's successes, the Shubert brothers, J.J. and Lee, had developed their *Passing Show* franchise, done periodically as were the *Follies* and other recurring revues. At first, the Shubert shows did well based on their "snappier songs and broader sketches,"[24] but then as more producers got into the game, each *Passing Show* put more emphasis on sex. Again from Baral's *Revue*:

> The *Passing Show* still leaned on burlesk [sic], frequently smutty.... Revue competition grew stronger and stronger and THE GREAT BROADWAY PERIOD was ready to break wide open. Rival revues were picking up the formula; the best thing was to load the Winter Garden runway with girls and more girls. Anything was an excuse to bring them out.[25]

Popularity of revue and their girlie aspects had waxed and waned for decades from the beginning of the century, but by 1950, the form had mostly disappeared in the shadows of book shows.

Showman Todd thought the time ripe for a re-emergence of the revue. Conflict in Korea had been growing for months, dictating "a popular entertainment for a troubled time."[26] Reviews of *Peep Show* were good in Philadelphia and audiences flocked to the show, wanting to "put away the thoughts of a possible war in the East and concentrated on such other basic topics as beautiful, bare showgirls and low, rowdy comedians."[27] The war broke out three days before the New York opening. The critics recognized *Peep Show* for what it was — well-decorated burlesque. After the show opened, local authorities came down on the producer, forcing him to change scenes with striptease and other off-color material. One of these involved Rome's song,

"Gimme the Shimmy!," the changes to which he explained to Lehman Engel: "The other [song] was a girl who revolves tassels on her tits in opposite directions at the same time — which the New York censor made them take out — the revolving I mean."[28]

A songwriter at the time could make a living wage with a few songs in a show, and fortunately for Rome, his "I Hate a Parade" and "The Model Hasn't Changed" were to be used in *Peep Show*. According to an agreement signed in April of 1950, Rome was to be paid $175 per week for each week the revue was presented. Three weeks later, two more Rome songs were added, "Gimme the Shimmy!" and "Pocketful of Dreams," for an additional $175 per week.[29] At the time, the income was important to Rome: "*Peep Show* opened to so-so-reviews but business seems to be pretty good. I hope it hangs on for a long time because it's my only income at present. One of the highpoints of the show is 'Pocketful of Dreams,' I'm glad to say."[30]

But as producers often did, most notably Florenz Ziegfeld, Todd was living from show to show, barely making ends meet. *Peep Show* opened June 28, and by mid–August, Todd was in arrears to Rome. On August 25, lawyer William Fitelson sent Rome a check with an explanation:

> This check is the result of phones [*sic*] and a telegram, reading as follows:
> DEAR MIKE: OVER TWO THOUSAND DOLLARS IS NOW OWING TO HAROLD ROME FOR PEEP SHOW ROYALTIES WHICH HE BADLY NEEDS. HE MUST HAVE HIS CHECK FOR THESE ROYALTIES NO LATER THAN NOON TOMORROW OR AN ACTION WILL BE STARTED.[31]

The amount of the check was not mentioned. The songs continued to be performed in the show through its closing in February of 1951.

As for the music and not the legal matters, Rome's songs for *Peep Show*, while good revue material, did nothing outside of the theater. The best of them, "Pocketful of Dreams," was sung by an assemblage of comedians rather than as a featured solo and was never picked up by a solo recording artist. This song was one of several songs he wrote about money, admitting that he was fascinated by opportunities for humor in money.[32] Other prominent money songs were "The Money Song" from *That's the Ticket* in 1948 and "The Sound of Money" from *I Can Get It for You Wholesale* in 1962.

Following the mixed successes of *Alive and Kicking* and *Michael Todd's Peep Show*, Rome focused on *Bless You All*. When it premiered in New Haven, Connecticut, on November 13, 1950, among the sketches and songs were the following[33]:

| Idea | Song |
|---|---|
| Penchant of Southern writers for discussing family morals | "Don't Wanna Write about the South" |

| Idea | Song |
|---|---|
| Woman bricking in her husband in the cellar of their home | "Little Things Meant So Much to Me" |
| Presidential candidate running campaign from TV studio | "Love That Man"; "Just a Little White House"; "Voting Blues" |
| Satire of the dance crazes of the fifties | "The Roaring '20's Strike Back" |
| Miracle cold remedies flooding the market | Sketch only |

This was true revue with little to unify these songs and sketches except (1) the audiences' appreciation for ridicule of the foibles of the day and (2) an abundantly talented cast. The *Theatre Arts* critic felt it had met requirement (1): "*Bless You All* satisfies basic revue requirements by providing a lively, occasionally charming collection of disconnected vignettes set to pleasant music. In addition, it marks the season's first triumph of satire over slapstick.... *Bless You All* should be blessed itself for giving the captive audience a chance to laugh intelligently at its manic tormentors."[34] A reviewer of the Philadelphia tryouts added to this train of thought: "A revue, of course, is just glorified vaudeville: an old-fashioned variety show with scenery and choruses. The producers of this one have not monkeyed with the pattern — just scratched the 'supper acts' and dressed it fit to kill."[35]

As for (2), an abundantly talented cast, featured players in the program included Pearl Bailey, Valerie Bettis, Mary McCarty, and Jules Munshin, and they all delivered. The latter two were the comedic staples of the production with McCarty delighting the house with her song as she bricked in her boring spouse, "Little Things Meant So Much to Me." With her other scenes, as one critic put it: "Whenever Miss McCarty is on the stage the fun seems effortless."[36] Munshin received like praise.

The other two standouts were Pearl Bailey and Valerie Bettis, the latter dancing several scenes and winning unanimous raves. Her ballet "The Desert Flame" was described by New York critic John McClain as "one of the most exciting things I've seen in the theater since 'Slaughter on Tenth Avenue.'"[37] Bailey was not in as many scenes as the three other featured players, and as one clever reviewer surmised: "She stopped the show only twice at last night's opening but that was because she sang only twice."[38]

Born in Virginia, Bailey had won an amateur contest in Philadelphia, rising from there to clubs across the country, USO tours, and a stint with the Cootie Williams band.[39] Postwar she was featured in Harold Arlen and Johnny Mercer's ill-fated *St. Louis Woman* along with Ruby Hill, the Nicholas Brothers, and Rex Ingram, who had been featured in Rome's *Call Me Mister*.[40] Bailey stopped the Arlen show with "A Woman's Prerogative" and in 1950, did a similar thing with "There Must Be Something Better Than Love" in *Arms and the Girl* with songs by Morton Gould and Dorothy Fields.[41] Bailey's delivery of a song was truly original, referred to as "conversational singing,"[42] well before Rex Harrison made it to Broadway. Her style was best explained by the same critic:

> [T]he tunes are unimportant because if you know Miss Bailey you know she doesn't bother much about them. What does matter are the words which are funny, and the way she intermingles singing and conversation, spaces or clips her notes, and virtually talks with eyes, expressions, and gesture. She can't be imitated and she simply can't be beat.[43]

Though not tied to the book, the songs "When" and "You Never Know What Hit You (When It's Love)" were important to her and to Rome. He tailor-made them to her singing, and it showed. She sang both in front of the curtain, in entr'acte format. She received raves in every review. The remainder of Rome's score was generally well-received, especially his lyrics, with critical comments that included "eloquent and pertinent," "deft and intelligent," and "literate and neatly edged with satire."[44]

"You Never Know What Hit You" and "Take Off the Coat" had both been recycled from a 1948 flop, *That's the Ticket*.[45] Another song from that show, "I Shouldn't Love You," was modified by Rome years later for *Fanny*, and the aforementioned "Cry, Baby" was added to *Alive and Kicking*. Originally titled *Alfred the Average*, *That's the Ticket* was noted by one race-track minded critic to be "by *Connecticut Yankee* out of *Of Thee I Sing*,"[46] while another thought it more "*One Touch of Venus* meets *Of Thee I Sing*."[47]

Julius and Philip Epstein wrote the book for *That's the Ticket*, having had recent successes with the screenplays for *Yankee Doodle Dandy* (1942), *The Man Who Came to Dinner* (1942), *Casablanca* (1943), and *Arsenic and Old Lace* (1944).[48] Julius would go on to write the screenplay for *Fanny* in 1960. The show was an election-year, political satire and, like *Of Thee I Sing*, involved a mythical political party. The party slates an enchanted prince to run for president, and to combat this, the opposing party transforms him into a frog. *That's the Ticket* featured place and time transformation of a main character as did *A Connecticut Yankee* and *One Touch of Venus*. Rome did an excellent job with a duet "Dost Thou," an homage to "Thou Swell" from *A Connecticut Yankee*.

*That's the Ticket* was the first Broadway musical directed by Jerome Robbins, who was "coerced" into the job by producer Joe Kipness, a former enforcer for organized crime.[49] The show ran less than ten performances, never making it to Broadway. As with most flops, the book was highly criticized. Robbins, too, came in for a good share of the blame. Star Kaye Ballard put it bluntly regarding the new director: "He didn't know how to give direction."[50]

Rome's score came in for praise that included "song patter ... catchy as well as humorous"[51] and songs that "give the show what pungency and wit it has."[52] Fortunately for his tunes, Ballard delivered them with charm and exuberance, stopping the show with both "You Never Know What Hit You" and "Take Off the Coat."[53] "Love Is Still Love," a ballad sung by the female lead Patricia to the knight Alfred, is especially touching and old-fashioned. Two of the songs — "The Money Song" and "Gin Rummy Rhapsody" — were Rome at his song-of-the-common-man best. "The Money Song" received air play and earned some royalties, mostly from recordings by the Andrews Sisters for Decca Records and Dean Martin and Jerry Lewis for Capitol.

In 2002, *That's the Ticket* was presented as part of the *Musicals Tonight!* series produced by Mel Miller at the 14th Street YMCA in New York.[54] It had a planned eleven-day run and came in for much praise, best summarized by a May 3, 2002, review: "*Musicals Tonight!*, which stages forgotten American musicals, has given the show its New York premiere with charming, humorous results."[55] No 1948 cast recording was ever done, but one was done for this 2002 edition. Most forgotten musicals are forgotten for a reason. Not so *That's the Ticket*, if judged by this compact disc. It is a good exhibition of Rome's versatility, and soprano Rita Harvey and baritone David Staller perform especially well on their duets of "Dost Thou" and "I Shouldn't Love You."[56] In all, its score is one of Rome's strongest, fits the book well, and featured a variety of song styles.

Rome knew he had written good songs for *That's the Ticket* and because of their limited exposure in a show that never went to Broadway, he was able to pull a few out of his trunk and fit them into *Bless You All*. He also included a song with social significance, but it was deleted early on in the production. Still capable of infusing a song with his liberal thinking, the composer said of this cut: "I was the only one who wrote an anti–McCarthy song, in a revue titled *Bless You All*. But they didn't want to listen. Times change."[57]

In the New Haven and Philadelphia tryouts, the sketches and songs of *Bless You All* were considered vintage revue, the cast was impeccable, and the sets and costumes were lavish. Audiences and critics mostly raved, the three weeks in Philadelphia were sellouts, and one critic declared: "It must be reported that there were occasional first night lapses. A few of the sketches were fillers and some of the cues were missed. But the faults were so obvious and the remedies so apparent that there seems at this moment, little standing between *Bless You All* and success."[58] The old team from *Call Me Mister* appeared to have found the right formula, and as musical director Lehman Engel observed: "In Philadelphia, therefore, no real work was done."[59]

The show opened at the Mark Hellinger Theatre on December 14, 1950, with a confident cast and team of creators. Based on pre–Broadway reviews and a reliable creative team, *Bless You All* had good pre-opening sales. A summary of an accounting statement for a week in late December of 1950 showed a promising profit with the following numbers[60]:

| | | |
|---|---:|---:|
| Box office receipts | | $48,692 |
| Theater owner's share | | (12,173) |
| Producer's share | | 36,519 |
|     Company (performers & staff) | 14,310 | |
|     Stage crew & wardrobe | 3,328 | |
|     Musicians | 1,431 | |
| | | (19,069) |
| Royalties: | | |
|     Authors | 3,530 | |
|     Director | 974 | |
|     Choreographer | 486 | |
|     Set & costume designers | 150 | |
| | | (5,140) |
| Publicity & advertising | | (2,819) |
| Departmental (tradesmen & rentals) | | (1,644) |
| Administrative & office | | (2,439) |
| Net profit week ending December 23, 1950 | | 5,408 |

This was not a huge profit but certainly enough to sustain a show and eventually return investors' money. Of particular interest in this statement is the bulk of royalties that go to the authors, which usually means the book or sketch writer and song composer. A program from the New Haven run lists only Rome and Auerbach in those roles,[61] although musical arranger Don Walker and ballet music arrangers Mischa and Wesley Portnoff wrote music for a few dances.[62] Presumably, Rome and Auerbach received the lion's share of the authors' royalties, giving them each approximately fifteen hundred dollars a week, a good income for 1950.

As it turned out, things were amiss as house numbers steadily declined. The fifteen hundred a week for Rome and Auerbach was not to last. Though praise had been heaped on performers and creators alike, the overall pace of the show was found wanting with comments like "occasionally loses pace and zest,"[63] "goes throughout the evening, from attic to cellar," and "parts of it fall below the level which it originally promises."[64] Various sketches were found unnecessary, and although the score was appreciated overall, none of the songs became a hit.

The competition it had should also be noted. If a theatergoer wanted to attend only one musical for the Broadway season, there was quite a choice, all successful book musicals[65]:

| Show | Stars | Total Performances |
|---|---|---|
| *Call Me Madam* | Ethel Merman | 644 |
| *Gentlemen Prefer Blondes* | Carol Channing | 740 |
| *Guys and Dolls* | Vivian Blaine, Robert Alda | 1,200 |
| *Kiss Me Kate* | Anne Jeffreys | 1,077 |
| *South Pacific* | Mary Martin | 1,925 |

Years later, John Kander and Fred Ebb's first musical, *Flora the Red Menace*, met a similar fate. Despite a creative team that included director George Abbott, orchestrator Don Walker, producer Hal Prince, and Liza Minnelli, it failed at the box office when up against *Hello, Dolly!* and *Fiddler on the Roof*.[66]

Also around this time, the medium of television was emerging, keeping people at home to watch comedy and variety. According to *The History of North American Theater*:

> A combination of economic factors contributed to Broadway's decline, but the swift rise of television was also a major culprit. By 1949, for example, there were about two million television sets in operation in the United States, receiving hundreds of hours of free news, drama, and variety entertainment. A decade later, eighty-five percent of the population had access to a television. As television programming expanded and advanced in sophistication, the audience for theater contracted.[67]

As Rome kidded to an interviewer in 1982, the title of the show was short for "*Bless You All* for coming to the theater instead of sitting home and watching *Howdy Doody*."[68] But television was a threat to Broadway, especially to the revue, which was already faltering as book musicals had taken over Broadway, typified by the aforementioned list. Sheldon Harnick, who wrote the lyrics for one of Broadway's most successful book musicals, *Fiddler on the Roof*, had done extensive work in revues just as Rome had. Harnick said of the inroads television made on the revue genre:

> As television got more and more popular, and as television variety shows became more popular, they just obliterated the Broadway revues. There was no need for them. They could do them quicker and faster, they could do them with stars, they could make them truly topical, which we couldn't. Revue, by and large, disappeared....[69]

An extreme example of the effect television had on Broadway musical entertainment is the story of *Cinderella*. Written for television by Richard Rodgers and Oscar Hammerstein II, it was the most widely seen show in their careers. Aired on March 31, 1957, it garnered nearly the largest television audience for a single show up to that time:

> According to CBS, the program was seen by 107,000,000 viewers, which was the equivalent, it was computed, of sellout performances at the

Majestic Theatre eight times a week for 214 years, or more people than had seen every one of the preceding Rodgers and Hammerstein shows combined.[70]

The best efforts of those involved with *Bless You All* could not overcome the tepid New York reviews plus competition on Broadway and television; the show closed after eighty-four performances. The initially confident Engel admitted in *This Bright Day*, his 1974 autobiography: "This one fooled us."[71] In his short treatise "How to Write a Hit Musical," Rome quoted friend and collaborator Jerome Chodorov: "More shows have been killed by good reviews out of town than by bad reviews on Broadway."[72]

*Chapter 10*

# Liberal Politics and the Right Wing

"They knew I was not a member of the Communist Party or anywhere near it and they wouldn't have gotten anything out of me."—Harold Rome

Harold Rome's various liberal, pro-labor, and pro–Soviet activities landed him in the 1950 publication *Red Channels: The Report of Communist Influence in Radio and Television*.[1] It was published by a small, independent group of "anti-communist smear specialists" under the innocuous name of American Business Consultants. *Red Channels* was designed to expose "the 'communist front' and foreign associations of 151 people working in radio and television."[2] The "communist front" referred to inroads made by the Communist Party as manifested in various associations and committees. *Red* in its title meant communist influences and *Channels* referred to a phrase taken from Congressional testimony by FBI Director J. Edgar Hoover in 1947: "[Communist Party] members and sympathizers have not only infiltrated the airways but they are now persistently seeking radio channels."[3] As explained in the introduction to *Red Channels*:

> Party organizers double and redouble their efforts to spawn organizations, rallies, "benefits" and committees for this-and-that. No cause which seems calculated to arouse support among people in show business is ignored: the overthrow of the Franco dictatorship, the fight against anti–Semitism and Jimcrow [sic], civil rights, world peace, the outlawing of the H-bomb,are all used.[4]

Just as the House Committee on Un-American Activities (HUAC) in the late forties had investigated communist influences in the entertainment industry, mostly Hollywood, *Red Channels* was looked upon as a "blacklisting in the broadcasting industry as a continuation of earlier attacks that equated Jews and communism."[5] Rome had never testified at the HUAC hearings and thus avoided being either blacklisted or forced to testify against friends and

## 10. Liberal Politics and the Right Wing

co-creators. Although he attributed this mostly to the fact that he had done almost no work in Hollywood, he also firmly stated to an interviewer: "They knew I was not a member of the Communist Party or anywhere near it and they wouldn't have gotten anything out of me."[6]

Among the Broadway and radio entertainers in the *Red Channels* list of 151 were the following prominent names[7]:

| | | | |
|---|---|---|---|
| Larry Adler | Stella Adler | Leonard Bernstein | Marc Blitzstein |
| Abe Burrows | Jerome Chodorov | Lee J. Cobb | Aaron Copland |
| Howard Da Silva | Alfred Drake | Howard Duff | Jose Ferrer |
| John Garfield | Jack Gilford | Ruth Gordon | Morton Gould |
| Ben Grauer | Uta Hagen | Dashiell Hammett | E. Y. Harburg |
| Lillian Hellman | Judy Holliday | Lena Horne | Langston Hughes |
| Burl Ives | Sam Jaffe | Garson Kanin | John LaTouche |
| Arthur Laurents | Gypsy Rose Lee | Burgess Meredith | Arthur Miller |
| Zero Mostel | Dorothy Parker | Samson Raphaelson | Edward G. Robinson |
| Hazel Scott | Pete Seeger | Artie Shaw | William L. Shirer |
| Helen Tamiris | Louis Untermeyer | Orson Welles | Josh White |

Individuals on the *Red Channels* list had participated in one or more activities deemed by American Business Consultants as pro-communist with each person's litany of activities detailed after his or her name. Leading the group with four-page entries each were composer Marc Blitzstein and poet Langston Hughes. Rome's one page, typical of most, appeared as follows[8]:

### HAROLD ROME
*Composer*
*Reported as:*

| | |
|---|---|
| National Council of the Arts, Sciences and Professions | Signer. Advertisement in support of Hollywood Ten. *Variety*, 12/1/48. Sponsor. Committee to Abolish House Un-American Activities Committee. *Journal-American*, 12/30/48. Signer for Wallace. *Daily Worker*, 10/19/48, p. 7; *NY Times*, 10/20/48. |
| Progressive Citizens of America | Writer. Arts, Sciences and Professions Division of New York Progressive Citizens of America. "Show Time for Wallace" cabaret. *Daily Worker*, 4/5/48, p. 12. Sponsor. Arts, Science and Professions Division "Conference on Cultural Freedom and Civil Liberties," 10/25/47. Official Call. |

| | |
|---|---|
| Independent Citizens Committee of the Arts, Sciences and Professions | Affiliated. Un-Am. Act. Com. *Review of Scientific and Cultural Conference for World Peace*, 4/14/49, p. 2. |
| American Committee for Protection of Foreign born | Sponsor, "Status of Liberty Anniversary Dinner," 10/27/46. Official program. |
| American Council on Soviet Relations | Signer. Open letter to the President.Official leaflet. |
| Committee for the First Amendment | Signer. Advertisement *Hollywood Reporter*, 10/24/47. *Un-Am. Act. in California, 1948*, p. 210. |
| Open Letter to 81st Congress | Signer. Letter called for abolition of House Un-American Activities Committee. *Daily Worker*, 1/3/49, p. 7. |
| Scientific and Cultural Conference for World Peace | Sponsor, 3/49. Official program. |
| National Council of American-Soviet Friendship | Sponsor, 1948. *Un-Am. Act. in California, 1948*, p. 324. |
| People's Songs | Member, Board of sponsors. *Bulletin of People's Songs*, 5/47. Sent birthday greetings. *Bulletin of People'sSongs*, 2, 3/47, p. 19. |
| Voice of Freedom Committee | Associate Chairman. Program, 3/5/47. |

*Red Channels* had variable effects on those included in it, as many were theater people, involved only peripherally in mass media. However, it became a "kind of Bible" for producers and agents in radio and television broadcasting and adversely affected dozens of careers in those fields.[9] Rome told interviewer Martin Bookspan that an appearance in the early fifties on Ed Sullivan's *Toast of the Town* had been altered. Rome, director Joshua Logan, and principal cast members from *Fanny* were originally scheduled to appear on the show. Sullivan was conservative and right-wing, and when he and his staff became aware of Rome's listing, his role in the segment was cancelled. As a consolation, he was introduced from the stage, sitting in the audience.[10] Rome also felt that a passport application around that time was delayed due to his inclusion in *Red Channels*.[11] He was interviewed by FBI agents at the time and asked about the numerous petitions and the like that he had signed during the past few years. When Rome was vague about the number, they quickly informed him that there were "twenty-one."[12]

For the most part, the publication of *Red Channels* galvanized the theater community in their strong beliefs for First Amendment rights of free speech. More than any other professional organization in America, Actors' Equity was supportive of these rights and stood behind its members, forming a protective shield. With exceptions such as Marc Blitzstein, blacklisting occurred rarely in the theater, which led one witch-hunter to describe Broadway as "New York's Great Red Way."[13] None of this seems to have affected Rome or made him back off from his convictions. Thirty years later, he told Bookspan: "I'm still a Democrat. I still have my liberal feelings."[14]

*Chapter 11*

# Wish You Were Here

"Rome was the ideal songwriter for this milieu; he had virtually grown up with the characters."—Ethan Mordden

Create a fictitious adult Jewish summer camp in upstate New York. Add a few romances, a cad, and a few musclemen. Engage them in a swimming pool, a basketball game, and a weenie roast. Give Leland Hayward, Joshua Logan, Harold Rome, and a few other veteran Broadway creators a chance at it, and one has the basis for a musical.

In the show, the action takes place at a camp described in the program: "Camp Karefree, a summer camp for adults, 'where friendships are formed to last a whole lifetime through,' is located in the heart of Vacationland. It could be the Berkshires, the Adirondacks, the Poconos, the White Mountains—or even the Catskills."[1] Such camps were popular in the rural, mountainous areas of the northeast. They attracted young, mostly Jewish adults who would book a week or two, looking for fun and romance, "where the women hoped to snag a husband and the men tried to settle for a date."[2] These places typically had musical entertainment, usually in the form of talent shows for the employees and attendees, if the latter were confident enough to perform.

Rome learned his revue songwriting at such a camp. In the mid-thirties, he had been working in dance bands, orchestras, and dance studios as a pianist while attending Yale University. He began writing songs at Yale and, based on these early efforts, was hired to create musical entertainment at Green Mansions in Warrensburg, New York. He started there in 1935 at $150 for the summer plus room and board.[3] This resort and Camp Tamiment in the Pocono Mountains of Pennsylvania were crucibles for stage talent, attracting numerous artists who went on to distinguished careers[4]:

| | | | |
|---|---|---|---|
| Lee Adams | Stella Adler | Woody Allen | Bea Arthur |
| Jerry Bock | Lloyd Bridges | Carol Burnett | Imogene Coca |

| | | | |
|---|---|---|---|
| Barbara Cook | Sylvia Fine | Betty Garrett | Jack Gilford |
| Sheldon Harnick | Danny Kaye | Elia Kazan | Joe Layton |
| Max Liebman | Dorothy Loudon | Jerome Robbins | Mary Rodgers |
| Herb Ross | Dick Shawn | Neil Simon | Michael Stewart |
| Lee Strasberg | Charles Strouse | Jonathan Tunick | |

When starting at Green Mansions, Rome wanted to add more consistency to the entertainment, and according to composer Charles Strouse, "[H]e started the tradition of doing an original revue every Saturday night."[5] Under the usual schedule, campers would stay for two weeks and three weekends, requiring three separate shows, but then these could be rewritten and improved for each group of newcomers.[6] Such work prepared him for his job of composing songs for the ever-changing ILGWU revue *Pins and Needles*. It would also provide Rome with a collection of songs which he would try to sell a few years later to producers, entertainers, and the publishers in Tin Pan Alley, mostly to no avail.

He definitely knew the territory and the type of people who went to Green Mansions, as Ethan Mordden explained: "Rome was the ideal songwriter for this milieu; he had virtually grown up with the characters.... For these naïve people, Rome somehow contrived a canny yet artless-seeming

*Left to right:* Rome, producer Leland Hayward, director Joshua Logan, and book writer Arthur Kober, creators of *Wish You Were Here* (1952), based on Kober's 1937 play *Having Wonderful Time* (courtesy of the Museum of the City of New York).

score ... above all, there's naturalism: a score made of the way this culture speaks and thinks."⁷ Another critic added to this thought: "[H]is specialty was writing songs in his own New York Jewish vernacular ... [and] he gravitated to subjects and songs that were directly connected to that background."⁸ Also attuned to that milieu was Arthur Kober, the author of the play *Having Wonderful Time*, the basis of *Wish You Were Here*. *Having Wonderful Time* was a risqué comedy written in 1937, then toned down for a 1938 film starring Ginger Rogers and Douglas Fairbanks, Jr. Joshua Logan said of Kober and Rome: "The two of them knew the Catskill syndrome thoroughly."⁹ A Boston journalist described the setting as a place where "the Sophies, Sarahs and Rebeccas of the Bronx, with the Mannys, Abes and Sols — their boyfriends — strive to make the best of the two weeks with pay allotted to them."¹⁰

*Having Wonderful Time* was a "simple play about simple people," "'Hillbillies from the Bronx,' the Cinderellas who seek to fulfill the yearnings of their lives in two weeks."¹¹ It had run for 372 performances in 1937 and was considered part of the "twenties-thirties folk play movement, in which a play incorporated a subculture in its very language and lore."¹² Most famously, *Porgy* in 1927 and *Green Grow the Lilacs* in 1931 were successful folk plays later turned into successful musicals, *Porgy and Bess* and *Oklahoma!*, respectively. Each of these three plays had the dialect of an area and subculture (Brooklyn, South Carolina, and Oklahoma), using it to express the ethos of the people and provide a backdrop for the story.

Kober had penned a kind, loving novel of this subculture, providing the starting point for him and Logan to write the book of the musical. With New York and theater-going audiences, the authors knew they could use ethnic phrases, idioms, and speech patterns. The same could be said of the later production in Chicago. When *Wish You Were Here* had a London production in 1954, the creators knew it would be a bit tougher. Rome was confident of its success there despite the differences in cultures, telling his attorney William Fitelson: "I was pleased with the unanimity with which all the producers agreed that *Wish You Were Here* would make a very good show for London. They know vacation camps well in England and it would only be necessary to change a few local jokes."¹³ Ultimately, *Wish You Were Here* was "largely de-Judaized" for the British with several "reorientated lyrics."¹⁴

But even with two writers true to their upbringings and capable of capturing a subculture, a Broadway musical needed some pizzazz to counter the competition from the growing medium of television and the improved sound and picture qualities of movies. The adult camp scene had lots of possibilities. A basketball game, a weenie roast with campfire, and other activities were staged over the course of the evening, and master set designer Jo Mielziner had his work cut out:

Jo Mielziner constructed a series of elaborate settings that depicted all sections of the camp including the picnic grounds, complete with a glowing barbecue pit; a social hall; the woods surrounding the camp; the interior of the cabins; and a basketball court. In addition, he created a realistic rainstorm and a fire that burned down part of the camp.[15]

To capture the hustle and bustle of a camp, there were fifty-four cast members, the majority of whom were often on stage together.[16] As he had done in *South Pacific* with large groups, Logan used this population to emphasize the scene:

> In this show he has brought the cast down front to perch on tree stumps or to sit, kneel and lie at the very edge of the stage. They frame the picture and their foreground silhouette adds an illusion of depth.... [H]e has gone so far as having them hang their legs over into the orchestra pit....[17]

To accommodate all this activity, there were forty stagehands and twenty-seven musicians. Quite an undertaking. Then there was the swimming pool!

Despite Mielziner's protests, Logan insisted on the pool. There had been one previous swimming pool on Broadway, for *Viva O'Brien* in 1941 at the Majestic Theater.[18] For *Wish You Were Here*, this was to be no casual, above-ground pool but one large and deep, containing forty tons of water. It required workmen to dig into the floor beneath the Imperial Theater stage to provide concrete reinforcement.[19] It was estimated to have cost between $30,000 and $100,000,[20] was covered up most of the time and used mostly in a fifteen-minute first act closing scene. Mielziner gave Logan a pool that became one of the hits of the show, "with lights and mirrors that made the interior of the pool visible to the entire audience."[21]

The swimming pool was problematic for more than Mielziner and the tradesmen at the Imperial Theater. Pre-Broadway venues could not justify the cost of the pool, nor could potential national tour theaters with the exception of Chicago's Shubert Theater which hosted the show for two months in 1953–54. What no out-of-town performances meant was that Logan, Rome, and their team had to have previews in New York, seldom a good idea. When a show previews in Boston, New Haven, Philadelphia, etc., there are reviewers in these towns, and of course, some curious New Yorkers.[22] More specifically, with out-of-town openings, there was often another group, mostly unwanted at this point: "The 'wrecking crew.' Those theatrical agents, ticket brokers, movie company executives and scouts, all the 'wise money...'"[23] Oscar Hammerstein II referred to these groups as the "grave-diggers" or "smarties."[24] Agnes de Mille, who revolutionized choreography on Broadway with *Oklahoma!*, had cynical comments about the "wrecking crew" that came to New Haven to see the early versions of that show:

> "Oh, they were all there," says de Mille. "The 'wrecking crew' from New York, that's the name Ruth Gordon gave them, up to New Haven to see

this show. It certainly wasn't the show you see today, but all the good songs were there. So a lot of them left early, and most of their reactions were, 'Well, too bad. This means the end of the Theatre Guild.... This is their last flop.'"[25]

If a show is not doing well and the out-of-town critics are hard on it, changes can be made gradually, without day-to-day scrutiny. This is the whole idea behind a pre–Broadway tryout period. Songs may not fit, scenes need cutting, and worst of all, cast members are not fit for their roles. These are just a few of the problems that can be worked out on the road. But with *Wish You Were Here* and its New York previews, "[h]ourly bulletins were generally forthcoming from those who seemed to have made a career on keeping up with events around the Imperial."[26] Critic John Chapman added to this with harsher words:

> For another handicap there was the Broadway mob — the wise ones who hear all, see all, and tell all.... It held its tryouts in the theater.... This resulted in the Broadway mob knowing everything that was going on — and telling. It seems to me that every New Yorker who follows the theater closely was going around saying, "I hear it isn't so good."[27]

Despite the gossip and the naysayers, *Wish You Were Here* premiered on June 25, 1952. Opening night reviews were tepid, New York was in the middle of a heat wave, and a few second-night critics did not even bother to use their tickets.[28] Producer Leland Hayward and Rome began to lose confidence.[29] Logan, on the other hand, had just begun to fight. *Wish You Were Here* had two weeks of sold-out performances, mostly benefits, giving the creative team a bit of wiggle room. Changes in New York were to continue for over a month, almost unheard of on Broadway. In an interview years later with Lehman Engel, Rome explained Logan's strategy at this point:

> The plot didn't seem to be working right and Josh wouldn't give up and he invited critics ... from out of town to see it.... [H]e wanted me to have a conference with him and Elliot Norton who had great reservations about the show.
> And I said, "No, I've had enough of that and I don't want to have anything more to do with any critics."
> He pumped Elliot Norton for three hours and came away with an idea for changing the plot that would help and we did it.[30]

Most of Logan's changes involved the book. For one, critics felt that the charm and humor of the original play had been lost. One put it quite bluntly: "The touching Bronxish lilt of Arthur Kober's original play seems oddly to become stilted, without wit or tenderness, in transition."[31]

Logan thought that the audience lost interest early on in the female protagonist, Teddy. He asked for a new song to soften Teddy's image, and Rome obliged with the sweet, sympathetic "There's Nothing Nicer Than People," replacing "Goodbye, Love."[32] Because of the late changes, the latter song was recorded for the cast album.[33] In all, Logan presented the cast with changes that involved thirty-three pages of script and eight scenes.

A positive development was the popularity of the title song "Wish You Were Here." During the production delays and alterations, singer Eddie Fisher had recorded it for RCA Victor, and it became a gold record for him, lasting several weeks on *Your Hit Parade*.[34] A decade later, another show in trouble, Ervin Drake's *What Makes Sammy Run?*, benefited greatly when its star Steve Lawrence recorded "A Room Without Windows."

"Wish You Were Here" anchored the second act, a beguine sung dramatically by the waiters at Camp Karefree with a solo by star Jack Cassidy. The song was a late addition to the score requested by the director. Logan claimed Rome had made twenty-three tries to come up with a title song, stealing a musical phrase from a second act song, "Who Could Eat Now?," with the same cadence as the title words.[35] Rome felt the song—"Wish You Were Here"—out of place as everybody important to the story was there at Camp Karefree. He wondered to whom it was being sung and wondered what Logan wanted from the song. Again from the Engel interview:

> And then I couldn't get the end of it and Logan kept saying, "There is not enough sex in it. I want that ending to say fuck, fuck, get together, sex, sex, sex, fuck, fuck, fuck."
>
> And I kept bringing in different endings. Then we had a conference and I brought in "They're not shining the stars as bright, they've stolen the joy from the night."
>
> He said, "That's exactly what I meant!"[36]

Logan promised he would fit it in, doing so quite successfully, about which Rome would later say, "This is against all the rules."[37] Rome learned over the years that one of Logan's best talents was his staging of songs, and although Rome had no confidence in "Wish You Were Here," he knew Logan would give it a proper treatment. In the days of revue, there would be a sketch, then a song, then perhaps a dance, with no particular integration of the three. To maintain the flow of a musical, a good director does not just get the dialogue spoken, then have a song sung, then stage a dance related to it. He wants the dialogue to flow naturally into the song, almost demanding it; songs should be done when the emotions of the story become too high to be spoken. The song can then be embellished by a dance. If done properly and seamlessly, dialogue, song, and dance are synergistic, producing a wonderful effect. Hundreds of Broadway songs have had such an effect. Those which come to mind: "Shall We Dance" (*The King and I*), "I'm Only Thinking of Him" (*Man of La Mancha*), "It Only Takes a Moment" (*Hello, Dolly!*), and "I'm Gonna Wash

*11. Wish You Were Here* 91

Rome (right) with Eddie Fisher in 1952, the time of the singer's hit recording of "Wish You Were Here" (courtesy Gilmore Music Library, Yale University).

That Man Right Outa My Hair" (*South Pacific*). The last of these was staged by Logan. This is part of the art of the book musical. This is what made for a good director — like Joshua Logan.

"Wish You Were Here" was a hit in the show with the title words repeated ten times in each chorus, resulting in the audience singing it in the exit aisles. "Wish You Were Here" enjoyed a modicum of success with other singers besides Fisher, being recorded by Bing Crosby, Peggy Lee, and Jerry Vale, among others.[38] It resurfaced in 1971 in *The Last Picture Show*, playing prominently in the background of a motel scene with Cybill Shepherd and Timothy Bottoms.

This ballad, along with several other songs in the score, was a significant departure for Rome. He had left revues and "social significance" behind and proved himself in a Broadway musical with lyrics "surprisingly free of the political slant he had heretofore shown."[39] He also added to this a new "richness of musical style."[40] Complimentary words used by the critics included "lively and clever," "memorable and diverse," "pleasant," "sweet," and "wit and brilliance."[41] The situations and emotions of the book had dictated his songs, and he let them lead "with every number a funny, culturally specific treat."[42] Among other standouts in the score was another for Cassidy and female lead Patricia Marand, "Where Did the Night Go?," a ballad that should have gone further but was overshadowed by the title song. Reminiscent of his hit from *Call Me Mister*, "South America, Take It Away," was a clever song with a Latin tempo, "Don Jose of Far Rockaway," done by Sidney Armus.

Logan — the songwriter's director — was particularly fond of "They Won't Know Me," which he called "an ecstatic outburst as sung by our hero." Logan felt it was a Rome song that advanced the character, adding, "This is a song that never reached the *Hit Parade*, but in the show it always received the solidest round of applause of the evening."[43] Perhaps most Rome-like was "Certain Individuals," sung by Sheila Bond, in a Tony-winning supporting role. The lyrics speak tongue-in-cheek of someone in love, whom everyone at Camp Karefree knows about, but the name is never spoken. As one blogger said of it: "That's good lyric writing: simple yet cleverly rhymed, suggestive of everyday speech without being a carbon copy of it, full of specific images and fresh takes on familiar expressions."[44]

After the sold-out previews, audiences were sparse with weekly grosses reaching a nadir in mid–July at $25,000.[45] Investors had to come up with a total of $50,000 more after their initial $250,000. But gradually, the critics were ignored, the heat wave broke, and prospective ticket buyers were led by positive word-of-mouth.[46] More surprisingly, Walter Winchell got involved. Years earlier, Rome and Winchell, the syndicated reporter of the *New York Daily Mirror*, had a falling-out over Rome's "When I Grow Up" ("The G-Man Song") which was a satire of J. Edgar Hoover and the FBI. The conservative Winchell disliked the song and according to Rome, "Winchell refused to mention his name or any of his shows for ten years after *Pins and Needles*."[47] But the sentence must have run its course because Winchell, with prompting by Logan, took a particular interest in the faltering show:

> Logan ... began furnishing Winchell with exclusive tidbits about the show ..., whereupon Winchell turned around and adopted "Wish You Were Here" as his pet. He called it a "small hit musical" ... and he took the view that it was he who singlehanded, had, as he characteristically put it, "jumped into the *Wish* pool and saved it from going glug glug."[48]

*Wish You Were Here* surprised the Broadway mob. By mid–October, what had been called "the season's most successful flop"[49] became standing room only with weekly grosses exceeding $52,000.[50] As Logan told E.J. Kahn, Jr., of *The New Yorker* in a two-part profile: "It was fabulous. It was the dark horse copping the race, the long shot winning the pennant. It was the lost, starving woods-man finding that rutabaga root in the forest. It was everything."[51]

The musical based on Arthur Kober's sweet play ran for 598 performances from June of 1952 through November of 1953, Joshua Logan pulled off "perhaps the biggest upset in theatrical history,"[52] and composer Harold Rome found his voice in the changing American musical theater.

*Chapter 12*

# Movie Work and Shows Gone Awry

> "I had a motion picture songwriter when I should have chosen a popular songwriter." — Alfred Hitchcock

Although always leery of Hollywood and its attitude toward composers, Rome became involved in the Alfred Hitchcock film *Rear Window* (1954). The story revolves around the observations of a commercial photographer (James Stewart) confined to his apartment for several weeks because of an injury. His room overlooks several apartments in a complex with a large inner courtyard, and through his telephoto lenses and binoculars, he surmises that an occupant of another apartment has murdered his wife. Among the characters living in the complex are a dancer, Miss Torso, a single woman, Miss Lonelyhearts, and a songwriter who works frequently at his piano.

Micromanager Hitchcock wrote a nineteen-page list of directions for dubbing of the movie's music for composer Franz Waxman and film editor George Tomasini. Most of the songs to be used were popular standards, but Hitchcock specified that an original, popular song should be "composed" by the songwriter as the story progressed, the melody emanating from his piano and window. It was to be played by him in its finished form during the closing scene.[1] Entitled "Lisa," the name of Grace Kelly's character, the evolving melody and lyrics of the song were to express the evolving relationship of Lisa and Jeff (Stewart).

Through an association with Waxman, Rome was asked to write the lyrics and ultimately wrote three sets of them, two entitled "Lisa," the other one "Love You." One set of Rome's "Lisa" lyrics was used in the closing scene.[2] German-born Waxman had worked for Hitchcock on three previous films and had won two Academy Awards for Best Score for *Sunset Blvd.* (1950) and *A Place in the Sun* (1951).[3] He was one of several European-born or -influenced composers responsible for the development of American film music in the thirties and forties. Other important composers included Herbert Stothart, Erich Wolfgang Korngold, Alfred Newman, Max Steiner, Bernard Herrmann, and Miklos Rozsa.[4] These gentlemen were known for beautiful, creative scores, but despite obvious melodic talents, wrote few popular songs.

*Rear Window* was a huge success, the score had strong jazz elements, and movie historians felt the song played a crucial role in the film.[5] Unfortunately, "Lisa" was heard mostly in snippets throughout the movie — Hitchcock's plan — and when played in its entirety in the final scene, the listener gets little sense of a popular song. Beyond this, Rome's lyrics are all but inaudible. Unlike Lisa, whose character strengthened as the story progressed, the song of the same name was of little note and had no life outside the film. This was a common occurrence in Hollywood. To directors and producers, songs were mere props, like pieces of scenery used to add to the overall effect of the films. Hitchcock and his producers may have figured that if a composer — Waxman — can write a score, why not a song? Mere songwriting could not be that hard. Watch the ending scene of *Rear Window*. The melody can hardly be considered a popular song, and the words: Rome could have written his best lyric ever and no one would know.

Franz Waxman's son, John, said of the song: "Hitchcock knew what he wanted — he always did — and he wasn't getting it from my father. He wanted a hit song, and my father was after something else."[6] Though Hitchcock was pleased with the score overall, he complained specifically about that final song: "I was a little disappointed in the lack of structure in the title song. I had a motion picture songwriter when I should have chosen a popular songwriter."[7]

Quite an irony with Harold Rome close at hand.

\* \* \*

A top flight team of creators never insures that a musical will be a hit or even open. Rome learned that when his efforts with Broadway legends George Kaufman and Moss Hart —*Sing Out the News*— went awry. Broadway history is filled with sure bets that went wrong. A sampling of them[8]:

| Show | Year | Creative team | Broadway run |
|---|---|---|---|
| Greenwillow | 1960 | Frank Loesser; George Roy Hill; Joe Layton | 95 |
| Breakfast at Tiffany's | 1961 | Bob Merrill; Abe Burrows; Michael Kidd | Closed in tryouts |
| Anyone Can Whistle | 1964 | Stephen Sondheim; Arthur Laurents; Kermit Bloomgarden | 9 |
| Flora the Red Menace | 1965 | John Kander; Fred Ebb; George Abbott; Harold Prince | 87 |
| Rex | 1976 | Richard Rodgers; Sheldon Harnick; Edwin Sherin; Richard Adler | 48 |

| Show | Year | Creative team | Broadway run |
|---|---|---|---|
| *The Baker's Wife* | 1976 | Stephen Schwartz; David Merrick; Joseph Stein | Closed in tryouts |
| *Dance a Little Closer* | 1983 | Alan Jay Lerner; Charles Strouse | 1 |

In 1953, Rome was part of a team doing a musical adaptation of *Saints and Sinners*, a short story written by Paul Vincent Carroll and made into a movie by Alexander Korda.[9] The show's creative team included Rome as lyricist, composer Frederick Loewe, and writers Joseph Fields and Jerome Chodorov, all Broadway veterans. Rome had avoided working as only a lyricist on shows, but when a project with Loewe came along, he could not turn it down. Loewe and lyricist–book writer Alan Jay Lerner had already had a surprise hit with *Brigadoon* in 1947, followed by a lesser hit, *Paint Your Wagon*, a show with several beautiful Loewe melodies.[10] In September of 1952, Loewe and Lerner had abandoned their project to musicalize George Bernard Shaw's *Pygmalion*.[11] The royalty agreement at the time for *Saints and Sinners* was as follows[12]:

| | |
|---|---|
| Paul Vincent Carroll (author) | 1% |
| Jerome Chodorov and Joseph Fields (book) | 4% |
| Frederic Loewe (music) | 3½% |
| Harold Rome (lyrics) | 2½% |

This agreement demonstrated Loewe's prestige on Broadway and his ability to command a favored contract, as composer and lyricist were normally paid equally.

By mid–1953, Rome and Loewe had finished several songs, but the book was lagging as Fields and Chodorov were finishing *The Girl in Pink Tights* which was to open in March of 1954.[13] The book for *Saints and Sinners* took better shape by late summer of 1954 but was still unfinished. The progress of the musical, now titled *Dancin' Day*, began to languish, mostly due to problems with British producer Jack Hylton.[14] This was particularly disappointing as there were other producers interested in doing the show, including actor Burgess Meredith.[15] As late as the summer of 1955, there was talk about the show with Edwin Lester of the Los Angeles and San Francisco Civic Light Opera companies.[16] Loewe returned to his work with Lerner on their musical adaptation of *Pygmalion*, a show they had begun calling *My Lady Liza*. When Loewe became immersed in this, production of *Dancin' Day* was abandoned. The loss of this project was a disappointment to Rome.

Not only was Loewe, the composer of *My Lady Liza*, distracted from a Rome project, but likewise its director, Moss Hart. Rome and Hart had known each other since working on *Sing Out the News* in 1940 and had discussed numerous projects over the years. In the spring of 1955 they focused their talents on a show inspired by "a magazine article that explained the psychological reasons for the popularity of pink in this country."[17] It was to be called *In the Pink*, a satire on big business featuring an Aimee Semple McPherson–style evangelist. To accomplish all this, Rome, Hart, and book writer Jerome Chodorov holed up in mid–June of 1954 in Beach Haven, New Jersey.[18] They hoped to begin rehearsals in August and open out-of-town tryouts in the fall.[19] As they were all fast workers, progress was made until *My Lady Liza* intruded again.

Numerous producers, writers, and songwriting teams — including Rodgers and Hammerstein — had given up or never tried to adapt *Pygmalion*. Everyone thought the transition to a musical impossible.[20] Shaw himself had not wanted his works to be put to music. In 1907, Oscar Straus wrote an operetta, *The Chocolate Soldier*, based on Shaw's *Arms and the Man*. Despite the immense success of the operetta, Shaw is said to have "loathed" it and "ruled all his work off musical limits" thereafter.[21] It was not until after Shaw's death in 1950 that his estate relented and permitted projects to be pursued.

Hart up to this time had wanted to avoid the Shaw project. Moreover, being deep into *In the Pink* with Rome, he did not want to be tempted by a different musical. One of the true talents of the theater, he was particularly adept at knowing what would work early on in a project and how music and story would play out. Lerner and Loewe were well aware of Hart's skills and after several phone calls from the persistent pair, Hart agreed to just listen to what they had written. According to Frederick Loewe, "[A]fter the fourth number all of a sudden he said, 'You sons of bitches, I'm hooked!'"[22] Hart would later write that he never should have permitted himself to listen to Lerner and Loewe do their songs, saying of such situations: "It is a fatal enticement. A composer and lyricist generally perform their own work with uncommon skill."[23]

Hart knew a great project when he heard one. Soon after his meeting with Lerner and Loewe, he knew he had to postpone work on *In the Pink*. As Kitty Carlisle Hart remembered it: "Moss went to the Chodorovs and the Romes and threw himself on their mercy. Never have friends been more generous in their understanding of Moss's having to postpone their project, even though it might mean that it might never come to pass."[24]

*My Lady Liza* became *My Fair Lady*; the rest is history. It did not open until March 1956 but then ran for 2,717 performances and garnered six Tony Awards, including one for Hart for Best Director.[25] The show took a lot out of Hart, and he knew he could not go back to work on another show too soon. Rome remembered: "It was ready to go, we even had the money, when Moss Hart came to me, on my birthday, and said that the book isn't right, and he was too tired to fix it."[26] Rome and Chodorov were greatly disappointed. *In the Pink* never was completed, and the unlikely Shaw musical ultimately robbed Rome of two great collaborators and two promising shows.

\* \* \*

During work on *Dancin' Day*, Rome was asked to become involved in the Yale Collection of the Literature of the American Musical Theater,[27] a project of Goddard Lieberson, executive vice-president of Columbia Records. He had become well-known for his original cast recordings of Broadway shows. This had been a much ignored genre of the industry, but when Columbia introduced the long-playing (LP) record in 1948, cast recordings became plausible. Lieberson oversaw the recordings of numerous shows including *The Pajama Game*, *The Sound of Music*, *West Side Story*, *Gypsy*, *Camelot*, and *My Fair Lady*. The last of these became a #1 best-selling album on *Billboard* charts.[28]

Lieberson had been asked by Yale University Library personnel to establish a committee to encourage the growth of their musical theater collection, of which Lieberson said: "Personally, I feel that this Yale collection, comparatively small as it is now, is the nucleus of something that can be of great importance to the serious study of the American musical theater. This, I am sure, is as close to your heart as it is to mine."[29] Those asked by Lieberson to be on the committee included:

| | | |
|---|---|---|
| Irving Berlin | Noël Coward | Max Dreyfus |
| Ira Gershwin | Oscar Hammerstein II | Eva Kern |
| Frank Loesser | Cole Porter | Richard Rodgers |
| Harold Rome | Lotte Lenya Weill | |

Rome informed Lieberson that as a Yale alumnus, he was already involved in the collection, but would help the committee in whatever capacity he could.[30] Rome would later donate his professional papers to Yale University; they are kept at its Gilmore Music Library. Other important collections at the Gilmore related to the musical theater include Mildred Bailey, Lehman Engel, E.Y. Harburg, Lotte Lenya, Goddard Lieberson, Cole Porter, Kay Swift, and Kurt Weill. The original Yale Collection which Lieberson organized became part of the Yale Music Library and the Yale Collection of Historical Sound Recordings.[31]

*Chapter 13*

# *Fanny*

> "Putting the right song in the right place at the right time is what counts." — Harold Rome

In a tongue-in-cheek treatise in 1967, "How to Write a Hit Musical," Rome wrote down several rules for success, one of which included:

> START WITH A BASIC, SIMPLE BOOK
> NO PROBLEMS, NO MESSAGES, PURE ENTERTAINMENT

This rule doesn't work very well. As the American musical grows, the book has become all important. The more meaning and depth the story has, the greater the impact on the audience. Every show has "social significance." The very fact that it may avoid it is socially significant.[1]

The book musical had become the standard for Broadway with such 1940s shows as Rodgers and Hart's *Pal Joey*, Rodgers and Hammerstein's *Oklahoma!*, Lerner and Loewe's *Brigadoon*, and Lane and Harburg's *Finian's Rainbow*. In 1954, *The Pajama Game* by Adler and Ross was selling out. The songs for these works had to be beautiful and hummable but they had to propel the story, and that story better be a good one. Dramaturgy, the art and technique of writing story and drama, had not been of great importance in Broadway musical entertainments until shows like these emerged, and then it became crucial.

David Merrick, a lawyer and budding Broadway producer from St. Louis, knew the importance of a story and for several years had thought that the *Marseilles Trilogy* by Marcel Pagnol—*Marius, Cesar, Fanny*—following two families on the Marseilles waterfront, was rich in plot and characters and perfect for Merrick's first musical effort.[2] Unfortunately, Pagnol did not share this opinion although he had consented to straight play and movie adaptations of his stories over the years[3]:

| Year | Title | Medium | Stars |
|---|---|---|---|
| 1930 | *Marseilles* | Play | Dudley Digges, Guy Kibbee, Frances Torchiana, Alexander Kirkland |
| 1931 | *Marius* | Movie | Raimu, Pierre Fresnay |
| 1932 | *Fanny* | Movie | Raimu, Pierre Fresnay, Fernand Charpin |
| 1936 | *Cesar* | Movie | Raimu, Pierre Fresnay |
| 1938 | *Port of Seven Seas* | Movie | Wallace Beery, Frank Morgan, Maureen O'Sullivan, John Beal |

To the French, the *Marseilles Trilogy* was a literary treasure, etched in their minds by Raimu's films.

Pagnol had been approached before regarding a musical but had always rebuffed his suitors; not David Merrick. After countless letters, phone calls, and a few European trips, Merrick went to Monte Carlo and all but camped on Pagnol's doorstep. He secured the rights in September of 1951, paying the Frenchman $30,000 plus royalties for his story.[4] Pagnol told columnist Art Buchwald of the *Paris Herald* years later:

> I didn't think they could make a successful musical out of it. I told David Merrick when he approached me on the idea four years ago that he was crazy to try it. But he said he wanted to do it anyway.[5]

With rights in hand, Merrick put together a creative team of Albert Hackett and Frances Goodrich, husband-and-wife screenwriters with limited musical experience. He added Harold Arlen and E.Y. Harburg to do the score. But after Merrick announced his team in June of 1952, the writers proved inadequate as librettists and Arlen and Harburg soured on the project.[6] Merrick then turned to Joshua Logan, one of Broadway's premier directors, successful with *Annie Get Your Gun*, *Mister Roberts*, and *South Pacific*. Merrick offered him a package as director, writer, and co-producer which the multitalented Logan could not turn down.[7] It was Merrick's hope that Logan could bring in Richard Rodgers and Oscar Hammerstein II to produce and write the score. Logan had worked successfully with them on *South Pacific*, although there had been controversy over writing credits between Logan and the powerful twosome.

Logan arranged a meeting of Merrick, Rodgers, and Hammerstein as the latter two, especially Hammerstein, had been impressed by the possibilities when they saw the French movie *Fanny*. Despite Hammerstein's enthusiasm, Rodgers took an instant dislike to Merrick and refused to give him billing even as associate producer.[8] Merrick recalled the incident in an interview with music director Lehman Engel years later:

> The billing I asked for was Richard Rodgers and then in small type, about 4 point type, "in association with David Merrick." The smallest type I could ask for. You know, they refused it. When I say they, Oscar Hammerstein didn't say anything.

Richard Rodgers went on. And he said, "We can't give you any billing. It would dilute our presence in it."[9]

Merrick acknowledged the talent of Rodgers but had nothing but dislike for him thereafter. Being Merrick, he wanted to settle the score, as he described to Lehman Engel:

> So I vowed that I would ultimately do something about him. And I did.... And I started a series of stunts. For example, if I would go out to some place where they had a band for dancing and everything — I would go to the conductor and give him a bill and say, "No Richard Rodgers music, please."... Of course, he heard about it.[10]

Merrick's mischief aside, Hammerstein regretted the decision to not produce *Fanny*, asking Logan years later: "Why the hell did we give up *Fanny*? What on earth were we trying to prove? My God, that's a great story and look at some of the junk we've done."[11]

After this debacle, Merrick sought the services of Burton Lane and Alan Jay Lerner. Lane was not available and Merrick and Logan disagreed on Lerner. Merrick had been impressed with *Brigadoon* as well as Lerner's film work on *An American in Paris*. According to Merrick, Logan said: "I don't think much of his work.... If you think Alan Lerner has any talent, I don't know whether I should do this show with you." Then Merrick finished the story: "So I shrugged.... And of course, Alan Lerner had to blame somebody, so he blamed me. It was Josh who made the decision. Nevertheless, he blamed me. He wouldn't speak to me for a long time after that."[12]

From then on, Logan took up the cause of Harold Rome to be the composer and had to convince co-librettist S. N. Behrman of Rome's abilities. While not experienced with writing musicals, Behrman was well-respected in the theater for plays for Alfred Lunt and Lynn Fontanne, comedienne Ina Claire, and the Theatre Guild. Behrman was hesitant to work with Rome until Logan played him the entire scores of *Call Me Mister* and *Wish You Were Here*.[13]

Rome and Logan were enjoying a long run with the latter musical, based on the adult summer camps in upstate New York. Merrick had passed on that project a few years earlier, partly because of Rome's reputation as a composer of revues of "social significance," thinking the score not "classy" enough. But with the run of *Wish You Were Here* and the success of its title song and "Where Did the Night Go?," Merrick reappraised Rome as a composer and took him on for the new musical.[14]

All the creators were aware that compressing seven hours of a cinematic trilogy, adding songs, and coming down with an eleven o'clock curtain was a daunting task. Rome said, "We talked for six months before practically a word was written."[15] Songs took on a great importance as a well-written one that advanced the story could replace pages of dialogue; this was a key to the book musical. Over the next two years, Rome began as always writing lots of songs, usually more than necessary. In the aforementioned piece, "How to Write a Hit Musical," Rome expounds in Rule 9: "My principle is simple. Always write twice as much as you need. It's easier to cut and discard than to find new material in a crisis out of town. You've always got what you've written, but you might get something better if you keep on going."[16] He met Marcel Pagnol in Paris, discussed the story and learned how important Pagnol felt it was that Rome should visit the south of France "to absorb some of the atmosphere in Marseilles itself." As he often did, Rome wrote his friend-attorney William Fitelson about his work and travels in France:

> I must say it was a stimulating experience to see the play [*Marius*] actually performed and to hear the audience's response to the warm and humorous story. It made me feel, more than ever, that the play has a universal quality which would be wonderfully exciting if we could catch it in our musical.
>
> I also did some research on the French folk songs of the Marseilles area, unearthed several collections of French folk songs and heard some others....
> I think my new score will gain freshness in flavor as a result of what I heard and saw.[17]

Logan and Behrman labored, first translating the Pagnol plays, then focusing on the story of Fanny within the trilogy. Working on his first musical, Behrman described the methods of the threesome:

> I went to Mr. Logan's house in Stamford, Connecticut, to work; Mr. Rome took a house across the street so he could run in and out to culminate emotion. We generated plenty! Mr. Logan early explained to me that while, surely, Mr. Rome would come in for the kill with his music and lyrics at the end of each scene, we must contrive what should be the content of those lyrics, what they should say.[18]

In Pagnol's stories, Fanny, the daughter of an oyster woman from Marseilles, falls in love with Marius, son of Cesar, a local bar owner. Torn between Fanny and his love of the sea, Marius decides to ship out on a five-year voyage and unknowingly leaves her pregnant. Convinced that her child needs a father, Fanny is persuaded to marry Panisse, an older, wealthy sail maker. He is delighted, and their family thrives. Marius returns but is not welcomed into the family. Panisse takes ill and, worried about his young family, is pleased that Marius will step into his place. *Fanny* closes with a touching death scene, most uncommon for a musical.[19]

There were plenty of spots for songs for the four principals — Fanny, Marius, Cesar, and Panisse — although the creators felt Panisse was the key, casting the role with particular care. Early on, there was much interest in

Walter Slezak, an avuncular, rotund, multilingual Austrian actor who could sing, dance, and had movie and Broadway experience. He had begun on Broadway in Kern and Hammerstein's *Music in the Air* in 1932, then appeared in Rodgers and Hart's *I Married an Angel* in 1938.[20] Slezak had held out on *Fanny* for months, most of which was spent on a New York run and national tour of *My Three Angels*, a play directed by Jose Ferrer.[21] Slezak completed the tour and showed up for an audition, asking Rome to accompany him. Louis Calta, Broadway columnist of the *New York Times*, described the audition: "When Mr. Rome inquired if the key was too high for him, Mr. Slezak impressed everyone by showing off his top register. Of his dancing talents, he was a bit more modest.... 'I was a wonderful dancer about one hundred pounds ago. Now I'm not so sure.'"[22]

To cast the remainder of the principals, Logan et al. turned to *South Pacific*. For Cesar, father of Marius, they engaged Ezio Pinza, who had originated the role of Emile de Becque in *South Pacific* opposite Mary Martin, putting his stamp on "Some Enchanted Evening." A tall, handsome bass, he had enjoyed years at the Metropolitan Opera House as well as European companies. Pinza's matinee idol–like popularity from the run of *South Pacific* and Walter Slezak's reputation on stage and screen, as well as the collaborative triumvirate of Logan, Rome, and Behrman, generated interest on Broadway. This permitted Merrick to raise the initial investment of $280,000 within a few days. Logan himself invested $55,000, RCA Records $24,750, and Behrman, Slezak, and designer Jo Mielziner $5,500 each.[23] No record could be found that Rome had invested in the show.

Rome found out that Pinza did not read music but had learned his numerous operatic roles by rote, listening to the melody on piano. Rodgers and Hammerstein had run into this during *South Pacific*, wanting to give the basso a second-act song late into rehearsals. He balked at their first submission, but when they handed him "This Nearly Was Mine," he decided he could accelerate his learning.[24] Pinza requested the songs for *Fanny* six months ahead of rehearsals, and beyond this, was averse to change. As the premiere approached, Rome came to him with a new song and played it for Pinza, who said "My boy, it's a great song, but we open in four weeks."[25] The song, "Let's Talk about a Woman," never made it into *Fanny*. Years later, Rome tried to use it for *Destry Rides Again*, but it was cut once more.[26]

For the role of Marius, William Tabbert was chosen. He had begun his theater career as an usher at the Chicago Civic Opera where he then sang. His numerous Broadway credits, mostly in the chorus, included *What's Up*, *Follow the Girls*, *Billion Dollar Baby*, *Three to Make Ready*, and a lead role in *Seven Lively Arts* along with Dolores Gray (who would later star in Rome's *Destry Rides Again*).[27] Like Pinza, Tabbert had been in the original *South*

*Pacific* for nearly five years, playing Lieutenant Cable, a role which was to go to Howard Keel until he signed a movie contract with MGM.[28] Tabbert had sung "Younger Than Springtime" and "You've Got to Be Carefully Taught" in *South Pacific* to critical acclaim. He was athletic and boyish, perfect for the part of the young man destined for the sea.

The title role went to Florence Henderson, a twenty-year-old Kentuckian whose route to *Fanny* included the original chorus of *Wish You Were Here*, a show in which she nearly got the lead. She then spent a season as Laurie in the national touring company of *Oklahoma!*[29] Rome was high on her talent, thought her perfect as Fanny, and claimed they got her because "a big Hollywood studio didn't have sense enough to sign her to a contract after she made a screen test."[30] Prior to signing Henderson, other names had come up including Mary Martin, Julie Harris, Maureen O'Hara, and operatic soprano Patrice Munsel.[31] Nearly a year before the opening, Fanny was Martin's role for the asking. Even though she was forty, the idea of reuniting her and Pinza was a box office dream, but delays with *Fanny* led her to abandon the role.[32] Instead, she chose the Jule Styne-Betty Comden-Adolph Green version of *Peter Pan*. This became her signature role and was done on television in 1955 with Cyril Ritchard as Captain Hook. The role of Fanny was a plum for Henderson as the only female lead with three prominent males, but as the show evolved, the two older males dominated the score, and Henderson ended up with only one solo, "I Have to Tell You." Nonetheless, she loved the role and working with Rome.

With Slezak, Henderson, and the *South Pacific* duo, principal casting for *Fanny* was finished, but not the book and score. Logan and Behrman worked on their story for two years, creating what Pinza called "a character play."[33] In the middle of it all, Logan had a mental breakdown, finally going back to work at the urging of his wife Nedda and Merrick. The writers synthesized the plots of the Pagnol trilogy, limited the storyline of the young lovers, and ended with a book that emphasized parental love and responsibility. Merrick's biographer, Howard Kissel, put this into perspective: "Rome himself felt the reason the material spoke so deeply to him and Logan is that at the heart it was about parenthood.... [B]oth the Logans and the Romes had adopted children. This may account for the deep poignancy in the musical's frequent assertions that true fatherhood comes from love and care, not simply physical paternity."[34]

To express this, Rome wrote several songs for the older characters, not showstopping ballads but character pieces with lyrics expounding on life. Theater historian Glenn Litton expressed the situation well:

> A story with so many views of love inspired Rome to write a copious score of short, direct songs. The lighter, more humorous ones were given to Panisse and Cesar, whose notions of love were moderated by their age and

paternal concerns.... Their final scene was a musical-comedy actor's dream: Panisse's death and the parting of two lifelong friends.[35]

Pinza's Cesar sang "Why Be Afraid to Dance?," "Welcome Home," and "Love Is a Very Light Thing." Pinza was especially pleased with these songs and expressed this to the composer in a letter the week that *Fanny* opened:

> Many, many thanks for your very kind letter, and most important of all, for the glorious music you have given me as "Cesar."
> I shall never tire of singing my music in *Fanny*, not only because the melodies are so beautiful, but because the lyrics are so real, so moving, and yet so poetic.[36]

Rome returned Pinza's compliments, saying of the basso that he was "the most exciting, magnetic man [he] ever worked with."[37] Notwithstanding his success with "Some Enchanted Evening," the Italian basso had tired of hearing it played whenever he made an appearance. During *Fanny* tryouts in Boston, he commented on the matter and discussed Rome's music:

> I began to wish they would play something else.... Perhaps I shall be fortunate enough to have people prefer "Love Is a Very Light Thing" from my new show, *Fanny*. Myself, I think the music is beautiful. Or perhaps they will like "Welcome Home. "It will be very agreeable to have a change in the music that is played in my honor.[38]

Pinza recorded "Welcome Home" on *Ezio Pinza Presents: Dinner Music* with George Melachrino and His Orchestra in 1958.

Slezak's character, Panisse, sang "Never Too Late for Love," "To My Wife," and "Panisse and Son." Boston critic Elliot Norton wrote of the last song: "[N]othing could be gayer than his song about his unborn son who will, in the distant future, become a member of his firm — 'Panisse and Son.'"[39] These characters, particularly Cesar and Panisse, became the lifeblood of the show, generating word of mouth business and an uncommon number of repeat customers. London critic Robert Tee would write to Rome a few years later: "I feel I must say (however hackneyed it may sound) that the more one hears the *Fanny* score, the fonder one becomes of it."[40] This would become a frequent comment about Rome's music.

*Fanny* sold out its three-week run in Boston, setting a one-week record for the Shubert Theater there at $50,151.[41] The creators felt they could have sold out all six weeks but wanted the reactions of a different audience in Philadelphia, the second tryout town.[42] Rome had been fooled a few years earlier when *Bless You All* was met with raves in Philadelphia and then was panned in New York. At about this time, Rome received a letter from New York producer Robert Fryer asking if Rome was interested in doing a musical based on the movie *Casablanca*. He tried to tempt Rome by saying that he and partner Lawrence Carr had gotten Marlene Dietrich interested in the project. He then informed Rome, deep into rehearsals for *Fanny* at that moment, that time is of the essence: "We have only a very short time to get the show together, since Warners wants to do a musical remake of the picture, but would forego this if there were to be a stage production."[43] Needless to say, Rome was unable to do such a project on short notice, and *Casablanca* never got a Broadway musical treatment.

To make changes as the show evolved from Boston to Philadelphia to New York, Joshua Logan was the man for the job.[44] Known as an efficient, creative play doctor, he had saved *Wish You Were Here* from sure failure during a month-long tryout period, all in front of New York audiences. The biggest problems to be addressed in *Fanny* were choreography and length. First, choreographer Helen Tamiris was brought in to replace James Starbuck, to better focus and shorten the length and number of dances.[45] The original Boston performances were well over three hours, but by the time the show reached Philadelphia, twenty minutes had been removed. More time would be clipped before New York.

Despite the show's problems, Boston critic Elliot Norton had been high on *Fanny*, putting it in the same league as *Carousel* and *South Pacific*. He referred to the trio as musical plays and delineated the difference between this genre and musical comedies: "The musical play, like *Fanny*, has songs and dances and jokes and, it too, is designed to entertain; but it has, also, a solid dramatic story and characters drawn from life, not from the back-stage ragbag."[46] In the integrated work that is a musical play, not only are the songs to have good lyrics and melody, but they have to be employed well. Rome was quick to complement his collaborators for their contributions to this: Logan, music conductor Lehman Engel, and orchestrator Philip Lang. Rome appreciated Logan's use of songs, as he never added a song to a scene as an afterthought, but created the scene around a song. Richard Rodgers was especially aware of this in Logan's direction of *South Pacific*, telling of "the extraordinary way he has managed to stage the songs as though they were both book and dialogue, not unpleasant little interruptions in the scheme of the place."[47] Logan was sensitive to lyricists, knowing their words could propel a story, and he always tried to get dialogue and stage action to reach an emotional level that necessitated a particular song. Rome said of Logan: "He can hardly read music, but he knows how to use it more originally, effectively and knowingly than any composer."[48]

Rome felt the same way towards songs and dances, that they should complement each other. In an interview with Engel years later, he stressed how important this was. They had had problems with Herbert Ross, the choreographer on *I Can Get It for You Wholesale* in 1962:

A choreographer who thinks you get the number over and then do the dance. We had terrible fights ... because we both said, "That's not the way you do a musical number. We've done lots of them and the whole thing should be one thing, you don't do the songs then stop and suddenly do one of the dances."[49]

There were other problems with Ross in a similar vein during *Wholesale*. To Rome and Engel, a dance was not just a dance, but one that should be interpreted and designed within the context of the scene, its characters, and the music. Rome told Engel:

> Do you remember in the "Bar Mitzvah" number where the son dances with his mother and it was a very well choreographed *pas de deux* which had nothing to do with the thing and I finally in desperation ran up to Herb and yelled:
> "For Christ's sake, this is a young boy dancing with his mother, it's not two dancers."
> And the choreographer said: "Oh, oh I see."[50]

Lehman Engel, music director for *Fanny*, was crucial to Rome and his score. He had served in that role in 125 Broadway shows up to that time. With such a large score as that of *Fanny*, Engel was busy in the orchestra pit. His helpfulness went far beyond his baton work as he had a fine sense of what would work musically with an audience. He also had a wonderful personality for the rigors of creating a show. Rome said of him: "He's a cheerful personality who enjoys what he's doing and makes it fun for everyone. You know, you hit some awfully low moments when you're putting on a show together. He knows how to help you over those times."[51]

Rome's third musical collaborator on *Fanny* was orchestrator Philip Lang. The best composers on Broadway usually relied upon orchestrators, musicians who could fill out their melodies for the large pit orchestras of the day. Kurt Weill was one of the exceptions, usually doing his own. The most prominent orchestrators included:

| | | |
|---|---|---|
| Robert Russell Bennett | Ralph Burns | Robert Ginzler |
| Hershey Kay | Irwin Kostal | Philip J. Lang |
| Sid Ramin | Ted Royal | Eddie Sauter |
| Hans Spialek | Don Walker | Larry Wilcox[52] |

Lang was a newcomer at the time, having made his reputation as co-orchestrator on *My Fair Lady* with Robert Russell Bennett. Several critics mentioned the *Fanny* orchestrations, focusing on his arrangement for "Restless Heart."[53] Rome's attitude toward orchestrations was expressed in a 1971 interview with *ASCAP Today*: "It's like the orchestrations, if you notice the orchestrations in a show, there is something wrong. You should only be thinking of the story itself, of the people, and how you're being moved."[54] Beyond his talent, Lang had an easygoing manner, worked well with Rome, and was able to ignore David Merrick's game-playing. Fellow orchestrator Donald Pippin said of Lang: "Phil would do as he was told, he'd nod and smile. When everyone else was fighting or arguing, he just wouldn't get involved."[55] Lang went on to become Merrick's main orchestrator, the favorite of Jerry Herman and Gower Champion, and crowned his career with *Hello, Dolly!*

*Fanny* opened at the Majestic Theater on November 4, 1954. The veteran team of stars and creators plus the optimistic words of the Boston and Philadelphia critics had led to a hefty advance sale of $900,000.[56] In all, reviewers agreed that it was an important musical with much to commend it, but the best summation was done by the reviewer from *Variety*: "There will obviously be diverse reaction to this rather somber musical. Some will find it tender, warm and moving, while to others it will seem slow, heavy and stubbornly lacking in gaiety or animation."[57]

One critic took *Fanny* to task: "Book and score, instead of being mutually helpful, appear to get in each other's way."[58] Fortunately, the consensus was that the show developed characters far beyond musicals of years earlier. As a Philadelphia critic had stated, Rome's score was "woven perfectly into the action."[59] Rodgers shared the same sentiment: "I found myself touched time and time again by the score and its remarkable integration with the play itself."[60]

So pleased was Rome with *Fanny*'s success and Marcel Pagnol's source material that in the spring of 1955 he went to Europe, visiting with Pagnol and sharing the good news of their show. During this time, they discussed further shows based on movies Pagnol had directed, most prominently his 1938 comedy *La Femme du Boulanger* (*The Baker's Wife*) and from 1940, *La Fille du Puisatier* (*The Well-Digger's Daughter*). Rome and Pagnol never collaborated again, but Stephen Schwartz's 1976 musical, *The Baker's Wife*, was based on Pagnol's film.

As much as anything in the show, Rome's score received high praise. John Chapman of the *Daily News* thought it "the best work Harold Rome has done yet" with lyrics of "a wide range of style and content."[61] Fellow composers Marc Blitzstein and Richard Rodgers paid Rome high compliments. Blitzstein thought the songs showed a "combination of reticence, taste, and occasional daring."[62] Rodgers said, "[T]his score places its composer at a level far above anything he has attained so far, and that's pretty damned high."[63] The director of a 2005 production of *Fanny*, Ian Marshall Fisher of Lost Musical troupe, worked with the original score and found it "extremely powerful." He was taken with the underscoring in the original: "There's a lot of underscoring. Rome keeps reprising the theme so that the show takes on the power of a film noir."[64]

Rome was fond of the score of *Fanny*. When asked about it in a 1968 interview, he said: "Every show is a challenge because it has to have a personality of its own.... *Fanny* was a special challenge. [Songs] had to be simple and have a little French quality about them, [which] made for a very homogenous score all the way through."[65] He told Boston critic Elinor Hughes: "The difficult thing to do, both in the book and the lyrics, was to avoid American equivalents for French slang and yet to suggest something of the flavor of the background of the characters which was the Marseilles waterfront."[66]

Two critics felt there was enough of a score for two shows, with a good variety of song types.[67] Rome had written twenty-six songs for the show and ended up with seventeen. The title ballad had already become a hit for Eddie Fisher, as had Rome's 1952 "Wish You Were Here." Tabbert introduced it in the first act, singing of his love for the sea over that for Fanny. In Act II, he, Pinza, and Henderson reprised it, turning the meaning of the song around for a most dramatic effect (Marius learning that Fanny's love is no longer his). Broadway shows are filled with reprises, often loosely fit into the second act merely to get a rehearing of an audience favorite. The song "Fanny" not only advances the plot in Act I, but then twists it in the reprise.

Ethan Mordden thought Rome's work inventive in doing this not only with "Fanny" but other songs in the show: "But Rome's main work lay in the establishing and then intertwining of character motifs — 'Restless Heart,' 'Fanny,' 'I Have to Tell You,' and 'Welcome Home' are not only reprised but combined, torn apart, and recombined, just as the characters themselves are."[68]

"I Have to Tell You," Henderson's only solo, enjoyed an outside recording when Dinah Shore released it as a 45 rpm on RCA Victor. The critic for *Variety* wrote: "This is class material which may not have immediate commercial impact, but it may be around for some time."[69] Slezak had two endearing songs, "Panisse and Son" and "To My Wife." Music director Lehman Engel was fond of the latter, referring to it as a charm song, "a song that embodies generally delicate, optimistic, and rhythmic music, and lyrics of light though not comedic matter."[70] Examples of other charm songs would be "The Surrey with the Fringe on Top" from *Oklahoma!* and "Wrapped in a Ribbon and Tied in a Bow" from *Street Scene*. As for "To My Wife," Lehman took credit for saving it from the axe in Boston:

> The song seemed to go well in rehearsal and the cast thought it touching. On opening night in Boston the audience was embarrassingly silent at the end.... [I]t was my idea to try expanding it a bit.... The orchestra reprised the chorus, and Panisse spoke a toast over the music, singing on the last few bars.... [I]t was received cordially and remained in the show.[71]

Less than a month after the opening, Joshua Logan and cast members appeared on Ed Sullivan's prime-time Sunday variety show *Toast of the Town*.

Florence Henderson and Lloyd Reese, who played her boy Cesario, sang "Be Kind to Your Parents," Henderson and William Tabbert did "Fanny," and the young couple and Ezio Pinza sang "Why Be Afraid to Dance?" In between these songs, Logan discussed *Fanny* with Sullivan, the show's laconic host.[72] Rome never performed on stage nor spoke with Sullivan but was introduced by him and took a bow from the audience. Rome was originally scheduled to be involved in the segment, but when the conservative Sullivan learned of Rome's politics and his blacklisting in the ultra-conservative publication *Red Channels*, it was decided to only acknowledge him.[73]

Exposure to a national television audience was a boon to the show and its songs. A *Variety* listing for the week of December 3–9, 1954, listed the "Top 30 Songs on TV," of which four songs were from *Fanny*.[74] On the listing of "Songs with Largest Radio Audience" was "Fanny," aided by the *Toast of the Town* appearance and the success of the Eddie Fisher recording. Before the New York opening, four of the songs were recorded on Decca Records by Fred Waring and His Pennsylvanians. Ultimately, only "Fanny" had any staying power in the American Popular Songbook. Rome was well aware of the difficulty of writing a well-integrated song that becomes a hit, as he explained to a reporter in pre–Broadway Philadelphia: "Writing for the musical stage today is really like writing a form of opera. Each number is keyed into the mood of the story and the song not only advances the action but develops the character of the singer."[75] He wanted a hit song as much as the next composer but was firm about the integration of songs. Again from his "How to Write a Hit Musical":

> ONE OR TWO BIG HITS IS ALL YOU NEED.
> Watch this rule. No question about it, they help. But a good musical is more than a collection of hit songs. Half of the score could be meaningless without the setting it was created for. Putting the right song in the right place at the right time is what counts. It may never be a hit, but it sure can help the show to be one.[76]

He emphasized to interviewer Martin Bookspan years later: "Unless the show is right, the songs aren't going to mean anything anyway."[77]

Though short on popular hits, *Fanny*'s book and score made it a smash, the first one of the 1954–55 Broadway season. It played to capacity audiences for over a year even though Merrick was asking top dollar for the time, $7.50 for the best seats. Beyond this, he had forged a deal with the theater owners that any gross above $46,000 was retained by him and his co-producer Logan, uncommon for the time.[78]

With eight performances weekly, *Fanny* was grossing $85,900, a hefty profit for its investors. Merrick was proud of his first foray into the Broadway musical, and he and Logan wrote a letter to their investors a few months into the run:

March 4, 1955

Dear Investor:

This is our first week in the black! The enclosed check representing 40 percent of the original capitalizationof *Fanny* is the final payment of the production cost. Your management has been able to recoup this large sum in sixteen and a half weeks, which is believed to be a record in musicals.

We are able to report that *Fanny* is still selling out.[79]

As good as the show was, the creators could not take all the credit. By this time in his budding career, Merrick was a master of promotion. Beyond the usual newspaper and billboard ads, Merrick's promotions merit listing[80]:

- affixing stickers to men's room walls asking "Have you seen *Fanny*?";
- erecting a naked statue of the show's belly dancer, Nejla Ates, in Central Park, and notifying the police and the press simultaneously;
- skywriting "When in New York see Fanny" over the beach in Monaco during the wedding of Grace Kelly and Prince Rainier;
- running full page ads in the *Times and Herald Tribune*;
- taking ads in fourteen out-of-town newspapers with mail order coupons for *Fanny*;
- asking the U.S. Weather Bureau to name its next hurricane Fanny, which was denied.

In all, Merrick spent an unprecedented $3,500 a week on promotion for the show. In a letter to Rome seventeen months into the run, Merrick explained that there has been a decline in receipts, believing it only temporary and taking credit for his promotional campaign: "In spite of the half royalty, as you see, we were just in the vicinity of an even break, due, of course, to the large advertising budget. It looks like it will be full royalty for the next eight or nine weeks, however."[81]

*Fanny* was featured in three issues of popular magazines: *Life*, September 20, 1954, which featured Florence Henderson during rehearsals; *Look*, November 16, 1954; and *Life*, November 29, 1954. The show ran over two years. A major cast change eighteen months into the run with Lawrence Tibbett taking over as Cesar and Billy Gilbert as Panisse did not deter audiences. It closed December 16, 1956, after 888 performances — a record Rome would never exceed — and went on to a successful national tour. It was revived in February of 2010 in New York as a part of the City Center *Encores!* series.

A 1956 production in Munich, Germany, was the first American musical done there. Theatergoers in Germany were fond of their operetta and although

*Fanny* featured aspects of that musical form, an American book musical was something new to them. This was true not only of audiences but of the creative personnel as well. Rome said of the experience: "I didn't realize what a new form the musical is to the Germans and my approach to the show was really an eye-opener to the critics, producer, and director."[82] Composers are particular about how their songs are done as a production continues or new ones are created. They have to attend performances periodically and tend to details of productions. Rome worked extensively with the director of the Munich production, writing to William Fitelson: "It was very important to make those corrections and changes because there were a lot of mistakes and if they were not corrected in this production, they would be duplicated in future productions in Germany, jeopardizing the chances for the show's success."[83]

Along similar lines — preservation of one's score — as the London run progressed, Janet Pavek in the title role was having difficulty with two of the songs. Musical director Michael Collins wrote to Rome about the show and various friendly personal matters, then added, "Musically, everything is still the same as when you left, but I take this opportunity to ask your permission to raise the keys by half a tone or so for a couple of Janet's songs, for she finds them, at present, tiring on her voice after eight performances a week."[84] To the untrained, this does not seem like much of a request, but to a Broadway composer, it was crucial. Rome replied a week later: "As to raising the keys for Janet Pavek, I would ask you not to do so. The keys are as high as they can possibly be now and raising them even one-half tone would damage both songs. Please tell her that I emphatically do not wish them any higher."[85] Presumably, the songs stayed as they were, and Pavek learned to live with the keys, performing the role in 1958 at the Highland Park (Illinois) Music Theatre, the Chicago area's first production of *Fanny*.

The London production launched in 1956 starred Robert Morley as Panisse and Ian Wallace as Cesar. Critical attitudes in London were negative almost across the board.[86] The reviewer for the *Evening News* stated: "Harold Rome has succeeded in composing a score that almost completely lacks charm."[87] Fortunately, audiences did not agree, and it ran 333 performances. The producer closed it as receipts dwindled, blaming it on an extremely bad winter and the closure of the Suez Canal. The latter led to gasoline rationing which caused a significant decrease in coach (bus) party bookings, popular in England.[88] Rome thought the run should have been a better one, writing to producer Sandor Gorlinsky: "I was sorry to hear the news of the closing of *Fanny*. I still have the feeling that we missed having a success by only a small margin but what can we do? That's the kind of business we're in. We will make up for it on the next one."[89]

## 13. Fanny

The London run of *Fanny* did not meet Rome's expectations, but real disappointment came with the handling of the movie.

Never crazy about Hollywood producers and their view towards Broadway musicals and composers, Rome had resented the treatment of *Call Me Mister*.[90] As for *Fanny*, Warner Brothers never intended to do it as a musical but as a romantic comedy, then changed it to a romantic drama. Studio head Jack Warner, Joshua Logan, who was to direct the film, and the principal cast members all knew about it. One of the stars, Leslie Caron, explained: "[T]he project was already without singing when it was offered to me — musical films were not so popular with the large public any more. I was not involved in pre-production and don't know when the decision was taken."[91]

Whenever the decision was made, it seems somebody forgot to tell Rome until the movie's Panisse, Maurice Chevalier, mentioned it casually over dinner after the final day of shooting.[92] When he found out, he was angry and hurt.

In apologetic letters in August and September of 1960, Logan attempted to pacify Rome, explaining that the decision had been made only two days

*Left to right:* Rome, Harold Arlen, Sammy Cahn, Arthur Schwartz, and Jimmy McHugh at CBS Television, circa 1960 (courtesy Gilmore Music Library, Yale University).

before Rome heard of it — two days too late and without final approval from Rome. Logan laid much of the blame on Warner Brothers, claiming they never wanted a musical, and reminded Rome that he had been aware of Jack Warner's attitude about big screen musicals when the contracts were signed.[93] Another problem had been the casting as Horst Buchholz, who was playing Marius, could not sing and Charles Boyer, as Cesar, not only refused to sing but also said no to having his voice dubbed.[94] Logan claimed that he had intended to use four songs and insisted to the studio that they shoot a song or two. Logan then explained to Rome what happened after "To My Wife" was filmed: "The moment it was seen in an otherwise straight dramatic picture everyone felt that it was a shock and change of style that would hurt the picture's chances immeasurably."[95] After that screening, any discussion of a musical was dropped.

In a letter to Florence Rome, attorney William Fitelson explained that the possibility of the songs being eliminated had been discussed with Harold and that he had signed the contract, not wanting to turn down a lucrative deal.[96] The total payment by Warner Brothers for the movie rights was $300,000 with $120,000 to the musicals' producers and $180,000 to the authors, the latter distributed as follows[97]:

| | |
|---|---|
| S.N. Behrman | $35,000 |
| Joshua Logan | $36,000 |
| Harold Rome | $55,000 |
| Paul Osborn | $9,000 |
| Marcel Pagnol | $45,000 |

Whether songs were used or not, songwriters received a significant share, and Rome as both lyricist and composer benefited doubly. Fitelson felt that Logan had acted in good faith, sincerely meaning to use several of the songs, and reminded Florence that financially, success of the picture was the important thing, whether a musical or a drama. In concluding, Fitelson gave her good counsel: "I do not despair of his reputation or future based on this picture. What happens to a musical or a dramatic property, when converted to a picture, is almost always a film company's prerogative."[98]

Rome's songs were used extensively for the film score of *Fanny*, which was scored by veterans Morris Stoloff and Harry Sukman. Rome was nominated for a Golden Globe for Best Original Score, while Stoloff and Sukman were nominated for an Academy Award.[99] Rome thought they used his score to such an extent that he should have been credited: "They used them exactly the way I arranged them for Broadway. The score came up for an Academy Award nomination, which went to the arranger and conductor. My name wasn't mentioned. I raised a terrible stink."[100]

The star power of *Fanny*—Chevalier, Boyer, Caron and Buchholz—made it a success worldwide, and it reaped a healthy profit for Warner Brothers and Rome. Nonetheless, he was bitter about the whole experience and did not speak to Logan for three years.[101] This split had been brewing for some time, and while each man respected the other's talent, Rome could be stubborn and Logan all but impossible to work with. Despite their success with *Wish You Were Here*, Rome had reservations about starting the *Fanny* project with Logan. He told Lehman Engel in their interview years later:

> Logan was a little hard to handle and after all the experience of *Wish You Were Here*, I said, "Well, I've had that. He's a great director, but the sanity is very important." But when *Fanny* came along, I said, "Well, it's worth another nervous breakdown. I may have to go into analysis again I'm sure after this show is over" and I did.[102]

On the same topic—dealing with Logan—he told another interviewer, Beverly Gary: "When I was doing *Fanny*, I had some trouble with Josh Logan, so I did a painting, *Josh Logan Followed by Two Consciences*."[103]

Although lighthearted in these interviews on the topic of his mental health, Rome suffered for decades with bipolar disease, mostly depression. Joshua Rome said that it could be overwhelming for his father. Rome went through years of therapy including psychotherapy, medications, and even electroshock therapy which was widely used in those years for depression. Joshua said that Rome was demanding of himself; even with a successful show and a majority of rave reviews, he would fixate on the one bad review or comment.[104] Joshua remembers his parents spreading out all the early papers and poring over the reviews, often foregoing the usual cast parties. Of his sensitivity to criticism, Rome admitted: "My analysis did a great deal for me. I'm less worried about my work and less sensitive about opening myself to attack. I've also learned to trust my instincts and let my subconscious work."[105] He also said on the subject:

> After a while, you learn to let your unconscious work for you.... Sometimes, I'll make a list of things that have to be done and let them sit for a while. Quite often, when I get up one morning, I find that somewhere during the night the problem has been solved for me, and I can go ahead and work on the song because it seems to have a direction by then.[106]

With long-term psychoanalysis and much support from family and friends, Rome slowly improved but depression was always a factor. Ultimately he learned to find criticism "helpful."[107]

As for *Fanny* the movie, the bottom line for Rome was that Logan and the studio had missed a great opportunity. Rome knew movies, well aware that the popularity of screen musicals was ebbing. He was cynical towards

Hollywood's second-rate treatment of songs and felt that when it came to understanding and filming a book musical, Tinseltown just didn't get it. He had told an interviewer fourteen years earlier: "[M]y philosophy will find tough going in Hollywood, where there's seldom any connection between the plot and the score. There hasn't been much integrated music since Rodgers and Hart scored the Maurice Chevalier musicals years ago."[108]

Nonetheless, he had faith in the book musical and in Logan: "He could have made the first movie musical in which the songs flowed naturally as an extension of the dialogue."[109] A few years later, Rome wrote an article in the *Journal-American* entitled "The Voice of Broadway: Rome Can't Get Films Wholesale," making his case: "My naïve assumption is that a good musical film will be a success, and a bad one will be a failure, and that it doesn't depend on any trend factor."[110]

The movie experience notwithstanding, Rome remained proud of his work on *Fanny*. It receives productions frequently, being especially popular on the summer theater circuit, and there were discussions for a 1984 Broadway revival that never materialized. Rome, Logan, and Behrman managed to take a beloved French trilogy and create an enduring American book musical. As for Hollywood producers:

> "My wife was sore, too," Rome recalls. "And when one of the producers said soothingly that *Wish You Were Here* was still good movie material and should be done, she told him, 'Why don't you do it as a silent?'"[111]

## Chapter 14

# *Destry Rides Again*

> "*Destry* has bounce and verve and a Harold Rome score that advances the plot lyrically in the same, sure way of the R. and H. musicals."
> — Peggy Doyle

Producer David Merrick felt the time was ripe for a musical Western, "a real Western musical comedy."[1] The Western had long been popular in literature and the movies, while in musical shows, only a western motif had been used. The best known of these include[2]:

| Year(s) | Title | Composers |
| --- | --- | --- |
| 1910 | *The Girl of the West* (opera) (*La fanciulla del West*) | Giacomo Puccini |
| 1912 | *The Red Petticoat* | Jerome Kern |
| 1924–26 | *Rose Marie* (operetta) | Rudolph Friml; Otto Harbach |
| 1928 | *Rainbow* | Vincent Youmans; Oscar Hammerstein II |
| 1930–31 | *Girl Crazy* | George Gershwin; Ira Gershwin |
| 1943–48 | *Oklahoma!* | Richard Rodgers; Oscar Hammerstein II |
| 1946–49 | *Annie Get Your Gun* | Irving Berlin |
| 1951–52 | *Paint Your Wagon* | Frederick Loewe; Alan Jay Lerner |

According to Merrick, a real Western had never been done on a Broadway stage, or anywhere else for that matter, and he wanted one "in the classic good-guys-versus-bad-guys movie tradition."[3]

The author of the musical's book, Leonard Gershe, was in full agreement, referring to the show as an "out and out horse opera,"[4] and elaborated on the idea of a musical Western in an article prior to the premiere in Philadelphia:

> I don't think Westerns are a novelty that became popular with the advent of television. They have always been popular—even in the earliest days of motion pictures. And why not?
>
> The stories are filled with colorful heroes and villains engaged in outrageous lawlessness. These stories must certainly be interesting to a society living in an era when jaywalking is a misdemeanor.[5]

Gershe's reference to television, a burgeoning medium in 1959, reflected the fact that at the time, seven of the ten most popular TV shows were Westerns[6]:

| | | |
|---|---|---|
| *Gunsmoke* | *Wagon Train* | *Maverick* |
| *Have Gun, Will Travel* | *The Rifleman* | *I've Got a Secret* |
| *The Danny Thomas Show* | *The Real McCoys* | *Tales of Wells Fargo* |
| *The Life and Legend of Wyatt Earp* | | |

The Western Merrick chose was based on the Max Brand novel *Destry*, which had spawned four productions on the big screen[7]:

| Year | Title | Director | Stars |
|---|---|---|---|
| 1932 | *Destry Rides Again* | Benjamin Stoloff | Tom Mix, Claudia Dell, Stanley Fields |
| 1939 | *Destry Rides Again* | George Marshall | Marlene Dietrich, James Stewart, Brian Donlevy |
| 1950 | *Frenchie* | Louis King | Shelley Winters, Joel McCrea, Paul Kelly |
| 1954 | *Destry* | George Marshall | Audie Murphy, Mari Blanchard, Lyle Bettger |

For the 1939 film, Frank Loesser and Frederick Hollander wrote "See What the Boys in the Back Room Will Have,"[8] sung by Marlene Dietrich in black net stockings standing on the bar. One movie critic referred to the scene as "a greater work of art than the Venus de Milo."[9] It was the intention of Merrick and Gershe to employ elements from the 1939 *Destry Rides Again*, the most popular of the four movies. At the same time, Gershe's text was to be more faithful to the Max Brand novel than any of the screenplays had been.

In late 1956, Merrick pitched the *Destry* idea to Rome, who immediately took to it. The two were still flush from the great success of *Fanny* which would close in December of that year after its 888-performance run. The problem was that Merrick did not yet have the rights to *Destry*, which were held by Universal Pictures. Fortunately, Rome was friends with Milton Rackmil, the head of Universal as well as Decca Records, and arranged for a meeting between Merrick and Rackmil, both tough negotiators. Theater writer Herbert Mitgang of the *New York Times* wrote of their meeting: "At the end of the negotiation, Mr. Merrick emerged with the Broadway musical rights, with the rights to sell the musical or make it as a film; Universal received a percentage of, and a favored position in bidding for, the future movie rights, and Decca the rights to record the original cast album."[10]

Knowing the novel and the 1939 movie, Rome began work soon after Merrick had secured the rights. It was Rome's *modus operandi* to start out with a slew of ideas from the original work and the libretto as it developed, write a lot of songs, then pare down from there to fit the show. Of course, there were numerous exceptions to this. After a 1973 interview with Rome, John Mahoney of the *Los Angeles Times* detailed the composer's work habits: "Rome writes up to 40 songs for a single production, always at least twice as many as will be used, before submitting to a weeding process."[11] He further clarified his work habits in an extensive interview in *ASCAP Today* in 1973:

> What usually comes to me first is the necessity for doing the song. The first thing you do is go over the book and find the high emotional points.... You find out what the situation or the scene has to say. You figure out the characters that are going to do it, and then you think of a song that will convey that — in music and lyrics.... I usually work on both of them at the same time.[12]

Unlike many other composers, he seldom dipped into his "trunk," the collection of songs that composers cut or never used in shows. Most did this regularly, among them Richard Rodgers, whose trunk was immense; he called these recycled songs "escapees." Rodgers and Lorenz Hart's "There's a Small Hotel" had "escaped" from *Jumbo* and became a hit a few years later in *On Your Toes*.[13] In one famous instance, Irving Berlin "took an old song of his trunk and refashioned it into 'God Bless America.'"[14] Cole Porter depended on his trunk of songs: "Generally, Cole found that if fourteen songs were called for, six or seven songs already completed would, with a bit of tinkering, be suitable. Whenever he took on a task of some enormity, the trunk gave him the feeling that he had already half completed it."[15]

Porter's hit "I Get a Kick Out of You" (from *Anything Goes*) was a trunk song. Rome was philosophically against this and in the case of *Destry* said: "I have written 36 songs for it, all new, none from the trunk. For David Merrick, you write new or get your hands chopped off. He doesn't want any trunk stuff."[16] How Merrick ever knew a song came from the trunk of Rome or any of his other composers is a mystery.

Although never given program credit for writing the books for any of his musicals, Rome was usually involved with them from the start. His writing skills had been honed on dozens of sketches for revues going back to his summers at Green Mansions camp in the Catskill Mountains and his writing for the war effort and soldier shows. Leonard Gershe had never done a stage musical but had written the screenplays for *Funny Face* and *Silk Stockings*. In the latter, Merrick felt his writing had been an improvement over the Broadway book. Regarding Merrick's Western, Gershe admitted, "I took it on because I felt I could do something with it because originally it wasn't a love story."[17] Up to that time, there could be no Broadway musical without a love story or two. As Gershe expanded the plot with a love story, Rome wrote his songs and gave Gershe some assistance with the book.

By this time in Rome's career, he was financially comfortable and able to invest in this show. Nearly two-thirds of the initial capitalization of $325,000 was provided by three investors:

| | |
|---|---:|
| Harold Rome | $48,750 |
| Max J. Brown | 81,250 |
| Byron Goldman | 78,000 |
| | $208,000 |

The latter two were friends and frequent backers of David Merrick productions. For his fifteen percent investment and contributions as composer-lyricist, Rome received:

- 7½% of the backers' shares (calculated after all expenses deducted);
- 5% of the profits figured prior to the above backers' shares;
- 1% additional of the backers' share;
- weekly royalties as composer-lyricist.[18]

This was a good contract and reflected the confidence that Merrick had in his composer and the idea of a musical Western. Over the years, Merrick had earned the reputation of being difficult to work with; in 1993, Howard Kissel wrote *David Merrick: The Abominable Showman: An Unauthorized Biography*, detailing this. Merrick's difficult side was "not part of Mr. Rome's memories," said Avery Corman after a 1991 interview of Rome. When asked about Merrick, Rome told the journalist: "He got us involved, he waited until we were ready to go, and then he went with it. He was a catalyst in those days, because he let the artist do the work. He did not fool around with the artistic end."[19]

Casting for the show began early in 1958, and Gwen Verdon was the first choice for the female lead. The role demanded a strong voice and dance skills, and Verdon, with recent successes in *Damn Yankees* (1955) and *New Girl in Town* (1957), fit the bill to a tee.[20] The male role was less demanding, calling for an actor with a passable voice. Andy Griffith came to Merrick's attention.

Griffith had gained a following on Broadway as the down-home, dumb-as-a-fox Will Stockdale in the play *No Time for Sergeants*. The production had started as an episode on *The United States Steel Hour*, then was expanded and moved to Broadway where it ran 796 performances from October 1955 through September 1957. Griffith won a Tony nomination for Best Featured Actor. The show was the Broadway debut of Don Knotts, later to team with Griffith in television's *The Andy Griffith Show* (1964–69). *No Time for Sergeants* then became a successful film of the same name in 1958 with much of the Broadway cast including Griffith and Knotts.[21] Griffith had also been the protagonist in Elia Kazan's anti–Fascist film *A Face in the Crowd*. With Griffith's triple exposure on television, Broadway, and film, producer Merrick felt he could attract an audience. Moreover, Griffith's stage persona was perfect for the title role, "the gangling knight with the syrupy drawl, without fear and beyond reproach."[22] But the creative team had reservations about his voice.

They had no such hesitations with their ultimate leading lady, Dolores Gray, a big voice in the mold of Ethel Merman, referred to by one critic as "the biggest, beltingest voice in the business."[23] Merrick signed Gray, his second choice, as Gwen Verdon was busy with *Redhead*. Gray had received a Tony for *Carnival in Flanders* in 1953, a James Van Heusen–Johnny Burke show that had lasted only six performances in New York. She had also played leading roles in Vernon Duke's flop *Sweet Bye and Bye* (1946), London's original *Annie Get Your Gun* which ran longer than the American original (1947), and the Jule Styne-Betty Comden-Adolph Green show *Two on the Aisle* (1951). Extensive nightclub work and MGM movies rounded out her résumé.[24] She could act and project the personality of a saloon lady.

With Gray, the problem was her dancing, but she wanted the opportunity to do it in this show:

> David and Michael [Kidd] promised me I'd dance. That's one of the things that made me do the show. I'm terribly disappointed in this. I admit I can't dance in the same world with Gwen Verdon, but let's say she's a dancer who can sing, and I'm a singer who can dance, and I've often asked them just to give me a chance.[25]

Merrick and director Kidd both denied they had promised her a dance, and when pushed on the subject, Kidd said: "Dolores was cast because she is a superb singer. We hired expert dancers to dance."[26] The differences of opinion over her dancing role in the musical boiled over during tryouts in Boston. A change in the scene "The Whip Dance," further reducing her dancing presence, was the last straw. She screamed at Kidd, and they ultimately slapped each other. A few days later, Gray's stage mother became involved and also slapped Kidd.[27] Apologies were not forthcoming, but for the good of the show the disagreement was tabled, and none of the threatened legal actions was ever taken.

Behind the scenes and prior to the "Whip Dance" fiasco, the creators of *Destry* faced problems with their casting. Scott Brady had been hired to play the town heavy; he had played in tough guy roles in movies and was hired for his acting ability and macho presence as the gang leader in Bottleneck.[28] A few songs had been written for his character, but when Brady came to New York, it was discovered he had hardly any voice. Rome explained the debacle to Lehman Engel years later:

> Engel: What was the name of the tall, good-looking movie star?
> Rome: Scott Brady. The guy couldn't sing.... I had a lovely song called "I'm a Handy Thing to Have Around the Place" which he was supposed

to have.... It was his song, and he couldn't sing a line. We had to throw it out.[29]

More importantly, when Dolores Gray and Andy Griffith first came to rehearsals, Rome and Kidd sensed no chemistry between them. Again, Rome and Engel:

> Engel: I will say that *Destry* is an example in my own opinion of a show that had it been cast properly would have been a great hit.... Dolores sang very well and Andy Griffith was all right but it should have been a charming boy and beautiful girl.
> Rome: No electricity there at all.
> Engel: None at all.[30]

Rome felt the creators had two choices: (1) call off rehearsals and recast, which would have been contractually difficult or (2) build a different kind of *Destry* around Gray, Griffith, and Brady.[31] They chose the latter and did the show with less of a love story. As songs panned out, the two stars had only one duet, the casual "Anyone Would Love You," and Brady's character ended up with no songs.

Out-of-town tryouts were booked for Philadelphia and Boston before the Broadway opening, so into the City of Brotherly Love Harold Rome brought his sheaf of three dozen songs, custom-fit for a musical Western. *Destry Rides Again* required the usual adjustments, rewrites, cuts, and late night meetings of the creative team during previews. Fortunately, there were no threats to close the show, no need for show doctors, and no classic second act trouble. Rome believed in his audiences and listened to them. For an article entitled "How a Show Gets the Works for a Run on Broadway," he told a Boston writer:

> You really have to have an audience before you know what kind of a show you've got. If it's too slow, or if things are getting past them — you know right away.
> They cough, they rustle their programs, they move around in their seats. Sometimes you can really hate an audience — but they're usually right![32]

Rome referred to this as "instant communication" with an audience.[33]

The plot involved a peace-loving sheriff, Tom Destry (Griffith), hired to clean up the town of Bottleneck, run by a gang of outlaws led by Kent (Brady) with saloon hostess Frenchy (Gray). With three principals, a group of gunslingers, etc., there were plenty of opportunities for Rome to write duets, ensemble songs, and dances. The score of the show was pure Rome with lyrics of "uncommon grace and humor"[34] and melodies displaying "an astonishing number of inventive variations on the clop-clop rhythm imposed by the familiar terrain."[35] As the critic for *Cue* raved: "Harold Rome's songs are in the

## 14. Destry Rides Again

Rome with the Yale University Band rhythm section — Dan Hunt (guitar), Martin Goldberg (drums), and John Stewart (bass) — in 1959 (courtesy Gilmore Music Library, Yale University).

new tradition. They are not all June-moon, juke-box numbers. They represent a variety of styles and moods — from the stirring 'Ballad of the Gun' to the satirical 'Are You Ready, Gyp Watson?'"[36] In a similar vein, a Boston critic felt *Destry* had "a Harold Rome score that advances the plot lyrically in the same, sure way of the R. and H. musicals."[37]

From his years of experience with revues, Rome was particularly adept writing entertaining novelties, and for *Destry*, this included "Respectability" and "That Ring on the Finger." There were also three engaging ballads: "Once Knew a Fella," "I Say Hello," and "Anyone Would Love You." The last was recorded by ten different artists, most notably The Four Aces on their *Hits from Broadway*.[38] With "Anyone Would Love You," Rome again exhibited his ability to write a love duet, like the one for *Fanny* in 1954, "The Thought of You," sung by Marius (William Tabbert) and Fanny (Florence Henderson).[39]

There was no real hit song in *Destry* as Rome had enjoyed with the title numbers of both *Wish You Were Here* and *Fanny*.[40] One song from *Destry* that stood out for many of the critics was a group effort by Frenchy (Gray) and the townspeople in a mock trial of a villain, "Are You Ready, Gyp Watson?"[41] Sung in six parts, "Gyp Watson" is in the same mold as other group efforts from Broadway, notably "Fugue for Tinhorns" from *Guys and Dolls*, Jerry Herman's "The Fox Hunt" from *Mame*, and Richard Adler's "The Cocoa Bean Song" from the ill-fated *Kwamina*.[42] Ethan Mordden, known for his decade summaries of Broadway musicals, singled out Rome's use of such multi-melody pieces:

> We should mention [Jerry Herman's] "The Fox Hunt," a number in a form that Harold Rome favored, in which as many as five or six melodies are sung separately, then all at once. Rome always used it as sheer music....
> We hear it in *Call Me Mister*'s "Going Home Train," *Fanny*'s "Birthday Song," *Destry Rides Again*'s "Are You Ready, Gyp Watson?," and even in Rome's last show, *Gone with the Wind*, in "Blissful Christmas."[43]

With his score, Rome was able to compose music for his dance-oriented director and also write for the varied voices of his principals. Two of them, Gray and Griffith, received Tony nominations that year. Most importantly, Rome was able to capture the spirit of the Wild West within the confines of a Broadway musical; as he put it: "*Destry* had to sound western ... and still it had to be modern."[44] Since many book musicals were written for a period, it was incumbent upon the book writers and composers to capture that period. Of the many composers who did this, Rome was especially impressed by the work of Frederick Loewe: "Fritz Loewe is a master at writing like the period or the place it's supposed to be and still making it completely original."[45] Rome singled out *Brigadoon* and *My Fair Lady* as exemplary of this. The critics were in agreement that *Destry* was a real Western, best expressed by *New York Times* critic Herbert Mitgang:

> [T]his is the first musical Western with the classical elements: the shy sheriff, the heart-of-gold dance hall hostess at the Last Chance Saloon, the wicked heavies in black hats, and if not horses, at least the sound of hoof beats thundering into a town called Bottleneck, stranger.[46]

As successful as the critics considered the score, the highest praise for the show was almost unanimous for Michael Kidd, not for his direction but for his choreography. When Kidd signed on, he saw numerous opportunities for dance and displayed much inventiveness around the Western theme. One critic concluded "[T]he show is a dance show from beginning to finish."[47] The high point of all of this was a whip dance — the scene in which Gray had demanded to be included but never was[48] — involving three bad guys, their dark clothes, and bull whips, a performance that would "make minor history."[49] Several reviews singled out the three dancers of this routine: Swen Swenson, Marc Breaux, and George Reeder. In 1986, "The Whip Dance" was one of fifteen dance numbers from Broadway musicals chosen for a dance revue, *The American Dance Machine*.[50] Ultimately, Kidd won a Tony Award for Best Choreography for *Destry*.

David Merrick had trade union problems during the show, and despite a respectable run of 472 performances, *Destry Rides Again* did not recoup its investment. Many thought it "never achieved the popularity or respect it deserved,"[51] being overshadowed by another Merrick production of that year, *Gypsy*. Not that Merrick had ignored the show. He worked hard to assemble an effective creative team and, among promotional efforts, hired a cowboy club to ride up and down 45th Street.[52] By his own admission, though, none of his promotions generated the publicity that the Gray-Kidd feud had.

Several months after *Destry* opened, Merrick asked Rome to write the score for a show to be called *Lili*, based on the 1953 movie of the same name.[53] Helen Deutsch had written the screenplay, prompting Merrick to get her to do the book of the musical. Initially, she was to work with French composer Gerald Calvi, but he proved unable to do English lyrics,[54] and Rome got the job. Fifteen years later, Rome and Calvi would collaborate on the American version of the Parisian revue *La Grosse Valise*. After logistical delays, Deutsch and Rome began work by late December of 1959 with Rome writing a few songs within a short time. By early January, the working relationship had soured from Deutsch's perspective. She told Merrick that Rome was "impossible to collaborate with,"[55] and she wanted out. Deutsch's agent from MCA called Rome wanting to explain the situation. Rome, "smelling a big size rat,"[56] insisted on speaking to his collaborator.

Their discussion went poorly as Deutsch claimed to already have been working on the project for a year with Bob Merrill. He had started his musical career as a novelty songwriter, then made his Broadway debut in 1957 with *New Girl in Town* and had achieved real success in 1959 with the Jackie Gleason vehicle *Take Me Along*. Deutsch wanted to resume the project solely with Merrill, leaving Rome "shocked and astonished." He said of their phone discussion:

> I told Miss Deutsch, as far as I knew, we had gotten along very well, I had three or four new songs, all ready to play for her, that I considered that Mr. Merrick had engaged me to do the score, with her approval, that I had been at work on this and I considered I had an oral contract that I would not, under any circumstances, relinquish this show and would do all in my power to prevent the score being done by anyone else but me.[57]

As was his wont, Merrick knew all about the situation, having often played one collaborator against another for reasons only he understood. He was to do that to the extreme a year later during the production of *I Can Get It for You Wholesale*, pitting director Arthur Laurents against Rome and book writer Jerome Weidman. The *Lili* issue remained pending into mid–January. Rome turned the matter over to attorney John Wharton, who let it fade away when Merrick employed Rome to work on *Wholesale*. As it turned out, Bob Merrill did do the score, but Deutsch never completed the book as Merrick found her too inexperienced to do a musical and replaced her with Michael Stewart. *Lili* became *Carnival!* and enjoyed a long run on the strength of its star Anna Maria Alberghetti and innovative staging.[58] Merrill had a huge hit with the show's theme, "Love Makes the World Go 'Round."[59]

*Destry Rides Again* was not the kind of show to become part of the stock repertory or amateur theater productions, and there have been no Broadway revivals. The only significant revival of *Destry* opened in London in 1982 after year-long negotiations.[60] It starred Jill Gascoine and newcomer Alfred Molina, lost a few songs from the original, eliminated the ladies of the Last Chance Saloon, and had actors doubling as musicians.[61] Though it lasted only forty performances and never made it to the West End, producer Ian B. Albery considered it "artistically successful."[62] English critic Rexton S. Bunnett wrote in the liner notes of the London cast recording: "[I]t focused the story on the leads and the conflict between good and evil that brought a close insight to western frontier violent life at the end of the nineteenth century."[63] Of the British revival, Rome said: "It isn't the show I wrote, but it's interesting."[64] Recordings of both the original and London casts are available.

*New York Post* critic Richard Watts, Jr., summed up the show's appeal in his opening night review:

> There are no pretensions about *Destry Rides Again*.... [It] is a Western melodrama with songs and dances, and it doesn't try to be anything else. It isn't a satire or a folk opera. At the same time, it never takes itself too seriously.[65]

And so it was. Rome, Merrick, and their co-creators had put a Western on Broadway.

*Chapter 15*

# I Can Get It for You Wholesale

"I didn't have to do any research for this; it was taken from my own blood, my own life."— Harold Rome

An unlikable protagonist — a cad as star — was not a common dramatic device in a Broadway musical. When Rome and Jerome Weidman decided to build a show around such a character, especially one from the garment district, they knew it was risky. But the two collaborators knew the garment trades and wanted to incorporate their experience into a show. Mostly a novelist, Weidman was new to the Broadway musical but had won a Pulitzer Prize for Drama in 1960 as co-librettist, with George Abbott, of *Fiorello!*[1]

As a basis for the book of their musical, Rome and Weidman went back to their work and experiences in the thirties. They had Weidman's first successful novel, *I Can Get It for You Wholesale*, published in 1937. His first job after school had found him in an office in the garment district. The personalities he encountered in that hectic, competitive arena formed a composite that became his protagonist, Harry Bogen, a heel. Weidman used Bogen for a trilogy of novels: *Ten O'clock Scholar*, *I Can Get It for You Wholesale*, and *What's in It for Me?*[2] The first found little audience or praise, but *Wholesale* caught the eye of readers and critics alike, engendering comments like this from the *Jewish Exponent*: "Jerome Weidman tore savagely into a milieu and its moral tone. His book raced fiercely through the idiom and people of Seventh Avenue. He had a social comment to make and he made it bitterly ... brilliantly."[3] Others felt that Weidman and other Jewish authors of the time were engaged in a "self-hating period."[4]

A group of Hollywood executives wanted two of Weidman's novels withdrawn from publication because of their anti–Semitism. Spokesman Nate Spingold was sent by the group to speak with Weidman and his publisher regarding *I Can Get It for You Wholesale* and *What's in It for Me?*, both novels critical of the garment industry which was predominantly Jewish. In his 1986 autobiography *Praying for Rain*, Weidman recalled the discussion with Spingold and the co-founder of the publishing house Simon & Schuster, Dick Simon. Weidman said of the film executives: "There were people beyond civilized intercourse. It was stupid to try to deal with them except in their own terms.... I said to Mr. Nate Spingold, 'Go fuck yourself,' and I walked out of Dick Simon's office."[5]

Rome's background contributions to the book for *Wholesale* went back to 1937–1938 when he had created a revue for the International Ladies' Garment Workers' Union, *Pins and Needles*, working with an all–ILGWU cast. Although he never worked in the garment industry, Rome immersed himself in its history, drawing ideas for songs and sketches from the stories told to him by the cast, stories telling of working with bosses like Harry Bogen. Ultimately, between Weidman and Rome's experiences, *I Can Get It for You Wholesale* "took a hard-boiled look at the cutthroat world of New York's garment district."[6]

Broadway audiences liked a hero as their star, winning the girl, defending a cause, and wrapping the show up in a joyous finale. Cads in starring roles in musicals have met with mixed success over the years. Most prominent among these were[7]:

| Show | Year | Character / Played by | Description | Performances |
|---|---|---|---|---|
| Pal Joey | 1940 | Joey Evans / Gene Kelly | "hollow, self-serving, two-timing little twerp" | 374 |
| Pal Joey (revival) | 1952 | Joey Evans / Harold Lang | | 572 |
| How to Succeed in Business Without Really Trying | 1961 | J. Pierrepont Finch / Robert Morse | "disarmingly opportunistic" | 1,416 |
| I Can Get It for You Wholesale* | 1962 | Harry Bogen / Elliott Gould | "cold, pushy, and determined" | 300 |
| What Makes Sammy Run? | 1964 | Sammy Glick / Steve Lawrence | newspaperman who steals material, marries boss's daughter | 540 |
| Kelly | 1965 | Hop Kelly / Don Francks | "the mean and petulant Mack the Knife–type title character proved universally unlovable" | 1 |
| How Now, Dow Jones* | 1967 | Charley / Anthony Roberts | "Merrick's second of three attempts at a caustic, 'business' musical" | 220 |
| Promises, Promises* | 1968 | Chuck Baxter / Jerry Orbach | "half slickie, half schlemiel, but always endearing" | 1,281 |

*These shows were produced by David Merrick.

*Pal Joey* was the prototype for these musicals, a show which "demonstrated that a musical could be set in a world completely removed from operetta-land and be about people who were not all peaches and cream."[8] Joey was a cad and his girlfriends were not paradigms of womanhood. A Philadelphia critic pointed out, "Gene Kelly played Pal Joey as though he didn't know he was behaving like a heel."[9] Harry Bogen knows throughout the story that he is one; the plot of *Wholesale* unfolds as the others discover it.

The score of *Pal Joey*, one of Rodgers and Hart's finest, had what *The New Yorker*'s critic called a "delicate brilliance" which "sharply defined and commented on the sleaziness of the hero and his special world."[10] The beauty of the songs contrasted with Joey's world. That same writer added that rather than contrasting with Bogen's own sordid life, Weidman's book and Rome's score complemented it:

> In *I Can Get It for You Wholesale*, the songs and dances and the production itself, in all their brash, melodic vitality and tension, merely match the comical, cutthroat frenzy of the special world *they* depict, and, in a couple of awful numbers called "Family Way" and "Too Soon," echo its putting-off sentimentality.[11]

Another one of the cad-as-star musicals, *How to Succeed in Business Without Really Trying* had garnered Tony awards and the Pulitzer Prize for drama and was just settling into its nearly four-year run near to the theater where *Wholesale* played. But its cad was more "funny and ingratiating,"[12] with Robert Morse playing him with "charm and ingenuity."[13] Morse's unique stagecraft "helped the creators envision a winning protagonist."[14]

Two years later, Steve Lawrence would distinguish himself as a heel in *What Makes Sammy Run?* Lawrence had a nice-guy image and had never starred on Broadway. Historian Glenn Litton said of his performance: "Lawrence was very credible as a ruthless egotist who hacks his way from newspaper copy boy to head of a motion picture studio, then finds himself alone and without the solace of knowing why he fought to get to where he is."[15] Of two of the other shows listed above, Litton said *How Now, Dow Jones* "compromised its honesty" in the end and *Promises, Promises* was not the "toughest of the tough shows."[16] Nonetheless, the latter ran 1,218 performances.

Rome, Weidman, and director Arthur Laurents knew they had an uphill climb with Harry Bogen as the main character. Weidman wanted to adhere to his *Wholesale* story, adding elements from its sequel, *What's in It for Me?*, both books dealing harshly with Bogen and his type. Rome had never been afraid to go against theatrical convention and had done so often in his work. For *Pins and Needles*, he was not afraid to write songs that were of social significance, although it often put off potential Broadway producers and backers. He continued in this vein with *Sing Out the News*. During and after World

War II, many artists were lampooning big government and the military, but no one did it like Rome in *Lunchtime Follies* and *Call Me Mister*.

Because the musical was going against the grain, the casting of its star, Harry Bogen, was an important one. Producer David Merrick's first choice had been rising film star Laurence Harvey, just off rave reviews in *Room at the Top*. Born Zvi Mosheh Skikne in Lithuania, he was a trained actor with a singing voice who would go on to play King Arthur in the London production of *Camelot*. Theater historian Ethan Mordden explained that the role appealed greatly to Harvey: "[H]e really wanted to play Weidman's Harry Bogen, through some deeply personal identification with the character, or perhaps just a desire to break out of the zombie roles that movie people were always offering him. Harvey was even willing to commit for nine months, a sacrifice for a movie actor who had just got hot."[17] Ultimately, Merrick overplayed his hand in contract negotiations, and Harvey turned the project down, leaving the show with a cast lacking a big name draw. Weidman, in particular, regretted the loss, as he thought Harvey would have generated real interest in *Wholesale*.[18] Harvey's next film, *Summer and Smoke*, opened when *Wholesale* opened in Boston. In it, Harvey played a reprobate young doctor, further establishing "his star persona of being a first-class heel."[19]

This episode was only one of many distasteful ones with Merrick. Rome and Weidman had problems with their producer almost from the start of *Wholesale*. Although he had brought the two of them together for a different project, Rome and Weidman had opted to develop one of their own — *Wholesale*. Their common interest and knowledge of the garment district had been a common source of inspiration. Reluctantly, Merrick agreed to do their show because of his faith in Rome, especially what he had done with *Fanny*. As was his wont, however, Merrick made it difficult for them, particularly during the period before contracts were signed. Rome was offended by Merrick, whom he considered a friend — although Merrick had few — and an associate with whom he could work.

Fortunately, Weidman was a tough New Yorker and felt they could wait Merrick out and get their show done. He blamed Merrick's behavior on the fact that during his early years as a producer, he had had to grovel to everyone: stars, composers, and other producers. Weidman felt that with the success of Merrick's *Carnival!* in early 1961, there had been a change in the producer:

> I think with *Carnival!* a crucial change took place.... [I]t took place under water, like an iceberg.... [H]e decided that he could now get up off his knees and walk like the man or producer the public had all this time thought he was.
> 
> ...I don't think it is personal... We happened to be crossing the street when he decided to step on the gas; so we got hit.[20]

Weidman felt that the script and songs would win the day and reassured Rome: "I have always found the best way to make them really wince is, when your turn at bat comes, to repay it with kindness. Oy; do they then kvetch their kishkes!"[21] Besides Weidman's patience, they had an ace up their sleeve: producer Billy Rose would have taken over the show without hesitation.[22] Ultimately, they didn't need him.

The search for Bogen went on, and despite his initial disappointment with losing Harvey, Weidman wrote to Rome: "I'd like a kid in this show to whom the show is his whole life ... not a star who wants to use it as a stepping stone in his career."[23] At the time, Merrick had a production on a successful run, *Irma La Douce*. In its chorus line was 23-year-old Elliott Gould. He had gotten into the entertainment profession at age eight and had been on Broadway in brief appearances in *Rumple, Say, Darling*, and *Hit the Beach*.[24] Mostly unknown, he fit the role as he could sing, dance, act, was tall and Jewish with "a confident bearing."[25] He played conniving and cocky well. He was Weidman's "kid." Gould would go on to his most famous role in Robert Altman's 1970 war satire *MASH* as a conniving and cocky Trapper John McIntyre.

Most of the featured players in *Wholesale* were Broadway veterans including Sheree North, Bambi Lynn, Marilyn Cooper, Jack Kruschen, Ken LeRoy, and Harold Lang, who had played the title character in the successful 1950 revival of *Pal Joey*. Returning to the stage after thirty years was Lillian Roth, a former child model and movie actress. She had performed on Broadway at age fourteen in *Artists and Models*, three editions of *Earl Carroll Vanities*, starred at the Palace Theatre, and had been one of the country's premier singers in the thirties, the period of *Wholesale*. Her alcohol-interrupted career was the subject of her 1954 autobiography *I'll Cry Tomorrow*, which sold seven million copies worldwide and renewed the public's interest in her. The book was turned into a hit movie starring Susan Hayward.[26]

The find of the cast was a young woman from Brooklyn who was appearing in a small night club at the time and had been a guest on *PM East/PM West*, a radio talk and variety show. Rome recalled her audition in an interview with Avery Corman of the *New York Times*:

> One afternoon we were holding auditions and this girl came in and she had a bundle of music and she came to the piano and she dropped the music. Then she finally got arranged and started to sing. And we sat up. We had her come back three times because it was such a pleasure to listen to her. And on the third time ... we said to her on the stage that she had the job, and she said, "Goody, goody. Now I can afford a telephone."[27]

The young talent was Barbra Streisand, and *Wholesale* launched her Broadway career. A few of the principal creators of the show were a bit harsh on her, her mannerisms, and lack of professionalism and punctuality.[28] Especially unkind was producer Merrick, who thought her too unattractive for the Broadway stage. In his unauthorized biography *David Merrick: The Abominable Showman*, author Howard Kissel related a scene when Merrick wanted to fire her:

> Rome, who, after all, had now been working for Merrick for some time, instantly knew how to handle the matter.
> "You can get her for scale," he said.
> "You're the most anti–Semitic guy I know," Merrick shouted at him.
> "You've hired every ugly Jew in town for this show, and now you want me to hire this meeskite."[29]

In the end, Streisand's talent won out, pinpointed by director Laurents: "When she sang, she was simple; when she sang, she was vulnerable; when she sang, she was moving, funny, mesmerizing, anything she wanted to be."[30] Fortunately for Streisand, the man writing the songs, Rome, "loved Barbra's voice which was a perfect match for the plaintive Jewish wail in his tunes."[31]

Rome at piano rehearsing with Lillian Roth (Mrs. Bogen) for *I Can Get It for You Wholesale* in 1962 (courtesy of the Museum of the City of New York).

Her only song, "Miss Marmelstein," had been written but dropped before the role was cast. Once she was signed, the song was reinstated and her role was enlarged. Weidman explained the logic behind this, other than the obvious desire to give a good voice more singing time: "When you have a talent that large on stage, you just can't let her wander around. You have to give her something to do or she'll kill you. She'll steal scenes, make up business, throw people off cues."[32] Besides "Miss Marmelstein," she was included in a duet, "He's Not a Well Man," and the ensemble songs "Ballad of the Garment Trade" and "What Are They Doing to

Us Now?" Rome said simply: "Somebody is that good, you try to use them as much as possible."[33]

During 1962, the 25th anniversary of the opening of *Pins and Needles* was celebrated with a revival of the cast album. Goddard Lieberson, president of Columbia Records and the unrivaled master of the cast recording, did not want Streisand to be part of it. He and his Columbia staff thought her "too way-out, too kooky, too obscurely offbeat."[34] Already enamored of her talent, Rome heard her perform some songs from the thirties, the period of *Pins and Needles*. It was at her own birthday party, and he said of her performance of these songs: "She's nineteen years old for heaven's sake! She's not a history student. She doesn't know a thing about the period, and yet she gets into the songs as if she'd been born to them."[35] It solidified his faith in her and, despite several other singers suggested by Columbia, he held out and got the job for Streisand. She did not disappoint and was even punctual and disciplined at the recording studio. She did a performance of "Nobody Makes a Pass at Me" better than Millie Weitz, the original singer, and as good a job as Beatrice Lillie had done in her cabaret act with "Not Cricket to Picket."[36]

Shortly after, Rome and Streisand had a falling out. He lamented to an interviewer: "I got her her first job, her first two albums, she's never done a song of mine since."[37] Soon after *Wholesale* closed, he attempted to call Streisand regarding his songs and was put off by a secretary. His final words on the matter: "I hung up. I'm too old, too talented and too long in the business to take that."[38] The composer's son Joshua said his father was particularly annoyed with her when she related to the host of a late night show the story of how she got her start on Broadway. She gave Rome absolutely no credit.[39]

One of the central problems for the creators of *Wholesale* was how evil to portray Harry Bogen, and secondarily, how Jewish. In Weidman's novel, Bogen was evil to the end and quite Jewish, but this was musical comedy and plot and character excesses had their limits. Rome had read Weidman's novel when it was published and had the story etched in his mind. Rome's viewpoint was simple, as he told David Dubinsky. The aging labor leader, who had made *Pins and Needles* possible, was hoping that *Wholesale* would be similar to that show. Rome set him straight: "But David, the garment trade isn't what the show's about. Sure, it's the Seventh Av. locale and has its flavor, but what it's about is a Jewish boy from the Bronx who goes wrong."[40]

Merrick had complained to Rome and Weidman that the show was "too Jewish" during their post-performance conferences in Boston. Rome told interviewer Lehman Engel: "He wanted to take out the 'Bar Mitzvah Song' and 'The Family Way' and everything and I just got up and walked out of the room and said, 'Why don't you close the show?'"[41]

Weidman's feelings toward his protagonist were harsh, based on his observations while working in the garment district, specifically a case of bankruptcy he had witnessed:

> The young man had gone to Seventh Avenue as a shipping clerk, just as I had gone to Seventh Avenue as an accountant's assistant, when he graduated from high school. In the frenetic, exciting, get-rich-quick, hit-or-flop atmosphere of the dress business of that period, he had seen his chances and had grasped them.[42]

Weidman's description of his Harry Bogen prototype ended on a tragic note, recalling the young man's "stunned, frightened face"[43] as his deeds became known to those involved in his bankruptcy. It was this evolution of Bogen's character that became problematic. Does the story stay true to the novel with a relentless Harry Bogen or does it portray Bogen as Weidman's remembered young man who eventually takes a fall?

At first, Weidman and Rome chose the former with Bogen's opening song, "The Way Things Are," projecting an eat-or-be-eaten philosophy. Boston critic Elliot Norton called Bogen "a heel without a soul or a saving grace, a monster who makes Pal Joey seem a mouse of virtue." Norton felt *Wholesale* was "the hardest-bitten musical the stage has yet produced" and asked the question: "But who would have believed that Broadway would have had the courage to toss him up on the musical stage?"[44] *New York Herald-Tribune* critic Walter Kerr, who wrote a rave review and followed it with a rave commentary a week later, called it "a restless, pushy, meticulously honest story"[45] that moved at a "cynical gallop."[46]

Attempts were made to soften Bogen's image with an early song "Momma, Momma, Momma," but this is followed by another song of greed, "The Sound of Money." Ethan Mordden concluded that "the show itself finds him so horrifying that it won't let him be its protagonist."[47] The romantic ballad of the show, "Have I Told You Lately?," rather than being sung by the lead, was captured well by a supporting character and his wife, played by Ken LeRoy and Bambi Lynn. If Bogen had sung it to his girlfriend, there would have been no credibility. In *Pal Joey*, the show's romantic hit "I Could Write a Book" is sung by Joey with a sarcastic subtext. In a like manner, Bogen sings a duet with his girlfriend, Marilyn Cooper, called "When Gemini Meets Capricorn," a seemingly delightful duet of a chance encounter. In reality, Bogen had it set up in order to borrow money from her.

The heel progresses through the show using business associates and personal friends alike, climbing over anybody in his way. Then Weidman softened his character with an ending not consistent with the novel. The same was done with a 1951 movie version of the same name starring Susan Hayward as Harriet Boyd, an ambitious model and fashion designer, with a screenplay that "changed practically everything except the title."[48] A 1992 play of *Wholesale* by the American Jewish Theater went back to the novel for its ending:

> [The AJT's] critically acclaimed production ... skipped the trumped-up happy version of the 1962 version which turned a garment center hustler who ruins his partner into a nice guy. This time, the creators, Jerome Weidman and Harold Rome, allowed the theater to use the original book and the character stayed a louse all the way through.[49]

AJT director Stanley Brechner admitted using junk bond king and Wall Street swindler Michael Milken, convicted in 1990, as a model for his Bogen.[50]

In Rome and Weidman's original, Bogen goes bankrupt — as did the young man from Weidman's past — a character "neither ruthless nor cunning enough to attain his goals."[51] Critic Elinor Hughes felt the audience and herself "a bit puzzled by the downbeat conclusion."[52] Her fellow Bostonian Elliott Norton, who had praised the hard edge of *Wholesale* and Bogen, was disappointed in this turn of the story: "[I]t lapses lamely at the end into sentimentality.... It must be played for all the toughness that is in it. To soften it is to sink."[53]

Perhaps most responsible for this evolution of the plot was Arthur Laurents, who had been a theater and screenwriter before becoming a director. He wrote a letter to Rome and Weidman six months prior to opening, detailing book and song suggestions, prefacing all of these with the following:

> The more work I do on the script, the more enthusiastic I become. And the fewer problems I see!...
> To restate, I think the show should be about a man who decides he has to be a son of a bitch to get to the top — and then finds he cannot be a big enough son of a bitch.[54]

Not Bogen but his mother puts all the pieces together in a song done brilliantly by Lillian Roth, "Eat a Little Something." Her feelings towards her ruined son go from attending to his basic needs to realizing what a flawed person she has raised; *Newsweek* called the song "a small, dramatic gem of self-revelation."[55] Laurents' advice on the song was: "She should run down like an old phonograph in the song — because she realizes Harry is her son and his morality is partly her doing."[56] Put emphatically by historian Mordden:

> She is trying to understand how she could have raised this monster; he doesn't care to understand, because understanding means considering how it feels to be one of his victims. As she feeds him, she begins to loathe him. There had never been anything this brutally honest in a musical comedy.[57]

Rome's view of "Eat a Little Something" he couched in reference to his own children: "There comes a point when you cannot dictate to your children any more and when you have to accept what they do and what they choose with love for them."[58] Momma Bogen had run short of love.

This song is Rome at his best, "writing songs in his own New York vernacular."[59] Beginning with a common phrase spoken by a Jewish mother — "Eat a little something"— the composer captures a multiplicity of emotions as the song progresses, having her repeat the phrase several times, in a tone "measured" and "quietly intense."[60] Rome is not only aware of Bogen's flaws but is sympathetic to his mother as well. Rome writes not a showstopper, but a quiet, contemplative song that sums up what has been going on. Rome told an interviewer: "The boy in *Wholesale* is a second generation Jew, and so am I. His mother and mine are in many ways alike. I didn't have to do any research for this; it was taken from my own blood, my own life."[61]

Another *Wholesale* song that only Rome could have written was "What Are They Doing to Us Now?," echoing the common man theme prevalent in *Pins and Needles*. The song begins in a light manner but gets progressively more serious, a protest song of sorts. Rome held strong feelings about the context of this song, thoughts which did not manifest themselves to him until after it was completed. The idea for the song came to him after a friend related a story:

> He was walking down a street on a miserable, slushy day. In front of him was a bum whose clothes were ragged and shoes tattered. The bum went to cross the street and suddenly sank almost up to his waist in slush. He turned around and said to Eddie: "What the hell are they doing to us now?"
>
> Actually, that song started out as a gag, but when I heard it sung, I suddenly found out it had a meaning far beyond what I had originally intended. It was the history of the Jews, their sense of oppression. I realized that here was the old cry of the Hebrew race, and I think maybe the audience realizes it, too.[62]

Rome's songs in *Wholesale* ran the gamut —"gay songs, love songs, marching songs, patter song and even a 'song of social significance'" — but he stayed on point with the characters of Seventh Avenue with a score of "extreme range and versatility,"[63] "perfectly integrated into the plot background."[64] Rome did not apologize for lyrics with ethnic, religious, and trade references. "Momma, Momma, Momma," "A Gift Today," "The Sound of Money," and "The Family Way" were filled with them.

Whether or not they bothered audiences is not clear, but whom they really bothered was director Laurents. To his "Dear Authors" in September of 1961, Laurents discussed a lyric and the characters involved in a scene: "It borders on what might seem as anti–Semitism to some. Incidentally, are there only Jews in the dress business? Couldn't one or two of the minor characters be Italian? or Spanish?"[65]

In a follow-up letter to Rome in October, with a variation on the same theme, Laurents pleaded with his composer:

> The whole script and score are too Yiddish. I have edited almost all of it from the script and Jerry agrees that the rest should go.... I would cut every single Yiddish expression from the songs with the exception of such words as have passed over into English as "schlemiel," "schlepper" and "cockamamie" (which isn't Yiddish anyway). The rest — O-U-T.[66]

In the same letter, Laurents made detailed suggestions for changes in the songs and book, emphatically telling his composer: "[T]his is not about immigrants nor is it about Second Avenue. It is about New Yorkers working on Seventh Avenue."[67] When Rome explained it to Dubinsky, he should have let Laurents in on it.

That background, Seventh Avenue and its Jewish inhabitants, was a frequent source of contention among Weidman, Rome, and Laurents. Weidman believed in his portrayal of the Seventh Avenue-garment district milieu and when criticized years later, along with Budd Schulberg, author of *What Makes Sammy Run?*, as being anti–Semitic in his novels, reacted strongly: "I have lived all my life with Jewish people, and I have to paint them, warts and all.... I admit that some of the people I write are not of the most estimable character. I am never apologetic about this."[68] He maintained the same unapologetic attitude with Laurents and Merrick. Rome, too, was in his element, both ethnically and musically. It seemed as if Weidman and Rome were more comfortable in their Jewish skin than the other two.

Rome and Weidman could take only so much ethnicity out of their musical. Whatever adjustments were made based on Laurents' comments, *I Can Get It for You Wholesale* remained a show with a heavily Jewish accent. One critic from Philadelphia, where it opened on February 12, 1962, found it too much so. Ironically, he cast blame on all three of the creators, Laurents included:

> Running through the show, and for this director Arthur Laurents and composer Rome must share the fault with Weidman, is what seems to me to be a heavy emphasis on the Jewish nature of the characters. At times it is heavy enough to be pure burlesque, although that is certainly not the intention.[69]

A later review in *Time* magazine was equally critical: "*Wholesale* relies heavily on Jewish folk and speech ways. But as comedy, Jewish dialect is in awkward transition, no longer funny and not yet English."[70]

Rome was capable of infusing an ethnic feeling into his songs yet keeping them much his own, true to the plot, and musically and lyrically artistic. In *Fanny*, he captured the flavor of Marseilles with tunes like "Oysters, Cockles, and Mussels" and "Why Be Afraid to Dance?" and in *Destry Rides Again* he gave audiences a feeling for the Wild West with "Are You Ready, Gyp Watson?" and "Once Knew a Fella." For *Wholesale*, he tapped numerous Jewish musical sources, successfully so, according to a different Philadelphia reviewer: "Harold Rome has dipped into Jewish musical sources for a score — a froelich [happy, jaunty piece], a chant of sorrow, even a Bar-Mitzvah ceremony; but he has successfully transplanted these into the musical comedy idiom."[71] Ethan Mordden added to this line of thought, saying of Rome's score:

> I believe Rome was using the songs *collectively* to summon up how these people felt as a whole. Each number adds more information — about the times, the garment-center workplace, the social code, the meaning of marriage, the use of English as a translation from a babble of diaspora.[72]

To write words and music of Broadway caliber and express an era or historical setting is a principal goal of theater composers. Rome had done this especially well in *Pins and Needles*, *Fanny*, and *Destry Rides Again*. Theater historian and frequent Rome collaborator Lehman Engel was music director and vocal arranger for *Wholesale*. In his thoughtful book *The American Musical Theater: A Consideration*, Engel discussed this aspect of composers, singling out, among others, Lerner and Loewe for *Brigadoon* and Frank Loesser for *Where's Charley?* In these works, Engel stressed that these composers wrote with their own individual styles, all the while enhancing the story and period settings of their shows. Including Rome in this group, Engel said:

> In *I Can Get It for You Wholesale*, Harold Rome infused many of the songs with a Jewish inflection.... It is, however, essential to understand than when Loesser suggests a Victorian flavor, or Rodgers an Oriental one, or Loewe a Scottish one, or Rome an American Jewishness, he has not altered that basic style which is inescapably his own.[73]

*Newsweek*'s critic called the music "a Harold Rome score that is a major adjunct of both character and plot,"[74] much like Walter Kerr's comment that Rome's score was "ready not so much to relieve the libretto as to mesh with it tactically so that both can advance at once."[75]

Show songs that mesh with the libretto do not often make hit songs, and various songwriters had mixed success with this. Rome felt strongly about his songs and their fit into a show. He told *Los Angeles Times* critic John Mahoney in an interview ten years after *Wholesale*:

> Hits come out of shows, but all of my songs are written to solve a specific problem in advancing the musical, to communicate ideas, character and story. What I want people to say as they exit the theater is "What a good show!" If they say anything else, we're in trouble.... One of the worst musicals I ever saw was Irving Berlin's *Louisiana Purchase*. There were maybe ten hit songs, just strung together, stopping the show.[76]

In his book *Lyrics*, written during his years of collaboration with Richard Rodgers, lyricist Oscar Hammerstein II discusses the importance of a well-integrated song. He focuses in his preface on the songs from *Oklahoma!* and discusses audience reactions, character development, and the overall effect of a given song within a musical. In a paragraph of summation, he restates Rome's feelings: "There are few things in life of which I am certain, but I am sure of this one thing, that the song is the servant of the play, that it is wrong to write first what you think is an attractive song and then try to wedge it into a story."[77]

In what seems almost blasphemous, Rome was critical of earlier Broadway shows. During an ASCAP symposium in the late sixties, he was quick to say that with the book musical, development of story and songs together was important.[78] To emphasize his points, he then offered an opinion that went beyond the original question:

> When they talk about the good old days and the Gershwin shows and the Cole Porter shows which had hits in them, they were terrible shows.... [T]he songs were good ... but the evening was, to say the least, rather dull. One of the reasons they can't be revived was the books were so bad, and actually, outside of the hit songs which we remember with pleasure, they were not well-constructed musical comedies and weren't intended to be that. That's the way they wrote them.[79]

Examples of notable shows with songs both integral to a show and appealing to the public were Frank Loesser's *Guys and Dolls* with at least six American Popular Song standards and Frederick Loewe and Alan Jay Lerner's *My Fair Lady* with an equal number. Numerous shows can claim similar numbers. Conversely, Loesser's later show *How to Succeed in Business Without Really Trying* had only one evergreen, "I Believe in You." Nonetheless, the songs of the Pulitzer Prize–winning musical fit "perfectly with the spirit and style of the book's satire."[80]

Rome had a few show songs which became *Your Hit Parade* numbers including the title songs for *Fanny* and *Wish You Were Here*, both of which were recorded by Eddie Fisher, but none of Rome's shows was ever loaded with hits. Most of Rome's score for *Wholesale* fell short of hit status and found little interest outside of the show, although certain songs were especially well-received by audiences. The touching, revealing "Eat a Little Something" sung by Lillian Roth left the audience quiet, nearly stunned on some nights.

Barbra Streisand's solo was the quirky "Miss Marmelstein," which she sang from an office chair, sliding around the stage. Despite being a Broadway novice, she had insisted upon this device during tryouts, giving director Arthur Laurents headaches over it. Just before the show opened in Philadelphia, he told her, "Do it in your goddamned chair!"[81] She did and brought down the house. She would later say, "I couldn't understand why they were mad at me for being right."[82] She would continue annoying cast and conductor during the run of *Wholesale* as she often experimented with the song and the role out of boredom, dropping gestures, adding business, etc. Rome remembered that "she would throw the conductor by altering tempi and phrasing."[83]

Only one song of the sixteen in the New York run received a recording outside of the cast album, "Have I Told You Lately?," a song which critic and ardent Rome fan Bruce F. Winston found especially charming as a couple's duet:

> A specialty among his songwriting abilities was the married couple's love song. Rome first essayed this ballad form in the musical *Fanny* (1954), for which he composed "To My Wife," a husband's tribute to his new, young bride. He repeated this song style in *I Can Get It for You Wholesale* (1962), where Rome had the middle-aged Bushkins sing "Have I Told You Lately?," about their still happy union after years of wedded life.... Finally, for his last musical, *Gone with the Wind* (London, 1972), Rome wrote "Strange and Wonderful," which finds Rhett Butler and Scarlett O'Hara blissful in their marriage. Rome patterned all of these songs after his own contented union to his charming wife, Florence, an accomplished authoress in her own right, which lasted 54 years. [84]

Ultimately, the "somber and predominantly cynical musical"[85] with the cad protagonist did just fair. After initially negative reviews for its two-week Philadelphia run, the show was shortened, re-written in several scenes, and songs were added and subtracted, all par for the course for pre–Broadway trials. Involved with all this, however, was much disagreement between Rome and Weidman on one side and Laurents on the other. The director had become increasingly critical of the book and songs and threatened to quit. The three creators and Merrick ironed it out with some eleventh hour dramatics. To believe Laurents' version in his 2000 autobiography *Original Story By*, he saved the show and everyone involved with it.[86]

Despite ongoing problems with their director and producer, Rome and Weidman enjoyed working on the show. There was a core of seasoned veterans who adapted well to the changes. Rome especially enjoyed Lillian Roth. Moreover, the remainder of the cast — with the exception of Streisand — was young and eager, especially Elliott Gould. Opening nights on Broadway usually include numerous telegrams of good wishes from friends and colleagues not involved in the show. In the case of *Wholesale*, Rome and Weidman sent their own cast a telegram, paraphrasing Rome's lyrics from "Have I Told You Lately":

> HAVE WE MENTIONED LATELY
> HOW YOU DELIGHT US,
>   HOW EACH PERFORMANCE ALWAYS BRINGS A TINGLE OR TWO?

WHEN WE COUNT UP ALL THE CAST WE COULD HAVE BEEN STUCK WITH,
WE SURE WERE IN LUCK WITH
   THE ONES WE DREW.
HAVE WE TOLD YOU LATELY
HOW MUCH YOUR AUTHORS LOVE YOU?[87]

The show opened in New York on March 22, 1962, to mixed reviews, commented on by Richard J. Watts:

> Critical differences of opinion are now notorious, but I can recall few occasions when the abyss between the applause and the hisses was as wide as over *I Can Get It for You Wholesale*. Where, for example, Walter Kerr seems to have found it virtually the high point in musical comedy since *Gypsy*, I snarled at nearly everything about it save Sheree North's figure.[88]

*Wholesale* ran for most of that year, closing December 8 after 300 performances. Total production costs by then had reached a modest $275,000 but only half of that was recouped. Audiences had not quite come to terms with the cad protagonist, but in 1963 real life Miss Marmelstein did, marrying Harry Bogen.

*Chapter 16*

# *Harold Rome's Gallery* and Artistic Endeavors

"...but when you paint, no one tells you what to do." — Harold Rome

In the mid-thirties, Rome began studying painting at the Art Students' League and the John Reed Club School of Art, both in New York. He gave it up within a few years after the success of *Pins and Needles*, deciding to devote his artistic skills to songwriting.[1] He only returned to art work in 1948 when a friend gave him a painting box and six canvases; Rome was hooked.[2] Over the years, he painted in small studios in lower Manhattan, first on Bleecker Street in Greenwich Village, then in the Bowery. He would travel downtown to paint in the afternoons, usually after a morning of composing. His art education continued at the Modern Museum Art School, and then he studied with Victor DePauw, modern art pioneer, caricaturist, and artist for *The New Yorker* and *Vanity Fair*.[3]

After completing a canvas, Rome would sometimes write a song to accompany it, though occasionally the order would be reversed. For one of his oils, he explained the process: "'Which Way Is Home?' hung above my piano for three weeks, then I woke up one morning and wrote it."[4] He was a believer in sleep and the subconscious. Between musicals in the mid-sixties, he put together a collection of his "mixed media"— painting and song — calling it *Stop, Look and Listen!*[5] He explained:

> Writing a song without a reason for it is almost impossible for me. Since I lead a double life as a composer in the morning and a painter in the afternoon, it occurred to me in the middle of a restless night that it could be fun to combine both fields — set myself a double problem — expressing a mood, an emotion, a fancy by painting, music and lyrics. Which came first? As always, the idea.[6]

### 16. Harold Rome's Gallery *and Artistic Endeavors*

Well-known composers had been inspired by art prior to this, most famously Gunther Schuller ("Seven Studies after Paul Klee") and Modest Moussorgsky ("Pictures at An Exhibition," based on paintings by Victor Hartmann).[7] But these were compositions about someone else's art, and Rome's concept was to do both, being encouraged by "the fact that nobody in the whole world has ever done this before."[8]

Rome in his Lower Manhattan studio with two paintings from his playing cards series in the background, circa 1974. He had given up cigarettes and taken up pipe smoking (courtesy of Joshua Rome).

His project came to fruition at the Marble Arch Gallery at 135 East 79th Street on Manhattan's Upper East Side in the fall of 1964. Twelve canvases, each accompanied by a song, were presented as a group, *Harold Rome's Gallery*. These were part of a total exhibit of forty paintings at the Marble Arch Gallery under the simple title *Harold Rome*. For the *Harold Rome's Gallery* section,

Rome (right) with Richard Rodgers at New York's Marble Arch Gallery for the 1964 opening of *Harold Rome's Gallery* (courtesy Gilmore Music Library, Yale University).

### 16. Harold Rome's Gallery *and Artistic Endeavors*

viewers were to listen to a song as they viewed a painting. The songs were sung variously by Betty Garrett, Jack Haskell, Rose Marie Jun, and the painter himself and were recorded by Columbia Records (KL 6091 and KS 6691).[9] In the introduction to the album, Richard Rodgers wrote in a most complimentary way of Rome:

> My friend Harold Rome happens to be a theater composer and a painter. Whether he painted an accompaniment to his songs or written songs to accompany his paintings is not important. What is important is that one art impinges on the other, explains it, and gives it depth. In this particular case each art lends the other beauty and wit. How lucky we are to be able to see and hear his talent at the same time.[10]

Included in the *Gallery* were[11]:

| Song / Painting | Song or picture described as | H x W in inches | Year | Singer |
| --- | --- | --- | --- | --- |
| Art in the Night (Self-portrait) | An artist dreams that he's forgotten who he is, then runs through the names of 110 other painters | 33 × 25 | 1964 | Harold Rome |
| The Audience* | Red canvas with disembodied faces in ghoulish white and nightmare blue; intriguing words and music | 50 × 48 | 1964 | Garrett, Haskell, Jun, and Rome |
| My Long Ago* | Lyrics that look back to a fondly remembered love; a fat, blank-faced, non-entity sitting primly on a hassock | 48 × 36 | 1964 | Jack Haskell |
| Shake Hands, Dear Mrs. Cow* | Chummy history of a cow, her services to mankind, and her tragic reward; cow with a dubious, aggressive look | 50 × 32 | 1960 | Betty Garrett |
| Which Way Is Home?* | A dozen creatures in frenetic motion searching for a home long since lost | 32 × 50 | 1964 | Jack Haskell |
| King of the Bushongo* | Investigation of the animal kingdom | 50 × 32 | 1960 | Harold Rome |
| Half-Forgotten Teddy Bear* | Memories of a teddy bear | 40 × 50 | 1964 | Rose Marie Jun |
| Stop Waltzing Around in My Mind* | A maddening waltz | 40 × 50 | 1963 | Haskell, Jun |
| Shy | Modernistic painting of a person tied in knots | 50 × 33 | 1960 | Rose Marie Jun |
| The Wolf That Swallowed Red Riding Hood* | Song explaining how to avoid the wolf that swallowed Red Riding Hood; gay, cuddlesome, yellow wolf | 32 × 50 | 1964 | Betty Garrett |

| Song / Painting | Song or picture described as | H x W in inches | Year | Singer |
|---|---|---|---|---|
| Tango Diabolo* | Follow-up to (South America, Take It Away) sung by Betty Garrett | 50 × 34 | 1960 | Betty Garrett |
| The Critics* | Fetus-like creatures dancing ring-around-the-rosy on a red floor; music is part tango, part calypso and satirizes the flowery clichés used in criticism, the kind that would condemn a show to fail | 25 × 33 | 1962 | Garrett, Haskell, Jun, Rome |

*Denotes similar painting with the same title stored at the Gilmore Music Library at Yale University.

Looking at this list of paintings, it is difficult to say if Rome had any favorite themes in his work. When asked that question years later by oral historian Martin Bookspan, Rome merely said, "It's hard to say; a painting is a painting."[12]

During these months of preparation for his art show, Rome was busy on the score for *Howe and Hummel.* Jerome Weidman was writing the book, a dark story based on the title characters William F. Howe and Abraham Hummel, high-profile criminal defense attorneys in New York at the end of the 19th century.[13] The producer was Diane Krasny, and Joe Layton was to direct and choreograph. Most of the work was done in 1964 but carried over well into 1965. In August of that year, Rome wrote to Lehman Engel about the progress of the show: "Did I tell you that your friend the demon producer Diana Krasny is dropping *Howe and Hummel.* She claims Jerry's book isn't good enough — but the plain truth is she's fucked everything up."[14]

Krasny had experience in the theater but not to the level of skill to which Rome had become accustomed. Why she actually lost interest was unclear, but the whole thing left Rome bitter towards her: "We have 6 mos. after she drops it to find another producer. We'll be looking around soon. Jesus Christ — 2 years work — I hope it doesn't go down the drain!"[15]

*Howe and Hummel* never made it to a stage, the fate of all the shows listed in the "Unproduced Shows Chronology" in the Appendix.

Writers for the theater, especially musicals, were frequently starting projects that met with dead ends. An idea would lead to a discussion which might lead to the start of a book and a few songs. Problems would arise, usually in the book, and of course, financing was not always forthcoming. A producer might take on the project and not like the book and/or its writer and switch plans in midstream. The creators might be attracted to another project and give up on the current one. The ideal star for a role might not be available or interested. Such were the vagaries of the Broadway musical process. It was a miracle a show ever made it to an opening.

But Rome always had his art, which was mostly a one-man show. His three-week exhibition *Harold Rome* opened November 10, 1964, and the artist admitted that during the previews, "I never felt more naked in my life."[16] One theater critic wrote, "At first glance, some of Rome's paintings resemble the Rorschach ink blot tests — random forms that suggest images."[17] But reviews were mostly complimentary as Rome's art was described by journalists as "jazzy, semi-abstract paintings *a la* Dubuffet,"[18] "richly painted, a stimulus to mind and eye,"[19] and work that has "[s]harp meaning — and an almost pictorial explicitness."[20] Marble Arch Gallery owner Sascha Robbins had encouraged Rome from the beginning and felt he had discovered him. He said of the paintings:

> His figures are amorphous creatures who seem to be spun from huge vats in brilliant clouds of color. At the moment of eruption, Rome skillfully fragmentizes his images and clots them in arrested motion. His paintings synthesize his intellectual ideas with his empathy for the world's peoples. The paintings are satiric and sensitive ... a wonderful assortment of human foibles.[21]

Rome's canvases on average were priced at $900 for the exhibit. How well they sold I do not know, but this was no doubt of little importance to him as he was by then wealthy on the strength of successful shows and ASCAP royalties. In 2002, one of Rome's paintings from this exhibit, "The Audience," was donated to the Museum of the City of New York by Felix H. Kent. The price for insurance and donation valuation, certified by an art expert, was $18,500.[22]

Rome felt he had talent beyond a casual amateur, had worked hard to be a painter, and wanted to be recognized as one. He confessed to Beverly Gary, a *New York Post* writer:

> This is a whole personal, private life, and one of the biggest kicks I've gotten from it is when a painter says I'm a painter. [Broadway caricaturist] Al Hirschfeld saw my work and said, "Hey, you're a painter." When someone says he likes my music, I enjoy hearing that, but it isn't the same kind of kick as the other.[23]

He apparently had a need to paint, as many artists do. It was a great source of achievement, stimulation, and relaxation to him, leading him to say: "And that's what I enjoy doing. I have to write, and I have to paint. It's like breathing. And no question of weighing what you want to do. That's the way it's worked out ... one reenforces the other."[24] Again to Gary: "[Painting is] the thing which has kept me sane. In this business, when you're not working on a show you've got to keep busy, so I study 12-tone music, write themes and sonatas, and paint. And I paint what I see in my mind."[25]

While painting was another creative outlet for him, it served a somewhat different purpose: It allowed him to work on his own. Hirschfeld recognized that it was often difficult for Rome to collaborate on a Broadway musical: "Hecky made very few compromises. When he felt a [song] was finished, that was it. He would be stubborn about making changes to suit anybody else."[26] Rome said of the difference between the two arts: "Working in the theater is a mass business, a cooperative effort. Half the time you don't know where you are, there are so many people involved, but when you paint, no one tells you what to do."[27]

The Marble Arch Gallery exhibition was his most important, although he had other well-publicized shows at the Fidelity-Philadelphia Trust Company in June of 1966, the Bodley Galleries in Manhattan in April of 1970 and the Museum of African Art of the Frederick Douglas Institute in Washington, D.C.[28] This 1978 exhibition not only included pieces from his African art collection but also oil paintings of each of the fifty-two playing cards. Rome, an inveterate card player, worked on the series over three years.[29] He based it on his collection of African art, as each face card incorporated an African tribal mask. Drawings of clubs, spades, hearts, and diamonds also included masks as well as other African art motifs.[30] The exhibition at the Museum of African Art was launched by a gala benefit dinner that included *Harold Rome Sings Harold Rome*.[31] Rome at his varied best: composer, lyricist, entertainer, artist, and art collector.

Rome often encouraged others to paint, including the dean of American songwriters, Irving Berlin. In a profile of Berlin on the 100th anniversary of his birth, Rome took credit for getting Berlin to start painting:

> "I used to go to Central Park in the old days with my watercolors," Mr. Rome said. "One day, as I was coming out of the park on my bike I ran into Irving Berlin. He said, 'What are you doing?' I showed him and he said, 'Gee whiz, that doesn't look too hard.' I said it is wonderful, a wonderful way to spend your time. He said he'd like to try it. He did and became a painter."[32]

Some people get all the talent.

*Chapter 17*

# The 1965 Shows and African Art

"Harold Rome was the perfect composer for the show. He was a man who 'had no borders toward people.'" — Joshua Rome

Late 1965 found Rome back on Broadway twice within a span of five weeks, returning to areas of expertise: social significance and revue. For the former, he was asked to write songs for a play with music, *The Zulu and the Zayda*, while the latter was to be additional songs for a revue from Paris, *La Grosse Valise*.

The book for *The Zulu and the Zayda* was to be co-written by Howard Da Silva and Felix Leon based on a short story by South African writer Dan Jacobson, "The Zulu and the Zeide."[1] Da Silva had been a jack-of-all-trades on Broadway, television, and Hollywood, including leading roles in the original productions of *The Cradle Will Rock* (1937), *Oklahoma!* as Jud Fry (1943), and *Fiorello!* as a crooked politician (1959). He had been a replacement director at Labor Stage during the later years of *Pins and Needles* when he and Rome became friends. He appeared in over sixty films including *Once in a Blue Moon*, *Abe Lincoln in Illinois*, *The Lost Weekend*, *Two Years Before the Mast*, and *David and Lisa*.[2] His career had suffered in the late forties when he was blacklisted by the House Un-American Activities Committee (HUAC). He returned to Broadway in 1950 at the insistence of Oscar Hammerstein II, who felt him perfect for a role in John Steinbeck's play *Burning Bright*.[3]

The souvenir program for *The Zulu and the Zayda* declared, "Felix Leon had written seven plays, about twenty-five television scripts, more than fifty comedy sketches and 'ten billion words' of radio continuity before he reached Broadway as co-author of *The Zulu and the Zayda*." Brooklyn-born Leon had written comedy for *Your Show of Shows* in the fifties and won drama awards for his plays *My Uncle Dom* and *The Year of Jubilee*.[4] Like Rome, he and Da Silva were writers with liberal, humanist points of view.

Dan Jacobson's early stories and novels were set in South Africa during apartheid — a government policy designating the segregation of blacks, whites, and other ethnic groups — which Jacobson "portrayed as emotional, psychological, and geographical isolation."[5] In the story, a Jewish grandfather, zayda in Yiddish, is brought to live with his son in a Jewish neighborhood in Johannesburg, and a young man, a Zulu, is hired to be his companion and sometime caretaker. There is a clash of cultures — ethnic, linguistic, age — as the grandfather is Yiddish, English-born, and set in his ways, while the young man was born of the Zulu tribe in South Africa and unaccustomed to foreigners. The grandfather is short and frail while the young man is tall and athletic. Worst of all, they have no language in common, as the older man speaks English, often lapsing into Yiddish, and the young man speaks Zulu, a Bantu language.

Their relationship develops in the setting of apartheid, a government policy sanctioned in South Africa starting in 1948 and expanding over the years. The government's claim was that "peaceful coexistence of the races was possible only if the races were separated from one another," when in fact, apartheid was being used to control the vast non-white majority in South Africa.[6] The setting of *The Zulu and the Zayda* was the current year, 1965, when apartheid was well-entrenched despite worldwide criticism. The United Nations General Assembly urged its members to break economic and diplomatic ties with South Africa until apartheid was abolished.[7]

Rome — topical, politically well-informed, and a staunch foe of any form of bigotry — was the perfect composer for the show; he was a man who "had no borders toward people."[8] He had written songs of social significance, particularly in his early career, songs which made Broadway producers balk at hiring him. This had started with his songs for the ILGWU revue *Pins and Needles* and continued on to *Sing Out the News*. In a 1940 interview, Rome explained: "It was only by coincidence that I got started writing this type of song satire. I'd like to get away from the label. Besides, there's a handicap and headache trying to write music with a message."[9]

Over the years, Rome's songs addressing freedom and persecution had been many:

| Song | Show | Year | Topic |
| --- | --- | --- | --- |
| "Doing the Reactionary" | *Pins and Needles* | 1937 | Right wing politics |
| "Four Little Angels of Peace" | *Pins and Needles* | 1937 | Oppressive dictators |
| "Franklin D. Roosevelt Jones" | *Sing Out the News* | 1938 | Racial equality |

| Song | Show | Year | Topic |
|---|---|---|---|
| "Let Freedom Swing" | Cabaret TAC song | 1938 | Personal freedoms for all |
| "Looking for a Candidate" | *That's the Ticket* | 1948 | Big government and presidential politics |
| "Mene, Mene, Tekel" | *Pins and Needles* | 1939 | Oppressive dictators |
| "Of the People Stomp" | *The Little Dog Laughed* | 1940 | Personal freedoms for all |
| "The Red Ball Express" | *Call Me Mister* | 1946 | Bigotry in hiring |
| "Sing Me a Song with Social Significance" | *Pins and Needles* | 1937 | Political freedom |
| "Stay Out, Sammy" | *Pins and Needles* | 1939 | Anti-war |
| "Tobacco — The Redman's Revenge" | *That Was the Week That Was* (TV) | 1973 | Mistreatment of Native Americans |
| "United Nations on the March" | Patriotic war song | 1942 | Freedom from military oppression in Europe and Russia |
| "What Are They Doing to Us?" | *I Can Get It for You Wholesale* | 1962 | Oppression of the common man |
| "Who's Gonna Investigate the Man Who Investigates Me?" | Political rally song | 1939 | Government interference in personal freedoms |
| "The Yanks Aren't Coming" | *Pins and Needles* | 1940 | Anti-war |

Along with his respect for personal and political freedoms, Rome had a touchstone to Africa in his love of its art and culture. He had collected African art for over twenty-five years, although he had never been there. He was exposed to it at an exhibition during a stopover in Paris after playing piano on an Atlantic Ocean cruise ship. At his first viewing, "I just went crazy about it.... It talked to me. And I resolved then — it was 1932 — that if I ever collected anything, it would only be African sculpture."[10] He waited until he had success with *Pins and Needles*, buying his first piece in 1939. From then on, he dove into African art with abandon, and as his career flourished, so did his collection. After a 1965 trip to Europe, he wrote producer Arthur Lesser: "Well, I'm safe back at home with all my African sculpture which I carried with me on the plane, air freight. It weighed two hundred and forty pounds. They were very pleasant with me in Customs here and I got everything through with a minimum of trouble."[11] He confessed years later to an art critic: "The funny thing is, I know every dealer in the world, but I've never been to Africa. My wife used to say that every time I had a hit, the drums would go in Africa, and they'd say, 'Start carving.'"[12]

As in his songwriting where there had to be an idea, such was the appeal of African art. Rome explained that there is "a directness about it.... This art was made for a purpose,"[13] and his collection reflected this as it included everyday utilitarian objects such as doors, locks, textiles, weapons, and farming implements, as well as numerous gold weights and implements, masks, ceramics, statues of humans and animals, and religious objects. Most interesting was Rome's collection of heddle pulleys, artistically carved pieces that were used as bobbins in weaving. Joshua Rome remembers more than once his father sitting on the floor of his Fifth Avenue apartment with an African art dealer trading and bartering heddle pulleys Rome had just picked up from a European trip.[14] At one point he had over 500 pulleys in his collection of 10,000 pieces.[15] He also had over 1,200 volumes relating to African art, archeology, and anthropology.[16]

An interviewer in 1962 spoke with Rome in his Fifth Avenue apartment near the Metropolitan Museum of Art and as their discussion ended, Rome gave the journalist a quick tour of his African art collection. The journalist commented that it would be competition for the Metropolitan, leading Rome to reply: "The Met doesn't have as good a collection.... They should have — but maybe they can't. I've sort of cornered the market..."[17] In 1963, he became the first donor to the Center for Cross Cultural Communication which later became the Frederick Douglas Institute/The Museum of African Art. This institution was incorporated into the Smithsonian Institution in 1979 and became the National Museum of African Art. From 1963 to 1980, Rome gave 197 objects to the NMAA.[18]

The size and quality of his acquisitions made it one of the most important collections in the field in America.[19] Rome continued to collect into the seventies, eventually selling off parts of the collection and donating others. He gave most of his books and 505 artifacts to the Schomburg Center for Research in Black Culture, part of the New York Public Library. The items listed in that institution's database under "The Harold and Florence Rome collection of African art" gives a view into the diversity of Rome's collection and interests[20]:

| | | | |
|---|---|---|---|
| 43 figures | 11 utensils | 3 busts | 1 fan |
| 4 weapons | 23 masks | 350 gold weights | 2 stools |
| 3 ivory horns | 8 musical instruments | 4 ornaments | 4 neck rests |
| 7 combs | 15 gold implements | 2 games | 1 pipe |
| 6 staffs | 4 canes | 7 locks | 2 boards |
| 1 bellow | 3 kuduos | 1 door | |

His pieces were often in demand for museums and exhibits, and he lent them generously.[21]

In the Africa of *The Zulu and the Zayda*, the two men develop their own "Yiddish-Zulu patois,"[22] and because of "their essential simplicity and humanity, create an insoluble bond."[23] Such a biracial relationship was prohibited by apartheid policies. Ironically, they discover the word "apartheid" at the same time, their reactions explained by book authors of the show,

## 17. The 1965 Shows and African Art 153

Howard Da Silva and Felix Leon: "When the Zulu and the Zayda are confronted with the Africans word apartheid they are not fully able to comprehend its meaning or unravel its logic. When introduced to the concept of separate buses, they ask: 'Why?'"[24] In the middle of the first act, Rome recognizes their relationship as they sang "It's Good to Be Alive (Lebe Is Gut)" while they dance steps reminiscent of a Jewish wedding. Rome's music and lyrics capture not only their love of life but the common humanity they share. Howard Taubman of the *New York Times* said that when this song is performed, "*The Zulu and the Zayda* is in its element."[25]

In 1959, Rome had become involved with a story that involved the clash of two societies, *Providence Island*, a novel by Jacquetta Hawkes, a British archeologist, poet, and amateur geologist. Rome had purchased the rights to musicalize the book which dealt with the discovery of a long-lost Stone Age tribe on a Pacific island. Rome saw a story with "serious overtones" and wanted the show's book to dwell on "the effects of the meeting of two civilizations."[26] The project fell through, but with *The Zulu and the Zayda*, Rome was again able to address the meeting and clash of two societies.

The star of the show was Menasha Skulnik, who had performed in Yiddish theater in New York for decades, often devising his own patter as the defenseless little man. His signature role had been in Clifford Odets' *The Flowering Peach* (1954). For *The Zulu and the Zayda*, Skulnik played "a Yiddish pixie full of wise Yiddish saws and instances."[27] To take advantage of his persona, Da Silva and Leon gave him plenty of lines of Yiddish humor and Rome provided songs such as "Oisgetzaichnet (Out of This World)" and "L'Chayim! (May Your Heart Stay Young)." In the show's souvenir program, Rome and his wife provided a Glossary of Zulu, Yiddish and English Terms, explaining the above phrases. One particularly humorous entry was the following from the Zulu section[28]:

### ZULU

**Awuyelelemama:** (Used in *Zulu Love Song*, also in *Tkambuza, Mighty Hunter*). (Ah-woo-yeh-lay-lay-ma-ma). An exclamation expressing many emotions, sad or joyous, depending on the tone of voice.
English equivalent: How about that?
Jewish equivalent: Oy!

Countering Skulnik's character was Louis Gossett, Jr., tall, dark, and handsome, with a deep baritone. Gossett made his Broadway debut in 1953 at age seventeen, starring in *Take a Giant Step*, and played in the original production of *A Raisin in the Sun* in 1961.[29] His solo numbers in *The Zulu and the Zayda* included "Zulu Love Song" and "Eagle Soliloquy."[30] Gossett went on to a distinguished movie and television career, winning the Best Supporting Actor Academy Award in 1982 for *An Officer and a Gentleman*.

Also prominent in the cast was Ossie Davis, who brought impressive credentials to the show, including Broadway performances in *The Wisteria Trees* (1950), the *Green Pastures* revival (1951), *Jamaica* (1957), and *A Raisin in the Sun* (1960), as well as extensive Hollywood and television credits.[31] *The Zulu and the Zayda* opened November 10, 1965, when the civil rights move-

Louis Gossett, Jr. (left), as the Zulu and Menasha Skulnik as the zayda in a scene from 1965's *The Zulu and the Zayda* (photograph by Friedman-Abeles © Schomburg Center, The New York Public Library).

ment in this country was gaining momentum. It is interesting to note that, for a show addressing racial segregation and starring a pioneer of desegregation in the performing arts in Ossie Davis, an article in the *New York Times* commented that there would be a "cast of 23, including eight Negroes."[32]

At the time Rome became involved in *The Zulu and the Zayda*, it was viewed by its producers, Theodore Mann and Dore Schary, as a play with music. Four months before the opening, Rome wrote to Lehman Engel, "Somehow, since the show isn't a musical, I feel curiously detached — which may be a good thing."[33] It was billed and perceived as a "play with music" rather than a book musical. Critic John S. Wilson felt it better described as "a play that is flavored with music, colored with music, deepened with music," adding that the play and songs "are unusually worthy complements to each other."[34] Wilson continued that the show had "a fine set of folk-based songs in which Rome expresses his natural heritage in lively and affecting fashion in the Jewish song and conveys an equally positive feeling in his Zulu songs."[35] Music historian Steven Suskin concurred, saying that Rome "provided a fascinating score in the styles of the two cultures."[36] Helping Rome with the music was orchestrator Meyer Kupferman, who performed the same function in Japan in 1972 when Rome wrote the score for the musical version of *Gone with the Wind*. The musical director was Michael Spivakovsky, who worked with a seven-piece orchestra.

There was negative criticism, with Suskin referring to *The Zulu and the Zayda* as "a left-wing soap opera"[37] and another reviewer stating that it relied on "all the trite devices of comedy and emotion."[38] In all, reviews were mixed, but the critics who count most, the audience, gave it only 179 performances. It was done again in 1966 at the Paper Mill Playhouse in New Jersey, with Menasha Skulnik both star and director, enjoying a brief run.[39]

\* \* \*

In late 1964, producers Joseph Kipness and Arthur Lesser took an interest in *La Gross Valise*, "a tiny show with little dialogue, music and dancing."[40] This was a French revue done in Paris by Robert Dhery,[41] a writer-director who'd had success in New York with *La Plume de Ma Tante*, a "spirited and droll revue," in 1959.[42] *La Gross Valise* — the big suitcase — takes place in Orly Airport in Paris when a clown attempts to get his "grosse valise" through customs. When he opens it for inspection, what spills out are not clothes and personal items but rather sketches, songs, and dance numbers.[43]

For the Paris production, Dhery had written little dialogue but pages and pages of stage directions, making book adaptation difficult for Joseph Fields.[44] There had been a few songs in Paris, but the New York producers wanted several more with music by the original composer Gerard Calvi and lyrics by Rome. Calvi was a theater and film composer who had done the music for Dhery's *La Plume de Ma Tante*.⁴⁵ He and Rome added to the comedy of the show with the songs "Hamburg Waltz," "Sandwich for Two," "Slippy Sloppy Shoes," and "Delilah Done Me Wrong."

A small show, *La Grosse Valise* required an initial investment of $250,000 of which $100,000 was provided by Mercury Records, which was given rights to the cast recording.⁴⁶ It was hoped that a song or two might be recorded prior to the opening, scheduled for December of 1965. Six months before this, Rome wanted to provide Mercury with the songs but there were contract problems with sheet music publisher Chappell and Company and the show's producers. Rome knew the power of a hit song promoting a show. He wrote to co-producer Arthur Lesser regarding the delays with Chappell: "Since I would like to give Mercury a few songs and let them get to work on them, it would be advisable to settle this business as quickly as possible."⁴⁷ Delays must have continued as none of the songs were recorded by any Mercury artist.

Rome had to go to Paris and work with a cast and chorus not too enthusiastic about rehearsals. He wrote to Lehman Engel: "Rehearsals have begun and the French they are a funny race. Nothing seems to start on time and everything sort of bumbles along. But it's a good company and I think things might turn out well."⁴⁸ Another problem appeared to be bad casting. In the successful Paris production, the clown had been played by a French comic actor with excellent pantomime skills. As things popped out of the trunk, his shock and surprise and the indignation of the customs officials provided the laughs. In rehearsals in America, several of the creators, including Rome, Fields, and Engel, felt that one of the key players, a customs officer, was not right for the role. Engel, who mentioned this little show in both his autobiography and his book *The American Musical Theater: A Consideration*, said of the situation: "[T]he English actor assigned the principal part was neither a comic nor a pantomimist — and in fact had little gift for, nor any experience with, these sort of things."⁴⁹

Despite these handicaps, the show went to Boston for a two-week tryout. The often too kind Boston critics gave it mixed reviews, but declared it a show "to enliven the Broadway doldrums"⁵⁰ and "lift the spirits of jaded theater-goers."⁵¹ Moreover, they adored Ronald Fraser, the very comic that Engel and others had wanted to replace.⁵² Although recognizing *La Grosse Valise* for what it was — a revue with an absurd premise — Beantown reviewers took time to single out the score; one wrote: "There are some great songs which are bound to be popular, including 'C'est Defendu' to a seductive tango, 'Happy Song,' the best salute to work since Walt Disney, 'Sandwich for Two,' [and] 'Slippy Sloppy Shoes'— the shoes are splendid."⁵³ Another said: "There are some good songs ... and these may possibly become memorable, although that is not important.... Its music is only incidental to its total concept, a novel entertainment."⁵⁴

Six songs from the original Parisian show had received English lyrics from Rome, and he and Calvi added seven more with new music and lyrics.⁵⁵ Two critics felt the English lyrics were often messed up by a primarily French-speaking cast.⁵⁶

The mixed reviews gave the producers a false sense of security, bringing Lehman to conclude: "The Boston reception was to prove *La Grosse Valise*'s kiss of death."⁵⁷ Few changes were made and two songs were added, but essentially, the show from Boston was taken to New York. Problems started immediately with the previews. The comedy and comics were not appreciated, the songs found little reception, and audiences "left noisily in droves during the first act."⁵⁸ Howard Taubman in the *New York Times* said:

> The imaginative level of *La Grosse Valise* is that of *Hellzapoppin'*.... The difference however is that *Hellzapoppin'* was performed at a mad, explosive clip by people who knew and loved their routines. *La Grosse Valise* is slapdash, unfocused, largely humorless.⁵⁹

The show opened on December 14, 1965, and closed after seven performances.⁶⁰

\* \* \*

David Merrick was difficult to work with. Although the most prominent producer of his era and capable of spending money on production and promotion, he was known to haggle over mere dollars in a contract, pit artists and creators against each other, stick to the fine print of a contract, deal harshly with labor unions, and use his front men to do his dirty work.

Few kind stories of Merrick emerge, but Rome was involved with one. In 1957, Merrick engaged George S. Kaufman, the elder statesman of the American theater, to direct and "Americanize" the book for *Romanoff and Juliet*. This play, a satire on the Cold War, had been written by actor Peter Ustinov. He had also directed and starred in the original London production and had even written a few ballads for the show.⁶¹ Rome's role in the New York production was to provide incidental music. When Ustinov arrived in the States, it was clear that the aging Kaufman was in no condition to either rewrite or direct a play. Kaufman himself was well aware of this.⁶² Ustinov became increasingly impatient with Kaufman, butting heads with him at every turn, wanting to save his play. Ultimately, he requested that Merrick let Kaufman go. Merrick's response to the Englishman: "I would rather have a flop than fire George Kaufman at this stage of his life and career."⁶³ Kaufman remained to direct his last play, and *Romanoff and Juliet* ran a respectable 389 performances.

So much for nice. Merrick produced his own shows with the help of a few of his front men — associates Michael Shurtleff, Jack Schlissel, and Neil Hartley — and a coterie of financial backers whom he could tap when a show was to be created. In 1946, Merrick had befriended his two most important backers, Max J. Brown and Byron Goldman. All three were smitten with the theater, supporting each other in their early years. Brown headed a construction company as well as a firm that sold flavoring oils, and Goldman was part owner of a large clothing manufacturer and had an affiliation with the financial firm of Goldman-Sachs.[64] Merrick and Brown drifted apart when Merrick, via fine print on a contract, excluded his backers, including Brown and the Theater Guild, from profits on *Hello, Dolly!*[65] Moreover, though dependent on these angels, Merrick never allowed them to specify which shows they wanted to back and which they wished to avoid. In the late sixties, Brown and Goldman tired of this arrangement. They quit Merrick about the same time, deciding to do a production themselves.[66]

Brown had been co-producer with Merrick on *Destry Rides Again*, which opened in 1959 and ran for 472 performances plus a successful production in London. Brown and Rome were well-acquainted and worked well together. Their project was to create a musical from the Mark Harris baseball novels *The Southpaw* (1953) and *Bang the Drum Slowly* (1956). When the latter was published, there had been options taken on it almost immediately for both screen and stage adaptations. At two separate times over several years, Merrick had owned the rights to produce a musical of it, hiring Robert Russell to do the book. In what may have been Merrick-like, pre-production hype, there was talk that the director-choreographer might be Gower Champion or Bob Fosse or even Jerome Robbins. When Merrick lost interest and his rights expired, Brown and Goldman took over the project in the summer of 1966 with plans to use the Russell book with songs by Rome.[67]

By early 1967, Goldman had dropped out, replaced by Edgar Lansbury, who had produced the successful drama *The Subject Was Roses*. Brown and Lansbury wanted to open by September of that year. Rome had most of the songs finished and was anxious to get the production done, writing to his attorney friend William Fitelson: "I want to make a date for you to hear the score of *The Southpaw* which I am very excited about and discuss what should be done to assure its production for the fall."[68] But then Brown and Lansbury decided to change book writers, opting for film writer Ring Lardner, Jr., delaying the project nearly a year.[69] By the fall of 1968, Rome convinced the producers to hold angel auditions even though he was unhappy with Lardner's new book. Rome wrote to Lehman Engel about his work on the score:

> I sat down to rehearse the numbers with myself for the audition and the next thing I knew, I was rewriting everything. I changed almost every number and rewrote some completely and worked like a dog, but it was fun, because being away from the score for four months had given me a perspective and as I changed the things kept coming right.[70]

Ultimately, despite a nearly completed score by Rome and much effort by Brown and Lansbury, the project was abandoned in early 1969.[71]

Rome, who did not want to give up, sent a recording of his music for *The Southpaw* to Mark Harris, who was quite pleased with it. Not a Broadway practitioner, Harris wrote Rome a warm letter discussing the situation: "It may ... be a sign from God, if you don't find a producer by May, that He didn't intend this particular project to set sail at all. You are an experienced man in this business, I know, and I suppose you have seen God in His eccentricity before."[72] Nothing came of the musical, but in 1973, a highly successful movie, *Bang the Drum Slowly*, was done by director John Hancock starring Michael Moriarty and Robert De Niro. In 1992, Harris wrote a dramatic play of the same name.

Along with *The Southpaw*, Rome made false starts on several musicals in the mid-late sixties as detailed in the Unproduced Shows Chronology in the Appendix. According to critic John Mahoney, Rome had completed four scores for various shows during this period, but none made it to opening night.[73] He was always on the lookout for a new show, but as the sixties came to a close, there was less demand for him and his contemporaries on Broadway. He was not sold on the newer musicals, but usually attending them early in their runs. In late 1968, shortly after the opening of *Promises, Promises*, he and Florence went to see that Burt Bacharach-Hal David show. He later wrote to Lehman Engel: "It's a blown up burlesque sketch and the music sounded like improvising over a vamp and the so-called rhythmic vitality made every song sound the same and the lyrics unintelligible — which judging by the few I did see was a blessing..."[74] He then adds with honesty: "[I]t's a big hit and I'm jealous." *Promises, Promises* was indeed a big hit, running for 1,281 performances with the title song and "I'll Never Fall in Love Again" becoming hits outside the show.[75]

One Rome contemporary was lyricist E.Y. "Yip" Harburg, who had a Broadway and Hollywood résumé to rival anyone. In 1975, *The Wiz*, an all-black version of *The Wizard of Oz*, opened on Broadway with new songs and libretto. After Harburg went to see it, he wrote to friends that he "walked out on it. There is nothing an author could do about it. I'm afraid the black people are not using their newly won *freedom* with good taste or sagacity.... [W]e must remember that men sing the hit songs but *time* sings the great ones."[76] These comments are interesting coming from a man whose liberalism was on a par with Rome's and whose 1947 musical *Finian's Rainbow* had dealt openly with bigotry and classism. Like *Promises, Promises*, *The Wiz* was a hit that ran 1,672 performances.[77]

\* \* \*

In the late sixties, Rome explored possibilities of television productions of his work. The medium had been evolving for over twenty years, starting with situation comedy and news. Cultural-educational slots were available on such programs as *The Bell Telephone Hour* and *Kraft Music Hall*. These shows would offer variety or musical entertainments, some original and others modified from previous productions. From Rome's notes at the time, now kept at the Harold Rome Collection at the Library of Congress, his considerations of television possibilities can be considered in four categories[78]:

*Produced musicals*

Pins and Needles
Destry Rides Again
I Can Get It for You Wholesale

Call Me Mister
Wish You Were Here
The Zulu and the Zayda

| *Musicals never produced* | *Book by* | *Work done by Rome* |
| --- | --- | --- |
| On Borrowed Time | Paul Osborn | Complete score |
| The Wonderful Door | Howard Fast | Six songs |

| *Compilations* | *Subject* |
| --- | --- |
| Harold Rome's Almanac | Rome songs from 1937–1966 |
| Man and Wife | Musical about a happy marriage with Rome songs |
| Oops Sorry or They Never Saw the Light of Day | Rome songs cut from produced shows or songs from shows never produced |

| *Music and Art* | *Subject* |
| --- | --- |
| Harold Rome's Gallery | Twelve Rome paintings with a song for each |

For one reason or another, none of these projects was ever produced for television.

\* \* \*

Rome was involved in liberal politics well into his sixties. With conservative presidential candidates for the Republican Party — Barry Goldwater in 1964 and Richard Nixon in 1968 — Rome answered the call to support the Democratic candidates, both musically and politically. In 1964, with a strong candidate in Lyndon Johnson, the Democratic Party was seeking the youth vote and organized a revue entitled *The Young Dem Bandwagon*. Rome was happy to donate his time and talent doing things he did well: revue-writing and spoofing politicians. Other artists involved included[79]:

| Songwriters | Performers | |
|---|---|---|
| Betty Comden | Hal March | Eydie Gorme |
| Adolph Green | Earl Wrightson | Lois Hunt |
| E.Y. Harburg | Mary Blyden | Judy Collins |
| Burton Lane | Kitty Kallen | Odetta |
| Carolyn Leigh | Peter, Paul and Mary | |

The ninety-minute show played a short while in New York, then toured the East and Midwest, targeting states and cities where no Democratic majority was assured. I do not know what Rome created for the show. Johnson won easily.

Four years later, when Johnson declined to run for re-election, the field opened wide and included Senators Robert Kennedy, Eugene McCarthy and George McGovern as well as Vice-President Hubert Humphrey. Humphrey didn't run in the primaries, but McCarthy — who had nearly beaten Johnson in the New Hampshire primary — and Kennedy went head to head, splitting delegates.[80] Rome became involved in the campaign for McCarthy, the anti-war–youth candidate from Minnesota. Democrats in New York organized the Citizens for McCarthy Committee. In addition to prominent politicians, civic leaders, and financial moguls, the committee included Rome, historian Henry Steele Commager, author Barbara Tuchman, and actors Eli Wallach and Anne Jackson.[81] Rome wrote a song dedicated to Eugene McCarthy entitled "Arouse, Arouse!" It is unclear whether it was used in the campaign.[82]

By the time of the protest-ridden Democratic Convention in Chicago in August of 1968, Robert Kennedy had been assassinated and the anti-war factions could not unite behind one candidate — McCarthy or McGovern. This shifted the momentum to Hubert Humphrey. Though identified with Johnson and his Vietnam War policies, Humphrey was still well-known as a progressive, thoughtful politician and had garnered the majority of delegates in the non-primary states. Humphrey won the nomination with Senator Edmund Muskie as his vice-president.[83] Rome was only minimally involved in their campaign but did get ink in *The New York Times* for his bicycle riding with Cyclists for Humphrey in Central Park a few weeks before the general election. Included among those riders were actor Douglas Fairbanks, Jr., singer Ella Logan from *Finian's Rainbow*, and Rome's old friend from the *Pins and Needles* days, president emeritus of the ILGWU, David Dubinsky.[84] No amount of bike riding or Democratic campaigning could beat former vice-president Richard Nixon, who won the electoral vote handily.

*Chapter 18*

# *Scarlett* in Japan

"All I can say is that this is going to be the goddamdest musical you've ever conducted." — Harold Rome

For the Broadway musical of Rome's day, out-of-town tryouts were workshops to assess a show's progress. Musicals would preview in New Haven, Boston, and Philadelphia and occasionally venture as far west as Chicago, Detroit, or Cleveland. Only one of Rome's shows did not follow that pattern, *Wish You Were Here*, because a swimming pool had to be built into the stage to accommodate the Kamp Karefree characters. All the tryouts and previews for that show were done in front of New York audiences.

The critics in the preview towns tended to be more forgiving, knowing that the shows they saw were undergoing changes. Their comments were often invaluable, indicating to the creators what might be missing or superfluous, where the book fell apart — usually the second act — and of course, overall length, as these early versions tended to be thirty minutes or more too long. Eventually, if the show was deemed presentable, it would open on Broadway after six to eight weeks on the road. What happened then was anyone's guess.

As time passed, production costs for a musical grew and out-of-town tryouts became more problematic. Music historian Max Wilk explained in the early 1990s: "Based on 1992 running costs, a touring show needs at least a full week in a theater, usually with subscription audiences, in order to turn some sort of profit. As for taking a *new* musical from New York anywhere out of town to try it out, such a venture these days would be hideously expensive, even disastrous."[1] While there are many exceptions, the technical productions of today's Broadway — think *Spiderman: Turn Off the Dark*—with elaborate sets, lighting, and stage mechanics continue to prohibit tryouts in other cities.

In 1968, Rome began work on a musical that would ultimately endure what he called "the world's longest out-of-town tryout."[2] It began with David O. Selznick, producer of the 1939 epic *Gone with the Wind*. He obtained the rights from author Margaret Mitchell's estate to do the story as a musical and approached Rome in 1959.³ Selznick went so far as to suggest song titles to Rome:

> Amongst the song titles that David Selznick has suggested as stemming almost inevitably from "Gone with the Wind" are the following:
> "The Land You Love Is Like Your Mother"
> "There's No Getting Away from It You're Irish"
> "Tara"
> "Fiddle-de-dee"
> "Tomorrow Is Another Day," and/or
> "I'll Think About That Tomorrow"⁴

It should be noted that many of the Hollywood producers were musically inept and often presumptuous in that area. Selznick talked with Richard Rodgers and Lorenz Hart about a song they had written for an MGM movie. William G. Hyland, a biographer of Rodgers, described the scene: "Selznick responded to one song by asking Rodgers whether he could improve it. The pair were told that they should try to sound more like Mack Gordon and Harry Revel, the two Hollywood writers who had composed 'Did You Ever See a Dream Walking?'"⁵

This to a Broadway songwriting team who by that time had written *Garrick Gaieties, Dearest Enemy,* and *A Connecticut Yankee.* In a similar vein, composer-arranger-conductor Andre Previn titled his memoir of his Hollywood days after the musical misconceptions of another Hollywood kingpin, Irving Thalberg. After hearing music in one of his movies that he did not like, Thalberg sent an interoffice memo that declared: "From the above date onward, no music in an MGM film is to contain a 'minor chord.'"⁶ Previn's book became *No Minor Chords: My Days in Hollywood.*

As for Selznick and *Gone with the Wind,* Rome and others on Broadway tossed the idea around, but he concluded: "I told him to come back in ten years time because it was still too early to do a musical; the film was still too fresh in people's minds."⁷ Though it had been twenty years since its premiere, *Gone with the Wind* was well-remembered. The novel had sold over one million copies. The movie is still the all-time leader in gross receipts when adjusted for inflation. For the curious, immediately following it are *Star Wars* (1977), *The Sound of Music* (1965), *E.T.: The Extra-Terrestrial* (1982), and *The Ten Commandments* (1956).⁸

By 1968, Selznick's rights had expired and Mitchell's estate and her brother, Stephens, sought a new buyer, preferably one far enough away that the book and movie would not exert undue influence over audiences and critics. Represented by Katharine Brown of Ashley Famous Agency, Stephens Mitchell signed an agreement with the Toho Company of Japan to musicalize

*Gone with the Wind.* Signed on January 29, 1968, the contract stipulated that the musical was to be done in Japan within two years and that Toho was to share rights for any productions done in Europe, Canada, or the United States.[9] At the time, Toho was one of two giants in the Japanese entertainment world, the other being Shochiku of kabuki theater fame.[10]

As a precursor to the musical, Toho's managing director, Kazuo Kikuta, had written a two-part, seven-hour dramatic play based on the novel. His play had been slated to run for one month but ran a total of eight, extremely long for Japan.[11] Why Rome was chosen by Kikuta to write the score, is unclear. He insisted that Rome and wife Florence fly to Japan in early February to see the epic play and be there when the contracts were announced to the press. Rome was "overwhelmed by the production and the faithfulness with which the drama followed the original."[12] If there was any doubt as to his writing the score, seeing the play won him over. After his trip, he wrote a most complimentary letter to Kikuta:

> Again I want you to know how deeply impressed I was with your production of *Gone with the Wind*. Everything about it ... the physical production, the acting, the direction ... was superb, and I congratulate you on a great concept brilliantly executed. It was very necessary for me to see it in order to realize the outstanding values a musical version could have.[13]

Florence Rome would later write to friends that "My Harold has that hooked look."[14]

Despite its Japanese premiere, production, and cast, the idea of Kikuta and other Toho personnel was to do an American musical, the first one ever done in Japan. They had committed to a budget of $1,500,000—more than any Broadway show of the time—and a cast of over 100.[15] An epic production for an epic story.

There were many hurdles ahead for the creators. For starters, Kikuta was to write a Japanese libretto for their "American musical" and send its translation to Rome. After this, the songs were to be written in English by Rome, then translated into Japanese for Kikuta. This was an uncommon work method for songwriting, fraught with hazards. The Japanese writer was well aware of this; according to a *Yomiuri* story: "Kikuta said that songs in his mind, therefore, might come out in words different from [Rome's]. He also predicted a difficult path lying ahead of Rome and himself because of possible clashes of ideas about songs to be featured in the musical."[16]

Clashes of ideas were not the problem early on; it was the lack of a book. Unused to the American musical, Kikuta did not appreciate the importance of the book in the development of a score. Rome and other writers of American book musicals believed that a song needed an idea. According to Rome: "The all important thing about songs is the idea itself. It doesn't matter how good the music is, if it's a bum idea the music is not carrying what it should."[17] For *Gone with the Wind*, Rome worked on songs for most of 1968, delivering a group of them to Kikuta in the late fall, still with no book from him. In *The Scarlett Letters*, her memoir of the creating of the musical and their travels to Japan, Florence Rome explained:

> Harold ... had to fulfill his contractual obligations by writing a certain number of songs as of a certain date. The contract, however, had been written with the idea in mind that there would be a book to which he could write the songs, and without it he was writing in a vacuum.[18]

A letter written by an assistant of Kikuta acknowledged the absence of the book, adding, "[Kikuta] believes that it is not fair for him to comment on the songs delivered at this stage of your work." In the next paragraph, however, Kikuta's rather harsh criticisms are mentioned:

> One fundamental feeling that Mr. Kikuta would like to express to you now is that the songs in general seemed to be in need of more forceful and more clearly defined character....
> He also asked me to ask you if the songs could be made more lyrical in feeling and more melodious?[19]

No letter of response could be found; Rome's reaction must have been something. To hear that one's songs should be more "lyrical" and "melodious" from a Japanese writer who had never done a book musical was not something Harold Rome would have suffered quietly.

Haggling over songs and contractual obligations continued well into 1969 with misunderstandings rampant. By July of 1969, Rome and Kikuta had done little face-to-face collaboration as Rome continued writing the score "on spec." In frustration, he wrote to attorney Ben Aslan:

> I made it clear to him that all those numbers were sketches made to meet contractual obligations to Toho and that I, by no means, considered them finished songs and since I had not had a chance to work with either director or writer, the final score would depend entirely on what the needs of the outline we would all develop together with Mr. Kikuta would demand.[20]

Rome concludes:

> ...This is basically a legal problem and threats of either or ultimatums by any of the parties involved have no place in the discussion.
> I have great faith in this project and am ready and impatient to go ahead full speed.[21]

Another problem during development was the reluctance of the Toho Company to bring over members of Rome's creative team — conductor-musical director, orchestrator, and dance music–vocal arranger. This was corporate penny-pinching and violated the terms of Rome's contract.[22] Moreover, it evinced the Japanese lack of knowledge regarding production of an American musical. Agent Katharine Brown became involved, writing a detailed letter to Kikuta and other Toho executives. She stressed that Rome having his creative team in place was crucial, detailing the importance of each position. She said that without these collaborators, the show "would be a Japanese musical and not an American musical."[23] Near the end, Brown presented an ultimatum: "I know that Mr. Rome wants to cooperate with you in every way possible as I do. I feel, however, that without the properly orchestrated score, and without giving Mr. Rome the proper tools to accomplish this, we will not accomplish our goal."[24]

By late 1969, songs and book began to mesh and Rome's creative staff arrived, including Meyer Kupferman to work on orchestrations and longtime Rome associate Trude Rittman for the vocal and dance arrangements. She was close to Rome on most of his shows, not only doing vocal and dance work but keeping notes and keeping Rome organized and on an even keel. During the creation of *Gone with the Wind*, his letters to Lehman Engel refer to Rittman only briefly, but always with phrases like "working like a dog,"[25] "working her ass off,"[26] and "busy writing notes all the time."[27] She was a jack of all trades whose career spanned from the early forties as a concert accompanist for Agnes de Mille through 2010 as a dance music arranger for a revival of *Finian's Rainbow*. Besides vocal, dance, and ballet music arrangements, she also worked on musical continuity, music coordination, and composed incidental music. She had worked with Rome in various capacities on *Wish You Were Here* and *Fanny*.[28]

Rome and director-choreographer Joe Layton called for rehearsals, creating another hurdle. Unbeknownst to the Americans, rehearsal time in Japan is limited, usually three to four days. On Broadway, 24 to 36 days is typical for a musical. Layton insisted on a 58-day period, causing more consternation on the part of Toho executives.[29] To compound this, before rehearsals there are auditions — another practice foreign to the Japanese theater. Toho, like many Japanese theatrical companies, had an ensemble of actors under contract and expected Layton et al. to draw from that group for casting. Toho's box office personnel had "charts showing how much each actor could be expected to draw at the b.o."[30] Moreover, the Japanese assured the Americans that even if they held auditions, few performers would show up. Rome's reply to this: "Show me an actor ... who isn't anxious to prove that he can play rings around everyone else in the part, and I'll show you an actor with a secret ambition to be a street cleaner."[31] As Layton explained it, for the Japanese it was apparently a matter of saving face: "They told us no one would come ... that people would be embarrassed to do it this way, afraid of being rejected and humiliated. We said it couldn't be done any other way."[32]

As Rome and Layton had anticipated, hundreds of actors appeared. Over several days, roles were filled satisfactorily from the viewpoints of both the American creative team and the Toho personnel. Then came the crucial role — Scarlett — and all hell broke loose. The Americans wanted Sakura Jinguji, "a great little actress, with a great big voice."[33] The Japanese wanted someone else, and a six-hour discussion-argument ensued. Layton put down an ultimatum:

> If we cannot have the people we feel we can work best with, Mr. Rome and I feel it would be impossible to take any responsibility for how the production would turn out. In that event, there is no use in our hanging around, and we have therefore decided to return to New York.[34]

Ultimately, the Americans got Sakura. Ironically, this feminine actress in a feminine role came to prominence in Japan playing male roles for the Takarazuka Opera Company under the name of Noboru Uchinoe. She had to dispense of a "throaty style" used for male roles at Takarazuka as well as an "exaggerated wobble" favored by most Japanese singers."[35] She did not disappoint, receiving standing ovations every evening in Tokyo.[36]

By November of 1969 rehearsals were going well with Joe Layton in charge. Layton was one of the directors who had started as a dancer-choreographer like Jerome Robbins, Bob Fosse, Danny Daniels, Michael Bennett, Tommy Tune, Agnes de Mille, Gower Champion, Michael Kidd, Peter Gennaro, and Susan Stroman.[37] He debuted on Broadway as a dancer in *Wonderful Town* in 1953; his credits through 1969 included[38]:

| Year | Musical | Position |
| --- | --- | --- |
| 1959 | *Once Upon a Mattress* | Choreographer |
| 1959 | *The Sound of Music* | Choreographer |
| 1959 | *On the Town* (revival) | Choreographer |
| 1960 | *Greenwillow* | Choreographer |
| 1960 | *Tenderloin* | Choreographer |
| 1961 | *Sail Away* | Choreographer |
| 1962 | *No Strings* | Director-choreographer |
| 1965 | *Drat! The Cat!* | Director-choreographer |
| 1965 | *My Name Is Barbra* (television) | Director |
| 1966 | *Color Me Barbra* (television) | Director |
| 1967 | *South Pacific* (revival) | Choreographer |
| 1967 | *The Belle of 14th Street* (television) | Director |
| 1968 | *George M!* | Director-choreographer |
| 1969 | *Dear World* | Director-choreographer |

Layton's overall conception for the show was to present singing and dialogue downstage with nearly continuous dancing — ballet and otherwise — serving as a backdrop upstage. This was a new concept and the main reason why Layton had insisted on such a long rehearsal period. One critic would say, "The background is continuously filled with swirling motion."[39] This had emerged from Layton's original concept for *Gone with the Wind* years before, which was to do the story as a full-length ballet.[40] Layton placed a note in each actor's script book, reminding them of "the unending panorama of the background ballet" and said of it all: "The concept is a free-flowing one. It's a choreographic idea — everything's constantly in motion. Nothing stops for anything."[41]

During rehearsals, Rome had written an enthusiastic letter to Lehman Engel regarding Layton's work:

> All I can say is that this is going to be the goddamdest [*sic*] musical you've ever conducted. Joe Layton's staging, at least at this stage, looks absolutely inspired.
> Joe is really the best-organized director I have ever worked with, and has a very good ear and instinct for what he wants musically, which makes things easier all around.[42]

The "Japanese-Broadway" musical based on the American novel *Gone with the Wind* opened as *Scarlett*. The name had been changed to provide a bit of distance from the movie and novel, fooling no one. The book Kikuta provided had nine scenes in two acts, workable for Layton's staging. Kikuta's story was more critical of the North than either the movie or the novel, more emphatic about the excesses of war.[43] This was why the novel, Kikuta's play, and the musical resonated with the Japanese audiences.

> With its special experience of atomic war, Japan has taken the Margaret Mitchell story peculiarly to heart....
> It appeals to our anti-war feeling ... and it makes a very strong impact because it is in "symbolic" rather than realistic form. We Japanese know the waste of war.[44]

Layton echoed and updated these sentiments: "The play ... is as up to date as the war in Vietnam, because it relates to war in general, with the unnecessary killing, the total destruction, and changes it makes in people."[45] Rome also weighed in on this matter, proud of the show's message: "This is the greatest anti-war show that I have ever seen and yet it doesn't say a word. Never one word, no one says 'War is hell.'"[46] This from the pacifist who composed "Stay Out, Sammy!" and "The Yanks Aren't Coming" in the early forties.

The story of *Gone with the Wind* and its anti-war subtext made the Tokyo production a solid hit, especially the staging. Audiences never expected the creators to burn down Atlanta on a musical stage, but it was done, night after night. This theatrical effect, conforming with Layton's theme of ever-present activity upstage, was achieved by building a set of Atlanta, burning it down, filming the fire, then showing it as a backdrop to the downstage drama.

What were less successful were Rome's songs which had suffered in translation. English and Japanese are a world apart, where "three words in English usually come out twelve in Japanese."[47] Though Rome felt the differences were not that great, it made for longer songs and took away the beautiful match between words and music that is a well-crafted Broadway song. To him, the bigger problem was the lack of rhyming in Japanese songs. Florence explained: "Japanese songs and poetry are never rhymed, as so many words have identical endings."[48]

Rome's experience as a vocal coach paid off in Tokyo. The Japanese performers had good voices and could sing the notes, but they could not always get the idea that a song advanced story and characterization. This was particularly evident with Akira Takarada, the first Rhett Butler in Japan. Florence explained: "Harold had not worked on his voice, which was adequate if not operatic, but on the technique of making a song mean something within the context of a show."[49] The Harold Rome Papers at Yale contain an endearing picture of Rome working with Mariko Togawa, the child playing Rhett and Scarlett's daughter Bonnie. He is not teaching her the words or notes, but appears to be trying to get some characterization across to her as they both look into a mirror.

Another hurdle Rome found in presenting his songs was the aforementioned throat wobble used by most Japanese singers. Music director Lehman Engel, choral arranger Trude Rittman, and the vocal coaches were able to minimize this in most of the cast, but the actress playing Belle Watley would not give it up; she was a television star with an exceptional wobble. Rome was philosophical: "We can't control it ... and anyway the Japanese love it."[50]

As if this were not enough of an adjustment for a Broadway songwriter, there was one more to be made: applause. Japanese audiences did not applaud, cheer, show emotion, or even change expression until the end of a performance.[51] An essential element of a Broadway musical is the showstopper, the song that brings strong applause and temporary suspension of the action. These can be solo numbers or ensemble efforts. The ultimate showstoppers are the title songs from *Hello, Dolly!* and *Oklahoma!* The latter was not put into the show until weeks into the out-of-town tryouts, and conductor Jay Blackton said simply: "They went wild! The number stopped the show, dead."[52] The lyricist for that show, Oscar Hammerstein II, appreciated the importance of applause and knew how to end a song so that a singer could hold a note as long she wanted and pull applause. He gives an example of using a word with long "o" to end a song. He summed up the situation: "There is nothing wrong with pulling applause. No matter how much an audience enjoys a song, it likes to be cued into applause."[53] In *Making American: Jews and the Broadway Musical*, historian Andrea Most discussed the evolution of the musical and the role of applause:

Rome rehearses a number with Mariko Togawa playing Bonnie (Scarlett and Rhett's daughter) in *Scarlett* in Tokyo in late 1969 (courtesy Gilmore Music Library, Yale University).

> Numbers have clear beginnings, when a character begins to sing, and endings, when the audience applauds. The role of applause — or, more accurately, of audiences — is central to musical comedy... The separation of musical numbers from the scenes allows audiences to participate in the play by applauding and even determining some of the course of the play by calling for encores.[54]

Rome was no stranger to such songs. His most prominent showstoppers include:

| Song | Performer | Show |
|---|---|---|
| "Sing Me a Song with Social Significance" | Ensemble | Pins and Needles |
| "F.D.R. Jones" | Rex Ingram / Chorus | Sing Out the News |
| "South America, Take It Away" | Betty Garrett | Call Me Mister |
| "Wish You Were Here" | Jack Cassidy / Chorus | Wish You Were Here |
| "Fanny" | Florence Henderson / William Tabbert | Fanny |
| "Miss Marmelstein" | Barbra Streisand | I Can Get It for You Wholesale |

In *Scarlett*, there would be no showstoppers. This meshed well with Layton's concept of the show as a flowing, ever-changing story with music and dance. Florence Rome put it well:

> I began to understand why Joe had insisted that there should not be any showstoppers.... His direction was such that no song quite ended but went directly into the dialogue or dance which followed it, for his conception was that the show must not lose its flow at any point. It was the same with the ballets.[55]

To be certain, this was not conventional for a book musical. It took him awhile, but Rome signed on to this "no mid-show applause" and "no showstoppers" idea. Writing to Engel, Rome admitted: "Everything flows — it's a mixture of drama, ballet, and music to tell the story, and it seems to work."[56] A veteran of over one hundred Broadway shows, Engel was to become involved in the show soon after this. He understood that Layton's *Scarlett* was dependent on a constant flow of all the elements, and in no need of showstoppers. From his autobiography *This Bright Day*:

> This production was different from all others. The differences took two forms. The songs were imbedded in an almost endless musical texture that became underscoring for dialogue between sung phrases and music for dancing and pantomime. Second, the dramatic scenes were generally acted down in front ... while frequently behind these there was continuous ballet.[57]

Of all of Rome's collaborators during his career, Lehman Engel was the most indispensable. They had known each other since the early months of *Pins and Needles* in 1938 when Rome had introduced himself to Engel after a performance. Engel's first Broadway position as musical director was for Kurt Weill's *Johnny Johnson* in 1937. He worked steadily on Broadway for the next forty years, his first show with Rome being *The Little Dog Laughed* in 1941.[58] Rome had been impressed with Engel's work on that show and a year later wrote a letter of recommendation for Engel: "I consider him one of the finest musical directors in the country today. Coupled with an all around musical knowledge and background, he has an ability for organization and handling of people that makes it a pleasure to work with him."[59] Rome treasured their longstanding friendship and professional association — and Engel's fondness for gin rummy. The two of them were part of a gin rummy group that also included Arthur Kober, playwright Paul Osborn and his wife Millicent, and occasionally Richard Rodgers.[60] After the 1959 opening of *Destry Rides Again*, Rome sent Engel the following telegram:

> LOVE FORTISSIMO, RESPECT MAESTOSO, FRIENDSHIP CRESCENDO, GIN RUMMY STINKO
> HECKY[61]

Rome and Florence kept up correspondence with Engel over the years until his death from cancer in 1982. In letters, they both addressed him as "Lehmsieboo."

Music directors like Engel had to be multi-taskers to accomplish their duties:

- conduct the orchestra and chorus for rehearsals and shows;
- coordinate the orchestra's work with the singers and dancers;
- collaborate with the dance and vocal arrangers;
- ensure that orchestrations were workable and sounded good from the pit;
- ensure that the score worked well for everyone;
- determine the ideal keys for the singers;
- cue everyone properly;
- keep tempos correct and consistent during shows and the entire run.

For a music director, assembling *Scarlett* was particularly problematic as the Japanese orchestra and singers were unaccustomed to occidental music, extended rehearsals, and nearly continuous music and dancing. It was Engel who helped sort this all out, as detailed by Florence Rome:

> The entire cast, once they're upon that stage, depends on him. Not simply for tempo, but for mood. Hecky has always insisted on Lehman to conduct a show of his because Lehman has the most extraordinary rapport with all the people with whom he works. He gets more out of an orchestra than they have to give, and he fills singers with confidence.[62]

Despite all the usual problems putting on a musical and the uniqueness of doing so in Japan, the spectacle that had started out as *Gone with the Wind* premiered at the Imperial Theater in Tokyo on January 2, 1970, as *Scarlett*. There were two performances a day: 12:30 P.M. and 5:30 P.M. The cast totaled

*18. Scarlett in Japan* 173

Rome in front of friend Ed Weiss's portrait of him, circa 1970. Rome's image is juxtaposed in the painting with an African mask (courtesy of Joshua Rome).

seventy-six members and a horse which carts Scarlett offstage depicting her leaving Atlanta to escape General Sherman's troops. The principal players were made up to look Caucasian, but not the minor role players or the chorus.[63] The premiere performance lasted four hours and eleven minutes and was met with thunderous applause — all at the end.

*Chapter 19*

# *Gone with the Wind* in London and America

> "It was then that I realized for the first time that a musical version of *Gone with the Wind* had its own personality." — Harold Rome

Harold Rome and Joe Layton wanted to get their musical version of *Gone with the Wind* to Broadway. To do so, they were going to have to go through London — and their show had to be modified for British audiences in more than language only. They had come to appreciate Kazuo Kikuta's book for *Scarlett*, which had focused on a more universal anti-war theme; but for London, there had to be more of a Southern story and more Miss Scarlett. Rome and Layton were retained by Harold Fielding, the British producer who had acquired the rights for a London production. He had done successful musicals in London including *Charlie Girl* and *The Great Waltz* and was responsible for the revival of *Showboat* which was running in late 1971.[1]

Fielding hired American veteran writer Horton Foote to redo the book. Foote had begun as an actor but turned to playwriting early in his career. His writing had a regional character to it as he often turned to his native Wharton, Texas, for inspiration, focusing on ordinary people and Southern settings. He came to national prominence for his 1962 screenplay for *To Kill a Mockingbird*, which won an Academy Award for him and for Gregory Peck as Best Actor. Three years later, Foote wrote the screenplay for *Baby, The Rain Must Fall* which starred Steve McQueen and was based on Foote's own *The Traveling Lady*. Foote had also written numerous teleplays in the early days of television for shows such as *The United States Steel Hour* and *Playhouse 90*. Although well-versed in drama and the South, he had never written a book for a musical.[2]

Rome and Layton were aware of the reluctance of early seventies Broadway to welcome a traditional book musical. The Broadway hits of 1971 had included *Oh! Calcutta!, Follies,* and *Jesus Christ Superstar,* hardly standard book musicals.[3] Overall, Rome's outlook was more optimistic. The ovations in Tokyo convinced him that "he had a hit in any language." He told interviewer Kay Gardella of *Show* magazine: "It was then that I realized for the first time that a musical version of *Gone with the Wind* had its own personality. It wouldn't have to compete with the movie."[4] Rome felt that a good show was a good show and would supersede the presence of any particular climate. He had felt this strongly at the time of the movie version of *Fanny.* Joshua Logan and the studio felt that movie musicals were no longer popular. Rome disagreed, thinking that if one did a good movie musical, it could be a hit, popular tendencies be damned. His musical was never filmed.

Layton was more negative about Broadway than Rome, saying, "[A]nyone who would attempt to make a theatrical or musical version of *Gone with the Wind* was regarded as either a lunatic or a genius. So Broadway has taken an attitude of aloofness, waiting for the appearance of a lunatic or genius."[5] This reticence towards Broadway and the fact that Fielding was ready to invest $400,000 for a production in London made it clear that the show would be stopping off there. Layton et al. estimated that an American-Broadway production would have cost over one million dollars, money that simply was not available at the time.[6] Moreover, London audiences were more favorable towards such a project. American baritone Harve Presnell, who had been brought in to play Rhett Butler, said of the American theater climate: "It's rough to be in musical now. There's a negative feeling about Broadway. There's a negative feeling about Hollywood. Here [London] you don't hear a negative word."[7]

Work on the British production began in late 1971 and by February of 1972, Layton was able to report good progress to the Romes. He was especially buoyed by the advance ticket sales and Fielding's ability to book coach tours, the lifeblood of London theater.[8] Layton liked Presnell's baritone and acting ability and asked Rome to add three songs, two of which would expand the Rhett Butler role. Veteran Presnell had starred with Tammy Grimes in Meredith Willson's *The Unsinkable Molly Brown* in 1960. True to his principle for the book musical — no song without an idea or purpose — Rome was able to fit these three new songs to the story and advance it. The *London Times* critic would say of the score: "Even the songs not up to that quality are generally related firmly to character and situation, and open to dramatic development."[9] Most notable of these were "Two of a Kind," "Lonely Stranger," and "Blueberry Eyes." Of the last one, Rome explained the beauty of a well-integrated song to an interviewer for *ASCAP Today*:

> The songs can take the place of a lot of dialogue. In the span of a song you can do what it takes a hundred pages in the book to do. For instance, there's a lullaby in [*Scarlett*] called "Blueberry Eyes." Now when that starts, the baby is born, and when that song finishes six minutes later, the baby is five years old. We've told the whole story while the song is going on, and when you see it you don't notice it because you're too interested in the story.[10]

Rome was also confident that the period writing of his lyrics would be appreciated in English-speaking London with nothing lost in translation as had been in Japan. When composers write period pieces, they attempt to capture the flavor of the show's era without hitting the audience over the head with it. Richard Rodgers said of his writing for *Oklahoma!*:

> Oscar sent me an impressively thick book of songs of the American Southwest which he thought might be of help; I opened the book, played through the music of one song, closed the book, and never looked at it again. If my melodies were going to be authentic, they'd have to be authentic on my own terms.... All a composer — any composer — can do is make an audience believe it is hearing an authentic sound without losing his own musical identity.[11]

Historian David Lehman expanded on this thought in three songs of Rodgers, including "Surrey with the Fringe on Top" (*Oklahoma!*), "Bali Ha'i" (*South Pacific*), and "The March of the Siamese Children" (*The King and I*): "Those melodies may sound wonderfully foreign and exotic, but they have nothing whatsoever to do with the indigenous music of Polynesia or Southeast Asia. Rodgers was exercising both his genius and his artistic license."[12]

As for Rome's ability to write period songs, he had been successful in capturing the essence of the Old West in *Destry Rides Again* and of the Marseilles waterfront in *Fanny*. Joshua Logan, who had worked on *South Pacific*, said of Rome's songs in the latter show: "He had a very difficult task in writing the score in *Fanny*.... Harold's songs must not offend the ear of French-speaking people, nor must it be too French and impossible to understand by American audiences. It must suggest France but at the same time be universal."[13] Of *Gone with the Wind* and its era, Rome declared:

> This is a Southern show about the Civil War, so everything must have the flavor of the South and those people and yet must be fresh enough for a modern audience.
>
> You just get yourself soaked in that period — and then you forget it! You start to write but you never really forget it because you have observed [*sic*] a kind of feeling.[14]

Rome's attention to period is elucidated in a letter exchange with broadcaster Thaddeus Holt in November of 1971, during work on the London production. Holt had written a long letter to Rome commenting on several of the lyrics. Rome's reply illustrates how deep a songwriter may go to flesh out his characters and story in lyrics. Holt's comments coupled with Rome's responses are most telling[15]:

| Song | Holt comment | Rome reply |
|---|---|---|
| "Bonnie Blue Flag" | This was a real song. | I know ... I did extensive research on Southern songs of the period before I did the score. |
| "Time for Love/What Is Love" | Belle Watling has gotten mighty intellectual... | I thought it might give her an extra dimension and help to explain Rhett Butler's attachment to her. |
| "Blueberry Eyes" | Watermelon seed hair? | Since all the descriptive references have to do with fruit, I wanted something that would describe the black shiny beauty of Bonnie's hair ... seemed to me unusual and apt enough. |
| "Little Wonders" | "It wonders me" sounds Pennsylvania Dutch ... | I was trying to express the way a five-year-old might think ... a child's point of view and a child's way of expressing it... |
| "Bonnie Gone" | "Mill-pond stone" doesn't quite work.... How about "grist-mill stone"? | "Mill-pond stone" I'm afraid is a compromise. I meant Grist Mill stone but that doesn't sound as well. It doesn't have the gentle sound that Mill-Pond stone has. It's less accurate but more poetic. |

Harold and Florence were a theater couple, often on the town or working, and had much help raising their children from a nanny. As parents, they were concerned about this but realized that they were engaged in a professional atmosphere that had its demands. For the London rehearsals of *Gone with the Wind*, they brought their son Joshua and daughter Rachel. By this time, both were in their teens and benefited greatly from the exposure to another culture and a musical-in-progress. In a letter to Lehman Engel at this time, Florence Rome reveals much about their family relationships:

> [The kids] are enjoying every minute I think, and [they] are profiting very much from this excursion — both from the standpoint of what they are seeing and doing, and from their (enforced) exposure to us on a different level than it has ever been. They seem not to mind in the least, and they are getting a view of their parents, father in particular, which they have never had.... They sit open-mouthed at rehearsals, are amazed at the discipline it takes to produce a result....[16]

In all of the correspondence in the Harold Rome Papers and Lehman Engel Collection at the Gilmore Music Library at Yale, this letter was the most conspicuous comment regarding the Rome family. In the several interviews of Rome that were available from various institutions, almost no mention is made of his children. The greater part of Rome's theater work was in New York, and he lived with his family there, mostly in their apartment on 1035 Fifth Avenue, across from Central Park and near the Metropolitan Museum of Art. His children were young during the time of his biggest shows and seldom were involved in any way with them. Son Joshua does remember going to the set of *Destry Rides Again*, climbing around the catwalks, and being shown the special effect of how the saloon lights were shot out.[17]

In London, Rome felt it was time to leave the non-applauding Japanese behind and bring out a few showstoppers. In extensive notes to Layton in early 1972, after several suggestions for cuts, Rome discusses the staging of the songs "Today's the Day" and "Lonely Stranger." The former is a hopeful, spirited song for Scarlett, and the composer wanted it showcased properly:

> Something is still wrong with the freeze at the end of the song. The applause is stifled because the movement suggests the action is going right on. Please see what you can do to clarify this, so as not to inhibit the audience's obvious desire and need to applause [sic].[18]

Of "Lonely Stranger," a song for the Belle Watley character, Rome declares:

> I feel she should complete the song — sing the last phrase, instead of giving it to a slide trombone. Also, instead of silence, the explosions have been coming too soon and stopping the applause.... Please give Belle a chance. Let her sing the whole thing and delay the explosions. Why must we again frustrate the audience?[19]

Continuing on — the quintessential composer promoting his music — Rome requests a sixteen-bar reprisal of "Tomorrow Is Another Day," explaining: "It is now a big empty hole. This is a chance for the audience to hear the melody again. It may be cliché musical, as you remarked to me, but after all we are doing a musical."[20]

In the remainder of these detailed notes, Rome also comments on orchestrations, Scarlett's characterization, and the libretto. Wisely, he makes no comments about choreography. Aware that he has been complaining for three pages, Rome ends on a most positive note: "As I have told you, I think this is the best and most imaginative staging any musical has ever had and I am grateful."[21]

There are another three pages of notes, these handwritten, in the Harold Rome Papers. In this second set, Rome focuses on specific singers, mostly June Ritchie, the London Scarlett. Like many pianist-composers — Harold Arlen, Jerry Bock, Hugh Martin, Cole Porter, Richard Rodgers, Ann Ronell, and Jule Styne — Rome worked early in his career accompanying rehearsals, recitals, and by necessity, coaching singers. He understood phrasing and voicing, especially when it involved his own songs. Of Ritchie's rehearsals, Rome's comments include:

> She must sing it ["Which Way Is Home?"] with the same intensity she would sing a spiritual. Her first statement "Which way is home" must be a strong complaint — not constipated....
> "Tomorrow Is Another Day" is not a sad song — it's a hopeful one. Scarlett's character is not weak and complaining but stubbornly optimistic in the face of everything....
> One great thing wrong is that she was taught by rote to sing the song exactly as it was written, and she's still singing notes instead of words.[22]

Another performer singled out was Harry Goodier, playing a minor role. After two and a half pages on Ritchie-Scarlett, Rome spends the last half-page on Goodier, telling Layton:

> I would like to have a half hour to work on Harry Goodier, on interpretation, voice shading and meaning. He has a habit of taking breaks in the wrong places — for instance
> fields of rich____red earth
> Deep in your dear half____Irish heart
> This is not a matter of music alone. It's a matter of what the song is trying to say....[23]

But the most emphatic criticism was directed at a singer's changing his notes on a song, a dislike shared by all composers. Rome was especially miffed about June Ritchie's taking liberties with "Today's the Day": "I cannot countenance changing a melody I have written without consulting me. The star does not rewrite my music, please."[24] Rome expressed similar feelings — "Don't touch my songs!" — when an Australian production was being planned: "Under no circumstances would I allow any changes in the music and lyrics to be made without my personal approval and presence. This means round trip passage for Mrs. Rome and me plus the set fee of 15 Pounds per diem."[25]

Despite these problems, the show opened in London on May 3, 1972, entitled *Gone with the Wind*. The critics and audiences were generally favorable. Layton's staging and choreography were rated the show's greatest strengths. One London reviewer explained, "The basic concept is a human drama played out downstage against a kaleidoscopic background of [the] Civil War."[26] Another writer said of Layton's work: "[His] fluid, continuous action staging was remarkable, telling a sprawling story in eight sequences (four to an act) which combined song, dialogue, dance, and movement and propelled the action forward without a break."[27]

As for Rome, comments on his score were mixed. Critics in a given city are normally mixed in their reviews of a show. Unanimity is rare but does occur, particularly negative. Strong evidence for this exists in Ken Mandelbaum's interesting read *Not Since Carrie: 40 Years of Broadway Musical Flops*. London critics were noted for kinder reviews than those in America but were seldom unanimous. To illustrate this and give an idea what show creators face with the vagaries of critics, the following chart reveals comments by London reviewers of the same show, *Gone with the Wind*, mostly the same performance, with comments on the same topic, Rome's score[28]:

| *Negative* | *Positive* |
|---|---|
| "lacks ... memorable melodies" | "tuneful" |
| "one melancholy dirge after another" | "melodic verve which makes their reprise a pleasure" |
| "sow his score with more authentic Civil War minstrelsy" | "music matches the moods of the action" |
| "production values ... substitute for musical content" | "choreography and music are brilliantly blended" |
| "vapid lyrics" | "songs ... related firmly to character and situation" |
| "songs ... go in one ear and straight out the other" | "evocative music, shrewdly paced and tastefully scored" |
| "advances in sophistication made by the American musical over the past few decades are blithely ignored" | "a product of sound craftsmanship and devotion to story" |
| "overcrowded score" | "exceedingly competent show music" |

Truly mixed reviews.

Eight months into the London run, another problem arose for Rome, this one regarding sheet music sales of the score. Before the phonograph was invented, the public would be exposed to new songs through sheet music which was then played on the family piano by one or more household members. It was common for a hit song to reach several hundred thousand copies in sales and even a million.[29] While the days of enormous sales were gone as radio and the recording industries grew, songwriters could count on modest royalty income for the sheet music of their songs.

For a musical, arrangements were made with a publisher to print several songs if not an entire score of a show if it had had some degree of success. In London, *Gone with the Wind* rights had been given to an old-line publisher, Chappell and Co. In January 1973, Rome discovered that the publisher had been making little or no effort to promote the music. He wrote to producer Harold Fielding who had stipulated that Chappell be the song publisher:

> Imagine my amazement, astonishment, and indignation... There is a fine display of current musical attractions in London in the front window in which *Gone with the Wind* is conspicuously absent.
> 
> This seems to be nothing but a deliberate sabotage of our show. I am

shocked that you have not taken action. I am appalled that my publisher in a music store bearing their name can allow this to happen.[30]

As it turned out, Fielding was aware of the problem but had been slow to act on it. He was miffed at Chappell because he was about to embark on an extensive television advertising campaign and wanted tie-ins with the sheet music and Chappell stores. Fielding wrote to one of the publisher's executives:

> I am of course appalled by the contents of the letter which I have received this morning from Mr. Harold Rome.
> The accent of this scheme is "NOW GREATER THAN EVER AS A STAGE MUSICAL," and I would be grateful for some space to be made available next week in the store....[31]

The television ad campaign met with some success as *Gone with the Wind* ran for several more months. Audiences liked it more than the critics and gave it a total of 397 performances. How successful the sheet music campaign was is not clear.

Rome and Layton looked ahead to a U.S. production which was to open in Atlanta — where else? — and then move to Broadway. But financial backing other than Fielding was thin as Broadway backers continued to keep their distance. The tour schedule had to be changed drastically, as detailed by Rome in the spring of 1973[32]:

| City | Planned Opening | Planned Run | Theater |
| --- | --- | --- | --- |
| Los Angeles | August 28, 1973 | 8 weeks | Dorothy Chandler Pavilion |
| San Francisco | October 1973 | 7 weeks | Curran Theatre |
| Denver | December 1973 | | |
| Chicago | December 24, 1973 | 4 weeks | |
| Cleveland | January 21, 1974 | 2 weeks | |
| Indianapolis | February 1974 | | |
| Washington, D.C. | April 22, 1974 | 4 weeks | Kennedy Center |

Other cities to be included but without specific dates: Detroit, Toronto, Pittsburgh, Baltimore, and Philadelphia.

*Gone with the Wind*, a.k.a. *Scarlett*, had now undergone three productions — Tokyo, London, and Los Angeles — and a myriad of changes, especially the score. Songs may be added or deleted from a show for a variety of reasons, including:

- addition or deletion of a scene;
- repositioning of a song within a show, necessitating lyric changes;
- inability of a cast member to sing the song as the composer imagines it;
- poor response by the audience to a song;

- consolidation of two or more songs for reasons of time or plot development;
- replacement of a dance number by a song or vice versa.

As an example of what songwriters go through as shows evolve, the following is a list of songs presented in each of the three productions of *Scarlett–Gone with the Wind* in order of their presentation[33]:

| *Tokyo* | *London* | *Los Angeles* |
|---|---|---|
| "He Loves Me" | "Today's the Day" | "Today's the Day" |
| "Gambling Man" | "We Belong to You" | "Cakewalk" |
| "Which Way Is Home?" | "Tara" | "We Belong to You" |
| "We Belong to You" | "Two of a Kind" | "Scarlett" |
| "Scarlett" | "Blissful Christmas" | "Bonnie Blue Flag" |
| "Two of a Kind" | "Home Again" | "Bazaar Hymn" |
| "Blissful Christmas" | "Tomorrow Is Another Day" | "Virginia Reel" |
| "My Soldier" | "Lonely Stranger" | "Quadrille" |
| "Goodbye My Honey" | "A Time for Love" | "Two of a Kind" |
| "Lonely Stranger" | "Which Way Is Home?" | "Blissful Christmas" |
| "A Time for Love" | "How Often, How Often" | "My Soldier" |
| "What Is Love?" | "If Only" | "Tomorrow Is Another Day" |
| "Bonnie Blue Flag" | "A Southern Lady" | "Where Is My Soldier Boy?" |
| "O'Hara" | "Marrying for Fun" | "Why Did They Die?" |
| "The Newlyweds Song" | "Blueberry Eyes" | "Johnny Is My Darling" |
| "Strange and Wonderful" | "Strange and Wonderful" | "Lonely Stranger" |
| "Blueberry Eyes" | "Little Wonders" | "If Only" |
| "Little Wonder" | "Bonnie Gone" | "How Often" |
| "Bonnie Gone" | "It Doesn't Matter Now" | "A Southern Lady" |
| | | "Marrying for Fun" |
| | | "Brand New Friends" |
| | | "Miss Fiddle-Dee-Dee" |
| | | "Blueberry Eyes" |
| | | "Bonnie Gone" |
| | | "It Doesn't Matter" |

Rehearsals for a production in the States took place during the summer of 1973. Rome was working essentially with the music team from the London production which included advisor Ray Cook, orchestrator Keith Amos, conductor Jay Blackton, and of course, Trude Rittman. Engel was ill at the time, and although not working on the show, he was keenly interested. Rome assured him, "We've got a great music department."[34] He was also pleased with his new Rhett Butler: Pernell Roberts. Roberts, best known for his TV role in the popular *Bonanza* series, was classically trained and had done primarily theater. Rome had been satisfied with his Rhett in Tokyo, Kinya Kitaoji, and in London, Harve Presnell, but he felt the role could have been much more. Rome and Layton had wanted Rhett to be more on a par with Scarlett throughout the story and thought it best done in song. Rome wrote to Engel:

"Pernell Roberts is a great Rhett. He sings fine, but is a wonderful actor, and the part is coming out like it never could in London with Harve. We've given him a lot more to do — 3 new songs and more vocal bits."[35]

These three songs had been added to accommodate changes in the libretto and staging which Layton had requested. If he had an idea for the song and could see its usefulness in advancing the story, Rome was always willing to add a song or two — or three. Layton had agreed to stage the new songs with endings more conducive to applause from the American audiences.[36] Despite his positive comments to Engel, Rome concluded like the veteran theater man he was: "Of course, with everything going so well, I am waiting for the shit to hit the fan which it undoubtedly will — but that's to be expected."[37]

*Gone with the Wind* opened August 28, 1973, at the Dorothy Chandler Pavilion under the auspices of the Los Angeles Light Civic Opera Association and its long-time artistic director, Edwin Lester. Despite score and libretto changes, the production faltered after negative reviews. Rome had made numerous suggestions to Layton with which Lester agreed. He felt the show ran too long, but Layton did not want to cut it. Lester told Rome: "The day of the 11:30 curtain, which Rodgers and Hammerstein and one or two other classic works got away with, is over..."[38] Lester also had a few unkind words about Layton: "It is rather a pity that Joe has been accorded so much autonomy and that even though he professes to listen, he ends up doing just what he pleases."[39]

Lester was especially fond of the score, although he recognized that it was slow to win over the listener:

> We all know from long experience that critics, and even most musicians, are not capable of a fair evaluation of a score on first hearing. (I can recall two reasonably qualified critics who covered *Kismet* in its Los Angeles premiere who said unequivocally that the score lacked "hit songs." This is a typical example.)[40]

Rome's score for *Fanny* was said to have been better on the second hearing, perhaps a manifestation of Rome's need to fit the song to the book and not worry about an individual song being a hit. Fortunately, the songs of that show advanced the plot and characterization so well that audiences came around to it and gave the show an 888-performance run.

A month later, when *Gone with the Wind* had collapsed, Lester summarized the reactions of the Los Angeles audiences:

> The professionals in general do not like it because they are so reminiscent of the greatness of the picture and the superlative cast.... The less sophisticated theatergoers were definitely taken by the production stunts and the style and we have almost no complaint on the music.[41]

Historian Ken Mandelbaum would say later of the musical: "Of all the movies ever adapted to the musical stage, perhaps none cried out to be left alone as much as *Gone with the Wind*."[42] Like the Los Angeles critics, Rome was much aware of the movie and that it would be used as a measuring stick for the musical, prompting him to request a title change to *Scarlett*, the title in Tokyo. He was particularly worried that the first act of the musical's book followed the movie too closely.[43] The title change back to *Scarlett* was never made.

Negative audience and critic reactions continued into San Francisco. Several songs were added, as evidenced by the above list, and Layton had made attempts to consolidate the action. The critic of the *San Francisco Examiner* had kind words for Lesley Ann Warren as Scarlett and for parts of Layton's staging, but that was about it. He was particularly hard on Rome's score, referring to "pedestrian musical numbers," songs that were "quite pleasant, but none really memorable," with lyrics that were "insipid."[44] The show folded, the rest of the tour was cancelled, and nothing further was mentioned of a Broadway opening. Rome had had high hopes for *Gone with the Wind* and seems to have been particularly upset over its failure. He wrote an open letter to the cast which was posted on the backstage bulletin board expressing his appreciation for their efforts.[45] He wrote to conductor Jay Blackton: "What is there to say at a time like this? It's so sad to see all our efforts and hard work coming to an end. Some day we will get together and reminisce. Right now I am too stunned by the blow to even want to examine what happened and blame anybody."[46]

Like the South after the Civil War, *Gone with the Wind* was to rise once more, in Dallas, Texas. Rome and Horton Foote, along with Kay Brown representing the Mitchell estate, agreed to have Tom Hughes of the Dallas Summer Musicals series present the show.[47] Rhett Butler was to be played by David Canary who, like Pernell Roberts, had played in television's *Bonanza* for several years and possessed a wonderful baritone. The role of Scarlett went to Sherry Mathis. She had much experience with musicals, particularly the Broadway version of *A Little Night Music*. She had been understudy for six different roles in that show and was on stage nearly every night for the eighteen-month run.[48]

With a $250,000 budget, the Dallas *Gone with the Wind* was to be a two-and-a-half-hour production in keeping with the format of the series. Focus was to be placed on Scarlett and the three characters surrounding her: Rhett, Ashley Wilkes, and Melanie Wilkes. New materials were to be written and Rome was to rewrite several lyrics. Meyer Kupferman's original orchestrations from *Scarlett* in Tokyo were to be resurrected.[49] Newspaper advertisements referred to it as "the southwestern premiere of a totally new musical."[50]

Because the show had struggled on the West Coast, Rome was concerned more than ever about its connection to the movie. He wanted songs and plot elements to diverge from the film and he passed on specific ideas about this to Tom Hughes. He was directing the production for the Dallas Summer Musicals organization, which Rome hoped would tour the States and then go on to Broadway. After the Dallas shows, Rome wrote to Hughes: "Right now we have a first act ending which is exactly the same as the ending of the first part of the movie which I think is a distinct handicap and cannot help remind the audience of the climax of the first part of the movie."[51]

Rome then suggested a first act closing number, "O'Hara," from the Japanese production. He explained that the words come mostly from the novel and explain Scarlett's family tree in an entertaining manner. His intention was to have an effective first act closing: "This way it would end on a positive musical note and the audience would go out in intermission not thinking of the movie, I hope, but of how much more fun a musical can be."[52]

Sherry Mathis and David Canary displayed confidence and were also anxious to put the movie behind them. Canary said of his role: "The film and musical we're doing are such completely different entities that there is no temptation for me to imitate Clark Gable.... I'm lousy at imitations anyway."[53] Equally assertive, Mathis stressed: "I am playing Scarlett — not Vivien Leigh."[54]

*Dallas Morning News* critic Harry Bowman was positive about the production and felt it "far superior to the London production," though still flawed. He felt that Rome's songs were "quite successful in catching the period," and singled out "The Lady Is," a song Rome had added for the Dallas production. Most importantly for Rome, no doubt, was Bowman's appreciation of the integrated score: "One may not be able to recall the songs on the way home but they fit neatly into their surroundings inside the theater."[55]

Soon after Dallas, Rome inserted a song into the show, "A Time for Healing." This was a biblical phrase and had been used by the Jimmy Carter presidential campaign as one of its slogans. The country had been adversely affected by the Watergate scandal and subsequent resignation of President Richard Nixon. Rome used the song late in the show, as the Civil War was ending. In the summer of 1976, he offered the song to the Carter campaign but little came of it.[56]

Toward the middle of July in Atlanta on through August in Miami Beach, *Gone with the Wind* limped along with small audiences and tepid reviews. The Miami Beach critic found Rome's lyrics sometimes "maudlin," but at other times "singable ... something of a triumph nowadays."[57] As late as July 30, Rome was still working to maintain show quality. He was particularly upset over the production as it moved into Miami Beach. He complained about an inadequate orchestra, insufficient rehearsals, and a shaky opening night. As always, guarding his score, he told producer-director Hughes: "Every tempo was just a shade fast and kept getting faster. By the time they got to 'Bonnie Gone' it sounded like they were racing after the coffin. There wasn't a moment of relaxation in the whole show."[58]

The end of the run for the show came when it closed in Miami Beach. No further theaters had been booked and no financing could be obtained for a Broadway opening. If *Gone with the Wind* were to continue, the impetus would have to come from Tom Hughes and the Dallas Summer Musicals organization. After productions in Dallas, Kansas City, Atlanta, and Miami Beach and much thinking about the project, Hughes wrote to Rome:

> A part of me is still convinced that there is a "show" and a "great piece of theatre" contained in all of that wonderful material.
>
> However, as I studied the press books and the attendance figures from the four cities, I more and more realized that we are facing almost insurmountable odds. There would always be the film to overcome, and I think we all concur that a major rewrite would again be necessary.[59]

Rome felt the same way and was not surprised at Hughes' conclusions. He thanked him for his "courage and taste to do the project." On a positive note, he felt that good had come from the four-city run: "At least in the process we have restored the show to some of its original form and intent which would have been impossible if you hadn't come along."[60]

In all, the music-dance extravaganza envisioned by Joe Layton had enjoyed raves in Tokyo and a respectable run in London. The score of *Gone with the Wind* was tuneful and had blended well with Layton's staging and choreography. Rome was proud of this and told interviewer Bruce Winston:

> *Gone with the Wind* had more music in its score than any musical written up to its time, including *The Most Happy Fella* and possibly *Porgy and Bess*. It has music going continuously all the way through recalling things, like an interwoven tapestry, going further than any other musical in the use of music to connect a story.[61]

When it came to America, critics and audiences apparently wanted a more typical Broadway musical, and of course, there was always the movie. Rome concluded the story: "We didn't get that good a reception. The critics were a little hurt that we would take a cinema masterpiece and make it into a 'vulgar musical.'"[62]

The longest tryout period for a pre–Broadway musical ended. *Gone with the Wind* never made it to New York.

*Chapter 20*

# Later Years

"The output of this composer-lyricist is highly impressive as well as various; he's one of the most underrated figures of his time." — Robert Gottlieb and Robert Kimball

In March of 1973, Rome was called on to perform *An Evening with Harold Rome* during the third year of the *Lyrics and Lyricists* series presented at the 92nd Street YMCA on Manhattan's Upper West Side. Founded by Maurice Levin under the auspices of the Billy Rose Foundation, *Lyrics and Lyricists* focused on the words of well-known composers of the American Popular Songbook. Also featured during 1973 were Stephen Schwartz, Hal David, John Kander and Fred Ebb, and Carolyn Leigh.[1] The organization also did a show entitled *Stage Door Canteen: Broadway Responds to World War II*. Three of Rome's songs were included: "Victory Symphony, Eight to the Bar" from *Lunchtime Follies* and "Military Life" ("The Jerk Song") and "Little Surplus Me," both from *Call Me Mister*.[2]

In the mid-seventies, Rome worked on *Give My Regards to Broadway and Remember Me to Harold Rome*, a musical of mostly his creation which never made it into production. He did perform some of the songs from this show as part of the *Broadway at the Ballroom* series in New York in 1976. He explained to an interviewer about being approached by a nightclub owner to do the show: "I told him I wasn't a nightclub performer. Then I asked him how much he paid. He said $2,000 a week. I told him, 'I'm a night club performer.'"[3]

One of the songs from the nightclub show was "Pink," a listing of things pink or possibly pink, done with "Jimmy Durante intensity" and described by the composer as "a hell of an operative number."[4] It had been part of a show on which he had worked with Jerome Chodorov and Moss Hart in 1953–54, *In the Pink*. A more representative Rome song for his *Broadway at the Ballroom* stint was "Tobacco — The Redman's Revenge," the scoring of which included coughing. The setting of the song was three Native Americans looking down from Heaven and commenting on smokers and their plight. Rome had written it for *That Was the Week That Was*, a satirical NBC television series that aired in 1964–65. His song was cut during rehearsals because of complaints from a cigarette company sponsor.[5] Rome said of the song: "A funny thing is that when I play it for a group of friends, despite the message, people light up cigarettes right in the middle of it. That's how effective it is!"[6]

This *Ballroom* series allowed Rome to perform his Broadway songs and engage the audience with stories about them. In addition to complimenting Rome's songs and patter, critic John S. Wilson found Rome, who was sixty-eight at the time, to have "weathered the years well."[7] Rome told an interviewer in 1978 about the experience: "I did a week at The Ballroom in New York, and a couple who couldn't have been more than 22 or 24 years old came up and said they had a wonderful time. I realized they'd never heard these songs before."[8]

In August of that year, he did *An Evening of Harold Rome* at the White Barn Theatre in Norwalk, Connecticut. Rome did the same show at the Foreign Correspondents' Club of Japan in December. A year later, the Joseph Jefferson Theatre Company in Manhattan performed *Lyrical and Satirical: The Music of Harold Rome* at the Little Church around the Corner. The title of the show seemed particularly apt and was adopted for the title of this biography. Rome's songs in his early career were mostly satirical in shows like *Pins and Needles*, *Sing Out the News*, and *Call Me Mister*. His talent in that genre of song was on a par with the best songwriters of the day. As the forties closed and the book musical dominated Broadway, his writing became more lyrical or melodic, with shows like *That's the Ticket*, *Wish You Were Here*, and *Fanny*.

Rome continued to showcase his songs and was filmed doing so by a crew from *Camera Three*. This was a regular presentation from 1956 through 1979 by WCBS-TV in New York featuring the performing arts. In 1978, Rome was asked to do "Songs from *Pins and Needles*" for an episode of *Camera Three*. In a small studio, Rome sat at the piano singing occasionally, commenting on many of the songs, and accompanying one female and five male singers. In addition, there were two other piano accompanists, reminiscent of the "orchestra" from the original *Pins and Needles*. Rome was comfortable on camera with a wonderful sense of humor and a tuneful, slightly raspy voice that did justice to his songs. The singers included Elaine Petricoff, David Berman, Daniel Fortus, Tom Offt, and Dennis Perren, while the two additional pianos were played by Philip Campanella and Marc Segan.[9] A videotape of the entire program is available at New York's Paley Center for Media.

Rome continued to look for projects into the late seventies, finding them in a variety of sources, often far-flung. He had long been interested in Jean

Anouilh's 1952 play *La Valse des toreadors*. Like George Bernard Shaw, Anouilh had refused to consent to a musical adaptation of any of his plays. Rome persisted, explaining how he had convinced the French playwright: "I told him, 'Mr. Anouilh, you have to consider the musical as your son. It walks like you, looks like you, has your features, but it has to leave home and have a life of its own.'"[10] Rome finally acquired the rights in 1978 and began writing songs for a show to be called *Waltz of Love*. Seventy at the time, he told interviewer Ernest Leogrande: "I believe in writing about what you know about, and that play is about growing old."[11] Rome could not generate interest from producers or a book writer; *Waltz of Love* was abandoned. From all available records, it appears that this was the last musical he worked on.

As he had most of his life, Rome continued to write classical music into the seventies. For the most part, these were exercises in composition. The Gilmore Library at Yale contains holographic manuscripts of the following compositions, all piano works except the final listing, a string quartet[12]:

| Piano Work | Type of piece | Year |
|---|---|---|
| "Chaconne Sentimentale" | Sketches | 1937 |
| "Dover Beach" | | n.d. |
| "Geneva" | Satirical ballet | 1938 |
| "Passacaglia in E Minor" | | 1937 |
| "Piano Inventions: | | |
| Nos. 1, 2, 4–6 | | n.d. |
| Nos. 8, 10, 11" | | 1946 |
| "Oh Insomnia" | From suite *In America* | n.d. |
| "Piano sketches" | | 1941–77 |
| "Snake in the Parlor" | | n.d. |
| "Sonatas: Nos. 1–5" | | 1944 |
| "Sonatinas: Nos. 1–2" | | 1944 |
| "String Quartet in F Major" | | 1975 |
| "Variations on an Unsuspecting Theme" | | n.d. |

Even in classical works, Rome's sense of humor and satire emerged with titles like "Oh Insomnia" and "Snake in the Parlor." No evidence was found that Rome ever performed these pieces or that any were ever published or printed. In 1970, he also wrote several "Experimental songs" with typical popular song titles: "Just Me," "Land of Might Have Been," and "Guilty." They are also at the Gilmore Music Library.

In 1982, Rome was elected to the Songwriters' Hall of Fame (SHOF) of the National Academy of Popular Music. His recognition came late in his career, over twenty years after his outstanding run of 1950s musicals (*Wish You Were Here*, *Fanny*, and *Destry Rides Again*). This point was not lost on fellow lyricist Howard Dietz: "Lucinda [his wife] and I congratulate you, but we couldn't believe you weren't already in, however you are in brilliantly distinguished company. I couldn't believe you weren't already in until I saw that some of the greatest writers weren't in either. You're all younger, that's what it is!"[13]

Dietz's reference to "some of the greatest writers" referred to those from the early years of the twentieth century, composers of American Popular Song not yet in the SHOF. With their year of inclusion, these overlooked songwriters included Rome, Rube Bloom (1982), Meredith Willson (1982), Ervin Drake (1983), Noël Coward (1988), and Max Steiner (1995). Steiner had made his mark mostly as a film composer. It is of note that candidates for this award were to have been in professional songwriting for at least twenty years, and by this time, Rome had been a songwriter for well over forty-five. Critic Dan O'Leary said of Rome's talent: "In a career that spanned over four decades, Harold Rome managed to combine lyrics that were brilliant without being strained with melodies that were memorable without being derivative. His was a style often characterized as 'ripe for the times.'"[14]

Inducted with Rome into the SHOF in 1982 were Rube Bloom, Bob Dylan, Jerry Herman, Gordon Jenkins, Paul Simon, and Meredith Willson.[15]

An even more distinguished award was given to Rome in 1985. The ASCAP Foundation Richard Rodgers Award recognizes lifetime achievement

Hal David (ASCAP president), Rome, and Dorothy Rodgers at the presentation of the ASCAP Foundation Richard Rodgers Award recognizing lifetime achievement by Broadway composers and lyricists in 1985 (courtesy Gilmore Music Library, Yale University).

by Broadway composers and lyricists. It was established in 1983 by Dorothy Rodgers, Richard's widow. The list of awardees is a who's who of Broadway songwriting[16]:

| Year | Recipient | Year | Recipient | Year | Recipient |
|---|---|---|---|---|---|
| 1983 | Howard Dietz | 1984 | Harold Arlen–Arthur Schwartz | 1985 | Harold Rome |
| 1986 | Jay Gorney | 1987 | Edward Eliscu | 1988 | Jule Styne |
| 1989 | Irving Caesar | 1990 | Hugh Martin–Ralph Blane | 1991 | Burton Lane |
| 1993 | Harvey Schmidt–Tom Jones | 1995 | George Forrest–Robert Wright | 1996 | Marshall Barer |
| 1997 | Betty Comden–Adolph Green | 1998 | Jerry Herman | 1999 | Charles Strouse |
| 2000 | Cy Coleman | 2001 | Richard Adler | 2002 | Stephen Sondheim |
| 2003 | Lee Adams | 2006 | Marvin Hamlisch | 2011 | Stephen Schwartz |

N.B. The award is not given every year, nor is it given posthumously.

Rome's work was also honored by the Drama Desk, a committee made up of New York theater writers, critics, and editors that recognizes achievements in theater of all types, from Broadway to not-for-profit organizations. Since 1976, the Drama Desk Special Awards have brought to light the work of individuals, groups, and institutions that have advanced theater in America. In 1991, Rome received the award for "his distinctive contribution to musical theater."[17] Like the Richard Rodgers Award, this one is given to artists still living. Other Broadway composers who have received it include Jule Styne, John Kander, and Fred Ebb. In the same year, Rome was inducted into the Theater Hall of Fame. This was founded in 1971 to honor contributors to theater in all areas of expertise. The committee is made up of theater historians, members of the Hall of Fame, and members of the American Theatre Critics Association. There are over 400 Theater Hall of Fame members and the name of each member is inscribed in gold letters on the walls of the upper rotunda of the Gershwin Theatre on 51st Street.[18]

It was most fitting that Rome received the Theater Hall of Fame induction. He was, more than anything, a real theater man. On his shows, he was credited only as composer and lyricist, but he usually contributed to shows in numerous ways. In his early revues, he was involved with writing of the sketches and coordinating them with his songs. Although it is little documented, it can be presumed that he was closely involved with the writing of the books of all his musicals. Most of the composers were, especially the lyricists; Cole Porter may be considered an exception to this. Rome worked with several experienced literary people and/or book writers: George S. Kaufman, Moss Hart, Julius and Philip Epstein, Arthur Kober, Joshua Logan, and

Jerome Weidman. He was quick to respect a fellow artist, but would just as quickly stand up to them if he didn't think the book and score were jelling.

Rome was friends with numerous theater people and among his closest were Jerome Chodorov, Vernon Duke, Lehman Engel, Moss Hart, Joshua Logan, Paul Osborn, Richard Rodgers, and Jerome Weidman. When he created shows, he often had friends critique them and was open to suggestions. He and Lehman Engel were well aware of this comradeship in the theater which Rome expressed during their interview:

> I'll tell you the nice thing about the theater, Lehman. When you're out of town, if you have friends they come down and they do anything for you. Moss Hart came down to *Destry Rides Again*. I came down to *My Fair Lady*. Anything that we could possibly do, we did....
>
> When you're in trouble, if you have friends they are there to help you and they're there because they want to help you, not for any other reason. That I'm sure isn't true in TV or any other place.[19]

Although he doesn't single it out, Rome was no doubt referring to Hollywood and the film industry in his last comment. Fortunately for Rome, most of his friendships were of the theater and lasted lifetimes. Well into his eighties, he was still playing gin rummy with a few of them. By the time of his retirement, Harold and Florence Rome had moved to 69th Street. He died from complications of a stroke on October 26, 1993, at age 85. He was survived by Florence, children Joshua and Rachel, and two grandchildren.

\* \* \*

An argument could be made that Harold Rome "got no respect." It is of interest to note his absence in various mentions of theater composers over the years. In *The History of the North American Theater*, authors Londre and Watermeier discuss Broadway musicals of the fifties and sixties, listing the notable hits. To have *Fanny* go unmentioned in such a list is difficult to understand.[20] In another history, *Making Americans: Jews and the Broadway Musical*, Rome's name is omitted from a list of Jewish-American musical theater writers. The list includes[21]:

| | | |
|---|---|---|
| Richard Adler | Irving Berlin | Leonard Bernstein |
| Jerry Bock | Eddie Cantor | Betty Comden |
| Dorothy Fields | Herb Fields | George Gershwin |
| Ira Gershwin | Adolph Green | Oscar Hammerstein II |
| E.Y. Harburg | Sheldon Harnick | Lorenz Hart |
| Moss Hart | George S. Kaufman | Jerome Kern |
| Alan Jay Lerner | Frank Loesser | Frederick Loewe |
| Richard Rodgers | Jerry Ross | Stephen Sondheim |
| Kurt Weill | | |

It should be noted that the songwriting team of John Kander and Fred Ebb, both Jewish, was also omitted.[22] Their biographer, James Leve, summarized a major thesis of *Making Americans*: "Andrea Most views the history of Jewish acculturation in America and the development of the musical as intertwined and inextricable from each other. Jewish writers, Most claims, negotiated their concerns about race and ethnicity through the musical theater genre."[23]

Rome, as much as anyone on the list, addressed race and ethnicity in his shows. *Pins and Needles* was a revue about, for, and by the ILGWU, a union with a high percentage of Jewish members. David Dubinsky, a well-known Jewish labor leader, was its president. "Chain Store Daisy" and "It's Better with a Union Man" were songs with ethnic subtexts to them. This was 1938, long before many of the popular songwriters would address such issues. Two years later, in *Sing Out the News*, he fashioned a song for a Harlem block party celebrating the birth of a baby boy in "Franklin D. Roosevelt Jones."

In 1952, Rome along with Arthur Kober, wrote *Wish You Were Here*. This musical focused on the adult summer camps of upstate New York, "greatly fancied by people of Russian or Polish antecedents, who, each summer flock by the thousands into the Catskills where there are literally hundreds of lodges, camps and resorts which cater to this particular clientele."[24] As cited earlier: "Rome was the ideal songwriter for this milieu; he had virtually grown up with the characters."[25]

Rome's third ethnic musical was *I Can Get It for You Wholesale*, again dealing with the garment trade but from a management perspective. It featured a heel as a protagonist — Harry Bogen — whom Rome described to David Dubinsky as "a Jewish boy from the Bronx who goes wrong."[26] With *Wholesale*, Rome made no apologies and wrote songs to match the hard-bitten novel and libretto of Jerome Weidman. Joshua Rome felt it was the musical that best fit his father's persona.[27] *Wholesale* songs with a definite Jewish flavor included:

| | |
|---|---|
| "Ballad of the Garment Trade" | "Eat a Little Something" |
| "The Family Way" | "A Gift Today" |
| "Miss Marmelstein" | "Momma, Momma, Momma" |

This last ethnic musical of Rome's was joined in the early sixties by others with a similar focus, including *Milk and Honey* (1961), *Fiddler on the Roof* (1964), and *What Makes Sammy Run?* (1964). *Fiddler on the Roof* director Jerome Robbins did not want it to appear too ethnic, focusing on family and people's responses to change. As director Harold Prince said: "The show was a success because for non–Jews it wasn't Jewish; it was about family."[28] The same could be said of *Wholesale*, with climactic scenes played between Harry Bogen and his mother, more family but still ethnic.

In his biography of Jerry Bock and Sheldon Harnick, *To Broadway, to Life!*, Philip Lambert cites several dramas and musicals that emerged in the sixties that succeeded with "realism and style in the portrayal of Jewish themes and characters."[29] His list includes:

| Show | Year | Composer(s) |
|---|---|---|
| Gideon* | 1961 | Paddy Chayefsky* |
| Milk and Honey | 1961 | Jerry Herman |
| A Family Affair | 1962 | John Kander–William Goldman |
| Seidman and Son* | 1962 | Elick Moll* |
| I Can Get It for You Wholesale | 1962 | Harold Rome–Jerome Weidman |
| Funny Girl | 1964 | Jule Styne–Bob Merrill |

*Denotes drama and dramatist

Any list of Jewish-American Broadway musical theater writers has to include Harold Rome.

In a similar vein, historian Ethan Mordden discusses New York City musical comedies in his *Beautiful Mornin': The Broadway Musical in the 1940's*, citing *On the Town* as the quintessential New York musical comedy. Mordden goes on to mention what he refers to as "just urban shows using a bit of New York flavor": *Irene, Good Boy, Face the Music, One Touch of Venus, Street Scene, Bells are Ringing, Promises, Promises, Annie,* and *The Life*. He ignores Rome's *I Can Get It for You Wholesale*, a show about as New York as it gets.[30] Also passing Rome by was recognition of him as a songwriter — words and music — in the pantheon of the best songwriters. Those who wrote both were uncommon, the most prominent among them being Irving Berlin, Cole Porter, Frank Loesser, and Stephen Sondheim. Historian David Lehman in *A Fine Romance* mentions only the first three and omits both Rome and Sondheim, including them as among "a very few others" who wrote words and music.[31]

\* \* \*

How songs are written has long been a topic of discussion, summarized by the question: "What comes first, the words or the music?" Each team of songwriters worked differently; there was no set formula. Jerome Kern insisted on writing the music first, then turning it over to his collaborator. Richard Rodgers was more malleable. Out of necessity, he would write the melody first, then attempt to corner Lorenz Hart long enough to put down a lyric. When Rodgers switched partners in the early forties to Oscar Hammerstein II, the order was reversed. Hammerstein preferred to set a lyric, then give it to Rodgers, whose facile mind could produce melodies at a fast pace when he was given a phrase or a rhythmic pattern from which to work. Lyricist Leo Robin, who wrote *Gentlemen Prefer Blondes* with Jule Styne, corroborated all this. Robin said, "The music guys could write a lot faster that the word guys." As for Rodgers, he could "write a number ... between dessert and port."[32]

When poet Langston Hughes began his work with Kurt Weill on *Street Scene*, he was eager to please his distinguished collaborator. Within a week of signing his contract, he provided Weill with a dozen or so lyrics. A week later, he sent fourteen more. This was all to Weill's liking as he always preferred the words first.[33] Jule Styne, another prolific melodist, provided a melody for Sammy Cahn. He explained:

> Now let me try to explain what my lyric writing is about. First, I am not sure what brings about an instant title when I hear a melody, but it seldom if ever fails me — a title flashes into my head.... What I do is sort of trigger it with the title and then follow wherever it leads.[34]

As for composer-lyricists, they generally wrote words and music simultaneously, polishing both sides after the majority of the song was written. Rome expanded on this: "Sometimes I get a phrase of music first. Sometimes I get a lyric phrase, but most often it's a lyric phrase. Since I write both music and lyrics, I have found my own way to work, and usually I work on both of them at the same time."[35] He was an enthusiastic worker, whether composing or painting. After breakfast and the papers, he would toil in his apartment for most of the morning, usually at the piano, putting together his words and music. His attitude for whatever he did was encapsulated by what he told reporter John Mahoney of the *Los Angeles Times* regarding songwriting: "When you are working on a new song, you have to feel that it is the greatest one you have ever written. If you don't feel that way, you should throw it away."[36]

Rome came to the art of songwriting later than many of the biggest names, but he evolved as they had, from revue to musical comedy to book musicals. He was viewed neither as an innovator nor an imitator; but like most of the successful composers and lyricists, he had his own style and voice. Theater caricaturist and observer Al Hirschfeld said of his friend: "I thought Hecky was unique. He didn't fit into the categories of the composer-lyricist field. He invented himself actually. I wouldn't know how to place him."[37]

Rome felt that his songs and scores were overlooked by critics and recording artists. Bruce F. Winston discussed this issue with Rome during an interview and in a long piece on the web:

> [T]here was evidence given by Mr. Rome's comments that although he was proud of the outcome of his numerous musical efforts through the years ... that his songs, in general, were not sung nearly enough by popular recording artists and that critics did not frequently understand or sufficiently appreciate the approach he took in writing.[38]

Rome's best score was *Fanny*, which for some was an acquired taste. People seeing it a second time appreciated it more. Part of this was due to Rome's belief that a song should fit within the libretto and advance character and plot. He told an interviewer in 1971: "The all-important thing about songs is the idea itself. It doesn't matter how good the music is.... If a song is communicating with the people who hear it, it transmits a mood or expression of something, an opinion or feeling about something."[39]

The corollary to this was that the songwriter not be concerned whether he was writing a hit or not. Numerous composers could do both — write a well-adapted song that achieved hit status. Irving Berlin focused not on shows, but on the songs from those shows, a practice Rome was critical of, particularly in Berlin's *Louisiana Purchase*.[40] To Rome, hits with no context made for a bad show, although his admiration for Berlin was immense. Ethan Mordden put Berlin beyond category: "Unlike all his songwriting colleagues in the Golden Age, Berlin alone kept open a pop shop. Yes, he wrote for both Broadway and Hollywood, but what he mainly did was write songs.... The other guys wrote shows; Berlin wrote music."[41] Rome said of all this: "I have never deliberately set out to write a hit song, with the single exception of 'All of a Sudden My Heart Sings,' which I wrote on a dare."[42]

As he got older and was interviewed and spoke at symposiums, Rome stressed the need for communication with an audience. He emphasized that the music and especially words should resonate with listeners, not only within the context of the musical but also within their lives. His first hit, *Pins and Needles*, was exemplary of this as his songs appealed especially to the early audiences — the ILGWU members. Eight years later, the same phenomenon occurred with *Call Me Mister*, as thousands of returning servicemen and women roared at Rome's view of military life and the civilian world they would be facing. For both shows, the early viewers set the tone, but more general audiences caught on as well as Rome made sure that they got the joke or caught the emotion of a song. He said: "In the theater, verbal communication is all-important. Your audience has to understand what the song is saying, and has to be with it. You stand in the back of the theater; you hear them coughing. You know that you're not getting across."[43] In his interview with Lehman Engel, the two frequent collaborators embellished on this idea as they concluded:

> Rome: The whole thing that I think people forget and composers and writers forget is that in the theater there's one key note, that's instant communication.... And writers forget that. And especially new writers forget. They say, "Look at this beautiful counter melody." What they forget is that the only thing that counts is what the audience hears and understands.

Engel: And reacts to.
Rome: And if they don't, no matter how good it is, they may have written a cantata better than Bach, if it doesn't help the show and the audience doesn't get it, you are in great trouble.
Engel: Of course, always that audience communication. The audience tells you and you better listen.[44]

Rome's best songs are of great variety, uniqueness, and communication with his audience:

| Song | Source | Song | Source |
| --- | --- | --- | --- |
| "(All of a Sudden) My Heart Sings" | Anchors Aweigh[M] | "Anyone Would Love You" | Destry Rides Again |
| "Be Kind to Your Parents" | Fanny | "Call Me Mister" | Call Me Mister |
| "Certain Individuals" | Wish You Were Here | "Don't Wanna Write About the South" | Bless You All |
| "Dost Thou" | That's the Ticket! | "Fanny" | Fanny |
| "Franklin D. Roosevelt Jones" | Sing Out the News | "Have I Told You Lately?" | I Can Get It for You Wholesale |
| "I Have to Tell You" | Fanny | "I Say Hello" | Destry Rides Again |
| "Love Is a Very Light Thing" | Fanny | "Love Is Still Love" | That's the Ticket! |
| "Mene, Mene Tekel" | Pins and Needles | "Miss Marmelstein" | I Can Get It for You Wholesale |
| "The Money Song" | That's the Ticket! | "Nobody Makes a Pass at Me" | Pins and Needles |
| "Pocketful of Dreams" | That the Ticket! | "Restless Heart" | Fanny |
| "Sing Me a Song with Social Significance" | Pins and Needles | "South America, Take It Away" | Call Me Mister |
| "Sunday in the Park" | Pins and Needles | "Take Off the Coat" | That's the Ticket! |
| "To My Wife" | Fanny | "Wish You Were Here" | Wish You Were Here |
| "You Never Know What Hit You (When It's Love)" | That's the Ticket! | | |

M — movie. All other sources listed are musicals.

These songs cover a wide range of melodies, rhythms, and lyrics. In 1941, *Chicago Daily Tribune* writer Cecil Smith said that Rome seldom pushed musical forms in his songwriting, adhering to the popular sixteen- or thirty-two–bar choruses with four-measure musical sentences. Smith added: "His rhythmic patterns are borrowed from ragtime, Charleston, rumba, Gilbert and Sullivan — whenever an appropriate model comes to hand."[45] Smith was positive towards Rome's songwriting and declared: "If a visitor from another country were interested in discovering the typical nature of good American show music, I should send him to Harold Rome..."[46] Of his own music at the time, Rome said: "I can't imagine why anyone should want to study my music. I just think of it as show music, and if it works with an audience, it is good. There is nothing to analyze or to take particularly seriously in any of it."[47]

Rome's songs improved from show to show. Starting with *Pins and Needles*, the strength of Rome's songs was more in the lyrics than the music. His lyrics continued to improve but with *That's the Ticket!* in 1948, his melodies in songs like "Dost Thou," "Love Is Still Love," and "Take Off the Coat" took a leap forward. By the time he worked with Joshua Logan in the early fifties, the director would say: "It is my prediction that in the years to come, he will be known chiefly for his music, and his lyrics, though they will remain as good as they are now, and perhaps even improve, will take second place to his gifts in the musical field of our theater."[48]

Rome himself thought his scores were "increasingly sophisticated."[49] Musical historians Robert Gottlieb and Robert Kimball summed Rome up well in their *Reading Lyrics*: "The output of this composer/lyricist is highly impressive as well as various; he's one of the most underrated figures of his time."[50]

# Appendices

## A. Chronology

5/27/1908 — Born Harold Jacob Rome in Hartford, Connecticut, father Louis Rome, owner of the Connecticut Coal and Charcoal Company, and mother Ida (Aronson).

1913–24 — Begins piano at age seven and writes a song for war bonds at age ten. Joins local musicians' union in Hartford as a teenager, playing piano in dance bands. Attends Hartford public schools, graduating from high school in 1924.

1927 — Begins college in Hartford at Trinity College, then transfers to Yale, studying liberal arts, and soon begins working as pianist for Eddie Wittstein's band.

1929 — Receives bachelor of arts degree from Yale, earning money during school writing arrangements for dance bands and playing piano; also plays in the University Orchestra, making four trips to Europe with it.

1934 — Graduates from the Yale School of Architecture with a B.F.A., working first for the Works Progress Administration and then for a New York architectural firm.

1935 — Begins a three-year summer stint at Green Mansions adult summer camp writing and producing shows and composing over 100 songs during this time.

11/27/1937 — *Pins and Needles* opens, a revue written for the International Ladies' Garment Workers' Union with songs by Rome, most notably "Sunday in the Park."

1937–38 — Becomes involved with Cabaret TAC, a political cabaret developed by the Theatre Arts Council, writing "One Big Union for Two" for these shows.

9/24/1938 — *Sing Out the News* opens at the Music Box Theatre, with words and music by Rome, runs only 105 performances, but includes the popular "F.D.R. Jones."

2/03/1939 — Marries Florence Miles, a radio advertising writer from Chicago.

4/24/1939 — *Sing for Your Supper* opens, a WPA Federal Theatre project, to which Rome contributes "Papa's Got a Job." The show closes after 60 performances.

6/19/1939 — Jimmy McHugh's *Streets of Paris* opens, runs six months. Rome's song, "The French Have a Word for It," is sung by Carmen Miranda in the finale.

1939 — Rome's hit is renamed *Pins and Needles 1939*, then is moved to the Windsor Theater and again renamed, this time as *New Pins and Needles*.
Writes patriotic song "We Sing America" and a political one, "Who's Gonna Investigate the Man Who Investigates Me?"

6/22/1940 — *New Pins and Needles* closes after 1,108 performances, the record for a Broadway musical, later to be broken by *Oklahoma!*

8/13/1940 — Rome's first book musical, *The Little Dog Laughed*, opens in Atlantic City and closes in Boston, eleven days later.

4/07/1942 — Writes sketches and songs for *Gratefully Yours*, a benefit for the American Theatre Wing War Service and British Ambulance Corps.

1942–43 — Writes sketches and songs for a series of revues, *Lunchtime Follies*, designed to provide entertainment for defense plant employees.

6/24/1942 — Writes "The Bunny" for a Broadway burlesque revue, *Star and Garter* (produced by Michael Todd), which runs 609 performances.

10/05/1942 — Writes song for a Youth Theatre revue, *Let Freedom Ring*, a commercial flop.
Writes the lyrics to "The Song of Meeting," movie music of Dmitri Shostakovich, re-titled "The United Nations March" and used at patriotic rallies.

1943 — Inducted into the army, first stationed at the New York Port of Embarkation in Special Services, then in an entertainment unit at Fort Hamilton, Brooklyn. *Stars and Gripes*, songs by Rome, plays stateside then extensively overseas.
Works with composer Vernon Duke on *Nantucket* which never gets produced.

4/01/1943 — Contributes songs to revue *Ziegfeld Follies of 1943*, runs 553 performances; his song, "The Micromaniac," is sung by star Milton Berle.

1944 — Composes songs along with Army Private Frank Loesser for the U.S. 8th Air Force production of *Skirts*, which plays in London.

1945 — Writes lyrics for "(All of a Sudden) My Heart Sings," a French song adapted for the movie *Anchors Aweigh*, sung by Kathryn Grayson.

3/19/1946 — Receives U.S. Treasury's Silver Medal for substantial contributions in radio to the War Finances Division through various war bond drives.

4/18/1946 — *Call Me Mister* opens, entire score by Rome, drawing its talent from the armed forces with hit song "South America, Take It Away" sung by Betty Garrett.

1/10/1948 — *Call Me Mister* closes after 734 performances.

9/24/1948 — Another social commentary, *That's the Ticket*, opens in Philadelphia but lasts only ten days despite one of Rome's best scores.

Summer 1949 — *Pretty Penny* plays regional theaters on the East Coast but never Broadway.

1950 — Contributes songs to two revues, *Alive and Kicking* and *Michael Todd's Peep Show;* the latter includes "Pocketful of Dreams" and runs 278 performances.
Listed in *Red Channels*, an anti-communist, right wing publication targeted at artists involved in radio and theater.

## A. Chronology

12/14/1950 — *Bless You All* opens, produced by Michael Todd, with the showstopper "You Never Know What Hit You" introduced by Pearl Bailey.

1951 — *Call Me Mister* made into movie starring Betty Grable and Dan Dailey with much different plot and limited use of Rome's songs.

6/25/1952 — *Wish You Were Here* opens, based on Arthur Kobel's play *Having Wonderful Time*, runs 598 performances; title song becomes hit for Eddie Fisher on *Your Hit Parade* for fifteen weeks.

1953 — Florence and Harold Rome adopt two children, Joshua and Rachel.

1954 — Writes words to "Lisa" with Franz Waxman's music for theme used in *Rear Window*, Alfred Hitchcock thriller with James Stewart and Grace Kelly.

11/04/1954 — *Fanny* opens, an adaptation of a French novel of the same name by Marcel Pagnol; title song becomes another hit for Eddie Fisher.

7/18/1955 — Purchases cooperative apartment in Manhattan, at 1035 Fifth Ave., at 85th Street, after living on Central Park West for over ten years.

12/16/1956 — *Fanny* closes after 888 performances.

April /1957 — Admitted to Yale Club of New York.

10/10/1957 — Contributes incidental music for *Romanoff and Juliet* which stars Peter Ustinov and runs 389 performances.

4/23/1959 — *Destry Rides Again* opens, derived from a well-known Western movie, and stars Andy Griffith and Dolores Gray, closing after 472 performances.

1961 — Movie made of *Fanny* but songs are dropped by director Joshua Logan and used only as background music, much to Rome's displeasure.

3/22/1962 — Opening of *I Can Get It for You Wholesale*, a show which deals with the garment trade and features the Broadway debut of Barbra Streisand.

11/10/1964 — Exhibits forty of his paintings at the Marble Arch Gallery in New York, including *Harold Rome's Gallery*, one dozen paintings each accompanied by a song.

11/10/1965 — *The Zulu and the Zayda* opens with cross-cultural themes, runs 179 performances.

12/14/1965 — *La Grosse Valise*, a French revue, opens but lasts only a week.

1/02/1970 — *Scarlett*, based on *Gone with the Wind*, opens in Tokyo with a Japanese cast.

5/03/1972 — *Scarlett* is rewritten, becomes *Gone with the Wind*, and opens at the Drury Lane Theater in London.

8/28/1973 — *Gone with the Wind* is produced in Los Angeles, tours the States in various productions, but never makes it to Broadway.

December 1977 — *Lyrical and Satirical: The Music of Harold Rome*, produced by Joseph Jefferson Theater Company, opens at the Little Church around the Corner in Manhattan.

3/15/1982 — Election to the Songwriters' Hall of Fame.

1985 — Receives ASCAP's Richard Rodgers Award.

circa 1988 — Move to cooperative apartment on the Upper East Side (69th Street).

1991— Receives Drama Desk Special Award for "distinctive contribution to musical theater." Elected to the Theater Hall of Fame.
10/26/1993 — Dies in his home in Manhattan from complications of a stroke, survived by his wife Florence, children Joshua and Rachel, and two grandchildren.

# B. Songs

| Song | Year | From[1] | Collaborator |
|---|---|---|---|
| "The Advertising Song" ("I Believe!") | 1943 | Ziegfeld Follies of 1943 | |
| "Ah Ah Ah Ah" ("The Songs That Haunts My Heart")[2] | | | Raymond Asso[U] Marguerite Monnot[U] Harold Rome[L-English] |
| "All GI's Got Rights" | 1943 | Army orientation program | |
| "(All of a Sudden) My Heart Sings" ("Ma Mie") | 1945 | Anchors Aweigh[F] | Henri Herpin[M] Jean Marie Blanvillain[L-French] Harold Rome[L-English] |
| "Alone" | 1943 | Nantucket[7] | |
| "Along with Me" | 1946 | Call Me Mister | |
| "Anthem of the Union of Soviet Social Republics" (aka "Hymn of the...") | 1944 | War programs | A.V. Aleksandrov[M] Sergei Mihalkov & El-Registan[L-Russian] Harold Rome[L-English] |
| "Anyone Would Love You" | 1959 | Destry Rides Again | |
| "Anything" | 1950 | The Sing Song Man[9] | |
| "Arab Song" | 1954 | Fanny | |
| "Are You Ready, Gyp Watson?" | 1959 | Destry Rides Again | |
| "The Army Service Forces" | 1944 | Stars and Gripes | |
| "Arouse, Arouse!" | 1968 | Eugene McCarthy Campaign | |
| "Art in the Night" | 1964 | Harold Rome's Gallery[Art] | |
| "Ashley's Departure" | 1970 | Gone with the Wind[10] | |
| "Ask Me" | | | Joseph Bovet[U] Harold Rome[U] |
| "Atlanta Burning" | 1970 | Gone with the Wind[10] | |
| "The Audience" | 1964 | Harold Rome's Gallery[Art] | |
| "Aye Aye Aye" | 1965 | The Zulu and the Zayda | |
| "Back to Work" | 1939 | Pins and Needles | |
| "(Ballad of a) Social Director" | 1952 | Wish You Were Here | |
| "The Ballad of Marcia LaRue" | 1948 | That's the Ticket! | |
| "The Ballad of Sloppy Joe" ("Flippy, Floppy, Mopey, Dopey, Sloppy Joe") | 1943 | Lunchtime Follies | |

## B. Songs

| Song | Year | From[1] | Collaborator |
|---|---|---|---|
| "Ballad of the Garment Trade" | 1962 | *I Can Get It for You Wholesale* | |
| "Ballad of the Gun" | 1959 | *Destry Rides Again* | |
| "Bazaar Hymn" | 1970 | *Gone with the Wind*[10] | |
| "Be a Folk Singer" | 1950 | *Bless You All* | |
| "Be Calm" | 1942 | *Let Freedom Sing* | |
| "Be Kind to Your Parents" | 1954 | *Fanny* | |
| "Because I'm So in Love" | 1951 | *The Mating Season*[F] | |
| "A Big One" | 1965 | *La Grosse Valise* | Gerard Calvi[8] |
| "Birthday Song" | 1954 | *Fanny* | |
| "Bless You All" | 1950 | *Bless You All* | |
| "The Blind Mice" | 1938 | Cabaret TAC[3] | |
| "Blissful Christmas" | 1970 | *Gone with the Wind*[10] | |
| "Blueberry Eyes" | 1970 | *Gone with the Wind*[10] | |
| "Bonnie Blue Flag" | 1970 | *Gone with the Wind*[10] | |
| "Bonnie Gone" | 1970 | *Gone with the Wind*[10] | |
| "Boombah" | | | |
| "Bottleneck" | 1959 | *Destry Rides Again* | |
| "The Boy Rangers Song" | | | |
| "Brand New Friends" | 1970 | *Gone with the Wind*[10] | |
| "Bright College Days" | 1952 | *Wish You Were Here* | |
| "Bunny, Bunny, Bunny" ("The Bunny") | 1942 | *Star and Garter* | |
| "Burlesque" | | *Opus — New York* | |
| "C'est Defendu" ("It's Forbidden") | 1965 | *La Grosse Valise* | Gerard Calvi[8] |
| "Cakewalk" | 1970 | *Gone with the Wind*[10] | |
| "Call Me Mister" | 1946 | *Call Me Mister* | |
| "Camp Karefree" | 1952 | *Wish You Were Here* | |
| "Campaign Song" | 1948 | *That's the Ticket!* | |
| "Certain Individuals" | 1952 | *Wish You Were Here* | |
| "Cesario's Party" ("Cirque Francais") | 1954 | *Fanny* | |
| "Chain Store Daisy" ("Vassar Girl Finds Job") | 1937 | *Pins and Needles* | |
| "Clank! Clank!" | 1948 | *That's the Ticket!* | |
| "Clip Clop Song" ("Le Fiacre") ("The Cab Song") | 1942 | | Leon Xandroff[M/L] Harold Rome[L-English] |
| "Cold Cream Jar Song" | 1954 | *Fanny* | |
| "Color Blind" | | | |
| "Congressional Minstrels" | 1938 | *Sing Out the News* | |
| "Could Be" | 1952 | *Wish You Were Here* | |
| "Couplet for Alfred" | 1948 | *That's the Ticket!* | |
| "The Crazy Song" | 1950 | *The Sing Song Man*[9] | |
| "Cream of Mush Song" | 1937 | *Pins and Needles* | |
| "Creative Thirties" | | | |
| "The Critics" | 1960 | *Harold Rome's Gallery*[Art] | |
| "Crocodile Wife" | 1965 | *The Zulu and the Zayda* | |
| "Cry, Baby" | 1948 | *That's the Ticket!* | |
| | 1949 | *Pretty Penny* | |
| | 1950 | *Alive and Kicking* | |

| Song | Year | From[1] | Collaborator |
|---|---|---|---|
| "Dance with Me" ("Danse avec moi") | 1954 | *The Last Time I Saw Paris*[F] | Frances Lopez[M] Andre Hornez[L-French] Harold Rome[L-English] |
| "Dancing with You" | 1950 | | |
| "Day Dream" | | | |
| "Dear Joe" | 1943 | *Lunchtime Follies* | |
| "Decca Blues" | | | |
| "Delilah Done Me Wrong" ("The No Haircut Song") | 1965 | *La Grosse Valise* | Gerard Calvi[8] |
| "Desert Flame" | 1950 | *Bless You All* | |
| "A Determined Woman" | 1948 | *That's the Ticket!* | |
| "Diddle Daddle" | 1943 | *Nantucket*[7] | |
| "Do a Favor for Adolf, Please" | 1943 | Army orientation program | |
| "Do You Know a Better Way to Make a Living?" | 1950 | *Bless You All* | |
| "Doing the Reactionary" | 1937 | *Pins and Needles* | |
| "Don Jose of Far Rockaway" | 1952 | *Wish You Were Here* | |
| "Don't Wanna Write about the South" | 1950 | *Bless You All* | |
| "Dost Thou" | 1948 | *That's the Ticket!* | |
| "Dream Express" | | | David Kapp[U] Harold Rome[U] |
| "The Drugstore Song" | 1946 | *Call Me Mister* | |
| "Easy Does It" | 1940 | *The Little Dog Laughed* | |
| "Eat a Little Something" | 1962 | *I Can Get It for You Wholesale* | |
| "Eating Is Such Fun" | | | |
| "Economics I" | 1937 | *Pins and Needles* | |
| "Enlloro" | 1944 | *Hollywood Canteen*[F] | Obdulio Morales[4] Julio Blanco[4] |
| "Entre Nous" | 1938 | *Sing Out the News* | |
| "Every Once in a While" | 1959 | *Destry Rides Again* | |
| "Everybody Love Everybody" | 1952 | *Wish You Were Here* | |
| "Everything Happens to Me" | 1943 | *Stars and Gripes* | |
| "Fa-La-La" | 1948 | *That's the Ticket!* | |
| "The Face on the Dime" | 1946 | *Call Me Mister* | |
| "The Fair Sex" | 1948 | *That's the Ticket!* | |
| "Fair Warning" | 1959 | *Destry Rides Again* | |
| "The Fairy Tales Are All Untrue" | 1940 | *The Little Dog Laughed* | |
| "The Family Way" | 1962 | *I Can Get It for You Wholesale* | |
| "Fanny" | 1954 | *Fanny* | |
| "First Impression" | 1937 | *Pins and Needles* | Charles Friedman[L] Harold Rome[M & L] |
| "First Tuesday" | | | |
| "Flattery" | 1952 | *Wish You Were Here* | |
| "Floradora" | 1938 | *Sing Out the News* | |
| "For Charity, Sweet Charity" ("I'm Doing It for Charity") | 1936 | Specialty number for Gypsy Rose Lee | |
| "For You" | 1965 | *La Grosse Valise* | Gerard Calvi[8] |

## B. Songs

| Song | Year | From[1] | Collaborator |
|---|---|---|---|
| "Forward" ("Song of the Red Army Tank Parade") | 1943 | War programs | Dan Pokrass[M] Dimitri Pokrass[M] Harold Rome[L] |
| "Four Little Angels of Peace" | 1938 | *Pins and Needles* | |
| "Franklin D. Roosevelt Jones" ("Man of the Year") | 1938 | *Sing Out the News* | |
| "Franklin D.–Winston C.–Joseph S. Victory March" | 1942 | War programs | |
| "The French Have a Word for It" | 1939 | *Streets of Paris* | |
| "French with Tears" | 1949 | *Pretty Penny* | |
| | 1950 | *Alive and Kicking* | |
| "A Friend of Mine, a Hero" | 1940 | *The Little Dog Laughed* | |
| "A Funny Thing Happened" ("On My Way to Love") | 1962 | *I Can Get It for You Wholesale* | |
| "The Galloping Comedians" | | | Dimitri Kabalevzky[M] Harold Rome[L] |
| "Gambling Man" | 1970 | *Gone with the Wind*[10] | |
| "Gee, But It's Cold in Russia" | 1942 | *Lunchtime Follies* | |
| "The General Unveiled" ("A Satirical Ballet") | 1937 | *Pins and Needles* | |
| "Geneva" | | | |
| "Giddy Ap" | | | Marcel Bertrou[U] Francisco Lopez[U] Louis Poterat[U] Harold Rome[U] |
| "A Gift Today" ("The Bar Mitzvah Song") | 1962 | *I Can Get It for You Wholesale* | |
| "Gigolette" | 1952 | | Virgilio Panzutti[U] Giancarlo Testoni[U] Harold Rome[U] |
| "Gimme the Shimmy" | 1950 | *Michael Todd's Peep Show* | |
| "Gin Rummy Rhapsody" | 1948 | *That's the Ticket!* | |
| "The Girl That Waits for Me" | | | |
| "Give a Viva!" | 1942 | *Let Freedom Sing* | |
| "Glimpse of Love" | 1952 | *Wish You Were Here* | |
| "Go to Hell Congress" | | | |
| "Goin' Home Train" | 1946 | *Call Me Mister* | |
| "Gone with the Revolution" | 1938 | *Sing Out the News* | |
| "Gone with the Wind" | 1970 | *Gone with the Wind*[10] | |
| "Good Little Girls" | 1938 | Cabaret TAC[3] | |
| "Goodbye Darling, Hello Friend" | 1951 | | Maurice Chevalier[U] Friedrich Goldbaum[U] Harold Rome[L-English] |
| "Goodbye Love" | 1952 | *Wish You Were Here* | |
| "Goodbye My Honey" | 1970 | *Gone with the Wind*[10] | |
| "The Goodnight Song" | 1950 | *The Sing Song Man*[9] | |
| "Grab Them While You Can" | | | |
| "The Gripers" | 1943 | Army orientation program | |

## B. Songs

| Song | Year | From[1] | Collaborator |
|---|---|---|---|
| "A Guitar Serenade" | | | Franz Funk[M] |
| | | | Harold Rome[L] |
| "Hail Yale '29" | | | |
| "Half-Forgotten Teddy Bear" | 1964 | Harold Rome's Gallery[Art] | |
| "Hamburg Waltz" | 1965 | La Grosse Valise | Gerard Calvi[8] |
| "Handy Thing" | | | |
| "Happily Ever After" | 1940 | The Little Dog Laughed | |
| "Happy Song" | 1965 | La Grosse Valise | Gerard Calvi[8] |
| "The Harmony Boys" | 1939 | Pins and Needles | |
| "Have I Told You Lately?" | 1962 | I Can Get It for You Wholesale | |
| "Hawaii" | 1965 | La Grosse Valise | Gerard Calvi[8] |
| "He Loves Me" | 1970 | Gone with the Wind[10] | |
| "Heigh Ho" | | | |
| "Henry" | 1965 | The Southpaw | |
| "His Old Man" | 1946 | Call Me Mister | |
| "History Eight to the Bar" | 1942 | Let Freedom Sing | |
| "History Is Made at Night" | 1939 | Streets of Paris | |
| "Holding Hands" ("J'ai ta Main") | | | Raoul Breton[U] |
| | | | Charles Trenet[U] |
| | | | Harold Rome[L-English] |
| "Home Again" | 1970 | Gone with the Wind[10] | |
| "A Home of Our Own" | | | |
| "Hoop-de-Dingle" | 1959 | Destry Rides Again | |
| "Horror Boys of Hollywood" | 1936 | One in a Million[F] | Lester Lee[M/L] |
| | | | Harold Rome[M/L] |
| "How Cold, Cold, Cold an Empty Room" | 1965 | The Zulu and the Zayda | |
| "How Long Can Love Keep Laughing?" | 1938 | Sing Out the News | |
| "How Lucky" | 1970 | Gone with the Wind[10] | |
| "How Often, How Often" | 1970 | Gone with the Wind[10] | |
| "How Peaceful Is the Evening" | 1948 | That's the Ticket! | |
| "Hup! Tup! Thrup! Four!" ("Jack the Sleepy Jeep") | 1943 | Stars and Gripes | |
| "I Can Hear It Now" | 1950 | Bless You All | |
| "I Did It for Defense" | 1942 | Let Freedom Sing | |
| "I Don't Want to Be Gay!" | | | |
| "I Hate a Parade" | 1950 | Michael Todd's Peep Show | |
| "I Hate Him" | | | |
| "I Have a Song" | 1940 | The Little Dog Laughed | |
| "I Have to Tell You" | 1954 | Fanny | |
| "I Knew You Well" | 1943 | Nantucket[7] | |
| "I Know Your Kind" | 1959 | Destry Rides Again | |
| "I Like You" | 1954 | Fanny | |
| "I Married a Republican" | 1938 | Sing Out the News | |

## B. Songs

| Song | Year | From[1] | Collaborator |
|---|---|---|---|
| "I Never Learned to Waltz" | 1949 | *Pretty Penny* | |
| "I Say Hello" | 1959 | *Destry Rides Again* | |
| "I Shouldn't Love You" | 1948 | *That's the Ticket!* | |
| "I Want Romance" | 1940 | *The Little Dog Laughed* | |
| "I Want to Bivouac with a WAC" | 1943 | *Stars and Gripes* | |
| "If Only" | 1970 | *Gone with the Wind*[10] | |
| "I'll Never Need the Moon" | | | Gaetano Oliviero[U] |
| | | | D. Titomanglio[U] |
| | | | Harold Rome[U] |
| "I'll Take the Check" | 1950 | *Bless You All* | |
| "I'm a King" | 1940 | *The Little Dog Laughed* | |
| "I'm Heading Home" | | | |
| "I'm Just Nuts About You" | 1939 | *Pins and Needles* | |
| "(I'm Not a) Well Man" | 1962 | *I Can Get It for You Wholesale* | |
| "Investigation" | | | |
| "It Doesn't Matter Now" | 1970 | *Gone with the Wind*[10] | |
| "It's a Small World" | 1943 | Army orientation program | |
| "It's Better with a Union Man" ("Bertha, The Sewing Machine Girl") | 1939 | *Pins and Needles* | |
| "It's Fun to Be Free" | 1942 | *Let Freedom Sing* | |
| "It's Good to Be Alive" ("Lebe Is Gut") | 1965 | *The Zulu and the Zayda* | |
| "It's Great Fun Living Alone" | | | |
| "It's the Principal of the Thing" | | | |
| "I've Always Loved You" | 1946 | *I've Always Loved You*[F] | Aaron Goldmark[M; 5] |
| "I've Got the Nerve to Be in Love" | 1939 | *Pins and Needles* | |
| "Je T'aime — I Love You" | 1943 | *Nantucket*[7] | |
| "Johnny Is a Hoarder" | 1942 | *Let Freedom Sing* | |
| "Johnny Is My Darling" | 1970 | *Gone with the Wind*[10] | |
| "Jumping to the Jukebox" | 1943 | *Stars and Gripes* | |
| | 1944 | *Skirts!* | |
| "Just a Little White House" | 1950 | *Bless You All* | |
| "Just Across the Street" | | | Michael Erner[U] |
| | | | Harold Rome[U] |
| "Just an Ordinary Guy" | 1938 | *Sing Out the News* | |
| "Kamp Karefree" | 1952 | *Wish You Were Here* | |
| "King of the Bushongo" | 1960 | *Harold Rome's Gallery*[Art] | |
| "La Grosse Valise" | 1965 | *La Grosse Valise* | Gerard Calvi[8] |
| "La Java" | 1965 | *La Grosse Valise* | Gerard Calvi[8] |
| "Ladies" | 1959 | *Destry Rides Again* | |
| "The Lady Is a WAAC" | 1942 | *Let Freedom Sing* | |
| "The Lady's on the Job" | 1943 | *Lunchtime Follies* | |

# B. Songs

| Song | Year | From[1] | Collaborator |
|---|---|---|---|
| "Latrine Duty" | 1943 | Stars and Gripes | |
| "Lesson in Etiquette" | 1937 | Pins and Needles | |
| "Let Freedom Swing" | 1938 | Cabaret TAC[3] | |
| "Let's Go to the Movies" | | | |
| "Let's Talk about a Woman" | 1954 | Fanny | |
| "Letter to General McArthur" | | | |
| "Like the Breeze Blows" | 1965 | The Zulu and the Zayda | |
| "Lisa" ("Theme from Rear Window") | 1954 | Rear Window[F] | Franz Waxman[M] Harold Rome[L] |
| "The Little Brown Suit My Uncle Gave Me" | 1943 | Stars and Gripes | |
| | 1944 | Skirts! | |
| "Little Fishes" | 1958 | Wonderful Things![F] | |
| "Little Miss Victory Jones" | 1942 | Let Freedom Sing | |
| "Little Surplus Me" | 1946 | Call Me Mister | |
| "Little Things (Meant So So Much to Me)" | 1950 | Bless You All | |
| "Little Wonders" | 1970 | Gone with the Wind[10] | |
| "Lonely Stranger" | 1970 | Gone with the Wind[10] | |
| "Look Up" | | | Willy Hernert[U] Jopp Leur[U] Harold Rome[U] |
| "Looking for a Candidate" | 1948 | That's the Ticket! | |
| "Love Has to Wait" | 1943 | Stars and Gripes | |
| "Love Is a Very Light Thing" | 1954 | Fanny | |
| "Love Is Like an Elephant" | 1943 | Nantucket[7] | |
| "Love Is Still Love" | 1948 | That's the Ticket! | |
| "Love It Hurts So Good" | 1950 | Alive and Kicking | |
| "Love Letter to Manhattan" | 1950 | Bless You All | |
| "Love Remains the Same" | 1946 | Call Me Mister | |
| "Love Sometimes Has to Wait" | 1943 | Stars and Gripes | |
| "Love That Man" | 1950 | Bless You All | |
| "Lullaby to a Landlord" | | Opus—New York | |
| "Made in Nantucket" | 1943 | Nantucket[7] | |
| "Make Your Vote Count" | | | |
| "The Man Behind the Man Behind the Gun" | 1943 | Lunchtime Follies | |
| "March Tito" | 1946 | American Committee for Yugoslav Relief[6] | Harold Rome[M] Lehman Engel[M] |
| "Marrying for Fun" | 1970 | Gone with the Wind[10] | |
| "May Day" | | | |
| "May Your Heart Stay Young" ("L'Chayim!") | 1965 | The Zulu and the Zayda | |
| "Meadowland" ("Cavalry of the Steppes") | 1943 | War programs | Lev Knipper[M] Albert Sirmay[M] |
| "Men Awake" | 1937 | Pins and Needles | |
| "Mene, Mene, Tekel" | 1939 | Pins and Needles | |
| "Mess Call" | 1943 | Stars and Gripes | |

## B. Songs

| Song | Year | From[1] | Collaborator |
|---|---|---|---|
| "The Micromaniac" | 1943 | *Ziegfeld Follies of 1943* | |
| "Military Life" ("The Jerk Song") | 1946 | *Call Me Mister* | |
| "Miss Fiddle-Dee-Dee" | 1970 | *Gone with the Wind*[10] | |
| "Miss Marmelstein" | 1962 | *I Can Get It for You Wholesale* | |
| "Mister Chucklehead" | 1942 | War song | |
| "Mix and Mingle" | 1950 | *Wish You Were Here* | |
| "The Model Hasn't Changed" | 1950 | *Michael Todd's Peep Show* | |
| "Modern Floradora Girl" | | | |
| "Momma, Momma, Momma" | 1962 | *I Can Get It for You Wholesale* | |
| "The Money Song" | 1948 | *That's the Ticket!* | |
| "Music Lessons" | | | Rafe Crabtree[U] |
| | | | Paul Misrachi[U] |
| | | | Leslie Sarony[U] |
| | | | Ralph Stanley[U] |
| | | | Harold Rome[U] |
| "My Cowboy Song" | 1950 | *The Sing Song Man*[9] | |
| "My Friend Franklin" | | | |
| "My Heart Decided" | 1943 | *Nantucket*[7] | |
| "My Heart Is Unemployed" | 1938 | *Sing Out the News* | |
| "My Long Ago" | 1964 | *Harold Rome's Gallery*[Art] | |
| "My Lost Melody" | 1951 | *The Mating Season*[F] | Raymond Asso[U] |
| | | | Marguerite Monnot[U] |
| | | | Harold Rome[U] |
| "My Pinup Girl" | 1943 | *Stars and Gripes* | |
| | 1944 | *Skirts!* | |
| "My Soldier" | 1970 | *Gone with the Wind*[10] | |
| "Never Too Late for Love" | 1954 | *Fanny* | |
| "The Newlyweds Song" | 1970 | *Gone with the Wind*[10] | |
| "Newsreel" | 1948 | *That's the Ticket!* | |
| "Nobody Makes a Pass at Me" ("Dear Beatrice Fairfax") | 1937 | *Pins and Needles* | |
| "Not Cricket to Picket" | 1937 | *Pins and Needles* | |
| "Not Guilty" | 1959 | *Destry Rides Again* | |
| "Nothing" | 1950 | *The Sing Song Man*[9] | |
| "Nothing Is Too Good" | 1943 | *Nantucket*[7] | |
| "Octopus Song" | 1954 | *Fanny* | |
| "Of the People Stomp" | 1940 | *The Little Dog Laughed* | |
| | 1942 | *Let Freedom Sing* | |
| "Oh, Give Me the Good Old Days" | 1940 | *Pins and Needles* | |
| "O'Hara" | 1970 | *Gone with the Wind*[10] | |
| "Okle Dokle" | 1950 | *The Sing Song Man*[9] | |
| "On Guard" | | | Edwin Goldman[U] |
| | | | Harold Rome[U] |
| "On That Old Production Line" | 1943 | *Lunchtime Follies* | |

210                                    B. Songs

| Song | Year | From[1] | Collaborator |
|---|---|---|---|
| "On the Avenue" | 1947 | | Marcel Betrou[U] |
| | | | Friedrich Goldbaum[U] |
| | | | Harold Rome[L] |
| "On the Swing Shift" | 1943 | *Lunchtime Follies* | |
| "On Time" | 1943 | *Lunchtime Follies* | |
| "Once Knew a Fella" | 1959 | *Destry Rides Again* | |
| "One Big Union for Two" | 1938 | Cabaret TAC[3] | |
| | 1938 | *Pins and Needles* | |
| "One of These Fine Days" | 1938 | *Sing Out the News* | |
| "Only Time Will Tell" | 1959 | *Destry Rides Again* | |
| "Ooh What You Did" | | | Bruno Bidoli[U] |
| | | | Harold Rome[U] |
| "Ordinary Guy" | 1938 | *Sing Out the News* | |
| "Other Hands, Other Hearts" | 1954 | *Fanny* | |
| "Our Boy" | | | |
| "Our Generals" | | | Albert Sirmay[M] |
| | | | Harold Rome[L] |
| "Out of This World" ("Oisgetzaichnet") | 1965 | *The Zulu and the Zayda* | |
| "Oysters, Cockles and Mussels" | 1943 | *Nantucket*[7] | |
| "Pals of the Pentagon" | 1950 | *Alive and Kicking* | |
| "Panisse and Son" | 1954 | *Fanny* | |
| "Papa Don't Love Mama Anymore" | 1939 | *Pins and Needles* | |
| "Papa's Got a Job" | 1939 | *Sing for Your Supper* | Ned Lehac[M] |
| | | | Hector Troy[L] (Rome) |
| | | | Robert Sour[L] |
| "Passing the Buck" | 1943 | *Stars and Gripes* | |
| "Penthouse Promenade" | | *Opus — New York* | |
| "Peter and the Wolf" | | | Sergei Prokofieff[M] |
| | | | Harold Rome[L] |
| "Pincus et Cie" | 1943 | *Nantucket*[7] | |
| "Pity the Poor Millionaire" | 1937 | *Pins and Needles* | |
| "Plaza 6–9423" | 1938 | *Sing Out the News* | |
| "The Pluto Boys" | 1939 | *Pins and Needles* | |
| "Pocketful of Dreams" | 1949 | *Pretty Penny* | |
| | 1950 | *Michael Todd's Peep Show* | |
| "Political Lady" | 1948 | *That's the Ticket!* | |
| "Public Enemy Number One" | 1937 | *Pins and Needles* | |
| "Read All About It" | 1948 | *That's the Ticket!* | |
| "The Red Ball Express" | 1946 | *Call Me Mister* | |
| "Relax" | 1952 | *Wish You Were Here* | |
| "Remember Thomas Jefferson" | | | |
| "Respectability" | 1959 | *Destry Rides Again* | |
| "Restless Heart" | 1954 | *Fanny* | |
| "Rhumba on the Right" | | | |
| "Ring on the Finger" | 1959 | *Destry Rides Again* | |
| "Ring Up the Curtain" | 1942 | *Let Freedom Sing* | |
| "Ringo Pingo Zingo" | 1950 | *The Sing Song Man*[9] | |
| "Rinso White Song" | 1943 | Advertising jingle | |

## B. Songs

| Song | Year | From[1] | Collaborator |
|---|---|---|---|
| "River of Tears" | 1965 | *The Zulu and the Zayda* | |
| "Roads" | | | Albert Sirmay[M] <br> Harold Rome[L] |
| "The Roaring 20's Strike Back" | 1950 | *Bless You All* | |
| "Room for One" | 1937 | *Pins and Needles* | |
| "A Rose Is a Rose" | 1950 | *Bless You All* | |
| "(Rose Lovejoy of) Paradise Valley" | 1959 | *Destry Rides Again* | |
| "Run Up the Curtain" | 1942 | *Let Freedom Sing* | |
| "Sandwich for Two" | 1965 | *La Grosse Valise* | Gerard Calvi[8] |
| "Scarlett" | 1970 | *Gone with the Wind*[10] | |
| "Serenade to a Traffic Light" | | *Opus — New York* | |
| "Shake Hands, Dear Mrs. Cow" | 1960 | *Harold Rome's Gallery*[Art] | |
| "She Rolled Up Her Sleeves — She Hitched Up Her Hose" | 1943 | *Lunchtime Follies* | |
| "Shika, Shika" | 1954 | *Fanny* | |
| "Shopping Around" | 1952 | *Wish You Were Here* | |
| "Shy" | 1960 | *Harold Rome's Gallery*[Art] | |
| "The Shy Sweetheart" | | | |
| "Sing Ho! for Private Enterprise" | | | |
| "Sing Me a Song with Social Significance" ("Why Sing of Skies Above?") | 1937 | *Pins and Needles* | |
| "The Sing Song Man" | 1950 | *The Sing Song Man*[9] | |
| "Slippy Sloppy Shoes" | 1965 | *La Grosse Valise* | Gerard Calvi[8] |
| "Slumming Party" | 1937 | *Pins and Needles* | |
| "Small World" | 1949 | *Pretty Penny* | |
| "The Social" | 1959 | *Destry Rides Again* | |
| "Social Director" | 1952 | *Wish You Were Here* | |
| "Solid, Solid Suzabelle" | 1943 | *Lunchtime Follies* | |
| "Some Things" | 1965 | *The Zulu and the Zayda* | |
| "Some Things a Man Must Have" | 1940 | *The Little Dog Laughed* | |
| "Song and Dance Man" | | | |
| "Song of Farewell" | | | |
| "Song of Our Love" | 1943 | *Nantucket*[7] | |
| | 1948 | *The Angry God*[F] | |
| "Song of Revenge" | | | |
| "Song of Stalingrad" | | | |
| "Song of the Ads" | 1937 | *Pins and Needles* | |
| "Song of the Baltic Fleet" | | | |
| "The Song of the Refugees" | 1938 | *Cabaret TAC*[3] | |
| "Song of the Sea" | | | |
| "Sophisticated Lulu" | | | |
| "The Sound of Money" | 1962 | *I Can Get It for You Wholesale* | |

## B. Songs

| Song | Year | From[1] | Collaborator |
|---|---|---|---|
| "South America, Take It Away" | 1946 | *Call Me Mister* | |
| | 1947 | *Starlight Roof* | London revue |
| "A Southern Lady" | 1970 | *Gone with the Wind*[10] | |
| "Spanish Dance" | 1965 | *La Grosse Valise* | Gerard Calvi[8] |
| "Special Service Makes Me Nervous" | 1944 | *Stars and Gripes* | |
| "Spring in December" | 1948 | | Vittorio Mascheroni[U] |
| | | | Gaincarlo Testoni[U] |
| | | | Harold Rome[L] |
| "Status Quo" | 1939 | *Pins and Needles* | |
| "Stay Out, Sammy!" | 1939 | *Pins and Needles* | |
| "Stop Walking Around in My Hand" | 1949 | *Pretty Penny* | |
| "Stop Waltzing Around in My Mind" | 1963 | *Harold Rome's Gallery*[Art] | |
| "Strange and Wonderful" | 1970 | *Gone with the Wind*[10] | |
| "Subway Nocturne" | | *Opus — New York* | |
| "Summer Afternoon" | 1952 | *Wish You Were Here* | |
| "Summer Dresses" | 1950 | *Bless You All* | |
| "Sunday in the Park" | 1937 | *Pins and Needles* | |
| "Surplus Blues" | 1946 | *Call Me Mister* | |
| "Take Me Back to My Flat in Manhattan" | | | |
| "Take Off the Coat (My Friend)" | 1948 | *That's the Ticket!* | |
| | 1950 | *Bless You All* | |
| "Tango Diabolo" | 1960 | *Harold Rome's Gallery*[Art] | |
| "Tara" | 1970 | *Gone with the Wind*[10] | |
| "Tell Me, Pretty Maiden" ("Modern Florodora Girl") | 1938 | *Sing Out the News* | |
| "Thanks for Thanksgiving" | | | |
| "That's Music" | 1938 | Cabaret TAC[3] | |
| "That's My Pop" | 1943 | *Lunchtime Follies* | |
| "There You Are Again" | 1943 | *Nantucket*[7] | |
| "There's Nothing Nicer Than People" | 1952 | *Wish You Were Here* | |
| "They Never Told Me" | 1943 | *Nantucket*[7] | |
| "They Won't Know Me" | 1952 | *Wish You Were Here* | |
| "This Is Our War" | 1942 | Patriotic war song | |
| "The Thought of You" | 1954 | *Fanny* | |
| "Thousands Cheer" | | | E.Y. Harburg[L] |
| | | | Herbert Stothart[U] |
| | | | Harold Rome[U] |
| "A Time for Healing" | 1976 | *Gone with the Wind* | |
| "A Time for Love" | 1970 | *Gone with the Wind*[10] | |
| "Tin Pan Alley Rag" | 1958 | *Lawrence Welk Show*[T] | Donald Phillips[U] |
| | | | Harold Rome[U] |
| "Tkambuza" ("Zulu Hunting Song") | 1965 | *The Zulu and the Zayda* | |
| "Tripping the Light Fantastic" | 1952 | *Wish You Were Here* | |
| "To My Wife" | 1954 | *Fanny* | |

## B. Songs

| Song | Year | From[1] | Collaborator |
|---|---|---|---|
| "Tobacco — The Redman's Revenge" | 1965 | *That Was the Week That Was* (TV show) | |
| "Today's the Day" | 1970 | *Gone with the Wind*[10] | |
| "Tomorrow Is Another Day" | 1970 | *Gone with the Wind*[10] | |
| "Tomorrow Morning" | 1959 | *Destry Rides Again* | |
| "Too Soon" | 1962 | *I Can Get It for You Wholesale* | |
| "The Toothbrush Song" | 1950 | *The Sing Song Man*[9] | |
| "Tripping the Light Fantastic" | 1952 | *Wish You Were Here* | |
| "The Two Friends" | | | |
| "Two of a Kind" | 1970 | *Gone with the Wind*[10] | |
| "United Nations on the March" ("United Nations March") ("United Nations Hymn") | 1942 | Patriotic war song | Dmitri Shostakovich[M] Harold Rome[L] |
| "Unlucky Pierre" | 1943 | *Nantucket*[7] | |
| "Up Fiorello" | | | |
| "Victory Symphony, Eight to the Bar" | 1943 | *Lunchtime Follies* | |
| "Viva America" | | | |
| "Virginia Reel" | 1970 | *Gone with the Wind*[10] | |
| "Voting Blues" | 1950 | *Bless You All* | |
| "The Water Wears Down the Stone" | 1965 | *The Zulu and the Zayda* | |
| "The Way Things Are" | 1962 | *I Can Get It for You Wholesale* | |
| "We Belong to You" | 1970 | *Gone with the Wind*[10] | |
| "Wedding Dance" | | | Jacques Press[U] Harold Rome[U] |
| "We'd Rather Be Right" | 1937 | *Pins and Needles* | Arthur Kraemer[L] |
| "Welcome Home" | 1954 | *Fanny* | |
| "We're Going Back" | 1948 | *That's the Ticket* | |
| "We're Ladies" | | | |
| "We Sing America" | 1939 | Council against Intolerance in America[6] | |
| | 1939 | *Pins and Needles* | |
| "We've Got the Song" | 1938 | *Sing Out the News* | |
| "We've Just Begun" | 1937 | *Pins and Needles* | Charles Friedman[L] Harold Rome[M&L] |
| "A Whaler's Life Is a Merry Life" | 1943 | *Nantucket*[7] | |
| "The Whaler's Return" | 1943 | *Nantucket*[7] | |
| "What Are They Doing to Us Now?" | 1962 | *I Can Get It for You Wholesale* | |
| "What Can I Do?" | 1949 | | Henri Betti[M] Edith Gassion[L-French] Harold Rome[L-English] |
| "What Good Is Love?" | 1937 | *Pins and Needles* | |
| "What Is Love?" | 1970 | *Gone with the Wind*[10] | |
| "What's in It for Me" | 1962 | *I Can Get It for You Wholesale* | |

| Song | Year | From[1] | Collaborator |
|---|---|---|---|
| "What This Party Needs" | 1939 | Pins and Needles | Arthur Kramer[L] |
| | | | Harold Rome[M&L] |
| "When" | 1950 | Bless You All | |
| "When Gemini Meets Capricorn" | 1962 | I Can Get It for You Wholesale | |
| "When I Grow Up" ("The G-Man Song") | 1939 | Pins and Needles | |
| "When It's Love" | 1943 | Nantucket[7] | |
| "When the Devil Played the Fiddle" | 1943 | Nantucket[7] | |
| "When We Meet Again" | 1946 | Call Me Mister | |
| "Where Did the Night Go?" | 1952 | Wish You Were Here | |
| "Where Is My Soldier Boy?" | 1970 | Gone with the Wind[10] | |
| "Which Way Is Home?"[11] | 1964 | Harold Rome's Gallery[Art] | |
| | 1970 | Gone with the Wind[10] | |
| "Whip Dance" | 1946 | Destry Rides Again | |
| "Whisper a Word of Love" | | | |
| "Who Could Eat Now?" | 1952 | Wish You Were Here | |
| "Who Knows?" | 1962 | I Can Get It for You Wholesale | |
| "Who's Gonna Investigate the Man Who Investigates Me?" | 1939 | Political rally | |
| "Why Be Afraid to Dance?" | 1954 | Fanny | |
| "Why Did They Die?" | 1970 | Gone with the Wind[10] | |
| "Wish You Were Here" | 1952 | Wish You Were Here | |
| "The Wolf That Swallowed Red Riding Hood" | 1960 | Harold Rome's Gallery[Art] | |
| "Wonderful Things" | 1958 | Wonderful Things![F] | |
| "Xanadu" | 1965 | La Grosse Valise | Gerard Calvi[8] |
| "The Yanks Aren't Coming" | 1940 | Pins and Needles | |
| "Yip Ahoy, or Adrift on the Old Prairie" | 1938 | Sing Out the News | |
| "You after All These Years" | 1943 | Nantucket[7] | |
| "You Never Know What Hit You (When It's Love)" | 1948 | That's the Ticket! | |
| | 1949 | Pretty Penny | |
| | 1950 | Bless You All | |
| "You're Your Highness to Me" | 1940 | The Little Dog Laughed | |
| "Yuletide, Park Avenue" | 1946 | Call Me Mister | |
| "Zulu Love Song" ("Wait for Me") | 1965 | The Zulu and the Zayda | |

Music and lyrics all by Harold Rome unless otherwise indicated. Missing years and other data could not be avoided. The above list was compiled from several sources, most prominently:

Lists of Published Music and Recordings, Harold Rome Papers, Yale University;
Songwriters' Hall of Fame, http://songwritershalloffame.org/index.php/songs;
ASCAP Ace Title Search, http://www.ascap/ace/search.cfm?requesttimeout;
*Lissauer's Encyclopedia of Popular Music in America: 1888 to the Present*, Facts on File, 1998;
Harold Rome and Vernon Duke Collections, Library of Congress;

Harold Rome, *Vocal Selections: Pins and Needles* (New York: Florence Music Company, 1968), Museum of the City of New York.

F — Film
T — Television show
U — Uncertain contribution
Art — Songs written to accompany paintings done for exhibit in *Harold Rome's Gallery* in 1964 at the Marble Arch Gallery, New York. Songs written in various years, not all in 1964.

# C. Song Recordings and Artists

*Song — Recorded by*[1]

"(All of a Sudden) My Heart Sings" Paul Anka (ABC-Paramount), Joe Basile, Tony Bennett, Polly Bergen, Blue Stars of France, Mel Carter (Imperial), Frank Chacksfield, Karen Chandler, Duke Ellington (Victor), Erroll Garner, Kathryn Grayson (MGM), Enrique Guzman, Roy Hamilton, Hildegarde (Decca), Dick Hyman, Johnnie Johnston (Capitol), Spike Jones, King Sisters (Bluebird), Kathy Kirby, Peggy Lee, The Lettermen, Liberace, Guy Lombardo Orchestra (Decca), Mantovani, Al Martino, Midland Radio Orchestra, Mathieu Mireille, Tommy Mottola, Odetta, Norrie Paramor, Danilo Perez, Martha Stewart (Blue Bird), Tommy Tucker (Columbia), Sarah Vaughan

"Along with Me" Jan Savitt and his Orchestra (ARA), Artie Shaw and his Orchestra (Musicraft), Charlie Spivak (Victor), Margaret Whiting

"Be Kind to Your Parents" Cincinnati Children's Choir, Michael Feinstein, Karen and Cubby (Disney), Pete Seeger

"Chain Store Daisy" Ruth Rubinstein (Decca)

"Doing the Reactionary" Nancy Stearns (Nancy Stearns-Greg Toroian)

"Fanny" Ames Brothers, Larry Elgart Orchestra, Eddie Fisher (RCA), Morton Gould, Living Strings, Henry Mancini, Fred Waring and His Pennsylvanians (Decca)

"Franklin D. Roosevelt Jones" Van Alexander (Blue Bird), Cab Calloway (Vocalion), Judy Garland (Decca), Hal Kemp (Victor), Living Strings, Glenn Miller, Chick Webb Orchestra with Ella Fitzgerald (Decca)

"How Long Can Love Keep Laughing?" Eddy Duchin (Brunswick), Leighton Noble (Vocal)

"I Have a Song" Vaughn Monroe (Blue Bird), Emile Petti (Decca)

"I Have to Tell You" Dinah Shore (RCA Victor), Eileen Barton

"I Like You" Darlene Gillespie (Disney)

"I Want Romance" Emile Petti (Decca)

"Mene, Mene, Tekel" Shep Fields (Blue Bird), Clarence Palmer

"The Money Song" Andrews Sisters (Decca), Dean Martin and Jerry Lewis (Capitol)

"My Heart Is Unemployed" Eddy Duchin (Brunswick), Hal Kemp Orchestra (Victor), Leighton Noble (Vocalion)

"**Nobody Makes a Pass at Me**" Millie Weitz (Decca)
"**One Big Union for Two**" Cab Calloway (Vocalion), Kay Weber and Sonny Schuyler (Decca)
"**Peter and the Wolf**" Shep Fields (Blue Bird), Guy Lombardo (Decca)
"**Plaza 6–9423**" Rudy Vallee (Varsity)
"**Pocketful of Dreams**" Eddie Howard
"**Ring on the Finger**" Ethel Smith (Decca)
"**Sing Me a Song with Social Significance**" Kay Weber and Sonny Schuyler (Decca), Nancy Stearns (Nancy Stearns-Greg Toroian), Janet Stecher and Susan Lewis (Reveille Music)
"**Sunday in the Park**" Frank Crumit (Decca), Ted Weems (Decca), Hudson-DeLange Orchestra / Mary McHugh (Brunswick)
"**South America, Take It Away**" Bing Crosby and the Andrews Sisters (Decca), Xavier Cugat with Buddy Clark vocal (Columbia), Betty Garrett, Ted Heath, James Last, Monica Lewis (Signature), George Paxton (Majestic), Mel Torme
"**United Nations March**" Igor Gorin (Victor), Paul Robeson (Keynote)
"**We Sing America**" The American Singers (Varsity)
"**What Can I Do?**" Yves Montand, Edith Piaf
"**When I Grow Up**" ("**The G-Man Song**") Vaughn Monroe (Victor)
"**Wish You Were Here**" David Allan Coe, Bing Crosby, Michael Feinstein, Eddie Fisher (RCA Victor), Jane Froman (Capitol), Peggy Lee, Guy Lombardo, Freddy Martin and Orchestra, Jerry Vale, Fran Warren

# D. Discography

*Album Title*                     *Recording Company / Label*

**Harold Rome**                  (Keynote Records —1938)
Rome performs songs from *Pins and Needles*. "Song of the Ads," "When I Grow Up" ("The G-Man Song")
**Harold Rome**                  (Decca — circa 1938)
Rome performs songs from *Sing Out the News*. "Plaza 6–9423," "Yip-Ahoy"
**Harold Rome Plays Fanny**          (Heritage Records —1954)
Rome performs songs from *Fanny*.
**Rome-antics**                   (Heritage Records —1956)
**And Then I Wrote**              (Coral Records —1956)
**Pins and Needles (25th Anniversary)**    (Columbia Records —1962)
Rome, Jack Carroll, Rose Marie Jun, Alan Sokoloff, and Barbra Streisand perform the songs from *Pins and Needles* on its 25th anniversary.
**Harold Rome's Gallery**             (Columbia —1964)
Rome performs songs from his art exhibition *Harold Rome's Gallery*. Other singers include Betty Garrett, Jack Haskell, and Rose Marie Jun. "Art in the Night," "The Audience," "The Critics," "Half-Forgotten Teddy Bear," "King of the Bushongo," "My Long Ago," "Shake Hands, Dear Mrs. Cow," "Shy," "Stop Waltzing Around in My Mind," "Tango Diablo," "Which Way Is Home?," "The Wolf That Swallowed Red Riding Hood"

*Harold Rome — A Touch of Rome* (DRG Records —1991)
Rome performs twenty-eight songs from his various shows. This is Rome at his best, playing piano and interpreting songs with his expressive voice. "Mene, Mene, Tekel," "Sunday in the Park," "It's Better with a Union Man," "F.D.R. Jones," "Military Life," "South America, Take It Away," "Call Me Mister," "The Money Song," "Gin Rummy Rhapsody," "You Never Know What Hit You," "I Shouldn't Love You," "Cry Baby," "French with Tears," "Don't Want to Write About the South," "I Can Hear It Now," "Pocketful of Dreams," "Where Did the Night Go?," "Don Jose of Far Rockaway," "Wish You Were Here," "Restless Heart," "Love Is a Very Light Thing," "Fanny," "Be Kind to Your Parents," "I Have to Tell You," "To My Wife"

# E. Cast Recordings of Harold Rome's Musicals

*Call Me Mister*—1946 New York cast  (Decca — 2003)
  (Part of Decca CD: Irving Berlin's All Soldier Show *This Is the Army*)
*Destry Rides Again*—1959 New York Cast  (Universal Classics Group — 2001)
—1982 London cast  (Jay Productions, Inc.— 2004)
*Fanny*—1954 New York Cast  (RCA Victor / BMG Music —1996)
*Gone with the Wind*—1972 London cast  (EMI Records —1972, 2011)
*I Can Get It for You Wholesale*—
  1962 New York Cast  (Columbia Records —1962)
*Scarlett*—1970 Japanese cast  (DRG Records —1970)
*That's the Ticket*— 2002 New York cast  (Original Cast Records — 2002)
*Wish You Were Here*—1952 New York cast  (Flare Records — 2008)

# F. Chronology of Produced Shows

| Opening | Closing | Show | Final City | New York Performances |
| --- | --- | --- | --- | --- |
| 11/27/37 | 6/22/40 | *Pins and Needles* | New York | 1,108 |
| 9/24/38 | 1/07/39 | *Sing Out the News* | New York | 105 |
| 4/24/39 | 6/30/39 | *Sing for Your Supper* | New York | 60 |
| 6/19/39 | 2/10/40 | *Streets of Paris* | New York | 274 |
| 8/13/40 | 8/24/40 | *The Little Dog Laughed* | Boston | * |
| 1942 | 1943 | *Lunchtime Follies* | East Coast | * |
| 4/07/42 | 4/12/42 | *Gratefully Yours* | New York | 6 |
| 6/24/42 | 12/04/43 | *Star and Garter* | New York | 609 |
| 10/05/42 | 10/11/42 | *Let Freedom Sing* | New York | 8 |
| 4/01/43 | 7/22/44 | *Ziegfeld Follies of 1943* | New York | 553 |
| 7/13/43 | # | *Stars and Gripes* | Brooklyn | * |
| 1/25/44 | # | *Skirts!* | London | * |
| 4/18/46 | 1/10/48 | *Call Me Mister* | New York | 734 |
| 9/24/48 | 10/02/48 | *That's the Ticket* | Philadelphia | * |
| 6/20/49 | + | *Pretty Penny* | Pennsylvania-Connecticut | * |
| 1/17/50 | 2/25/50 | *Alive and Kicking* | New York | 46 |
| 6/28/50 | 2/25/51 | *Michael Todd's Peep Show* | New York | 278 |

| Opening | Closing | Show | Final City | New York Performances |
|---|---|---|---|---|
| 12/14/50 | 2/24/51 | Bless You All | New York | 84 |
| 6/25/52 | 11/28/53 | Wish You Were Here | New York | 598 |
| 11/04/54 | 12/16/56 | Fanny | New York | 888 |
| 10/10/57 | 9/13/58 | Romanoff and Juliet[1] | New York | 389 |
| 4/23/59 | 6/18/60 | Destry Rides Again | New York | 472 |
| 3/22/62 | 12/08/62 | I Can Get It for You Wholesale | New York | 300 |
| 11/10/65 | 4/16/66 | The Zulu and the Zayda | New York | 179 |
| 12/14/65 | 12/21/65 | La Grosse Valise | New York | 7 |
| 1/02/70[2] | August/1976 | Gone with the Wind | Miami Beach | * |

+ The show ran several performances in East Coast regional theater, but the closing date is not clear.
\# These shows toured Europe or the Pacific theaters of war. Exact dates are unknown.
\* These shows never opened in New York.

# G. Chronology of Unproduced Shows[1]

| Show | Year | Collaborators |
|---|---|---|
| Give a Viva (Man from Mexicana)[2] | 1941 | Erskine Caldwell |
| Caleb Catlum's America[3] | 1941–42 | Valentine Davies; Vincent McHugh |
| Nantucket | 1943 | Vernon Duke; Samuel Hoffenstein; Gottfried Reinhardt |
| Impromptu | 1944 | New Opera Company |
| Sobbin' Women | 1947–48 | |
| Dancin' Day (Saints and Sinners) | 1953–57 | Joseph Fields; Jerome Chodorov; Frederick Loewe |
| Cinderella | 1953 | Billy Rose; Lively Arts Foundation |
| In the Pink | 1955 | Moss Hart; Jerome Chodorov |
| The Matchmaker | 1955 | |
| Lili[4] | 1959 | Helen Deutsch; David Merrick |
| Providence Island (Paradise Island) | 1959 | |
| Author! Author! | 1960 | Joseph Kipness; Arthur Kober |
| Holiday for Henrietta | 1960 | Joseph Kipness |
| Lucky's Transformation | 1960 | Eugene Ionesco; Leo Kerz |
| Fidelity Lane | 1960 | Jerome Chodorov; Joseph Kipness; Arthur Lesser |
| Untitled (in Roman world) | 1961 | Jerome Weidman; David Merrick |
| Man and Wife[5] | 1962–63 | |
| Such Stuff | 1962 | Jerome Weidman |
| Mr. Brink (On Borrowed Time) | 1962–64 | Paul Osborne; Leland Hayward |
| Casablanca | 1963 | Julius Epstein; David Merrick |
| Howe and Hummel | 1963–65 | Jerome Weidman; Joe Layton; Diana Krasny |
| Tourjours Forever | 1964–68 | Arthur Whitelaw; Selma Diamond |
| Wonderful Door | 1966–67 | Howard Fast |

| | | |
|---|---|---|
| *The Southpaw* | 1967 | Ring Lardner, Jr.; Max J. Brown; Gene Frankel |
| *Wee Bit O' Scotch* | 1970 | Jerome Chodorov |
| *Jonathan Wild* (*Jonathan the Great*) | 1971 | Joshua Logan; Edward Mann; Lalo Schifrin; Maurice Scofield |
| *The Waltz of Love* (*Waltz of Toreadors*) | 1975–78 | Jean Anouilh; Ed Anhalt; Ted Allan |
| *Operation Spring* | ? | Arnold Auerbach |

## H. Movie Work

| Year | Movie | Song[A] | Sung By | Producer |
|---|---|---|---|---|
| 1936 | *One in a Million* | "Horror Boys of Hollywood" M/L — Harold Rome and Lester Lee | Ritz Brothers | 20th Century–Fox |
| 1941 | *Babes on Broadway* | "Franklin D. Roosevelt Jones" | Judy Garland | MGM |
| 1943 | *December 7* | "United Nations on the March"[C] | | Navy / U.S. War Depts. |
| 1943 | *Thousands Cheer* | "United Nations on the March"[C] L — Harold Rome M — Dmitri Shostakovich | Kathryn Grayson | MGM |
| 1944 | *Hollywood Canteen* | "Enlloro" M/L — Obdulio Morales and Julio Blanco L — Harold Rome (English) | | Warner Bros. |
| 1945 | *Anchors Aweigh* | "My Heart Sings"[B] | Kathryn Grayson | MGM |
| 1946 | *Junior Prom* | "My Heart Sings"[B] L — Harold Rome M — Laurent Herpin | Freddie Stewart & Abe Lyman Orchestra | Monogram |
| | *I've Always Loved You* | "I've Always Loved You" L — Harold Rome M — adapted by Aaron Goldmark from Rachmaninoff's *2nd Piano Concerto* | | Republic |
| | *Young Widow* | "My Heart Sings"[B] | Hunt | Stromberg |
| 1948 | *The Angry God* | "Song of Our Love" L — Harold Rome M — Vernon Duke | Carlisle | |
| 1951 | *Call Me Mister* | "Call Me Mister" | Dan Dailey; Betty Grable | 20th Century–Fox |
| | | "Goin' Home Train" | Bobby Short & Male Chorus | |
| | | "Military Life" | Danny Thomas | |

|  | *The Mating Season* | "My Lost Melody"<br>"Because I'm So in Love" |  | Paramount |
|---|---|---|---|---|
| 1954 | *Rear Window* | "Lisa"<br>L — Harold Rome<br>(uncredited)<br>M — Franz Waxman<br>(uncredited) |  | Paramount |
|  | *The Last Time*<br>*I Saw Paris* | "Danse avec Moi"<br>("Dance with Me")<br>M — Frances Lopez<br>L–Andre Hornez (French)<br>L — Harold Rome (English) |  | MGM |
| 1958 | *Wonderful Things!* | "Wonderful Things" | Frankie<br>Vaughan | H. Wilcox<br>Productions |
|  |  | "Little Fishes" | Frankie<br>Vaughan |  |
| 1961 | *Fanny* | "Fanny" | Music only | Warner Bros. |
| 1971 | *The Last*<br>*Picture Show* | "Wish You Were Here" | Eddie Fisher | Columbia |
| 1994 | *It's Pat* | "Everybody Loves<br>Somebody" | Julia Sweeney | Touchstone |

A — Music and lyrics by Harold Rome unless otherwise indicated
B — Also listed as "(All of a Sudden) My Heart Sings"
C — Also known as "United Nations March"
Main sources — Imdb at http://www.imdb.com/title, s.v. "Harold Rome;" New York Public Library at http://catalog.nypl.org/search, s.v. "title."

---

# I. Political Endeavors

| Year | Association | Activity |
|---|---|---|
| 1936 | Federal Arts Council of the Workers Alliance | Songs for the *Spring Frolic* fund raiser |
| 1938 | Cabaret TAC (offshoot of Theatre Committee to Aid Spanish Democracy) | Songs and skits for shows |
| 1939 | Pro-Republican Spain | Protest of embargo of pro-communist, anti–Franco forces |
|  | Madison Square Garden rally against J. Edgar Hoover | Wrote song "Who's Gonna Investigate the Man Who Investigates Me?" |
|  | Council Against Intolerance in Americ | Wrote song "We Sing America" |
| 1941 | Solidarity with Soviet Jews | One of 200 American Jews supporting broadcast message pledging support and cooperation |
| 1942 | War effort | Wrote lyrics to "United Nations on the March" to music of Dmitri Shostakovich |
| 1943 | Players Stage and Political Cabaret | Songs and skits for Leo Shull and Genius, Inc. |

## I. Political Endeavors

| Year | Organization | Activity |
|---|---|---|
| 1946 | National Campaign Committee of the Independent Citizens Committee of the Arts, Sciences and Professions | Entertained at anti–Dewey rally against the incumbent governor of New York |
| | American Committee for Protection of Foreign Born | *Sponsor of Statue of Liberty Anniversary Dinner |
| 1947 | Progressive Citizens of America | *Sponsor of Conference on Cultural Freedom and Civil Liberties |
| | Committee for the First Amendment | *Signer of advertisement in *Hollywood Reporter*, 10/24 |
| | Voice of Freedom Committee | *Associate chairman |
| 1948 | National Council of the Arts, Sciences and Professions | *Signer of advertisement in *Variety*, 12/1, in support of the Hollywood Ten |
| | | *Sponsor of Committee to Abolish House Un-American Activities Committee in *New York Journal-American*, 12/30 |
| | National Council of American-Soviet Friendship | *Sponsor |
| | Wallace for President Campaign | Sponsor and entertainment |
| 1949 | National Council of the Arts, Sciences and Professions | *Support of Cultural and Scientific Conference for World Peace |
| | Letter to 81st Congress | *Signer, calling for abolition of House Un-American Activities Committee in *Daily Worker*, January 3 |
| 1956 | Anti–Tavern on the Green | Rally against New York restaurant incursion into Central Park for parking |
| | A.S.C.A.P. | Interviewed on Mike Wallace TV show re: A.S.C.A.P. vs. B.M.I. dispute |
| 1962 | WAIF-ISS | Financial support of WAIF, the inter-country adoption program |
| 1964 | Democratic National Party | Songs for *Young Dem Bandwagon*, revue for presidential campaign of Lyndon Johnson |
| 1966 | Student Nonviolent Coordinating Committee | Performance of songs at fund raiser |
| 1968 | Citizens for McCarthy Committee | Fundraising for presidential campaign of Senator Eugene McCarthy, Vietnam War opponent |
| | Cyclists for Humphrey | Bike ride–support for presidential campaign of Hubert Humphrey / Edmund Muskie |

*Entry from *Red Channels: The Report of Communist Influence in Radio and Television*, published in 1950 by American Business Consultants

# Chapter Notes

The following refer to large collections or sources of information regarding Harold Rome:

AJC — Harold Rome, interview by Martin Bookspan, November 22, 1982, transcript of recording, **P (Oral Histories, Box 64 no. 7), American Jewish Committee, Oral History Library, Dorot Jewish Division, New York Public Library.

ASCAP — "Harold Rome: Theatre Man." *ASCAP Today* (September 1971).

HRP — Harold Rome Papers, Irving S. Gilmore Music Library, Yale University, New Haven, CT.

HRC — Harold Rome Collection, Library of Congress, Washington, D.C.

LEC — Lehman Engel Collection, Irving S. Gilmore Music Library, Yale University, New Haven, CT.

MCNY — Broadway Production files and Collection on Theatrical Personalities, Museum of the City of New York.

## Preface

1. Theodore Goldsmith, "Of the Music and Lyrics by Harold Rome," *New York Times*, August 11, 1946.

## Chapter 1

1. AJC, 7.
2. AJC, 3–4.
3. Ibid.
4. John Mahoney, "Stage: Composer Sings Different Tune," *Los Angeles Times*, August 26, 1973; Andrew H. Older, "Done with *Pins and Needles*," *Hartford Courant*, January 30, 1938.
5. Roger Wolmuth, "The Arts," *Avenue* (May 1977), 24.
6. William Cockerham, "Songwriter Renews Links to City in Old Place Show," *Hartford Courant*, unidentified date, circa 1977, HRP.
7. Bruce F. Wiener, *A Rome with a View* (Rosemont, PA: Rosemont College, 2001), 1.
8. Whitney Bolton, "Theatre: Harold Rome's Rise in Theatre," *New York Telegraph*, April 2, 1959.
9. AJC, 4–5.
10. AJC, 16–20.
11. Harold Rome, interview by Lehman Engel, Box 6 / Folder 161, 4 LEC.
12. Frederick Nolan, *The Sound of Their Music: The Story of Rodgers and Hammerstein* (New York: Applause Theatre and Cinema Books, 2002), 27, 33; *DC Bar*, Jacob A. Stein, "Legal Spectator: Thanks for the Memory," http://www.dcbar.org/for_lawyers/resources/publications/washington_lawyer//october_2007 (accessed May 1, 2009), 2; William McBrien, *Cole Porter: A Biography* (New York: Alfred A. Knopf, 1998), 50.
13. Notes in musical selections, *Harold Rome's Gallery* (New York: Florence Music, 1964), 1; Norman Nadel, "Rome Harmonizes His Art," *New York World-Telegram and Sun*, November 7, 1964.
14. Rome, interview by Gene Bruck, ASCAP symposium on American music, n.d., *LDC 42652 [CD], Performing Arts Research Collections, Recorded Sound, New York Public Library.
15. Bolton.
16. ASCAP, 12.
17. Rome, interview by Engel, 1.
18. Allen M. Widem, "Coast to Coast," *Hartford Times*, April 11, 1959.
19. AJC, 28–9.
20. Rome, interview by Engel, 1.
21. George W. Clarke, "The Story Behind a Maestro," *Boston Advertiser*, August 24, 1940; New

Haven Evening Register, "Author of Shubert Musical Show Regards New Haven as Second Home," November 13, 1946.
22. Bolton.
23. Rome, interview by Martin Bookspan, ASCAP radio interview, n.d., interview *LDC 50232 [CD], tracks 13–16, Performing Arts Research Collections Recorded Sound, New York Public Library.
24. ASCAP, 13.
25. Rome, interview by Engel, 2.
26. Clarke.
27. Rome, interview by Bruck.
28. Clarke.
29. Wiener, 2; Wolmuth, 24; *WPAT Gaslight Revue Program Guide*, June 1962 (Paterson, NJ: Radio Station WPAT, 1962), 2, 59.
30. Dan O'Leary, liner notes for *Harold Rome: A Touch of Rome* (New York: DRG Theater, 1991).
31. Stanley Green, *The World of Musical Comedy: The Story of the American Musical Stage As Told Through the Careers of Its Foremost Composers and Lyricists* (New York: Ziff-Davis, 1960), 218.
32. William McBrien, *Cole Porter: A Biography* (New York: Alfred A. Knopf, 1998), 220.
33. Mahoney.
34. "Author of Shubert Musical Show Regards New Haven as Second Home," *New Haven Evening Register*, November 13, 1946.

## Chapter 2

1. Lehman Engel, *The American Musical Theater: A Consideration* (New York: Macmillan, 1967), 69–70.
2. Dan Sullivan, "Bargain in the Garment Center: *Pins and Needles* Only $2.50," *New York Times*, June 9, 1967, 51.
3. *Encyclopedia Americana: International Edition* (Danbury, CT: Scholastic Library Publishing, 2005), s.v. "International Ladies' Garment Workers' Union"; *The New Encyclopaedia Britannica*, 15th ed. (Chicago: Encyclopaedia Britannica, 2010), s.v. "International Ladies' Garment Workers' Union."
4. "International Ladies' Garment Workers' Union (1900–)," Western Historical Manuscript Collection, University of St. Louis-Missouri, http://www.umsl.edu-whmc/guides/whm0572.htm (accessed May 12, 2009), 1–2.
5. Amanda Ameer, "Life's a Pitch: We're Straight from the Shops," *Arts Journal*, http://www.artsjournal.com/lifesapitch/2008/09/were-straight-from-the-shops.html (accessed April 17, 2009), 1.
6. Michael Kantor and Laurence Maslon, *Broadway: The American Musical* (New York: Bulfinch Press, 2004), 169.
7. Ameer.
8. Michael Denning, *The Cultural Front: The Laboring of American Culture in the Twentieth Century* (London: Verso, 1998), 296.
9. Ameer, 3; Denning, 297.
10. Denning, 299.
11. Benjamin Stolberg, *Tailor's Progress: The Story of a Famous Union and the Men Who Made It* (New York: Doubleday, Doran, 1944), 296–7.
12. Ameer, 2.
13. Stolberg, 296.
14. "How *Pins and Needles* Was Born," *New York Herald Tribune*, January 30, 1938.
15. "Editor of the Paper," *New York Times*, February 13, 1938.
16. Deborah Jowitt, *Jerome Robbins: His Life, His Theater, His Dance* (New York: Simon & Schuster, 2004), 26–8.
17. Cecil Smith, "Harold J. Rome Composes with Easy Fluency," *Chicago Daily Tribune*, March 16, 1941.
18. Richard Carlin, *American National Biography* (New York: Oxford University Press, 1999), s.v. "Rome, Harold."
19. *The Encyclopedia of Popular Music*, 4th ed., Colin Larkin, ed. (Oxford: Oxford University Press, 2006), s.v. "Rome, Harold."
20. *The New Grove Dictionary of Music and Musicians*, 2nd ed., Stanley Sadie, ed. (London: Grove Press, 2001), s.v. "Rome, Harold."
21. "The Schillinger School of Music," http://www.theschillingerschoolofmusic.org/biog.php (accessed June 2, 2011), 1–2; *The New Grove Dictionary of Music and Musicians*, 2nd ed., Stanley Sadie, ed. (London: Grove Press, 2001), s.v. "Schillinger, Joseph"; "HAROLD ROME," personal notes, 1 HRP.
22. Ameer, 2.
23. "Talk of the Town: Leftist Revue," *The New Yorker*, December 25, 1937, 11.
24. Smith.
25. Denning, 301; AJC, 13.
26. Stanley Green, *The World of Musical Comedy: The Story of the American Musical Stage As Told Through the Careers of Its Foremost Composers and Lyricists* (New York: Ziff-Davis, 1960), 218; Charles Burr, liner notes, *Pins and Needles* (New York: Columbia Records, 1962), 6; Belmont Theatre program for *Pins and Needles*, directed by Charles Friedman, June 1936, HRC.
27. Hollis Alpert, *Broadway! 125 Years of Musical Theatre* (New York: Museum of the City of New York, 1991), 130.
28. Ameer, 1.
29. "Talk of the Town," 12.
30. Stanley Green, *Ring Bells! Sing Songs!: The Musicals of the 1930's* (New Rochelle, NY: Arlington House, 1971), 150.
31. Ethan Mordden, *Sing for Your Supper: The Broadway Musical in the 1930's* (New York: Palgrave Macmillan, 2005), 188.
32. Kantor and Maslon, 169.
33. Denning, 297–8.
34. Harry Goldman, "When Social Signifi-

cance Came to Broadway: *Pins and Needles* in Production," *Theatre Quarterly* 7, no. 28 (Winter 1977–78): 27.
35. Alpert, 130.
36. Gerald Bordman, *American Musical Theatre: A Chronicle* (New York: Oxford University Press, 2001), 614, 647.
37. Steven Suskin, *Show Tunes: The Songs, Shows, and Careers of Broadway's Major Composers*, 3rd ed. (New York: Oxford University Press, 2000), 163–4, 167, 214, 391, 394.
38. Green, *Ring Bells! Sing Songs!*, 151.
39. Suskin, *Show Tunes*, 318–327; *The New Grove Dictionary*, s.v. "Blitzstein, Marc."
40. *Internet Broadway Database*, s.v. "Pins and Needles," http://www.idbd.com/production.php?id=1066, (accessed November 14, 2008); *Absolute Astronomy.com*, "Pins and Needles," http://www.absoluteastronomy.com/topics/Pins_and_Needles (accessed April 15, 2009), 1.
41. Stanley Green, *Broadway Musicals: Show by Show* (Milwaukee: Hal Leonard Books, 1985), 100; David Ewen, *Popular American Composers from Revolutionary Times to the Present: A Biographical and Critical Guide* (New York: H.W. Wilson, 1962), 143.
42. Green, *The World of Musical Comedy*, 218.
43. Laurence Maslon, "Political Satire," *Broadway: The American Musical* http://www.pbs.org/wnet/broadway/p-political.html (accessed April 17, 2009), 2.
44. Green, 217.
45. Mordden, 188.

# Chapter 3

1. Alpert, 130.
2. *Internet Broadway Database*, 1–3; Liner notes, *Pins and Needles*, 2.
3. Burns Mantle, "Drama with Eva Le Gallienne Closes after Less Than a Week," *Chicago Daily Tribune*, November 6, 1938, E2; Robert Sell, "*Pins and Needles*, Produced by the International Ladies' Garment Workers, Is Appealing to the 'Carriage Trade' Just the Same," *St. Louis Post-Dispatch*, January 23, 1938, 4.
4. Robert Baral, *Revue: A Nostalgic Reprise of the Great Broadway Period* (New York: Fleet, 1962), 44–5, 75, 78, 201–2.
5. Suskin, *Show Tunes*, 193; *A Chronology of American Musical Theater*, Richard C. Norton, ed. (Oxford: Oxford University Press, 2002), 773–4.
6. Denning, 297.
7. Harry and Theresa Goldman, "*Pins and Needles*," *Performing Arts Review* 7, no. 3 (1977): 375.
8. Denning, 307.
9. Green, *Broadway Musicals*, 100.
10. T.E. Kalem, "Forty Years On," *Time*, July 17, 1978.
11. Engel, 70.
12. Kanter and Maslon, 170.
13. Harold Rome, "Sing Me a Song with Social Significance" (New York: Chappell, 1938).
14. Green, *The World of Musical Comedy*, 225.
15. Thomas S. Hischak, *Word Crazy: Broadway Lyricists from Cohan to Sondheim* (New York: Praeger, 1991), 92.
16. Kanter and Maslon, 169–70.
17. Rome, interview by Lehman Engel, Box 6 / Folder 161, 5 LEC; Harry Merton Goldman, "*Pins and Needles*: A White House Command Performance," *Educational Theatre Journal* 30, no. 1 (March 1978): 94.
18. Harry Merton Goldman, 94–95.
19. *Encyclopaedia Britannica*, s.v. "American Federation of Labor, International Ladies' Garment Workers' Union (ILGWU);" *Encyclopedia American*, s.v. "American Federation of Labor, ILGWU."
20. Bruce F. Wiener, *A Rome with a View* (Rosemont, PA: Rosemont College, 2001), 29.
21. Andrew H. Older, "Done with *Pins and Needles*," *Hartford Courant*, January 30, 1938.
22. Kalem.
23. Rome, interview with Martin Bookspan, ASCAP radio interview, n.d., interview *LDC 50232 [CD] tracks 13–16, Performing Arts Research Collections Recorded Sound, New York Public Library.
24. *Songwriters Hall of Fame*, s.v. "Harold Rome," http://songwritershalloffame.org/exhibits/C238 (accessed January 10, 2012), 1; *Answers.com*, s.v. "Harold Rome," http://www.answers.com/topic/harold-rome (accessed January 10, 2012), 2.
25. *Camera Three*, "Songs from *Pins and Needles*," WCBS-TV, July 30, 1978, B:70780, The Paley Center for Media, New York.
26. Claudia Cassidy, "On the Aisle: Rome's *Pins and Needles* Rueful Reminder of Social Significance with a Smile," *Chicago Tribune*, June 14, 1962.
27. Smith.
28. Rome, interview by Brooks McNamara, Spring, 1973, 4–5 HRP.
29. Goldman, *Theatre Quarterly*, 32, 34.
30. *Variety*, November 27, 1937.
31. Tom Prideaux, "Tailor-Made Hit of the 30's," *New York Times*, June 4, 1978, 34.
32. "Talk of the Town," 12.
33. Goldman, *Performing Arts Review*, 359–60.
34. Robert, 203.
35. "HAROLD ROME," 3.
36. Goldman, *Theatre Quarterly*, 36.
37. *Camera Three*.
38. Wiener, 37.
39. Goldman, *Educational Theatre Journal*, 96–7.
40. Goldman, *Theatre Quarterly*, 26.
41. Sullivan, 51.

42. Nan Robertson, "Roundabout Prospers in New Home," *New York Times*, August 19, 1986, C16.
43. Sullivan, 51.
44. Kalem; Richard Eder, "Stage: *Pins and Needles*," *New York Times*, July 7, 1978, C5.
45. Robin Brantley, "New Face: Corliss Taylor-Dunn: A Soprano That Audiences Want to Protect," *New York Times*, August 4, 1978, C4; Walter Kerr, "3 Tests of a First-rate Actor," *New York Times*, July 20, 1978, C15.
46. Kerr.
47. Mordden, 189–90.
48. Green, *Ring Bells! Sing Songs!*, 154.
49. Denning, 295.
50. David Dubinsky, liner notes, *Pins and Needles* (New York: Columbia Records, 1962), 8.

## Chapter 4

1. AJC, 29; Wiener, 5.
2. Jared Brown, *Moss Hart: A Prince of the Theatre: A Biography in Three Acts* (New York: Back Stage Books, 2006), 143.
3. Harold Rome, interview by Lehman Engel, Box 6 / Folder 161, 6 LEC.
4. Steven Suskin, *Show Tunes: The Songs, Shows, and Careers of Broadway's Major Composers*, 3rd ed. (New York: Oxford University Press, 2000), 32–3, 139–40.
5. Suskin, s.v. "Hart, Moss," "Kaufman, George S."; Stanley Green, *Encyclopedia of the Musical Theatre* (New York: Dodd, Mead, 1976), s.v. "Hart, Moss," "Kaufman, George S."
6. Suskin, 72–3.
7. Stanley Green, *Ring Bells! Sing Songs!: The Musicals of the 1930's* (New Rochelle, NY: Arlington House, 1971), 166.
8. Ethan Mordden, *Sing for Your Supper: The Broadway Musical in the 1930's* (New York: Palgrave Macmillan, 2005), 192.
9. Brown, 143–4.
10. Malcolm Goldstein, *George S. Kaufman: His Life, His Theater* (New York: Oxford University Press, 1979), 305.
11. John Mason Brown, "Two on the Aisle: *Sing Out the News* at the Music Box," *New York Post*, September 26, 1938, 6.
12. Goldstein, 306.
13. Burns Mantle, *Sing Out the News* a Revel: Radical, Riotous, Unrestrained," *New York Daily News*, September 26, 1938.
14. Michael Denning, *The Cultural Front: The Laboring of American Culture in the Twentieth Century* (London: Verso, 1998), 347; Green, *Ring Bells!*, 166–7.
15. Green, *Ring Bells!*, 166–7.
16. Rome, interview by Martin Bookspan, ASCAP radio interview, n.d., interview *LDC 50232 [CD] tracks 13–16, Performing Arts Research Collections Recorded Sound, New York Public Library.

17. George W. Clarke, "The Story Behind a Maestro," *Boston Advertiser*, August 24, 1940.
18. *ACE Title Search*, s.v. "F. D. R. Jones," The American Society of Composers, Authors and Publishers, http://www.ascap.com/ace/search.cfm?requesttimeout=300 (accessed December 25, 2009).
19. Rome, notes for guest article for columnist Alice Hughes, December 8, 1951, HRP.
20. Steven Suskin, *The Sound of Broadway Music: A Book of Orchestrators and Orchestrations* (Oxford: Oxford University Press, 2009), 539; Richard Lockridge, "The New Play: *Sing Out the News*, Rome-Friedman Revue, Opens at the Music Box," *New York Sun*, September 26, 1938, 12.
21. George Ross, "*Sing Out the News* Hit in Philadelphia," *Philadelphia Inquirer*, August 28, 1938.
22. Edwin H. Schloss, "Footlights: *Sing Out the News* Opens at Forrest," *Philadelphia Record*, August 30, 1938.
23. Brooks Atkinson, "The Play: *Sing Out the News*, a Topical Revue by the Authors of *Pins and Needles*," *New York Times*, September 26, 1938.
24. Sidney B. Whipple, "Exhilarating Entertainment in *Sing Out the News*," *New York World-Telegram*, September 26, 1938.
25. John Mason Brown.
26. Richard Watts, Jr., "The Theaters: New Deal Revue," *New York Tribune*, September 26, 1938, 6.
27. Felicia Hardison Londre and Daniel J. Watermeier, *The History of North American Theater: From Pre-Columbian Times to the Present* (New York: Continuum, 1998), 323.
28. Suskin, *Show Tunes*, 154, 163; Suskin, *Second Act Trouble: Behind the Scenes at Broadway's Big Musical Bombs* (New York: Applause Theatre and Cinema Books, 2006), 153.
29. John Mason Brown.
30. William A. Everett, *Sigmund Romberg* (New Haven, CT: Yale University Press, 2007), 151–2.
31. *The Encyclopedia of Popular Music*, 4th ed., Colin Larkin ed. (Oxford: Oxford University Press, 2006), s.v. "Hellzapoppin."
32. Rome, interview by Roland Winters, The Players Club, February 25, 1972, interview NCOW 35, Performing Arts Research Collections TOFT, New York Public Library.
33. *World Book Encyclopedia* (Chicago: World Book, 2011), s.v. "Munich Agreement"; *The New Encyclopaedia Britannica*, 15th ed. (Chicago: Encyclopaedia Britannica, 2010), s.v. "Munich Agreement."
34. AJC, 15.
35. Lockridge.
36. John Anderson, "*Sing Out the News* Comes to Music Box," *New York Journal-American*, September 26, 1938.
37. *A Chronology of American Musical Theater*,

Richard C. Norton, ed. (Oxford: Oxford University Press, 2002), 799.
38. Suskin, *Show Tunes*, 194.
39. Gerald Bordman, *American Musical Theatre: A Chronicle* (New York: Oxford University Press, 2001), 567.
40. Suskin, *Show Tunes*, 194.
41. Adolph Kaufman, Shubert Organization to William Klein, attorney, 20 March 1940, Shubert Archive.
42. Bordman, 568; *Internet Broadway Database*, s.v. "Streets of Paris," http://www.idbd.com/production.php?id=1066 (accessed November 14, 2008).
43. Program, *Playbill, Streets of Paris*, Broadhurst Theatre, week of August 7, 1939.
44. "Broadway Got Her from Brazil, Finds Her Really Good Neighbor," *New York Tribune*, June 2, 1939.
45. Hugh Martin, *Hugh Martin: The Boy Next Door* (Encinitas, CA: Trolley Press, 2010), 91–2.
46. Suskin, *The Sound of Broadway Music*, 549.
47. Martin, 93.
48. *Playbill*.
49. Bordman, 568.

## Chapter 5

1. Joshua Rome, interview with author, October 4, 2011.
2. "Spring Frolic," Federal Theatre Project Materials Collection, Special Collection & Archives, George Mason University Libraries, http://www.aladin.wrlc.org/gsdl/cgi-bin/library?e+d-01000-00---off-0-0ftpp (accessed May 23, 2009).
3. Michael Denning, *The Cultural Front: The Laboring of American Culture in the Twentieth Century* (New York: Verso, 1998), 326.
4. Ibid.
5. Theodore Strauss, "Night Club Notes," *New York Times*, December 18, 1938.
6. Hilton Als, forward to David Margolick, *Strange Fruit: Billie Holiday, Café Society, and an Early Cry for Civil Rights* (Philadelphia: Running Press, 2000), 16.
7. Denning, 326.
8. Margolick, 83.
9. Denning, 343.
10. Roger D. Kinkle, *The Complete Encyclopedia of Popular Music and Jazz: 1900–1950* (New Rochelle, NY: Arlington House, 1974), s.v. "Dowling, Eddie."
11. Elliot Norton, "Dowling's New Show at Shubert," *Boston Post*, August 21, 1940.
12. Norton.
13. Ethan Mordden, *Sing for Your Supper: The Broadway Musical in the 1930's* (New York: Palgrave, 2001), 190.
14. "Plays out of Town: Little Dog Laughed," *Variety*, August 21, 1940.
15. "Shubert Theatre: *The Little Dog Laughed*," *Boston Daily Globe*, August 21, 1940.
16. Helen Eager, "Dowling Show at Shubert," *Boston Traveler*, August 21, 1940; *Variety*; *Boston Daily Globe*.
17. Eager.
18. Joseph H. Weintraub, "*Little Dog Laughed* Is Sparkling Show," *Atlantic City Press*, August 14, 1940; *Variety*.
19. George W. Clarke, "The Story Behind a Maestro," *Boston Advertiser*, August 24, 1940.
20. Ibid.
21. John Bush Jones, *The Songs That Fought the War: Popular Music and the Home Front, 1939–1945* (Waltham, MA: Brandeis University Press, 2006), 59.
22. Eager.
23. Weintraub.
24. Lehman Engel, *This Bright Day: An Autobiography* (New York: Macmillan, 1974), 125.
25. Eager.
26. "New Dowling Musical Has Pier Opening," *Philadelphia Record*, August 14, 1940; *Variety*; *Boston Daily Globe*.
27. Steven Suskin, *The Sound of Broadway Music: A Book of Orchestrators and Orchestrations* (New York: Oxford University Press, 2009), 459.
28. Cecil Smith, "Harold J. Rome Composes with Easy Fluency," *Chicago Daily Tribune*, March 16, 1941.
29. Suskin.
30. AJC, 31.
31. Ibid., 32.
32. Jared Brown, *Moss Hart: A Prince of the Theatre: A Biography in Three Acts* (New York: Back Stage Books, 2006), 338.
33. Harold Rome, dedication to sheet music for "We Sing America," unpublished, HRP.
34. *Labor Arts*, http://www.laborarts.org/exhibits/playsam/exhibit.cfm?id=16 (accessed June 13, 2009), 1.
35. Rome, "Who's Gonna Investigate the Man Who Investigates Me?," unpublished, 1939, in *Labor Arts*.
36. Rome, interview by Roland Winters, The Players Club, February 25, 1972, interview NCOW 35, Performing Arts Research Collections TOFT, New York Public Library.
37. AJC, 16.
38. Glenn Collins, "Harold Rome, 85, Writer of Socially Pointed Songs," obituary, *New York Times*, October 27, 1993.
39. Rome, "Special lyrics written for the 1940 Roosevelt Campaign," unpublished, *Sing Out the News* folder, Broadway Production files, MCNY.
40. Jones, 92–3.
41. Ibid., 91.
42. Ibid., 91–2; *ACE Title Search*, s.v. "United Nations on the March," The American Society of Composers, Authors and Publishers, http://www.ascap.com/ace/search.cfm?requesttimeout=300 (accessed December 25, 2009), 1.

43. Baker's Biographical Dictionary of Musician's, 8th ed., Nicolas Slonimsky, ed. (New York: Schirmer Books, 1992), s.v. "Shostakovich, Dmitri"; The International Cyclopedia of Music and Musicians, 10th ed. (New York: Dodd, Mead, 1975), s.v. "Shostakovich, Dmitri."
44. All Music Guide: Classical Archives, "Dmitri Shostakovich — Counterplan, Op. 33," http://www.classicarchives.com/work/154148.html (accessed April 21, 2009).
45. Ibid.
46. Dmitri Shostakovich and Rome, "United Nations on the March" (New York: Am-Rus Music, 1942).
47. Denning, 317.
48. "Wallace to Speak Here," New York Times, September 8, 1946, 14.

## Chapter 6

1. Gerald Bordman, American Musical Theatre: A Chronicle (New York: Oxford University Press, 2001), 584.
2. Robert Baral, Revue: A Nostalgic Reprise of the Great Broadway Period (New York: Fleet, 1962), 19–20.
3. John Stewart, Broadway Musicals, 1943–2004 (Jefferson, NC: McFarland, 2006), 781.
4. Steven Suskin, Show Tunes: The Songs, Shows, and Careers of Broadway's Major Composers, 3rd ed. (New York: Oxford University Press, 2000), 4, 39, 89, 149.
5. Internet Broadway Database, s.v. "Star and Garter," http://www.idbd.com/ProductionSongs.aspxShowNo=8277&ProdNo=1206 (accessed November 14, 2008); Richard C. Norton, A Chronology of American Musical Theater (Oxford: Oxford University Press, 2002), 848–9.
6. Bordman.
7. Stewart.
8. Bordman.
9. "Harold Rome," unidentified interviewer, circa 1987, HRP; Cole Porter to Rome, 10 September 1962, HRP.
10. Ethan Mordden, Beautiful Mornin': The Broadway Musical in the 1940's (New York: Oxford University Press, 1999), 120.
11. The New Encyclopaedia Britannica: Micropaedia, 15th ed. (Chicago: Encyclopaedia Britannica, 2010), s.v. "United Service Organizations, Inc."
12. War and American Culture: A Historical Encyclopedia, ed. M. Paul Holsinger (Westport, CT: Greenwood Press, 1999), 320.
13. "About American Theatre Wing: History of ATW," American Theatre Wing, http://americantheatrewing.org/about/history_of_atw_2.php (accessed, June 11, 2009), 1.
14. "Ibid., 2; Malcolm Goldstein, George S. Kaufman: His Life, His Theater (New York: Oxford University Press, 1979), 362; Lewis Nichols,

"Lunchtime Follies," New York Times, June 13, 1943.
15. "About American Theatre Wing," 1.
16. Vernon Pope, "Factory Follies," Saturday Evening Post, January 19, 1943, 25.
17. "About American Theatre Wing," 2.
18. "Whistle While You Work," New York Times, June 23, 1943, 22.
19. Nichols.
20. "Lunchtime Follies, S.R.O.," New York Times, July 11, 1943.
21. "Lunch Follies to Tour," New York Times, September 9, 1942; Pope, 22–25; "About American Theatre Wing," 3.
22. "Lunchtime Follies S.R.O."
23. Goldstein, 362.
24. Jean Meegan, "Lunchtime Follies," Sunday World-Herald Magazine (Omaha), February 14, 1943, 22.
25. John Bush Jones, The Songs That Fought the War: Popular Music and the Home Front, 1939–1945 (Waltham, MA: Brandeis University Press, 2006), 191–2.
26. Jones, 192.
27. "Lunchtime Follies, S.R.O."; "About American Theatre Wing," 5; Jones, 52, 195–6.
28. "Lunchtime Follies, S.R.O."; Jones, 202.
29. "Lunchtime Follies Today," New York Times, October 23, 1942; "Lunch Follies to Tour"; "About American Theatre Wing," 3.
30. Meegan.
31. "Lunchtime Follies, S.R.O."
32. Wilella Waldorf, "Two on the Aisle: Let Freedom Sing Lifts Its Voice at the Longacre," New York Post, October 6, 1942; John Mason Brown, "Theater: The Youth Theater Stages Let Freedom Sing," New York World, October 6, 1942.
33. Burns Mantle, "Youth Has Plenty of Fling in Let Freedom Sing at Longacre," New York Daily News, October 6, 1942.
34. Norton, 854–5; program, Let Freedom Sing, Longacre Theatre, week beginning October 5, 1942, folder, Let Freedom Sing, MCNY.
35. Internet Broadway Database, s.v. "Let Freedom Sing," http://www.idbd.com/ProductionSongs.aspxShowNo=5345&ProdNo=1224 (accessed November 14, 2008).
36. Jones, 209.
37. Ibid.
38. Betty Garrett with Ron Rapoport, Betty Garrett and Other Songs (Lanham, MD: Madison Books, 1998), 59.
39. Garrett, 60.
40. Bordman, 585.
41. Tighe Zimmers, Tin Pan Alley Girl: A Biography of Ann Ronell (Jefferson, NC: McFarland, 2009), 66–7.
42. Mantle; Waldorf.
43. Mantle; Waldorf; Brown; Brooks Atkinson, "The Play," New York Times, October 6, 1942.
44. Waldorf.

45. Joshua Logan, souvenir program, *Fanny*, MCNY.
46. Program, *Playbill, Ziegfeld Follies*, Winter Garden Theatre, week of April 1, 1943, Shubert Archive.
47. Mordden, 24.
48. Adolph Kaufman, attorney, to Harry Kaufman, Shubert Organization, 17 December 1942, Shubert Archive.
49. Stewart, 657.
50. Max Wilk, *OK! The Story of Oklahoma!* (New York: Grove Press, 1993), 250.
51. Jones, 60.
52. Jones, 183.
53. Harold Rome, "Army Separation Qualification Record," HRP.
54. "Lusty New Soldier Show Gets a Good Start at Ft. Hamilton," *New York Daily News*, July 17, 1943; Lucius Beebe, "*Stars and Gripes*," *New York Herald Tribune*, July 17, 1943; *New York Herald Tribune*, "*Stars and Gripes* Opens Tuesday at Fort Hamilton," July 11, 1943; "*Stars and Gripes* Probably the Best Camp-Produced Show," *Variety*, July 21, 1943, 55.
55. "*Stars and Gripes* at Fort Hamilton," *New York Times*, July 16, 1943.
56. Alyn Shipton, *I Feel a Song Coming On: The Life of Jimmy McHugh* (Urbana, IL: University of Illinois Press, 2009), 169; Thomas L. Riis, *Frank Loesser* (New Haven, CT: Yale University Press, 2008), 39–40.
57. "All-Khaki *Stars and Gripes* Gets Top Rating at Newark Canteen," *The Billboard*, August 14, 1943.
58. Irving Drutman, "Soldier Revue Goes on to Win All Objectives," *New York Herald Tribune*, July 18, 1943.
59. "Soldier Songs," *New York Times*, July 25, 1943.
60. "*Stars and Gripes* Probably the Best," 3.
61. Drutman.
62. *Variety*; "*Stars and Gripes* at Fort Hamilton."
63. Jones, 106.
64. Andrea Marcovici: *I'll Be Seeing You: Love Songs of WWII* (Hollywood: Marcovici, 1991); Rosemary Clooney: *For the Duration* (Concord, CA: Concord Jazz, 1991).
65. Dick Jacobs and Harriet Jacobs, *Who Wrote That Song*, 2nd ed. (Cincinnati: Writer's Digest Books, 1994), 73, 104, 114, 116, 130, 142, 209.
66. Robert Coleman, "Theatre: Army Filming Its Hit with Kiss by Carole Lombard," *New York Daily Mirror*, August 9, 1943; *New York Post*, "Army Films *Stars and Gripes*," August 10, 1943.
67. "The U.S. 8th Air Force Presents *Skirts!*," *Go*, May 1945, 22.
68. *Go*; Suskin, 243.
69. Max Wilk, *They're Playing Our Song* (New York: Atheneum, 1973), 248.
70. Stewart, 777.
71. Riis, 39.
72. Jones, 168.

## Chapter 7

1. Roger D. Kinkle, *The Complete Encyclopedia of Popular Music and Jazz: 1900–1950* (New Rochelle, NY: Arlington House, 1974), s.v. "Duke, Vernon."
2. Harold Rome, "Nantucket Data," unpublished notes, HRP.
3. Ibid.
4. Steven Suskin, *Show Tunes: The Songs, Shows, and Careers of Broadway's Major Composers*, 3rd ed. (New York: Oxford University Press, 2000), 165.
5. Ibid.
6. Lewis Funke, "News and Gossip of the Rialto," *New York Times*, June 9, 1946, 45.
7. *Internet Movie Database*, s.v. "The Angry God," http://www.imdb.com/title/tt1147457/ soundtrack (accessed December 23, 2011).
8. Vernon Duke to Rome, 26 September 1960, HRP
9. Rome to Duke, 17 October 1960, HRP.
10. Rome to Duke, 22 September 1960, HRP.
11. "The Jingle Jangle," *Time*, May 6, 1957, 50.
12. Ibid.; "Lyres for Hire," *Time*, April 21, 1961.
13. "The Jingle Jangle."
14. Ibid.; "Lyres for Hire"; *Great Songs of Madison Avenue*, Peter and Craig Norback, eds. (New York: Quadrangle / New York Times Book, 1976), 105, 120; "The Jingle Hall of Fame," http://www.classicthemes.com/50sTVThemes/those-OldJingles.html (accessed May 1, 2009), 4; Philip Lambert, *To Broadway, To Life!: The Musical Theater of Bock and Harnick* (New York: Oxford University Press, 2011), 62–3, 185; James Leve, *Kander and Ebb* (New Haven, CT: Yale University Press, 2009), 307–9.
15. "Lyres for Hire."
16. "The Jingle Hall of Fame."
17. "Sanka Commercial," hand-written lyrics by Harold Rome, HRC.
18. "Lyres for Hire."

## Chapter 8

1. Richard Severo, "Arnold Auerbach, 86, a Comedy Writer," obituary, *New York Times*, October 21, 1998, C27; Ye Olde Vette, "All-Vet Show Big Broadway Hit," *Army Times*, May 4, 1946.
2. Irwin Stambler, *Encyclopedia of Popular Music* (New York: St. Martin's Press, 1965), 204; *Playbill* program, *Call Me Mister*, National Theatre, week beginning May 26, 1947, 40.
3. Severo.
4. *Playbill*.
5. Melvyn Douglas, "'Civvies' with Music," *New York Times*, April 14, 1946.
6. Herman Levin, interview by Edwin Wilson, *CUNY Spotlight*, circa 1990, interview NCOW 102, Performing Arts Research Collections TOFT, New York Public Library.

7. Douglas.
8. Lehman Engel, *The American Musical Theater: A Consideration* (New York: Macmillan, 1967), 5; Richard Kislan, *The Musical: A Look at the American Theater* (Englewood Cliffs, NJ: Prentice-Hall, 1980), 19.
9. Engel, 45.
10. Felicia Hardison Londre and Daniel J. Watermeier, *The History of North American Theater: From Pre-Columbian Times to the Present* (New York: Continuum, 1998), 290; Engel, 46.
11. William Everett, *Rudolf Friml* (Urbana: University of Illinois Press, 2008), 15; Everett, *Sigmund Romberg* (New Haven, CT: Yale University Press, 2007), 47; Kislan, 19.
12. Charles Higham, *Ziegfeld* (Chicago: Henry Regnery, 1972), 63–4.
13. Robert Baral, *Revue: A Nostalgic Reprise of the Great Broadway Period* (New York: Fleet, 1972), 265–88; Engel, 67; Leonard Sillman, *Here Lies Leonard Sillman: Straightened Out at Last* (New York: Citadel, 1959), various; Londre, 290; Wikipedia, s.v. "Leonard Sillman," http://en.wikipedia.org/Leonard_Sillman (accessed July 1, 2011), 1; Stanley Green, *Encyclopedia of the Musical Theatre* (New York: Dodd, Mead, 1976), s.v. "Leslie, Lew."
14. Everett, *Romberg*, 47–8.
15. Engel, 65.
16. Dan O'Leary, liner notes for *Harold Rome: A Touch of Rome* (New York: DRG Theater, 1991).
17. *American National Biography* (New York: Oxford University Press, 1999), s.v. "Rome, Harold."
18. *The Encyclopedia of Popular Music*, 4th ed., ed. Colin Larkin (Oxford: Oxford University Press, 2006), s.v. "Rome, Harold."
19. Harold Rome, interview by Gene Bruck, ASCAP symposium on American music, n.d., interview *LDC 42652 [CD], Performing Arts Research Collections, Recorded Sound, New York Public Library.
20. George Jean Nathan, "The Season's Showers Bring April Flowers," *New York Post*, April 19, 1946.
21. Baral, 209.
22. Theodore Goldsmith, "Of the Music and Lyrics of Harold Rome," *New York Times*, August 11, 1946.
23. Rome, interview by Martin Bookspan, ASCAP radio interview, n.d., interview *LDC 50232 [CD] tracks 13–16, Performing Arts Research Collections Recorded Sound, New York Public Library.
24. Abel Green, introduction to Robert Baral, *Revue: A Nostalgic Reprise of the Great Broadway Period* (New York: Fleet, 1962), 6.
25. Steven Suskin, *Show Tunes: The Songs, Shows, and Careers of Broadway's Major Composers*, 3rd ed. (New York: Oxford University Press, 2000), 50–1, 139–40, 161; Engel, 68–9; Richard C. Norton, *A Chronology of American Musical Theater* (Oxford: Oxford University Press, 2002), 625, 646, 663, 701, 783.
26. Engel, 67.
27. Ibid., 44.
28. Gerald Bordman, *Days to Be Happy, Years to be Sad: The Life and Music of Vincent Youmans* (New York: Oxford University Press, 1982), 151.
29. William McBrien, *Cole Porter: A Biography* (New York: Alfred A. Knopf, 1998), 70.
30. Baral, 213; Ethan Mordden, *Beautiful Mornin': The Broadway Musical in the 1940's* (New York: Oxford University Press, 1999), 181–2.
31. Malcolm L. Johnson, "Rome Comes Home with a Smash Fanny," *Hartford Courant*, August 10, 1986.
32. "Rome Must Be a Folk Singer," *Philadelphia Record*, March 22, 1946.
33. Lewis B. Funke, "News and Gossip of the Rialto," *New York Times*, March 3, 1946, X2.
34. Stanley Green, *The World of Musical Comedy: The Story of the American Musical Stage as Told through the Careers of Its Foremost Composers and Lyricists* (New York: Ziff-Davis, 1960), 220; Abe Laufe, *Broadway's Greatest Musicals*, rev. ed. (New York: Funk and Wagnall's, 1977), 380.
35. Funke; *Playbill*, 32–40.
36. Louis Calta, "Musical Planned by Harold Rome," *New York Times*, August 21, 1959.
37. Topics of skits gleaned from various reviews of *Call Me Mister* listed in the Bibliography.
38. Edwin H. Schloss, "*Call Me Mister* Opens at the Forrest Theater," *Philadelphia Record*, March 20, 1946.
39. Ibid.
40. Linton Martin, "Unpretentious Stage Show May Prove Most Appealing," *Philadelphia Inquirer*, March 24, 1946.
41. "The New York Play," *The Hollywood Reporter*, April 19, 1946.
42. "Arnold Horwitt Dies at 59; Writer and Lyricist for Broadway Shows," obituary, *New York Times*, October 23, 1977, 40; Suskin, 394–5.
43. Rome, "*Call Me Mister* as Seen by Its Composer," *New York Herald Tribune*, June 1, 1947.
44. Charlie Niles, "Fan Fare," *Hartford Times*, November 14, 1946.
45. John Chapman, "*Call Me Mister* a Fine, Funny, Brisk Revue by and with Ex-GI's," *New York Daily News*, April 19, 1946; Lewis Nichols, "The Play," *New York Times*, April 19, 1946.
46. Kaspar Monahan, "*Call Me Mister* Gay, Mocking Revue," *Pittsburgh Press*, April 1, 1947.
47. "Successful Military Operation," *New Yorker*, April 20, 1946.
48. Mordden, *Open a New Window: The Broadway Musical in the 1960's* (New York: Palgrave, 2001), 118.
49. Cartoon accompanying Rome, "*Call Me Mister* as Seen by Its Composer."
50. "Rome Must Be a Folk Singer."
51. Rome, interview by Roland Winters, The

Players Club, February 25, 1972, interview NCOW 35, Performing Arts Research Collections TOFT, New York Public Library.
52. *The Encyclopedia of Popular Music*, s.v. "Garrett, Betty."
53. Schloss; Nichols.
54. William F. McDermott, "*Call Me Mister* Fast and Amusing G.I. Musical Show Enlivens the Hanna Stage," *Cleveland Plain Dealer*, April 15, 1947.
55. Nichols.
56. Goldsmith.
57. Betty Garrett with Ron Rapoport, *Betty Garrett and Other Songs* (New York: Madison Books, 1998), 78–9.
58. Engel, *This Bright Day: An Autobiography* (New York: Macmillan, 1974), 151.
59. *ACE Title Search*, The American Society of Composers, Authors and Publishers, http://www.ascap.com/ace/search.cfm?requesttimeout=300 (accessed December 25, 2009), s.v. "South America, Take It Away."
60. Garrett, 80.
61. ASCAP, 13.
62. Mordden, *Beautiful Mornin'*, 46.
63. Vernon Duke to Rome, 4 April 1946, HRP.
64. Lt. David Levy, USNR, Chief of Radio Section to Rome, 19 March 1946, HRP.
65. Sam Zolotow, "News of the Stage," *New York Times*, May 30, 1946, 26.
66. Chapman, "*Call Me Mister* a Fine, Funny, Brisk Revue by and with Ex-GI's," *New York Daily News*, April 19, 1946.
67. AJC, 32–3.
68. Norton, 911–12.
69. McDermott; Leo Gaffney, "Fine Revue at the Shubert," *Boston Daily Record*, December 3, 1946.
70. Elinor Hughes, "*Call Me Mister*, G.I. Revue, Witty and Shrewd," *Boston Sunday Herald*, July 7, 1946.
71. David Ewen, *All the Years of American Popular Music* (Englewood Cliffs, NJ: Prentice-Hall, 1977), 445.
72. Lester Bernstein, "They're Real Civilians Now," *New York Times*, April 13, 1947, 67; Sam Zolotow, "Parish Play Ends Its Run Tomorrow," *New York Times*, April 18, 1947.
73. Henry T. Murdock, "*Call Me Mister* Regarded as Fast-stepping Musical," *Chicago Sun*, May 14, 1947.
74. Norton, 913; Louis Calta, "3 Plays to Leave Broadway Tonight," *New York Times*, January 10, 1948, 10.
75. Laufe, 381.
76. *Chicago Times*, May 14, 1947; "Entertainment Calendar," *Chicago Daily Tribune*, September 21, 1947.
77. Samuel L. Singer, "*Call Me Mister* Returns to Phila. on Shubert Stage," *Philadelphia Inquirer*, November 19, 1946; "*Call Me Mister*— at Shubert," *Philadelphia Daily News*, November 19, 1946.
78. "Nixon Gets a Show That's Fast, Bright," *Pittsburgh Post-Gazette*, April 1, 1947; Norton, 913.
79. Monahan; Claudia Cassidy, "On the Aisle," *Chicago Daily Tribune*, May 14, 1947.
80. Thomas F. Brady, "RKO Will Produce *The Window* Here," *New York Times*, October 28, 1947.
81. Roger Wolmuth, "The Arts," *Avenue*, May 1977, 25.
82. *Call Me Mister*, directed by Lloyd Bacon, 1951 (no place: Loving the Classics, 2008); *Internet Movie Database*, s.v. "Call Me Mister," http://wwww.imdb.com/title/tt0043370/ (accessed July 26, 2010), 7.
83. AJC, 28.
84. John Mahoney, "Stage: Composer Sings Different Tune," *Los Angeles Times*, August 26, 1973.
85. Charlotte Greenspan, *Pick Yourself Up: Dorothy Fields and the American Musical* (New York: Oxford University Press, 2010), 84.
86. Frederick Nolan, *The Sound of Their Music: The Story of Rodgers and Hammerstein* (New York: Applause Theatre and Cinema Books, 2002), 124.
87. Alyn Shipton, *I Feel a Song Coming On: The Life of Jimmy McHugh* (Urbana: University of Illinois Press, 2009), 110.
88. Gerald Bordman, *Jerome Kern: His Life and Music* (New York: Oxford University Press, 1980), 404–5.
89. Hugh Martin, *Hugh Martin: The Boy Next Door* (Encinitas, CA: Trolley Press, 2010), 173.
90. *Internet Movie Database*, 5; Lester Halliwell, *Halliwell's Film and Video Guide*, 12th ed., John Walker, ed. (New York: HarperPerennial, 1997), s.v. "Call Me Mister."
91. AJC, 10.
92. Ernest Leogrande, "Harold Rome Sharpens Up His 'Needles,'" *New York Daily News*, June 12, 1978.
93. *Camera Three*, "Songs from *Pins and Needles*," WCBS-TV, July 30, 1978, B:70780, The Paley Center for Media, New York.
94. ASCAP, 13.
95. "Seeing Things: The Order of the Ruptured Duck," *The Saturday Review*, April 25, 1946, 24.

## Chapter 9

1. William Hawkins, "Talent Jam-Packs *Bless You All*," *New York World-Telegram and Sun*, December 15, 1950.
2. Louis Calta, "*Bless You All* to Open Tonight," *New York Times*, December 14, 1950.
3. *The Encyclopedia of Popular Music*, 4th ed., Colin Larkin, ed. (Oxford: Oxford University Press, 2006), s.v. "Rome, Harold."
4. Theodore Goldsmith, "Of the Music and

Lyrics of Harold Rome," *New York Times*, August 11, 1946.
  5. ASCAP, 13.
  6. Max Wilk, *OK! The Story of Oklahoma!* (New York: Grove Press, 1993), 79.
  7. Agnes de Mille, *Dance to the Piper* (Boston: Little, Brown, 1951–52), 237.
  8. Robert Baral, *Revue: A Nostalgic Reprise of the Great Broadway Period* (New York: Fleet, 1962), 113.
  9. Baral, 59.
  10. Lehman Engel, *The American Musical Theater: A Consideration* (New York: Macmillan, 1977), 65–6.
  11. Comments and data gleaned from several reviews listed in the Bibliography.
  12. Richard Watts, Jr., "Two on the Aisle: Some Tall Girls and Low Comics," *New York Post*, June 25, 1950.
  13. John Stewart, *Broadway Musicals, 1943–2004* (Jefferson, NC: McFarland, 2006), s.v. "Alive and Kicking."
  14. Gerald Bordman, *American Musical Theatre: A Chronicle*, 3rd ed. (New York: Oxford University Press, 2001), 626.
  15. Harold Rome, interview by Lehman Engel, Box 6 / Folder 161, 13 LEC.
  16. *Variety*, "Alive and Kicking," January 25, 1950.
  17. John Chapman, "Creators of *Alive and Kicking* Turn Out Pretty Dull Revue," *Chicago Daily Tribune*, January 18, 1950.
  18. *Cue*, "Alive and Kicking," January 25, 1950.
  19. George S. Kaufman to Rome, circa 20 June 1943, HRP.
  20. Goldstein, 413; Louis Calta, "Equity Reprimand Voted for Burns," *New York Times*, July 21, 1949.
  21. Ethan Mordden, *Beautiful Mornin': The Broadway Musical in the 1940's* (New York: Oxford University Press, 1999), 136.
  22. *A Chronology of American Musical Theater*, Richard C. Norton, ed. (Oxford: Oxford University Press, 2002), 979.
  23. John Chapman, "Mike Todd Stages Stag Smoker, *Peep Show*, at Winter Garden," *New York Daily News*, June 29, 1950.
  24. Baral, 105.
  25. Ibid., 112.
  26. Watts, Jr.
  27. Ibid.
  28. Rome to Engel, circa summer, 1950, 2 LEC.
  29. Agreements between Rome and B.R.T. Corporation, 21 April 1950 and Rome and Michael Todd with B.R.T. Corporation, 9 May 1950, HRP.
  30. Rome to Engel, 2.
  31. H. William Fitelson to Rome, 25 August 1950, HRP.
  32. Rome, interview by Roland Winters, The Players Club, February 25, 1972, interview NCOW 35, Performing Arts Research Collections TOFT, New York Public Library.
  33. Comments and data gleaned from reviews listed in the Bibliography.
  34. *Theatre Arts*, "*Bless You All*" (February 1951), 18.
  35. R.E.P. Sensenderfer, "The Living Theater: *Bless You All*," *Philadelphia Evening Bulletin*, November 22, 1950.
  36. *Theatre Arts*.
  37. John McClain, "*Bless You All*: A Good Musical with Weak Spots," *New York Journal-American*, December 15, 1950.
  38. Sensenderfer.
  39. John McClain, "Pictorial Review," *New York Journal-American*, December 10, 1950; *The Complete Encyclopedia of Popular Music and Jazz: 1900–1950*, Roger D. Kinkle, ed. (New Rochelle, NY: Arlington House, 1974), s.v. "Bailey, Pearl."
  40. Steven Suskin, *Show Tunes: The Songs, Shows, and Careers of Broadway's Major Composers*, 3rd ed. (New York: Oxford University Press, 2000), 154–5.
  41. Suskin, 155; McClain, "Pictorial Review."
  42. Sensenderfer.
  43. Ibid.
  44. Brooks Atkinson, "At the Theatre," *New York Times*, December 15, 1950; McClain, "Pictorial Review"; Howard Barnes, "The Theaters: *Bless You All*," *New York Herald Tribune*, December 15, 1950.
  45. Suskin, *The Sound of Broadway Music: A Book of Orchestrators and Orchestrations* (Oxford: Oxford University Press, 2009), 555.
  46. "Plays out of Town: *That's the Ticket*," *Variety*, September 29, 1948.
  47. Amanda Vaill, *Somewhere: The Life of Jerome Robbins* (New York: Broadway Books, 2006), 152.
  48. *Musicals Tonight*, s.v. "That's the Ticket," http://www.musicalstonight.org/ARCHthatstheticket.html (accessed April 14, 2009).
  49. Vaill; Deborah Jowitt, *Jerome Robbins: His Life, His Theater, His Dance* (New York: Simon & Schuster, 2004), 145.
  50. Vaill, 153.
  51. Jerry Gaghan, "*That's the Ticket*, Shubert; Musical Satire Election Year," *Philadelphia Daily News*, September 25, 1948.
  52. Edwin H. Schloss, "*That's the Ticket* Makes Debut at Shubert," *Philadelphia Inquirer*, September 25, 1948.
  53. Gaghan; *Variety*.
  54. *That's the Ticket*, directed by Thomas Mills, compact disc (Georgetown, CT: Original Cast Records, 2002).
  55. Victor Gluck, *Backstage*, review of *That's the Ticket*, May 3, 2002.
  56. *That's the Ticket*, CD.
  57. John Mahoney, "Stage: Composer Sings Different Tune," *Los Angeles Times*, August 26, 1973.

58. Henry T. Murdock, "*Bless You All*, Musical, Has Premiere at Forrest," *Philadelphia Inquirer*, November 22, 1950.
59. Engel, *The American Musical Theater*, 187.
60. "Bless You All Company: Statement of Operations: Exhibit C," weeks ending December 16, 23, 30, 1950, HRC.
61. Program for *Bless You All*, Shubert Theater, New Haven, CT, November 13–18, 1950.
62. Norton, 984.
63. John Chapman, "*Bless You All* Is Bright Revue; Flaws Are Few," *Chicago Daily Tribune*, December 16, 1950.
64. McClain, "Pictorial Review."
65. Theater advertisements, *New York Post*, December 15, 1950; Suskin, *Show Tunes*, s.v. show name.
66. James Leve, *Kander and Ebb* (New Haven, CT: Yale University Press, 2009), 172–3.
67. Felicia Hardison Londre and Daniel J. Watermeier, *The History of the North American Theater: From Pre-Columbian Times to the Present* (New York: Continuum, 1998), 361.
68. AJC, 33–4.
69. Philip Lambert, *To Broadway, To Life!: The Musical Theater of Bock and Harnick* (New York: Oxford University Press, 2011), 25.
70. Frederick Nolan, *The Sound of Their Music: The Story of Rodgers and Hammerstein* (New York: Applause Theatre and Cinema Books, 2002), 237.
71. Engel, *This Bright Day: An Autobiography* (New York: Macmillan, 1974), 191.
72. Rome, "How to Write a Hit Musical," early draft, n.d., HRP.

## Chapter 10

1. *Red Channels: The Report of Communist Influence in Radio and Television* (New York: American Business Consultants, 1950), 124–5.
2. "Blacklisting," The Jewish Museum, http://www.thejewishmuseum.org/online/gallery_theme.php?id=blacklisting (accessed May 1, 2009), 1.
3. *Red Channels*, 1.
4. Ibid., 3.
5. "Blacklisting," 1.
6. AJC, 25.
7. *Red Channels*, 9–160.
8. Ibid., 124–5.
9. Eric A. Gordon, *Mark the Music: The Life and Work of Marc Blitzstein* (New York: St. Martin's Press, 1989), 347.
10. AJC, 27.
11. Joshua Rome, discussion with author, October 4, 2011.
12. AJC, 26.
13. Gordon, 348.
14. AJC, 50.

## Chapter 11

1. *Playbill* program for *Wish You Were Here*, Imperial Theatre, week beginning June 29, 1953, 17.
2. Ethan Mordden, *Coming Up Roses: The Broadway Musical in the 1950's* (New York: Oxford University Press, 1998), 55.
3. "News of the Stage," *New York Times*, May 8, 1936, 21; AJC, 7.
4. Charles Strouse, *Put on a Happy Face: A Broadway Memoir* (New York: Union Square Press, 2008), 48; Philip Lambert, *To Broadway, To Life!: The Musical Theater of Bock and Harnick* (New York: Oxford University Press, 2011), 23–4, 32; Deborah Jowitt, *Jerome Robbins: His Life, His Theater, His Dance* (New York: Simon & Schuster, 2004), 27–8; Richard Altman and Mervyn Kaufman, *The Making of a Musical: Fiddler on the Roof* (New York: Crown, 1971), 25.
5. Strouse, 48.
6. AJC, 7–8.
7. Mordden, 55–6.
8. Jaime J. Weinman, "Something Old, Something New: Thoughts on Popular Culture and Unpopular Culture," http://zvbxrpl.blogspot.com/2005/lyrics-by-harold-rome-certain.html (accessed April 14, 2009), 1.
9. Joshua Logan, *Josh: My Up and Down In and Out Life* (New York: Delacorte Press, 1976), 269.
10. George W. Clarke, "The Story behind a Maestro," *Boston Advertiser*, August 24, 1940.
11. Vernon Rice, "Curtain Cues: Amateur Night at Camp Karefree," *New York Post*, June 26, 1952.
12. Mordden, 55.
13. Harold Rome to William Fitelson, 7 January 1953, HRP.
14. Kurt Ganzl, *Encyclopedia of the Musical Theater* (New York: Schirmer Books, 1994), s.v. "Wish You Were Here"; John Stewart, *Broadway Musicals, 1943–2004* (Jefferson, NC: McFarland, 2006), 646.
15. Abe Laufe, *Broadway Greatest Musicals*, revised ed. (New York: Funk and Wagnall's, 1977), 166.
16. Sam Zolotow, "Musical Enters Imperial Tonight," *New York Times*, June 25, 1952, 24; Aline B. Louchheim, "Director 'Having Wonderful Time,'" *New York Times*, June 15, 1952, 38; Arthur Pollock, "Theater Time: *Wish You Were Here* Opens at the Imperial," *The Daily Compass*, June 26, 1952, 14.
17. Louchheim.
18. Stewart.
19. Lewis Funke, "News and Gossip Gathered on the Rialto," *New York Times*, March 9, 1952, X1; "*Two on the Aisle* Opens Here on Tuesday Night," *Chicago Daily Tribune*, May 4, 1952, H2; E.J. Kahn, Jr., "Profiles: The Tough Guy and the Soft Guy—II," *The New Yorker*, April 11, 1953, 40.

20. Claudia Cassidy, "On the Aisle: Lots of Production, Beef, and Brawn but Not Much of a Musical," *Chicago Daily Tribune*, December 9, 1953, D2; Stewart.
21. Laufe.
22. Milton Esterow, "Revisions during the Run," *New York Times*, April 23, 1961, 119.
23. Max Wilk, *OK! The Story of Oklahoma!* (New York: Grove Press, 1993), 3.
24. Ibid., 177.
25. Ibid., 180–1.
26. Rice.
27. John Chapman, "New Musical Hold Its Own against Odds," *Chicago Daily Tribune*, July 6, 1952, G4.
28. Stewart, 646; Logan, 271.
29. Kahn, Jr.
30. Rome, interview by Lehman Engel, Box 6 / Folder 161, 18 LEC.
31. William Hawkins, "Theater: *Wish You Were Here* Opens at Redecorated Imperial," *New York World-Telegram and Sun*, June 26, 1952.
32. Milton Bracker, "The Flop That Turned into a Hit," *New York Times*, January 25, 1953, X3; Mordden, 57.
33. Liner notes, *Wish You Were Here* (England: Flare Records, 2007), 8.
34. Bordman, 637; Ganzl; David Ewen, *All the Years of American Popular Music* (Englewood Cliffs, NJ: Prentice-Hall, 1977), 602.
35. Logan, 270.
36. Rome interview by Engel, 17.
37. Rome, interview by Gene Bruck, ASCAP symposium on American music, n.d., interview *LDC 42652 [CD], Performing Arts Research Collections Recorded Sound, New York Public Library.
38. *ACE Title Search*, s.v. "Wish You Were Here," The American Society of Composers, Author and Publishers, http://www.ascap.com/ace/search.cfm?requesttimeout=300&mode (accessed December 25, 2009).
39. Bordman.
40. Stanley Green, *The World of Musical Comedy: The Story of the American Musical Stage as Told through the Careers of Its Foremost Composers and Lyricists* (New York: Ziff-Davis, 1960), 225.
41. Chapman; Bordman; Robert Coleman, "The Theatre: *Wish You Were Here* Not Quite Up to Snuff," *New York Daily Mirror*, June 26, 1952; Liner notes, 3; Pollock.
42. Weinman, 1.
43. Joshua Logan, *Fanny*, souvenir program, MCNY.
44. Weinman, 2.
45. Bracker, X1.
46. Mary C. Henderson, *Mielziner: Master of Modern Stage Design* (New York: Back Stage Books, 2001), 191–2; Logan, 274–6.
47. John Corry, "Broadway: Old-time Burlesque is Musical Subject for Carol Channing," *New York Times*, May 26, 1978, C2.
48. Kahn, Jr., 40.
49. Mordden, 57.
50. Bracker.
51. Kahn, Jr., 42.
52. Kahn, Jr., "Profiles: The Tough Guy and the Soft Guy—I," *The New Yorker*, April 4, 1953, 38.

## Chapter 12

1. Steven DeRosa, *Writing with Hitchcock: The Collaboration of Alfred Hitchcock and John Michael Hayes* (New York: Faber and Faber, 2001), 47–8.
2. DeRosa, 50.
3. *The New Grove Dictionary of Music and Musicians*, 2nd ed., Stanley Sadie, ed. (London: Grove Press, 2001), s.v. "Waxman, Franz."
4. *The New Grove Dictionary of American Music*, H. Wiley Hitchcock and Stanley Sadie, eds. (New York: Macmillan, 1986), s.v. "film music."
5. DeRosa, 47–50; Jack Sullivan, *Hitchcock's Music* (New Haven, CT: Yale University Press, 2006), 169–82.
6. Sullivan, 175.
7. Alfred Hitchcock, "*Rear Window*," *Take One* (Nov–Dec, 1968), 18.
8. Steven Suskin, *Show Tunes: The Songs, Shows, and Careers of Broadway's Major Composers*, 3rd ed. (New York: Oxford University Press, 2000); Ken Mandelbaum, *Not Since Carrie: 40 Years of Broadway Musical Flops* (New York: St. Martin's Press, 1991). These shows are covered in both texts, although the Mandelbaum book focuses on flops.
9. *Internet Movie Database*, s.v. "Saints and Sinners," http://www.imdb.com/title/tt0041836/ (accessed June 7, 2011), 1.
10. Suskin, 223–4.
11. Edward Jablonski, *Alan Jay Lerner: A Biography* (New York: Henry Holt, 1996), 104.
12. Benjamin Aslan to Michael Halperin, 26 January 1954, HRP.
13. Sam Zolotow, "*Daphne* Opening Is Canceled Here," *New York Times*, September 18, 1953, 16.
14. Zolotow, "Guinness Stymied in Bid to Act Here," *New York Times*, June 11, 1954, 20.
15. Zolotow, "Katzka Discusses Spewack Musical," *New York Times*, July 21, 1954, 19.
16. Zolotow, "Malden to Leave Drama on Aug. 13," *New York Times*, July 29, 1955, 9.
17. Louis Calta, "Hart, Rome Finish Work on Musical," *New York Times*, November 1, 1955, 25.
18. Jared Brown, *Moss Hart: A Prince of the Theatre: A Biography in Three Acts* (New York: Back Stage Books, 2006), 338; Kitty Carlisle Hart, *Kitty: An Autobiography* (New York: Doubleday, 1988), 175.
19. Louis Calta, "Yiddish Theatre Gets 50

Backers," *New York Times*, June 7, 1955; Calta, "Hart, Rome Finish Work on Musical."
20. Frederick Nolan, *The Sound of Their Music: The Story of Rodgers and Hammerstein* (New York: Applause Theatre and Cinema Books, 2002), 229; Jablonski, 104.
21. Suskin, 224–5.
22. Brown, 339.
23. Ibid., 338.
24. Hart, 177.
25. Suskin, 224–5.
26. Malcolm L. Johnson, "Rome Comes Home with a Smash *Fanny*," *Hartford Courant*, August 10, 1986.
27. Robert Barlow, "Yale and The American Musical Theater," *The Yale Library Gazette* (April 1954), 144–49.
28. *Wikipedia*, s.v. "Cast Recording," http://en.wikipedia.org/wiki/Cast_recording (accessed June 8, 2012), 2, 6.
29. Goddard Lieberson to Harold Rome, 25 August 1954, HRP.
30. Rome to Lieberson, personal note on above letter, Lieberson to Rome.
31. Richard Warren, Curator of Historical Sound Recordings, Irving S. Gilmore Library, Yale University, email to author, January 27, 2012.

## Chapter 13

1. Harold Rome, "How to Write a Hit Musical," 1967, HRP.
2. Gerald Bordman, *American Musical Theatre: A Chronicle*, 3rd ed. (New York: Oxford University Press, 2001), 645.
3. *Variety*, September 15, 1954; "Shows on Broadway: *Fanny*," *Variety*, November 10, 1954; Leslie Halliwell, *Halliwell's Film and Video Guide*, 12th ed., John Walker, ed. (New York: Harper-Perennial, 1997), s.v. "Fanny"; *The Film Encyclopedia*, 5th ed. (New York: HarperCollins, 2005), s.v. "Raimu."
4. Steven Suskin, liner notes, *Fanny* (New York: BMG Entertainment, 1996), 8; Joshua Logan, *Josh: My Up and Down, In and Out Life* (New York: Delacorte, 1976), 286.
5. Art Buchwald, "Europe's Lighter Side: Pagnol on His 60th Birthday," *Paris Herald*, n.d., 1955, HRP.
6. Suskin, 8.
7. Ibid.
8. Logan, 286; Frederick Nolan, *The Sound of Their Music: The Story of Rodgers and Hammerstein* (New York: Applause Theatre and Cinema Books, 2002), 228.
9. David Merrick, interview by Lehman Engel, 3 LEC.
10. Merrick, 5–6.
11. Hugh Fordin, *Getting to Know Him: A Biography of Oscar Hammerstein II* (New York: Random House, 1977), 322.
12. Merrick, 7.
13. Logan, 287–8.
14. Suskin, 8–9; Howard Kissel, *David Merrick: The Abominable Showman: The Unauthorized Biography* (New York: Applause Theatre and Cinema Books, 1993), 93.
15. Rome, interview by Gene Bruck, ASCAP symposium on American music, n.d., interview *LDC 42652 [CD], Performing Arts Research Collections Recorded Sound, New York Public Library.
16. Rome, "How to Write a Hit Musical."
17. Rome to William Fitelson, 7 January 1953, HRP.
18. S. N. Behrman, "My Life with *Fanny*," *New York Times*, October 30, 1955, X1.
19. John Chapman, "*Fanny* a Warm and Captivating Musical with a Grand Big Cast," *New York Daily News*, November 5, 1954, 57.
20. Nolan, 67–8, 133.
21. George Keaney, *New York World-Telegram and Sun*, December 4, 1954, 10–11.
22. Louis Calta, "*Homeward Look* Opening Tonight," *New York Times*, June 3, 1954.
23. Suskin, 5; *Theatre Arts*, October 1954, 94.
24. Nolan, 187–8.
25. Kissel, 94.
26. Barry Kleinbort, phone discussion with author, November 15, 2011.
27. Robert Baral, *Revue: A Nostalgic Reprise of the Great Broadway Period* (New York: Fleet, 1962), 211; *Fanny*, directed by Joshua Logan, souvenir program, Museum of the City of New York.
28. Nolan, 182.
29. Marjorie Farnsworth, "Woman of the Week: On the Horizon, a Star," *New York Journal-American*, October 16, 1954, 8; George Clarke, "Around Boston: Ezio Pinza's 'Fadder' Looks Like Josh Logan," *Boston Daily Record*, September 20, 1954.
30. Clarke.
31. Suskin, 9–10; Sam Zolotow, "*Lullaby* Leaving Lyceum Saturday," *New York Times*, March 8, 1954, 23.
32. "Producers Trail Mary Martin," *New York Times*, June 19, 1953, 17; Sam Zolotow, "Musical Lined up for Mary Martin," *New York Times*, December 18, 1953, 39.
33. Herbert Kupferberg, "Pinza Grows Mustache for *Fanny*," *New York Herald-Tribune*, October 31, 1954.
34. Kissel, 93.
35. Glenn Litton and Cecil Smith, *Musical Comedy in America* (New York: Routledge/Theatre Arts Books, 1991), 228.
36. Ezio Pinza to Rome, 6 November 1954, HRC.
37. Bruce F. Wiener, *A Rome with a View* (Rosemont, PA: Rosemont College, 2001), 9.
38. Marjory Adams, "Ezio Pinza, Star of *Fanny*, Will Never Return to Opera," *Boston Globe*, September 19, 1954.

39. Elliot Norton, "The Theatre," *Boston Post*, September 21, 1954.
40. Robert Tee, *London Daily Mirror* to Harold Rome, 1 January 1957, HRP.
41. "*Fanny* $50,151, *Gertie* 10G, Hub," *Variety*, October 13, 1954.
42. Wayne Robinson, "Show Writer Keeps Young Composing Broadway Hits," *Philadelphia Evening Bulletin*, October 26, 1954.
43. Robert Fryer to Rome, 21 October 1954, HRP.
44. L.G. Gaffney, "*Fanny* Arty, Needs Revision," *Boston Daily Record*, September 22, 1954; Hamilton Dalton, "*Fanny* Opens at Shubert; Show Is Sure-Fire Hit," *Philadelphia Daily News*, October 13, 1954.
45. "Tamiris Staging *Fanny* Dances," *Variety*, September 29, 1954; Malcolm L. Johnson, "Rome Comes Home with a Smash *Fanny*," *Hartford Courant*, August 10, 1986.
46. Elliot Norton, "Second Thoughts of a First-Nighter: New Musical *Fanny* Rich in Promise," *Boston Post*, September 26, 1954.
47. Nolan, 186.
48. Rome, "What's Josh Logan like? I don't know.," personal notes, circa November 1954, HRP.
49. Rome, interview by Lehman Engel, Box 6 / Folder 161, 24 LEC.
50. Ibid., 25.
51. Harold Rubin, "A Jackson Downbeat for *Fanny*," *Times-Picayune* (New Orleans), October 31, 1954.
52. Suskin, *The Sound of Broadway Music: A Book of Orchestrators and Orchestrations* (Oxford: Oxford University Press, 2009), 24.
53. Chapman; Alvin Klein "Theater: Goodspeed Opera," *New York Times*, July 27, 1986, CN16.
54. ASCAP, 15.
55. Suskin, *The Sound of Broadway Music*, 70.
56. "Shows on Broadway: *Fanny*," *Variety*.
57. Ibid.
58. Richard Watts, Jr., "Two on the Aisle: The French Waterfront to Music," *New York Post*, November 5, 1954.
59. Henry T. Murdock, "*Fanny* New Musical at Shubert," *Philadelphia Inquirer*, October 14, 1954.
60. Richard Rodgers to Rome, 18 November 1954, HRP.
61. Chapman.
62. Marc Blitzstein to Rome, 4 December 1954, HRP.
63. Rodgers.
64. Rhoda Koenig, "Phantoms of the Musical," *The Independent*, http://www.independent.co.uk/arts-entertainment/theatre-dance/features/phantoms-of-the-musical (accessed April 15, 2009), 1.
65. Rome, interview by Martin Bookspan, ASCAP radio interview, n.d., interview *LDC 50232 [CD], tracks 13–16, Performing Arts Research Collections Recorded Sound, New York Public Library.
66. Elinor Hughes, "*Fanny* Composer Began Career as an Architect," *Boston Herald*, September 20, 1954.
67. Norton, "The Theatre"; Chapman.
68. Ethan Mordden, *Coming Up Roses: The Broadway Musical in the 1950's* (New York: Oxford University Press, 1998), 110.
69. Herm Schoenfeld, "Jocks, Jukes and Disks," *Variety*, September 29, 1954.
70. Lehman Engel, *The American Musical Theater: A Consideration* (New York: CBS Legacy Collection Book, 1967), 107.
71. Engel, *Their Words are Music: The Great Theatre Lyricists and Their Lyrics* (New York: Crown, 1975), 107.
72. TV.com, "Toast of the Town: Florence Henderson; Josh Logan; Teresa Brewer," http://www.tv.com/Toast+of+the+Town/Florence+Henderson%3B+Josh+Logan (accessed April 15, 2009).
73. AJC, 27.
74. "Songs with Largest Radio Audience," *Variety*, December 15, 1954.
75. Robinson.
76. Rome, "How to Write a Hit Musical."
77. Rome, interview by Bookspan.
78. Sam Zolotow, "*Sailor's Delight* Will Bow Jan. 13," *New York Times*, December 24, 1954; Kissel, 97.
79. Suskin, liner notes, 14.
80. Ibid., 10–11; Kissel, 95–6.
81. David Merrick to Rome, 3 April 1956, HRP.
82. Rome to H. William Fitelson, 21 January 1956, HRP.
83. Ibid.
84. Michael Collins to Rome, 21 January 1957, HRP.
85. Rome to Collins, 29 January 1957, HRP.
86. Reviews of *Fanny*, directed by Joshua Logan, Drury Lane Theatre, London, November 16, 1956: Milton Shulman, *Evening Standard*; Cecil Wilson, *Daily Mail*; Stephen Williams, *Evening News*; Elizabeth Frank, *News Chronicle*; uncredited, *Times*.
87. Williams.
88. S. A. Gorlinsky to Benjamin Aslan, 23 November 1956, HRP; Gorlinsky to Rome, 31 December 1956, HRP.
89. Rome to S.A. Gorlinsky, 20 August 1957, HRP.
90. John Mahoney, "Stage: Composer Sings Different Tune," *Los Angeles Times*, August 26, 1973.
91. Leslie Caron email to author, October 12, 2009.
92. Joshua Logan to Rome, 24 August 1960, 1, HRP; Mahoney.
93. Logan to Rome, 2.

94. Logan to Rome, 27 September 1960, 1, HRP.
95. Logan to Rome 24 August 1960, 2.
96. H. William Fitelson to Florence Rome, 24 August 1960, 1, HRP.
97. Benjamin Aslan to S.N. Behrman, Joshua Logan, Paul Osborn, Nedda Logan, David Merrick, and Harold Rome, 14 May 1958, 1, HRP.
98. Fitelson to Florence Rome, 2.
99. *Wikipedia*, s.v. "19th Golden Globe Awards" and "34th Academy Awards" http://en.wikipedia.org/wiki (accessed December 13, 2011).
100. Mahoney.
101. Ibid.
102. Rome, interview by Lehman Engel, Box 6 / Folder 161, 20 LEC.
103. Beverly Gary, "Closeup: Return to Seventh Av.," *New York Post*, April 8, 1962.
104. Joshua Rome, interview with author, October 4, 2011.
105. Gary.
106. ASCAP, 13.
107. Gary.
108. George W. Clarke, "The Story Behind a Maestro," *Boston Advertiser*, August 24, 1940.
109. Mahoney.
110. Rome, "The Voice of Broadway: Rome Can't Get Films Wholesale," *New York Journal-American*, June 18, 1962.
111. Douglas Watt, "Show Business: Rome in Old Haunts; A Successful Backer," *New York Daily News*, March 13, 1962.

# Chapter 14

1. Stanley Green, *The World of Musical Comedy: The Story of the American Musical Stage As Told Through the Careers of Its Foremost Composers and Lyricists* (New York: Ziff-Davis, 1960), 224.
2. Ibid.; John Chapman, "*Destry Rides Again* Whoops Up an Enjoyable Stage Ruckus," *New York Sunday News*, May 3, 1959; William Everett, *Rudolf Friml* (Urbana: University of Illinois Press, 2008), 35–6; Steven Suskin, *Show Tunes: The Songs, Shows, and Careers of Broadway's Major Composers*, 3rd ed. (New York: Oxford University Press, 2000), 11, 53, 71–2, 81–2, 104–5, 223–4.
3. Green.
4. Leonard Gershe, "Westerns Always a Hit," *Philadelphia Inquirer*, March 8, 1959.
5. Ibid.
6. Ibid.; *The Fifties Web*, "TV Ratings: United States," http://www.fiftiesweb.com/tv-ratings.htm#58–59 (accessed March 26, 1910).
7. *Internet Movie Database*, s.v. "Destry," "Destry Rides Again," "Frenchie," http://www.imdb.com/title (accessed March 13, 2010); Leslie Halliwell, *Halliwell's Film and Video Guide*, 12th ed., John Walker, ed. (New York: HarperCollins, 1997), 200, 280.

8. Max Wilk, *They're Playing Our Song* (New York: Atheneum, 1973), 246.
9. Halliwell, 200.
10. Herbert Mitgang, "Destry Rides, Again and Again," *New York Times*, April 19, 1959, X3.
11. John Mahoney, "Stage: Composer Sings Different Tune," *Los Angeles Times*, August 26, 1973.
12. ASCAP, 13.
13. Frederick Nolan, *The Sound of Their Music: The Story of Rodgers and Hammerstein* (New York: Applause Theatre and Cinema Books, 2002), 128.
14. David Lehman, *A Fine Romance: Jewish Songwriters, American Songs* (New York: Nextbook / Schocken, 2009), 179.
15. William McBrien, *Cole Porter: A Biography* (New York: Alfred A. Knopf, 1998), 228.
16. Whitney Bolton, "Theatre: Harold Rome's Rise in Theatre," *New York Telegraph*, April 2, 1959.
17. Kitty Hanson, "How a Show Gets the Works for a Run on Broadway," *Boston Daily News*, March 30, 1959.
18. "Songwriter Rome Has Hefty Deal on Royalties, Profits of *Destry*," *Variety*, June 24, 1959, 17.
19. Avery Corman, "Theater: Music? Lyrics? He Can Get Them for You," *New York Times*, March 3, 1991, II, 5.
20. Suskin, 252, 263.
21. *Wikipedia*, s.v. "No Time for Sergeants," http://en.wikipedia.org/wiki/No_Time_for_Sergeants (accessed March 26, 2010), 1–2.
22. Jerry Gaghan, "Andy Griffith Stars in *Destry* at Shubert," *Philadelphia Daily News*, March 10, 1959.
23. Walter Kerr, "First Night Report: *Destry Rides Again*," *New York Herald Tribune*, April 24, 1959, 10.
24. Suskin, 111, 166, 229; John McClain, "*Destry Rides Again*," *New York Sunday Journal*, April 9, 1959.
25. Sidney Fields, "War of Words and Blows behind *Destry*," *New York Mirror*, April 27, 1959.
26. Ibid.
27. Ibid; Mitchell Levitas, "There's No Business Like Show Business," *New York Post*, April 15, 1959; Don Ross, "*Destry* Folk Feudin' Like Wild Westerners," *New York Herald Tribune*, April 19, 1959.
28. *Wikipedia*, s.v. "Scott Brady," http://en.wikipedia.org/wiki/Scott_Brady (accessed November 29, 2011).
29. Harold Rome, interview by Lehman Engel, Box 6 / Folder 161, 23 LEC.
30. Ibid.
31. Barry Kleinbort, phone discussion with author, November 15, 2011.
32. Hanson.
33. Rome, interview by Martin Bookspan, ASCAP radio interview, n.d., interview *LDC 50232 [CD], tracks 13–16, Performing Arts Re-

search Collections Recorded Sound, New York Public Library.
34. John Chapman, "Bright Musical of 'Impossible West' Sweeps into New York," *Chicago Daily Tribune*, April 25, 1959.
35. Walter Kerr, "Bullwhips Snap, Musical Gallops," *New York Herald Tribune*, May 3, 1959.
36. *Cue*, "The Theatre: Michael Kidd's Wild West Show Is Tops," May 2, 1959.
37. Peggy Doyle, "*Destry* Rides into Town and Scores Smash," *Boston Evening American*, April 2, 1959.
38. *ACE Title Search*, s.v. "Anyone Would Love You," The American Society of Composers, Author and Publishers, http://www.ascap.com/ace/search.cfm?requesttimeout=300 (accessed December 25, 2009).
39. Paula J. Bishop, "Duets in Broadway Shows of the 1950's," http://people.bu.edu/pjbishop/BwayDuets.html (accessed April 17, 2009), 1, 3, 7.
40. Ethan Mordden, *Coming Up Roses: The Broadway Musical in the 1950's* (New York: Oxford University Press, 1998), 219.
41. Kurt Ganzl, *Encyclopedia of the Musical Theater* (New York: Schirmer, 1994), s.v. "Destry Rides Again."
42. Suskin, *Second Act Trouble: Behind the Scenes at Broadway's Big Musical Bombs* (New York: Applause Theatre and Cinema Books, 2006), 155.
43. Mordden, *Open a New Window: The Broadway Musical in the 1960's* (New York: Palgrave, 2001), 118.
44. Rome, interview by Bookspan.
45. Ibid.
46. Mitgang.
47. *Cue*.
48. Howard Kissel, *David Merrick: The Abominable Showman: The Unauthorized Biography* (New York: Applause, 1993), 156.
49. John McClain, "Yippee-e! Musical Is Best of Season," *New York Journal-American*, April 24, 1959.
50. Richard C. Norton, *A Chronology of American Musical Theater* (Oxford: Oxford University Press, 2002), 465; Schedule of Composers' and Lyricists' Royalties, *The American Dance Machine*, June 5, 1978, HRC.
51. Kissel, 159.
52. Martin Gottfried, *Broadway Musicals* (New York: Abradale Press / Harry N. Abrams, 1984), 143.
53. Suskin, *Show Tunes*, 264–5.
54. *Wikipedia*, s.v. "Carnival!," http://en.wikipedia.org/wiki/Carnival! (accessed April 28, 2011), 1.
55. Rome to John Wharton, 14 January 1960, 2, HRP.
56. Ibid.
57. Ibid.
58. *Wikipedia*, s.v. "Carnival!," 1.
59. Suskin, 265.
60. Benjamin Aslan and Ian B. Albery, Omega Stage Limited, London, multiple letters, January–May 1981, HRP.
61. Rexton S. Bunnett, liner notes, *Destry Rides Again* (London: Omega Projects Ltd., 1982).
62. Albery to Aslan, 15 November 1982, HRP.
63. Bunnett.
64. Malcolm L. Johnson, "Rome Comes Home with a Smash *Fanny*," *Hartford Courant*, August 10, 1986.
65. Richard C. Watts, "Two on the Aisle: A Western Melodrama with Music," *New York Post*, April 24, 1959.

## Chapter 15

1. Mel Gussow, "Jerome Weidman Dies at 85; Author of Novels and Plays," *New York Times*, October 7, 1998, C23; Steven Suskin, *Show Tunes: The Songs, Shows, and Careers of Broadway's Major Composers*, 3rd ed. (New York: Oxford University Press, 2000), 199–200, 257.
2. Jerome Weidman, *Praying for Rain* (New York: Harper & Row, 1986), 128.
3. S.S. Irving, "Stage: When the Sting Is Gone," *Jewish Exponent*, February 16, 1962.
4. Richard F. Shepard, "Jerome Weidman: Novel and Novelist," *New York Times*, May 28, 1978, BR3.
5. Weidman, 135.
6. Gerald Bordman, *American Musical Theatre: A Chronicle*, 3rd ed. (New York: Oxford University Press, 2001), 682.
7. Suskin, 102–3, 248, 400; Bordman, 576–7, 678–8, 690, 695, 712, 717; Suskin, *More Opening Nights on Broadway: A Critical Quotebook of the Musical Theatre, 1965–1981* (New York: Schirmer Books, 1997), 15, 219, 505–10, 699–702; John Chapman, "Hero of New Musical about Garment Trade a Real Heel," *Chicago Daily Tribune*, April 1, 1962, E11; Gerald Bordman, *The Oxford Companion to American Theatre* (New York: Oxford University Press, 1984), s.v. "Show-Off, The"; *Wikipedia*, s.v. "George Kelly (playwright)," http://en.wikipedia.org/wiki/George_Kelly_(playwright) (accessed November 21, 2010).
8. Frederick Nolan, *The Sound of Their Music: The Story of Rodgers and Hammerstein* (New York: Applause Theatre and Cinema Books, 2002), 139.
9. Henry T. Murdock, "Garment Shop Back on Stage," *Philadelphia Inquirer*, February 13, 1962.
10. *The New Yorker*, March 31, 1962.
11. Ibid.
12. Murdock.
13. John McClain, "Even at Retail, It's No Bargain," *New York Journal-American*, March 23, 1962.
14. Thomas L. Riis, *Frank Loesser* (New Haven, CT: Yale University Press, 2008), 177.

15. Glenn Litton, *Musical Comedy in America* (New York: Routledge/Theatre Arts Books, 1991), 276.
16. Ibid., 276–7.
17. Ethan Mordden, *Open a New Window: The Broadway Musical in the 1960's* (New York: Palgrave, 2001), 88.
18. Howard Kissel, *David Merrick: The Abominable Showman: The Unauthorized Biography* (New York: Applause, 1993), 235–6.
19. *Wikipedia*, s.v. "Laurence Harvey," http://en.wikipedia.org/wiki/Laurence_Harvey (accessed December 2, 2010), 2.
20. Jerome Weidman to Rome, 22 August 1961, 1–2 HRP.
21. Weidman to Rome, 15 July 1961, 3 HRP.
22. Weidman to Rome, 22 August 1961, 2.
23. Ibid., 3.
24. Liner notes, *I Can Get It for You Wholesale* (New York: Columbia Records, 1962), 14.
25. Ernest Schier, "*Wholesale* Is Musical of Garment Industry," *Philadelphia Evening Bulletin*, February 13, 1962.
26. Liner notes, 13–14; Roger D. Kinkle, *The Complete Encyclopedia of Popular Music and Jazz: 1900–1950* (New Rochelle, NY: Arlington House, 1974), s.v. "Roth, Lillian."
27. Avery Corman, "Music? Lyrics? He Can Get Them for You," *New York Times*, March 3, 1991, II, 5.
28. Arthur Laurents, *Original Story By: A Memoir of Broadway and Hollywood* (New York: Alfred A. Knopf, 2000), 220–22, 234–5; Kissel, 238–9; Lehman Engel, *This Bright Day: An Autobiography* (New York: Macmillan, 1974), 291–2.
29. Kissel, 238.
30. Laurents, 222.
31. Ibid., 237.
32. Randall Riese, *Her Name Is Barbra: An Intimate Portrait of the Real Barbra Streisand* (New York: Carol Publishing, 1993), 108.
33. Corman.
34. Donald Zec and Anthony Fowles, *Barbra: A Biography of Barbra Streisand*, (New York: St Martin's Press, 1981), 75.
35. Riese, 128–9.
36. Zec, 74–5.
37. AJC, 38.
38. Zec, 75.
39. Joshua Rome, interview with author, October 4, 2011.
40. Beverly Gary, "Closeup: Return to Seventh Avenue," *New York Post*, April 8, 1962.
41. Harold Rome, interview by Lehman Engel, Box 6 / Folder 161, 11 LEC.
42. Liner notes, 3, 6.
43. Ibid., 6.
44. Elliot Norton, "New Musical Here Has Heel as Hero," *Boston Record American*, February 28, 1962.
45. Walter Kerr, "First Night Report: *I Can Get It for You Wholesale*," *New York Herald Tribune*, March 23, 1962.
46. Kerr, "Walter Kerr on the Theater: Wholesale Delights," *New York Herald Tribune*, April 1, 1962.
47. Mordden, 90.
48. Thomas M. Pryor, movie review of *I Can Get It for You Wholesale*, directed by Michael Gorden, *New York Times*, April 5, 1951, 34.
49. Alex Witchel, "On Stage, and Off," *New York Times*, July 19, 1991, C2.
50. Corman, 24.
51. Bordman, *American Musical Theatre*, 682.
52. Elinor Hughes, "New Colonial Musical Could Become a Hit," *Boston Herald*, February 28, 1962.
53. Norton.
54. Arthur Laurents to Rome and Jerome Weidman, 10 September 1961, 1, HRC.
55. *Newsweek*, "Petit Guignol," March 26, 1962, 58.
56. Laurents to Rome and Weidman, 4.
57. Mordden, 90.
58. AJC, 22.
59. Jaime J. Weinman, "Something Old, Something New: Lyrics by Harold Rome: 'Certain Individuals,'" http://zvbxrpl.blogspot.com/2005/lyrics-by-harold-rome-certain.html (accessed December 16, 2010).
60. Mordden, 90.
61. Gary.
62. Ibid.
63. Murdock.
64. Murdock, "On Stage: Merrick Shows Way to Theater Economy in Two Musicals," *Philadelphia Inquirer*, February 18, 1962.
65. Laurents to Rome and Weidman, 3.
66. Laurents to Rome, 20 October 1961, 2, HRC.
67. Ibid.
68. Gussow.
69. Schier.
70. *Time*, "Delousing of Harry Bogen," March 30, 1962.
71. Jerry Gaghan, "*I Can Get It for You Wholesale* Opens," *Philadelphia Daily News*, February 13, 1962, 55.
72. Mordden, 92.
73. Lehman Engel, *The American Musical Theater: A Consideration* (New York: Macmillan, 1977), 133.
74. *Newsweek*.
75. Kerr, "Wholesale Delights."
76. John Mahoney, "Stage: Composer Sings Different Tune," *Los Angeles Times*, August 26, 1973.
77. Oscar Hammerstein II, *Lyrics* (New York: Simon & Schuster, 1949), 19.
78. Rome, interview by Gene Bruck, ASCAP symposium on American music, n.d., interview *LDC 42652 [CD], Performing Arts Research Collections Recorded Sound, New York Public Library.

79. Ibid.
80. Richard Watts, Jr., review of *How to Succeed in Business without Really Trying*, *New York Post*, October 15, 1961.
81. Riese, 2.
82. Ibid.
83. Zec, 74.
84. Bruce F. Winston, "In Gratitude: A Fan's Remembrance of Harold Rome," http://www.broadwayworld.com/article/In_Gratitude_A_Fans_Remembrance_of_Harold (accessed November 14, 2008), 2–3.
85. Frederick Guidry, "*I Can Get It for You Wholesale*: Weidman-Rome Musical Opens at the Colonial," *Christian Science Monitor*, February 28, 1962.
86. Laurents, *Original Story By*, 231–241.
87. Rome and Weidman, telegram to cast of *I Can Get It for You Wholesale*, Shubert Theatre, 22 March 1962, HRP.
88. Richard Watts, Jr., "Two on the Aisle," *New York Post*, April 1, 1962.

## Chapter 16

1. Notes in musical selections, *Harold Rome's Gallery* (New York: Florence Music Company, 1964), 1; Virginia Hagelstein Marquardt, "The American Artists School: Radical Heritage and Social Content Art," *Archives of American Art Journal* (Vol. 26, No. 4, 1986), 17.
2. Notes in musical selections.
3. Ibid; "The Art of De Pauw: As Unique and Multifaceted As the Man and His Life," http://depauwfineart.com/biography.html (accessed May 18, 2011), 1.
4. Harold Rome, interview by Paulette Attie, *Musical Playbill*, WNYC, July 14, 1966, RB: 27769, The Paley Center for Media, New York.
5. *Stop, Look and Listen*, personal notes of composer, July 13, 1964, HRC.
6. Notes in musical selections, Foreword.
7. Norman Nadel, "Rome Harmonizes His Art," *New York World-Telegram and Sun*, November 7, 1964.
8. Robert Daley, "Broadway Song Writer Mixes Oils and Music in Art Display," *New York Times*, November 12, 1964, 42.
9. Album cover notes, *Harold Rome's Gallery* (New York: Columbia Records, 1965).
10. Notes in musical selections, Introduction.
11. Daley; Nadel; Sascha Robbins, notes in catalogue, *Harold Rome* (New York: Marble Arch Gallery, November 10, 1964); "*Harold Rome's Gallery*," *High Fidelity* (February 1965), 101; album cover notes.
12. AJC, 47.
13. *Wikipedia*, s.v. "Howe and Hummel," http://en.wikipedia.org/wiki/Howe_and_Hummel (accessed April 19, 2010), 1–2.
14. Rome to Lehman Engel, 16 August 1965, 3 LEC.
15. Ibid., 4.
16. Daley.
17. Nadel.
18. "Other Gallery Exhibitions on the East Side Are Summarized," *New York Times*, November 21, 1964.
19. "Sunday Painters, Monday Artists," *New York Journal-American*, November 14, 1964, 8.
20. Nadel.
21. Robbins.
22. Papers regarding donation of Harold Rome painting, "The Audience," MCNY.
23. Beverly Gary, "Closeup: Return to Seventh Av.," *New York Post*, April 8, 1962.
24. ASCAP, 15.
25. Gary.
26. Bruce F. Wiener, *A Rome with a View* (Rosemont, PA: Rosemont College, 2001), 101–2.
27. Ernest Leogrande, "Harold Rome Sharpens Up His 'Needles,'" *New York Daily News*, June 12, 1978.
28. Ibid.
29. "Women Today: Rome's Philadelphia Holiday," *Philadelphia Evening Bulletin*, June 8, 1966.
30. "Harold Rome: Royal Flush," *Gamblers World*, (December–January 1974).
31. Program for *Harold Rome Sings Harold Rome* (Washington, D.C.: Museum of African Art, 1978), HRP.
32. Marilyn Berger, "Berlin at 100: Life on a High Note," *New York Times*, May 8, 1988, H1.

## Chapter 17

1. *Cyclopedia of World Authors*, 4th ed. (Pasadena, CA: Salem Press, 2004), s.v. "Jacobson, Dan."
2. Souvenir program, *The Zulu and the Zayda*, Broadway Production Files, MCNY.
3. Frederick Nolan, *The Sound of Their Music: The Story of Rodgers and Hammerstein* (New York: Applause Theatre and Cinema Books, 2002), 198.
4. Nina Sen, "Felix Leon, Local Playwright, Dies at 92," *Norwood News*, November 29, 2007; souvenir program.
5. *Cyclopedia*.
6. *The World Book Encyclopedia*, (Chicago: World Book, 2009), s.v. "apartheid."
7. Ibid.
8. Joshua Rome, interview with author, October 4, 2011.
9. George W. Clarke, "The Story Behind a Maestro," *Boston Advertiser*, August 24, 1940.
10. Roger Wolmuth, "The Arts," *Avenue* (May 1977), 22.
11. Harold Rome to Arthur Lesser, 2 June 1965, HRP.
12. Wolmuth, 24.

13. AJC, 2.
14. Joshua Rome.
15. Personal communication, e-mail, Bryna Freyer, Curator, National Museum of African Art, to author, 24 May 2011.
16. "The Schomburg Legacy Exhibition — Introduction," http://www.nypl.org/research/sc/WEBEXHIB/legacy (accessed April 15, 2009), 1, 7–8.
17. *WPAT Gaslight Revue Program Guide*, June-1962 (Paterson, NJ: Radio Station WPAT, 1962), 59.
18. Personal communications, emails, Bryna Freyer to author, 24, 26 May 2011.
19. "The Philadelphia Scene: The Showman's Art Show," unidentified clipping from Philadelphia newspaper, circa 1961, HRC; "The Schomburg Legacy Exhibition — Introduction," 7.
20. "The Harold and Florence Rome collection of African art," New York Public Library, http://catalog.nypl.org/search~S67?/Xrome%2C+harold&searchscope=67&SORT=D/Xrome%2C (accessed May 26, 2011), 1.
21. Samuel J. Wagstaff, Jr., "African Sculpture Comes of Age," *Courant Magazine* (Hartford, CT), September 29, 1963; "African Art Is Due at Allentown Museum," *Call-Chronicle* (Allentown, PA), March 21, 1971, F-5.
22. Howard Taubman, "Da Silva-Leon-Rome Play Opens at Cort," November 11, 1965, 59.
23. Irving Drutman, "Mr. Skulnik," *New York Times*, November 7, 1965, X1.
24. Howard Da Silva and Felix Leon, "Theater: They Talk across Hedges," *New York Herald Tribune*, October 24, 1965, 35.
25. Taubman.
26. Louis Calta, "Musical Planned by Harold Rome," *New York Times*, August 21, 1959.
27. Taubman.
28. Souvenir program, "Glossary of Zulu, Yiddish and English Terms," MCNY.
29. *Louis Gossett Jr. Official Web Site*, "About Louis Gossett Jr.," 1–2, "News Louis Gossett Jr.," 2–3, http://www.louisgossett.com (accessed January 14, 2012).
30. Richard C. Norton, *A Chronology of American Musical Theater* (Oxford: Oxford University Press, 2002), 187.
31. *Ossie Davis and Ruby Dee*, "Ossie Davis Stage Credits," "Ossie Davis Acting Credits," and "Ossie Davis Television Credits," http://www.ossieandruby.com/david-credits (accessed February 9, 2012).
32. Sam Zolotow, "Apartheid Story to Star Skulnik," *New York Times*, May 27, 1965.
33. Rome to Lehman Engel, 16 August 1965, 3 LEC.
34. John S. Wilson, "A Drama Deepened by Music," *New York Times*, January 2, 1966, 89.
35. Ibid.
36. Steven Suskin, *Show Tunes: The Songs, Shows, and Careers of Broadway's Major Composers*, 3rd ed. (New York: Oxford University Press, 2000), 200.
37. Ibid.
38. Taubman.
39. John Stewart, *Broadway Musicals, 1943–2004* (Jefferson, NC: McFarland, 2006), 804.
40. Lehman Engel, *The American Musical Theater: A Consideration*, (New York: Macmillan, 1967), 188.
41. Norton, 190.
42. Taubman, "Theater: French Musical," *New York Times*, December 15, 1965.
43. Stewart, 244.
44. Engel, *This Bright Day: An Autobiography* (New York: Macmillan, 1974), 296.
45. *Wikipedia*, s.v. "Gerard Calvi," http://en.wikipedia.org/wiki/Gerard_Calvi (accessed December 13, 2011).
46. "Production Planned Here for a Paris Musical," *New York Times*, March 30, 1965.
47. Rome to Lesser, HRP.
48. Rome to Engel, n.d., circa 1965, 1 LEC.
49. Engel, *American Musical Theater*, 188.
50. Alta Maloney, "A Bag Chock Full of Tricks ... All Winners!," *Boston Traveler*, November 16, 1965.
51. Frederick H. Guidry, "New French Musical: *La Grosse Valise*," *Christian Science Monitor*, November 16, 1965.
52. Bradford F. Swan, "Boston Stage: Musical *La Grosse Valise* Is New Shubert Offering," *Providence Journal*, November 17, 1965; Elliot Norton, "Elliot Norton Writes: *La Grosse Valise*," *Boston Record American*, November 16, 1965.
53. Maloney.
54. Swan.
55. Rome, "List of Songs for La Grosse Valise," typed notes, HRP.
56. Norton; Taubman.
57. Engel, *This Bright Day*, 189.
58. Engel, *American Musical Theater*, 298.
59. Taubman.
60. Stewart, 244.
61. Howard Teichmann, *George S. Kaufman: An Intimate Portrait* (New York: Atheneum, 1972), 154.
62. Malcolm Goldstein, *George S. Kaufman: His Life, His Theater* (New York: Oxford University Press, 1979), 453–4.
63. Teichmann, 154–5.
64. Howard Kissel, *David Merrick: The Abominable Showman: The Unauthorized Biography* (New York: Applause Theatre and Cinema Books, 1993), 72; Sam Zolotow, "A Merrick Angel to Try His Own Wings," *New York Times*, June 24, 1966, 29.
65. Kissel, 305–6.
66. Zolotow.
67. Ibid.
68. Rome to H. William Fitelson, 5 January 1967, HRP.
69. Sam Zolotow, "Lindsay Upheld on Theater

Fund," *New York Times*, December 5, 1967, 59; Rome, document "Re: *The Southpaw, Bang the Drum Slowly,* and *Ticket for a Seamstick* [sic]," February 21, 1968, HRP.
70. Rome to Engel, 24 December 1968, 2 LEC.
71. Rome, document / letter to Max Brown and Edgar Lansbury, 21 February 1969, HRP.
72. Mark Harris to Rome, 25 February 1969, HRP.
73. John Mahoney, "Stage: Composer Sings Different Tune," *Los Angeles Times*, August 26, 1973.
74. Rome to Engel, 1.
75. Suskin, 400.
76. E. Y. Harburg postcard to the Rev. and Mrs. S. Jackson, n.d., 1978, collection of the author.
77. Suskin, 403.
78. Rome, folder of Original Mss of Lyric Sheets, 1964–1967, HRC.
79. Louis Calta, "Democrats Plan Revue for Votes," *New York Times*, September 30, 1964, 39.
80. *Wikipedia*, s.v. "United States presidential election, 1968," http://en.wikipedia.org/wiki/United_States_presidential_election_1968 (accessed June 25, 2011), 1–9.
81. Clayton Knowles, "Finletter Aiding McCarthy Drive," *New York Times*, April 22, 1968, 21.
82. Songs, Sub-series I.B., 2 HRP.
83. *Wikipedia*, "Hubert Humphrey," http://en.wikipedia.org/wiki/Hubert_Humphrey.
84. "Cyclists Here Hoping to Pedal Humphrey into the White House," *New York Times*, October 21, 1968, 38.

# Chapter 18

N.B.: When "Rome" is cited, this is Harold Rome. His wife, Florence, is always cited as "Florence Rome."
1. Max Wilk, *OK! The Story of Oklahoma!* (New York: Grove, 1993), 164.
2. "Musical *Gone with the Wind* Still Drifting," *New York Times*, July 28, 1976, 16.
3. Florence Rome, *The Scarlett Letters* (New York: Random House, 1971), 12.
4. L. Arnold Weissberger to Rome, 27 August 1959, HRP.
5. William G. Hyland, *Richard Rodgers* (New Haven, CT: Yale University Press, 1998), 96.
6. Andre Previn, *No Minor Chords: My Days in Hollywood* (New York: Doubleday, 1991), 86.
7. "*Gone with the Wind* on London Stage," *New York Times*, April 27, 1972, 48.
8. *Box Office Mojo*, "All Time Box Office," http://boxofficemojo.com/alltime/adjusted.htm (accessed February 15, 2010), 1.
9. "*Gone with the Wind* to Become Musical," *The Yomiuri*, February 15, 1968.
10. Takashi Oka, "For Japan, Musical *Gone with the Wind*," *New York Times*, January 1, 1970, 17.
11. Ibid.; Florence Rome, 9.
12. "*Gone with the Wind* to Become Musical."
13. Rome to Kazuo Kikuta, 15 March 1968, HRP.
14. Florence Rome, 30.
15. "Japanese Musical Version of *GWTW* Bows Next Week," *Variety*, December 24, 1969.
16. "*Gone with the Wind* to Become Musical."
17. ASCAP, 13.
18. Florence Rome, 39.
19. Nobuko Uenishi Morris of Toho International, Inc. to Rome, 9 December 1968, HRP.
20. Rome to Benjamin Aslan, 11 July 1969, 1 HRP.
21. Ibid., 2.
22. Florence Rome, 30.
23. Katharine Brown of Ashley Famous Agency, Inc. to Kazuo Kikuta, 25 March 1968, 1 HRP.
24. Ibid., 2.
25. Rome to Lehman Engel, 12 November 1969, 2 LEC.
26. Rome to Engel, 21 November 1969, 2 LEC.
27. Rome to Engel, 13 August 1973, 1 LEC.
28. "Trude Rittman: Choral and Dance Music Arranger," *Variety*, March 14, 2006; *Internet Broadway Database*, s.v. "Trude Rittman," http://www.ibdb.com/person.php?id=12294 (accessed April 23, 2012).
29. Oka.
30. Florence Rome, 51
31. Ibid., 50.
32. Selig S. Harrison, "Scarlett O'Hara at Tokyo Tara," *International Herald Tribune*, January 18, 1970, K2.
33. Florence Rome, 51.
34. Ibid.
35. Harrison.
36. Oka, "*Scarlett*, Musical, and Star Cheered by Tokyo Audience, *New York Times*, January 3, 1970.
37. Wilk, 265.
38. Steven Suskin, *Show Tunes: The Songs, Shows, and Careers of Broadway's Major Composers*, 3rd ed. (New York: Oxford University Press, 2000), 456; Richard C. Norton, *A Chronology of American Musical Theater* (Oxford: Oxford University Press, 2002), s.v. "Layton, Joe."
39. Bart Mills, "...or Is It Southern Lilacs?," *Chicago Tribune*, May 14, 1972, Q7.
40. Kay Gardella, "*Scarlett*," pre-publication copy, n.d., circa July 1970, 4 HRP.
41. Mills.
42. Rome to Engel, 21 November 1969, 1, 3 LEC.
43. "Musical *Scarlett* a Hit in Tokyo," *Chicago Daily News*, January 5, 1970.
44. Harrison, K2.
45. William Leonard, "Tokyo *Wind* May Be

Headed for Broadway," *Chicago Tribune*, January 11, 1970, F1.
46. John London, "Rome Didn't Make It in a Day," *London Evening News*, April 22, 1972.
47. Harrison, K2.
48. Florence Rome, 103.
49. Ibid., 141.
50. Harrison, K2.
51. Gardella, 7; Florence Rome, 103.
52. Wilk, 203.
53. Oscar Hammerstein II, *Lyrics* (New York: Simon & Schuster, 1949), 25.
54. Andrea Most, *Making Americans: Jews and the Broadway Musical* (Cambridge, MA: Harvard University Press, 2004), 8.
55. Florence Rome, 142.
56. Rome to Engel, 12 November 1969, 2 LEC.
57. Lehman Engel, *This Bright Day: An Autobiography* (New York: Macmillan, 1974), 335.
58. Rome, interview by Lehman Engel, Box 6 / Folder 161, 5–8 LEC.
59. Rome to Lt. Commander E.E. Peabody, Great Lakes Naval Training Station, 21 March 1942, LEC.
60. Joshua Rome, interview with author, October 4, 2011.
61. Rome telegram to Engel, 23 April 1959, LEC.
62. Florence Rome, 150–1.
63. Robert Crabb, "Musical *Scarlett* Theatrical Blend of East and West," *Japan Times*, January 6, 1970.

## Chapter 19

1. Peter Waymark, "*Gone with the Wind* on London Stage in Spring," *Times-News* (London), December 8, 1971, P4.
2. Wilborn Hampton, "Horton Foote, Chronicler of America in Plays and Film, Dies at 92," *New York Times*, March 5, 2009, A28.
3. Norton, 256–70.
4. Gardella, 2.
5. Liner notes, *Scarlett* (New York: DRG Records Incorporated, 1970), 4.
6. Mills.
7. "*Gone with the Wind* on London Stage," *New York Times*, April 27, 1972, 48.
8. Joe Layton to Harold and Florence Rome, 20 February 1972, HRP.
9. Irving Wardle, "Sound Craftsmanship," *London Times*, May 4, 1972.
10. ASCAP, 15.
11. Wilk, 79–80.
12. David Lehman, *A Fine Romance: Jewish Songwriters, American Songs* (New York: Nextbook / Schocken, 2009), 24.
13. Joshua Logan, souvenir program, Broadway Production files, *Fanny*, MCNY.
14. London.
15. Thaddeus Holt to Rome, 17 November 1971; Rome to Holt, 23 November 1971, HRP.
16. Florence Rome to Engel, 25 April 1972, LEC.
17. Joshua Rome.
18. Rome, "NOTES TO JOE LAYTON: Musical Cuts," n.d., 1972, 2 HRP.
19. Ibid.
20. Ibid., 3.
21. Ibid.
22. Rome, "Notes for Joe Layton from Harold Rome Scarlett's songs," n.d., 1972, 1–3 HRP.
23. Ibid., 3.
24. Rome, "NOTES TO JOE LAYTON," 1–2.
25. Rome to Audrey Wood of International Famous Agency, 28 November 1972, HRP.
26. Henry Pleasants, "London: Musical *Gone with the Wind*," *International Herald Tribune*, May 5, 1972.
27. Ken Mandelbaum, *Not Since Carrie: Forty Years of Broadway Musical Flops* (New York: St. Martin's Press, 1991), 182.
28. These comments were gleaned from various reviews of *Gone with the Wind* listed in the Bibliography.
29. Gerald Bordman, *Jerome Kern: His Life and Music* (New York: Oxford University Press, 1980), 49.
30. Rome to Harold Fielding, 5 January 1973, 1 HRP.
31. Fielding to E.C. Holmes, Chappell Ltd., 5 January 1973, HRP.
32. Rome to Julian and Jean Aberbach, Hill and Range Songs, Inc., 13 April 1973, HRP.
33. *Wikipedia*, s.v. "Scarlett (musical)," http://en.wikipedia.org/wiki/Scarlett (accessed February 21, 2012), 2–3.
34. Rome to Engel, 13 August 1973, 1 LEC.
35. Ibid., 2.
36. Ibid., 3.
37. Ibid., 3.
38. Edwin Lester to Rome, 11 September 1973, HRP.
39. Lester to Rome, 10 October 1973, 1 HRP.
40. Lester to Rome, 8 October 1973, HRP.
41. Lester to Rome, 10 October 1973.
42. Mandelbaum, 180.
43. Rome, "Notes on a Projected First Class Tour of G.W.T.W.," July 30, 1976, 2 HRP.
44. Stanley Eichelbaum, "*Gone with the Wind* Goes Nowhere," *San Francisco Examiner*, October 24, 1973, 41.
45. Rome to San Francisco cast of *Gone with the Wind*, 26 November 1973, HRP.
46. Rome to Jay Blackton, 26 November 1973, HRP.
47. John Neville, "*Gone with the Wind* Will Open Musicals," March 3, 1976, 14 A.
48. Helen C. Smith, "Musical *GWTW* to Open Tuesday," *Atlanta Constitution*, July 9, 1976.
49. Patty Moore, "Stars Rising as Atlanta Flames Rise," *Dallas Morning News*, June 13, 1976.

50. Advertisement for Dallas Summer Musicals production of *Gone with the Wind*, *Dallas Morning News* and *Dallas Times Herald*, June 10, 1976.
51. Rome to Tom Hughes, Dallas Summer Musical, 9 July 1976, HRP.
52. Ibid.
53. Robert W. Butler, "Starlight's Rhett, Scarlett Careful Not to Imitate," *Kansas City Times*, July 1, 1976, 4E.
54. Smith.
55. Harry Bowman, "Revised *Wind* Comes Off Well," *Dallas Morning News*, June 15, 1976.
56. "Musical *Gone with the Wind* Still Drifting," *New York Times*, July 28, 1976, 16.
57. Shirley Green, "*Gone with the Wind* Comes to the Stage," *The Times* (Miami Beach), July 25, 1976.
58. Rome to Hughes, 30 July 1976, HRP.
59. Hughes to Rome, 22 September 1976, HRP.
60. Rome to Hughes, 11 October 1976, HRP.
61. Bruce F. Winston, "In Gratitude: A Fan's Remembrance of Harold Rome," http://www.broadwayworld.com/article/In_Gratitude_A_Fans_Remembrance_of_Harold (accessed November 14, 2008), 3.
62. Roger Wolmuth, "The Arts," *Avenue*, (May 1977), 25.

## Chapter 20

1. Nicholas Pavlik, Archivist, 92nd Street Y, email to author, 30 April 2012.
2. Jeannie Lieberman, "92 St. Y's Lyrics and Lyricists Stage Door Canteen: Broadway Responds to WWII," Theatre Scene.net, http://www.theatrescene.net/ts%5Carticles.nsf (accessed April 28, 2012), 1–2.
3. William Cockerham, "Songwriter Renews Links to City in Old Place Show," *Hartford Courant*, n.d., 1977, HRP.
4. John S. Wilson, "Harold Rome Sings Harold Rome," *New York Times*, November 25, 1976, 39.
5. Harold Rome, interview by Roland Winters, The Players Club, February 25, 1972, interview NCOW 35, Performing Arts Research Collections TOFT, New York Public Library.
6. Norton Mockridge, "The Red Man Gets Even," *Paterson* (NJ) *News*, January 15, 1973.
7. Wilson.
8. Mary Ellen Butler, *Washington Star*, 1978, n.d., HRP.
9. *Camera Three*, "Songs from *Pins and Needles*," WCBS-TV, July 30, 1978, B:70780, The Paley Center for Media, New York.
10. Ernest Leogrande, "Harold Rome Sharpens Up His 'Needles,'" *New York Daily News*, June 12, 1978.
11. Ibid.
12. Piano Works / Chamber Music / Songs, Folders 54–5, HRP.

13. Howard Dietz to Rome, 2 February 1982, HRP.
14. Dan O'Leary, liner notes for *Harold Rome: A Touch of Rome* (New York: DRG Theater, 1991).
15. *Songwriters' Hall of Fame*, http://songwritershalloffame.org/exhibits/year (accessed January 10, 2012), 1–3.
16. *ASCAP Foundation Awards*, http://www.ascap.com/eventsawards/awards/foundation/awards/rodgers.aspx (accessed February 7, 2012), 3–4.
17. *Wikipedia*, s.v. "Drama Desk Awards," http://en.wikipedia.org/wiki/Drama_Desk_Award (accessed February 7, 2010), 2.
18. *American Theatre Critics Association*, http://www.americantheatrecritics.org/theatre-hall-of-fame/ (accessed February 7, 2012), 1–2.
19. Rome, interview by Lehman Engel, Box 6 / Folder 161, 21–2 LEC.
20. Felicia Hardison Londre and Daniel J. Watermeier, *The History of North American Theater: From Pre-Columbian Times to the Present* (New York: Continuum, 1998), 427.
21. Andrea Most, *Making Americans: Jews and the Broadway Musical* (Cambridge, MA: Harvard University Press, 2004), 2.
22. James Leve, *Kander and Ebb* (New Haven, CT: Yale University Press, 2009), 31.
23. Ibid.
24. George W. Clarke, "The Story Behind a Maestro," *Boston Advertiser*, August 24, 1940.
25. Ethan Mordden, *Coming Up Roses: The Broadway Musical in the 1950's* (New York: Oxford University Press, 1998), 55–6.
26. Vernon Rice, "Curtain Cues: Amateur Night at Camp Karefree," *New York Post*, June 26, 1952.
27. Joshua Rome, interview with author, October 4, 2011.
28. Abigail Pogrebin, *Stars of David: Prominent Jews Talk about Being Jewish* (New York: Broadway Books, 2005), 297.
29. Philip Lambert, *To Broadway, To Life!: The Musical Theater of Bock and Harnick* (New York: Oxford University Press, 2011), 161–2.
30. Mordden, *Beautiful Mornin': The Broadway Musical in the 1940's* (New York: Oxford University Press, 1999), 126.
31. David Lehman, *A Fine Romance: Jewish Songwriters, American Songs* (New York: Nextbook/Schocken, 2009), 96.
32. Ibid., 107.
33. Arnold Rampersad, *The Life of Langston Hughes: Volume II: 1941–1967: I Dream a World*, 2nd ed. (Oxford: Oxford University Press, 2002), 110.
34. Sammy Cahn, *I Should Care: The Sammy Cahn Story* (New York: Arbor House, 1974), 74–5.
35. ASCAP, 13.
36. John Mahoney, "Stage: Composer Sings Different Tune," *Los Angeles Times*, August 26, 1973.

37. Bruce F. Wiener, *A Rome with a View* (Rosemont, PA: Rosemont College, 2001), 100.
38. Bruce F. Winston, "In Gratitude: A Fan's Remembrance of Harold Rome," http://www.broadwayworld.com/article/In_Gratitude_A_Fans_Remembrance_of_Harold (accessed November 14, 2008), 2.
39. ASCAP, 13.
40. Mahoney.
41. Mordden, *Beautiful Mornin'*, 114.
42. Mahoney.
43. ASCAP, 13.
44. Rome, interview by Engel, 27.
45. Cecil Smith, "Harold J. Rome Composes with Easy Fluency," *Chicago Daily Tribune*, March 16, 1941.
46. Ibid.
47. Ibid.
48. Joshua Logan, souvenir program, *Fanny*, MCNY.
49. Barry Kleinbort, phone discussion with author, November 15, 2011.
50. Robert Gottlieb and Robert Kimball, eds., *Reading Lyrics* (New York: Pantheon, 2000), 407.

## Appendix B

1. Titles in italics are musical shows unless otherwise indicated.
2. Parentheses indicate an alternate title.
3. Songs were written for performers at Cabaret TAC, mostly in 1938.
4. These two composers collaborated on music and Spanish lyrics.
5. Goldmark adapted the music of Sergei Rachmaninoff's *2nd Piano Concerto*.
6. Songs were written for political causes or fund raisers.
7. All *Nantucket* songs were music by Vernon Duke and lyrics by Harold Rome.
8. All *La Grosse Valise* songs were music by Gerard Calvi and lyrics by Harold Rome. Several French lyrics had been written by Andre Maheux.
9. This was an album of children's songs.
10. Songs listed *Gone with the Wind* may be from any of the versions including *Scarlett* (Tokyo, 1970) or *Gone with the Wind* (London, 1972, or Los Angeles, 1973).
11. These are probably two different songs, same title, different sources.
12. Show was never produced.

## Appendix C

1. No artists are listed if the recording was part of original cast recordings detailed below.

## Appendix F

1. Rome provided incidental music for this show. Ballads were written by Anthony Hopkins and Peter Ustinov, the latter having starred in and written the show.
2. This show opened in Tokyo as *Scarlett* on January 2, 1970. It was then rewritten and opened in London as *Gone with the Wind* on May 3, 1972. It opened in America in Los Angeles on August 28, 1973, as *Gone with the Wind*.

## Appendix G

1. None of these shows was produced, and only a few of them got far into development.
2. Alternate titles are given in parentheses.
3. Scenes of this were played at a war relief program, "Music at Work," on May 10, 1942.
4. *Lili* was done in 1961 by Bob Merrill and Michael Stewart as *Carnival!*
5. This was called "an operetta entertainment in six scenes and four commercials," and had been proposed as a presentation for television.

# Bibliography

## Books, Periodicals and Online

*Absolute Astronomy.com.* http://www.absolute astronomy.com/topics/Pins_and_Needles (accessed April 15, 2009).

Alpert, Hollis. *Broadway! 125 Years of Musical Theatre.* New York: Museum of the City of New York, 1991.

Ameer, Amanda. "Life's a Pitch: We're Straight from the Shops." *Arts Journal.* http://www.artsjournal.com/lifesapitch/2008/09/were-straight-from-the-shops.html (accessed April 17, 2009).

*American National Biography.* New York: Oxford University Press, 1999.

Baral, Robert. *Revue: A Nostalgic Reprise of the Great Broadway Period.* New York: Fleet, 1962.

Bolton, Whitney. "Theatre: Harold Rome's Rise in Theatre," *New York Telegraph* (April 2, 1959).

Bordman, Gerald. *American Musical Theatre: A Chronicle.* 3rd ed. New York: Oxford University Press, 2001.

_____. *Days to Be Happy, Years to be Sad: The Life and Music of Vincent Youmans.* New York: Oxford University Press, 1982.

Botto, Louis. *At This Theatre: 100 Years of Broadway Shows, Stories and Stars.* New York: Applause Theatre and Cinema Books, 2002.

Brown, Jared. *Moss Hart: A Prince of the Theatre: A Biography in Three Acts.* New York: Back Stage Books, 2006.

Citron, Stephen. *The Wordsmiths: Oscar Hammerstein 2nd and Alan Jay Lerner.* New York: Oxford University Press, 1995.

Clarke, George W. "The Story behind a Maestro." *Boston Advertiser* (August 24, 1940).

Collins, Glenn. "Obituary: Harold Rome, 85, Writer of Socially Pointed Songs." *New York Times* (October 27, 1993).

Corman, Avery. "Theater: Music? Lyrics? He Can Get Them for You." *New York Times* (March 3, 1991).

Denning, Michael. *The Cultural Front: The Laboring of American Culture in the Twentieth Century.* London: Verso, 1998.

DeRosa, Steven. *Writing with Hitchcock: The Collaboration of Alfred Hitchcock and John Michael Hayes.* New York: Faber and Faber, 2001.

Engel, Lehman. *The American Musical Theater: A Consideration.* New York: Macmillan, 1967.

_____. *This Bright Day: An Autobiography.* New York: Macmillan, 1974.

*Encyclopedia Americana: International Edition.* Danbury, CT: Scholastic Library Publishing, 2005.

*Encyclopaedia Britannica.* 15th ed. Chicago: Encyclopaedia Britannica, 2010.

Ewen, David. *All the Years of American Popular Music.* Englewood Cliffs, NJ: Prentice-Hall, 1977.

_____. *American Songwriters: An H.W. Wilson Biographical Dictionary.* New York: H.W. Wilson, 1987.

_____. *Popular American Composers from Revolutionary Times to the Present: A Biographical and Critical Guide.* New York: H.W. Wilson, 1962.

Everett, William A. *Sigmund Romberg.* New Haven, CT: Yale University Press, 2007.

_____. *Rudolf Friml.* Urbana: University of Illinois Press, 2008.

"Fanny." http://www.guidetomusicaltheatre.com/shows (accessed April 14, 2009).
Fordin, Hugh. *A Biography of Oscar Hammerstein II*. New York: Random House, 1977.
Gammond, Peter. *The Oxford Companion to Popular Music*. Oxford: Oxford University Press, 1991.
Ganzl, Kurt. *Encyclopedia of the Musical Theater*. New York: Schirmer Books, 1994.
Gary, Beverly. "Closeup: Return to Seventh Av." *New York Post* (April 8, 1962).
Goldman, Harry. "When Social Significance Came to Broadway: *Pins and Needles* in Production." *Theatre Quarterly* Vol. VII, No. 28 (Winter 1977–78), 25–43.
Goldman, Harry, and Theresa Goldman. "Pins and Needles." *Performing Arts Review* Vol. 7, No. 3, (1977), 356–377.
Goldsmith, Theodore. "Of the Music and Lyrics by Harold Rome." *New York Times* (August 11, 1946).
Goldstein, Malcolm. *George S. Kaufman: His Life, His Theater*. New York: Oxford University Press, 1979.
Gordon, Eric A. *Mark the Music: The Life and Work of Marc Blitzstein*. New York: St. Martin's Press, 1989.
Gottfried, Martin. *Broadway Musicals*. New York: Abradale Press/Harry N. Abrams, 1984.
Gottlieb, Robert, and Robert Kimball, eds. *Reading Lyrics*. New York: Pantheon Books, 2000.
Green, Stanley. *Broadway Musicals: Show by Show*. Milwaukee: Hal Leonard Books, 1985.
———. *Encyclopaedia of the Musical Theatre*. New York: Dodd, Mead, 1976.
———. *Ring Bells! Sing Songs!: Broadway Musicals of the 1930's*. New Rochelle, NY: Arlington House, 1971.
———. *The World of Musical Comedy: The Story of the American Musical Stage as Told through the Careers of Its Foremost Composers and Lyricists*. New York: Ziff-Davis, 1960.
Halliwell, Leslie. *Halliwell's Film and Video Guide*. 12th ed. New York: HarperPerennial, 1997.
"Harold Rome: Theatre Man." *ASCAP Today* (September 1971).
Harrison, Nigel. *Songwriters: A Biographical Dictionary with Discographies*. Jefferson, NC: McFarland, 1998.
Henderson, Mary C. *Mielziner: Master of Modern Stage Design*. New York: Back Stage Books, 2001.
Higham, Charles. *Ziegfeld*. Chicago: Henry Regnery, 1972.
Jasen, David A. *A Century of American Popular Music: 2000 Best-Loved and Remembered Songs (1899–1999)*. New York: Routledge, 2002.
Jablonski, Edward. *Alan Jay Lerner: A Biography*. New York: Henry Holt, 1996.
Jacobs, Dick, and Harriet Jacobs. *Who Wrote That Song?* 2nd ed. Cincinnati: Writer's Digest Books, 1994.
Jenness, David, and Don Velsey. *Classic American Popular Song: The Second Half-Century, 1950–2000*. New York: Routledge, 2006.
Johnson, Malcolm L. "Rome Comes Home with a Smash *Fanny*." *Hartford Courant* (August 10, 1986).
Jones, John Bush. *The Songs That Fought the War: Popular Music and the Home Front, 1939–1945*. Waltham, MA: Brandeis University Press, 2006.
Jowitt, Deborah. *Jerome Robbins: His Life, His Theater, His Dance*. New York: Simon & Schuster, 2004.
Kahn, E.J., Jr. "Profiles: The Tough Guy and the Soft Guy." *The New Yorker* (April 4, 1953; April 11, 1953).
Kantor, Michael, and Laurence Maslon. *Broadway: The American Musical*. New York: Bulfinch Press, 2004.
Kerr, Walter. "Walter Kerr on the Theater: Wholesale Delights." *New York Herald Tribune* (April 1, 1962).
Kinkle, Roger D. *The Complete Encyclopedia of Popular Music and Jazz: 1900–1950*. New Rochelle, NY: Arlington House, 1974.
Kissel, Howard. *David Merrick: The Abominable Showman: The Unauthorized Biography*. New York: Applause Theatre and Cinema Books, 1993.
Lamb, Andrew. *150 Years of Popular Musical Theatre*. New Haven, CT: Yale University Press, 2000.
Lambert, Philip. *To Broadway, To Life! The Musical Theater of Bock and Harnick*. New York: Oxford University Press, 2011.
Larkin, Colin, ed. *The Encyclopedia of Popular Music*. 4th ed. Oxford: Oxford University Press, 2006.
Laufe, Abe. *Broadway's Greatest Musicals: 1977 Revised Edition*. New York: Funk and Wagnall's, 1977.

Laurents, Arthur. *Original Story By: A Memoir of Broadway and Hollywood.* New York: Alfred A. Knopf, 2000.

Lawrence, Jack. *They All Sang My Songs.* Fort Lee, NJ: Barricade Books, 2004.

Lehman, David. *A Fine Romance: Jewish Songwriters, American Songs.* New York: Nextbook/Schocken, 2009.

Leogrande, Ernest. "Harold Rome Sharpens Up His 'Needles.'" *New York Daily News* (June 12, 1978).

Lerner, Alan Jay. *The Street Where I Live.* New York: W.W. Norton, 1978.

Lissauer, Robert. *Lissauer's Encyclopedia of Popular Music in America: 1888 to the Present.* New York: Facts on File, 1996.

Logan, Joshua. *Josh: My Up and Down, In and Out Life.* New York: Delacorte, 1976.

Mahoney, John. "Stage: Composer Sings Different Tune." *Los Angeles Times* (August 26, 1973).

Mandelbaum, Ken. *Not Since Carrie: 40 Years of Broadway Musical Flops.* New York: St. Martin's, 1991.

Maslon, Laurence. *Broadway: The American Musical.* New York: Bulfinch, 2004.

Mordden, Ethan. *Coming Up Roses: The Broadway Musical in the 1950's.* New York: Oxford University Press, 1998.

———. *Open a New Window: The Broadway Musical in the 1960's.* New York: Palgrave, 2001.

———. *Sing for Your Supper: The Broadway Musical in the 1930's.* New York: Palgrave, 2001.

Most, Andrea. *Making Americans: Jews and the Broadway Musical.* Cambridge, MA: Harvard University Press, 2004.

Nolan, Frederick. *The Sound of Their Music: The Story of Rodgers and Hammerstein.* New York: Applause Theatre and Cinema Books, 2002.

Norton, Richard C. *A Chronology of American Musical Theater.* Oxford: Oxford University Press, 2002.

O'Leary, Dan. Liner notes for *Harold Rome: A Touch of Rome.* New York: DRG Theater, 1991.

*Pins and Needles.* New York: Columbia Records, 1962.

"Pins and Needles." *Internet Broadway Database.* http://www.idbd.com/production.php?id=1066 (accessed November 14, 2008).

Pogrebin, Abigail. *Stars of David: Prominent Jews Talk about Being Jewish.* New York: Broadway Books, 2005.

*Red Channels: The Report of Communist Influence in Radio and Television.* New York: American Business Consultants, 1950.

Rome, Florence. *The Scarlett Letters.* New York: Random House, 1971.

Rome, Harold J., Papers. Gilmore Music Library. Yale University.

———. "How to Write a Hit Musical." Harold J. Rome Papers, Gilmore Music Library, Yale University, New Haven, CT, 1967.

———. Interview with Martin Bookspan. Dorot Jewish Division, New York Public Library. New York: American Jewish Committee, Oral History Library, 1982.

———. "The Voice of Broadway: Rome Can't Get Films Wholesale." *New York Journal-American.* (June 18, 1962).

———. "What's Josh Logan like? I Don't Know." Harold J. Rome Papers, Gilmore Music Library, Yale University, New Haven, CT, November 1954.

Rome, Joshua. Interview with author, unpublished. October 4, 2011.

Ruhlmann, William. *All Music Guide.* http://www.answers.com/topic/harold-rome-soundtrack (accessed April 10, 2009).

Sadie, Stanley, ed. *The New Grove Dictionary of Music and Musicians.* 2nd ed. London: Grove, 2001.

Smith, Cecil. "Harold J. Rome Composes with Easy Fluency." *Chicago Daily Tribune.* (March 16, 1941).

Songwriters Hall of Fame. "Harold Rome." http://www.songwritershalloffame.org/index.php/exhibits/bio/C238 (accessed April 10, 2009).

Stambler, Irwin. *Encyclopedia of Popular Music.* New York: St. Martin's, 1965.

Stewart, John. *Broadway Musicals, 1943–2004.* Jefferson, NC: McFarland, 2006.

Stolberg, Benjamin. *Tailor's Progress: The Story of a Famous Union and the Men Who Made It.* New York: Doubleday, Doran, 1944.

Sullivan, Jack. *Hitchcock's Music.* New Haven, CT: Yale University Press, 2006.

Suskin, Steven. *Show Tunes: The Songs, Shows, and Careers of Broadway's Major Composers.* 3rd ed. New York: Oxford University Press, 2000.

———. *The Sound of Broadway Music: A Book of Orchestrators and Orchestrations.* Oxford: Oxford University Press, 2009.

Weidman, Jerome. *Praying for Rain.* New York: Harper and Row, 1986.
Widem, Allen M. "Coast to Coast." *Hartford Times* (April 11, 1959).
Wiener, Bruce F. *A Rome with a View.* Rosemont, PA: Rosemont College, 2001. New York Public Library for the Performing Arts, Billy Rose Theater Collection.
Wilk, Max. *OK! The Story of Oklahoma!.* New York: Grove, 1993.
Wilson, John S. "Harold Rome Sings Harold Rome." *New York Times* (November 25, 1976).
Winston, Bruce F. "In Gratitude: A Fan's Remembrance of Harold Rome." http://www.broadwayworld.com/article/In_Gratitude_A_Fans_Remembrance_of_Harold (accessed November 14, 2008).
Wolmuth, Roger. "The Arts." *Avenue* (May 1977).

## Reviews

*Sing Out the News*, directed by Charles Friedman.
　August 30, 1938, Edwin H. Schloss, *Philadelphia Record.*
　August 30, 1938, George Ross, *Philadelphia Inquirer.*
　September 26, 1938, John Anderson, *New York Journal-American.*
　September 26, 1938, Brooks Atkinson, *New York Times.*
　September 26, 1938, John Mason Brown, *New York Post.*
　September 26, 1938, Richard Lockridge, *New York Sun.*
　September 26, 1938, Burns Mantle, *New York Daily News.*
　September 26, 1938, Richard Watts, Jr., *New York Tribune.*
　September 26, 1938, Sidney B. Whipple, *New York World-Telegram.*
*The Little Dog Laughed*, directed by Eddie Dowling.
　August 14, 1940, Philip Klein, *Philadelphia Daily News.*
　August 14, 1940, Uncredited, *Philadelphia Evening Bulletin.*
　August 14, 1940, Uncredited, *Philadelphia Record.*
　August 14, 1940, Joseph H. Weintraub, *Atlantic City Press.*
　August 21, 1940, Helen Eager, *Boston Traveler.*
　August 21, 1940, Leo Gaffney, *Boston Record.*
　August 21, 1940, Elliot Norton, *Boston Post.*
　August 21, 1940, Uncredited, *Boston Daily Globe.*
　August 21, 1940, Uncredited, *Christian Science Monitor.*
　August 21, 1940, Uncredited, *Variety.*
*Let Freedom Sing*, directed by Joseph C. Pevney.
　October 6, 1942, Brooks Atkinson, *New York Times.*
　October 6, 1942, John Mason Brown, *New York World.*
　October 6, 1942, Burns Mantle, *New York Daily News.*
　October 6, 1942, Wilella Waldorf, *New York Post.*
*Stars and Gripes*, directed by Pfc. Glenn Jordan.
　July 16, 1943, Uncredited, *New York Times.*
　July 17, 1943, Lucius Beebe, *New York Herald Tribune.*
　July 17, 1943, Burns Mantle, *New York Daily News.*
　July 18, 1943, Irving Drutman, *New York Herald Tribune.*
　July 21, 1943, George Rosen, *Variety.*
　August 14, 1943, Joe Cohen, *The Billboard.*
*Call Me Mister*, directed by Robert H. Gordon.
　March 15, 1946, F.R.J., *New Haven Journal-Courier.*
　March 15, 1946, Uncredited, *New Haven Evening Register.*
　March 20, 1946, Linton Martin, *Philadelphia Inquirer.*
　March 20, 1946, Edwin H. Schloss, *Philadelphia Record.*
　March 30, 1946, Uncredited, *The Billboard.*
　April 19, 1946, Howard Barnes, *New York Herald Tribune.*
　April 19, 1946, John Chapman, *New York Daily News.*
　April 19, 1946, Robert Coleman, *New York Daily Mirror.*
　April 19, 1946, George Jean Nathan, *New York Post.*
　April 19, 1946, Lewis Nichols, *New York Times.*
　April 19, 1946, Uncredited, *The Hollywood Reporter.*

April 22, 1946, Uncredited, *New Yorker*.
April 25, 1946, Uncredited, *The Saturday Review*.
April 28, 1946, John Chapman, *Chicago Daily Tribune*.
April 29, 1946, Uncredited, *Newsweek*.
May 4, 1946, *Ye Olde Vette*, Army Times.
July 7, 1946, Elinor Hughes, Boston Sunday Herald.
November 14, 1946, Charlie Niles, *Hartford Times*.
November 19, 1946, Samuel L. Singer, *Philadelphia Inquirer*.
November 19, 1946 Uncredited, *Philadelphia Daily News*.
December 3, 1946, Peggy Doyle, *Boston Evening American*.
December 3, 1946, Leo Gaffney, *Boston Daily Record*.
December 3, 1946, Elliot Norton, *Boston Post*.
April 1, 1947, Ronald V. Cohen, *Pittsburgh Post-Gazette*.
April 1, 1947, Kaspar Monahan, *Pittsburgh Press*.
April 15, 1947, William F. McDermott, *Cleveland Plain Dealer*.
May 14, 1947, Claudia Cassidy, *Chicago Daily Tribune*.
May 14, 1947, Henry T. Murdock, *Chicago Sun*.

Pretty Penny, directed by George S. Kaufman.
June 21, 1949, Max de Schauensee, *Philadelphia Evening Bulletin*.
June 21, 1949, Edwin H. Schloss, *Philadelphia Inquirer*.

Alive and Kicking, directed by Robert H. Gordon.
December 28, 1949, Jerry Gaghan, *Philadelphia Daily News*.
December 28, 1949, Henry T. Murdock, *Philadelphia Inquirer*.
December 28, 1949, R.E.P. Sensenderfer, *Philadelphia Evening Bulletin*.
January 18, 1950, Brooks Atkinson, *New York Times*.
January 18, 1950, Howard Barnes, *New York Herald Tribune*.
January 18, 1950, John Chapman, *Chicago Daily Tribune*.
January 25, 1950, Uncredited, *Variety*.

Michael Todd's Peep Show, directed by Hassard Short.
June 29, 1950, John Chapman, *New York Daily News*.
June 29, 1950, Robert Coleman, *New York Daily Mirror*.
June 29, 1950, Robert Garland, *New York Journal-American*.
June 29, 1950, Richard Watts, Jr., *New York Post*.

That's the Ticket, directed by Jerome Robbins.
September 25, 1948, Jerry Gaghan, *Philadelphia Daily News*.
September 25, 1948, Edwin H. Schloss, *Philadelphia Inquirer*.
September 29, 1948, Uncredited, *Variety*.

Bless You All, directed by John C. Wilson.
November 14, 1950, F.R.J., *New Haven Journal-Courier*.
November 22, 1950, Jerry Gaghan, *Philadelphia Daily News*.
November 22, 1950, Henry T. Murdock, *Philadelphia Inquirer*.
November 22, 1950, R.E.P. Sensenderfer, *Philadelphia Evening Bulletin*.
December 10, 1950, John McClain, *New York Journal-American*.
December 15, 1950, Brooks Atkinson, *New York Times*.
December 15, 1950, Howard Barnes, *New York Herald Tribune*.
December 15, 1950, William Hawkins, *New York World-Telegram & Sun*.
December 15, 1950, John McClain, *New York Journal-American*.
December 15, 1950, Richard Watts, Jr., *New York Post*.
December 16, 1950, John Chapman, *Chicago Daily Tribune*.
December 25, 1950, Uncredited, *Time*.
February 1951, Uncredited, *Theatre Arts*.

Wish You Were Here, directed by Joshua Logan.
June 26, 1952, Brooks Atkinson, *New York Times*.
June 26, 1952, Robert Coleman, *New York Daily Mirror*.
June 26, 1952, William Hawkins, *New York World-Telegram*.
June 26, 1952, John McClain, *New York Journal-American*.
June 26, 1952, Arthur Pollock, *The Daily Compass*.
June 26, 1952, Vernon Rice, *New York Post*.
June 27, 1952, John Chapman *Chicago Daily Tribune*.
July 6, 1952, John Chapman, *Chicago Daily Tribune*.

December 9, 1953, Claudia Cassidy, *Chicago Daily Tribune*.
*Fanny*, directed by Joshua Logan.
  September 21, 1954, Elinor Hughes, *Boston Herald*.
  September 21, 1954, Alta Maloney, *Boston Traveler*.
  September 21, 1954, Edwin F. Melvin, *Christian Science Monitor*.
  September 21, 1954, Elliot Norton, *Boston Post*.
  September 22, 1954, L.G. Gaffney, *Boston Daily Record*.
  September 22, 1954, Uncredited, *Variety*.
  September 26, 1954, Cyrus Durgin, *Boston Sunday Globe*.
  October 13, 1954, Hamilton Dalton, *Philadelphia News*.
  October 14, 1954, Henry T. Murdock, *Philadelphia Inquirer*.
  November 5, 1954, Brooks Atkinson, *New York Times*.
  November 5, 1954, John Chapman, *New York Daily News*.
  November 5, 1954, Robert Coleman, *New York Daily Mirror*.
  November 5, 1954, Thomas R. Dash, *Women's Wear Daily*.
  November 5, 1954, Walter F. Kerr, *New York Herald Tribune*.
  November 5, 1954, John McClain, *New York Journal-American*.
  November 5, 1954, Lee Rogow, *Hollywood Reporter*.
  November 5, 1954, Louis Sheaffer, *Brooklyn Eagle*.
  November 5, 1954, Richard Watts, Jr., *New York Post*
  November 10, 1954, Uncredited, *Variety*.
  November 13, 1954, John Lardner, *New Yorker*.
  November 27, 1954, George Jean Nathan, *New York Journal-American*.
*Destry Rides Again*, directed by Michael Kidd.
  March 10, 1959, Jerry Gaghan, *Philadelphia Daily News*.
  March 10, 1959, Ernie Schier, *Philadelphia Evening Bulletin*.
  April 2, 1959, Peggy Doyle, *Boston Evening American*.
  April 2, 1959, Elinor Hughes, *Boston Herald*.
  April 2, 1959, Elliot Norton, *Boston Daily Record*.
  April 24, 1959, Brooks Atkinson, *New York Times*.
  April 24, 1959, Robert Coleman, *New York Mirror*.
  April 24, 1959, Walter Kerr, *New York Herald Tribune*.
  April 24, 1959, John McClain, *New York Journal-American*.
  April 24, 1959, Richard Watts, Jr., *New York Post*.
  April 25, 1959, John Chapman, *Chicago Tribune*.
  May 2, 1959, Uncredited, *Cue*.
  May 3, 1959, John Chapman, *New York Daily News*.
*I Can Get It for You Wholesale*, directed by Arthur Laurents.
  February 13, 1964, Jerry Gaghan, *Philadelphia Daily News*.
  February 13, 1964, Henry T. Murdock, *Philadelphia Inquirer*.
  February 13, 1964, Ernest Schier, *Philadelphia Evening Bulletin*.
  February 16, 1964, S. S. Irving, *Jewish Exponent*.
  February 18, 1964, Henry T. Murdock, *Philadelphia Inquirer*.
  February 28, 1964, Cyrus Durgin, *Boston Globe*.
  February 28, 1964, Frederick H. Guidry, *Christian Science Monitor*.
  February 28, 1964, Elinor Hughes, *Boston Herald*.
  February 28, 1964, Elliot Norton, *Boston Record American*.
  March 23, 1964, John Chapman, *New York Daily News*.
  March 23, 1964, Walter Kerr, *New York Herald Tribune*.
  March 23, 1964, John McClain, *New York Journal-American*.
  March 23, 1964, Norman Nadel, *New York World-Telegram*.
  March 23, 1964, Howard Taubman, *New York Times*.
  March 23, 1964, Richard Watts, Jr., *New York Post*.
  March 26, 1964, Uncredited, *Newsweek*.
  March 30, 1964, Uncredited, *Time*.
  March 31, 1964, Uncredited, *New Yorker*.
  April 1, 1964, John Chapman, *Chicago Daily Tribune*.
  April 1, 1964, Walter Kerr, *New York Herald Tribune*.

*Scarlett*, directed by Joe Layton.
  January 5, 1970, Uncredited, *Chicago Daily News*.
  January 6, 1970, Robert Crabb, *Japan Times*.

*Gone with the Wind*, directed by Joe Layton.
  May 4, 1972, John Barber, *London Daily Telegraph*.
  May 4, 1972, Felix Barker, *London Evening News*.
  May 4, 1972, Michael Billington, *London Guardian*.
  May 4, 1972, Irving Wardle, *London Times*.
  May 5, 1972, Henry Pleasants, *International Herald Tribune*.
  May 13, 1972, Kenneth Hurren, *London Spectator*.
  May 14, 1972, Bart Mills, *Chicago Tribune*.
  May 21, 1972, Ronald Bryden, *New York Times*.
  October 24, 1973, Stanley Eichelbaum, *San Francisco Examiner*.

*Gone with the Wind*, directed by Lucia Victor.
  June 15, 1976, Harry Bowman, *Dallas Morning News*.
  June 17, 1976, Uncredited, *Dallas Times Herald*.
  July 1, 1976, Robert W. Butler, *Kansas City Times*.
  July 14, 1976, Helen C. Smith, *Atlanta Constitution*.
  July 25, 1976, Shirley Green, *Miami Beach Times*.

# Index

Numbers in *bold italics* indicate pages with photographs.

Abbott, Bud 32
Abbott, Charles 56
Academy Award 114
Actors' Equity 22, 73–74, 84
Adams, Lee 55
Adler, Philip 70
Adler, Richard 55–56, 95, 99, 192
advertising 48, 55–56, 111, 181
"The Advertising Song" 48
African art 3, 148, 151–52, *173*
Albery, Ian B. 126
*Alive and Kicking* 72–75, 77
"All of a Sudden My Heart Sings" 196–97
Allan, Lewis 35
Alvarez, Anita 12
amateurs 14–15, 17, 18, 22, 28, 31
American Business Consultants 82–83
American Federation of Labor (AFL) 20, 29, 34
American Jewish Theater 135
American Popular Songbook 1, 2, 110, 187
American Society of Composers, Authors, and Publishers (ASCAP) 56, 60, 139, 147, *190*
American Theatre Wing (ATW) 44–46
Amos, Keith 182
analysis 115
Anderson, John Murray 48, 59
Andrews Sisters 78
angel auditions 37–38, 58, 158
*The Angry God* 55
Annucci, Lydia 17
Anouilh, Jean 188–89
"Anthem of the Union of Soviet Socialist Republics" 40
anti-communist 19, 82
anti-Semitism 7, 127, 132, 136
anti-war 168
"Anyone Would Love You" 122–23, 197
apartheid 150, 152, 153
applause 169–71, 173
architect 7–9
"Are You Ready, Gyp Watson?" 123–24, 138

Arent, Arthur 15
Arlen, Harold 1, 27, 35, 38, 46, 48, 100, *113*, 178
Armus, Sidney 92
"The Army Service Forces" 53
Aronson, Ida 5
"Arouse, Arouse!" 161
Arsenal School 5
*Artists and Models* 59
ASCAP Foundation Richard Rodgers Award *190*–91
Ash, Frances 67
auditions 162
Auerbach, Arnold 15, 57–58, 62–63, 70–71, 79

Babchin, Sol 17
Bacharach, Burt 159
Bachelor of Fine Arts 7
"Back to Work" 18
Bailey, Mildred 98
Bailey, Pearl 76–77
"Ballad of the Garment Trade" 132, 193
"Ballad of the Gun" 123
Ballard, Kaye 77–78
bands 2, 5, *6*, 7, 12, 85, *123*
"The Bar Mitzvah Song" 107, 133
"Be Calm" 47
"Be Kind to Your Parents" 197
Behrman, S.N. 101–04, 114, 116
Bergersen, Baldwin 17, 48
Berle, Milton 48
Berlin, Irving 1, 12, 27, 39, 59, 61, 67, 68, 98, 117, 119, 138, 148, 192, 194, 196
Bernstein, Leonard 192
Bershadsky, Sadie 17
"Bertha the Sewing Machine Girl" 18
Best Lyric Writer award 66
Bettis, Valerie 76
Bird, Dorothy 12
"Birthday Song" 124
blacklisting 82–84, 110

253

# 254 Index

Blackton, Jay 169, 182, 184
*Bless You All* 57, 70–72, 75–81, 105
"Blissful Christmas" 124
Blitzstein, Marc 15, 16, 28, 41, 83–84, 108
Bloom, Rube 190
Bloomgarden, Kermit 44, 95
"Blueberry Eyes" 175–77
blueprint specials 51
Bock, Jerry 56, 178, 192, 194
Bolton, Guy 61
Bond, Sheila 92
"Bonnie Blue Flag" 177
"Bonnie Gone" 177, 186
book musicals 2, 27, 48, 58, 61, 70–71, 80, 99, 102, 108, 110, 116, 139, 164–65, 171, 174–75, 188, 196
Boone, Richard 69
Boretz, Allen 12
Borscht Belt 12
Bouvier, Yvonne 32
Boyer, Charles 114–15
Brady, Scott 121–22
Breaux, Marc 124
Brechner, Stanley 135
Brecht, Bertolt 15
Brent, Earl K. 67
Brest, Arthur G. 53
Brice, Fanny 20
Broadcast Music, Inc. (BMI) 56
Broadway 2–3, 6, 12, 17, 19, 25, 37, 42, 44, 49, 51–52, 58, 59–62, 67–68, 80, 91, 99, 106, 113, 117–20, 122, 124, 126–27, 134, 139, 147–50, 156, 162, 168, 174–175, 181, 186, **190**
*Broadway at the Ballroom* 187–88
Brown, Anne 17, **23**
Brown, Katharine 163, 166, 184
Brown, Lester 52
Brown, Max J. 120, 158–59
Brunswick Records 21
Buchholz, Horst 114–15
Bucks County Playhouse 73
"The Bunny" 42
burlesque 42–44, 58, 72–74
Burns, David 73–74
Burrows, Abe 95

Cabaret TAC 34–35
Caesar, Irving 46
Café Society 35
Cahn, Sammy **113**, 195
*Caleb Calum's America* 37
*Call Me Mister* 2, 15, 31, 46–47, 57–69, **64**, 70, 92, 101, 113, 130, 160, 187–88, 196
"Call Me Mister" 69, 197
Calloway, Cab 29
Calvi, Gerard 125, 155–57
*Camera Three* 188
Camp Tamiment 12, 85–86
Campanella, Philip 24
Canary, David 184–85

Cantor, Eddie 192
Carmichael, Hoagy 1, 2, 7, 55
Caron, Leslie 113, 115
Carr, Lawrence 106
Carroll, Earl 59
Carroll, Paul Vincent 96
Carter, Jimmy 185
*Casablanca* (musical) 105–06
Cassidy, Jack 90, 92
Catholic Theatre Movement 20
Catskill Mountains 8, 12, 57, 87, 119
"Cavalry of the Steppes" 40
CBS Television **113**
censorship 21, 22
"Certain Individuals" 92, 197
"C'est Defendu" 156
"Chain Store Daisy" 18, 20–21, 193
Champion, Gower 32, 37
Chaplin, Charles 35
Chappell 180–81
character play 104
charm song 109
Chayefsky, Paddy 194
Chen, Silan 34
Chevalier, Maurice 113, 115–16
children 177–78
Chodorov, Jerome 70, 73, 96–97, 187, 192
Chorus Equity 22
*A Chorus Line* 69
Citizens for McCarthy Committee 161
Clark, Bobby 32, 43
Clark, Harry 18
classical music 148, 189
Clooney, Rosemary 52
Coca, Imogene 12
Cole, Jack 72–73
Coleman, Cy 55
Collins, Michael 112
Comden, Betty 192
common man 19, 70, 78, 87
communication 196–97
communism/Communist Party 10, 15, 19–20, 36, 39, 82–84
Congress of Industrial Organization (CIO) 20, 29, 34, 41
conversational singing 77
Cook, Barbara 1
Cook, Ray 182
Cooper, Marilyn 131
Coots, J. Fred 52
Costello, Lou 32
Council Against Intolerance in America 38
Coward, Noël 60, 63, 98, 190
*The Cradle Will Rock* 15, 16, 24, 25
"Cream of Mush Song" 18, 21
Crosby, Bing 55
"Cry, Baby" 72–73, 77
Curto, Joan 1
Cyclists for Humphrey 161
Czitron, Rose 17

## Index

Dailey, Dan 67, 69
*Daily Worker* 20
Dallas Summer Musicals 184–86
Dameron, Tad 56
*Dancin' Day* 96, 98
Da Silva, Howard 19, 149–50, 153
Daughters of the American Revolution 15, 20, 36
David, Hal 159, **190**
Davis, Ossie 154–55
Dazieri, Vincent 17
"Delilah Done Me Wrong" 156
de Mille, Agnes 71, 88–89
demobilization 57–58, 61–62, 65–66, 69, 71
Democrat 39, 84, 160–61
DePauw, Victor 142
depression 115
Depression 7, 10, 11, 13, 36, 60
"The Desert Flame" 76
*Destry Rides Again* 2, 103, 117–26, 138, 158, 160, 172, 176, 178
Deutsch, Helen 125–26
"The Devil Played the Fiddle" 55
Dhery, Robert 155–56
dialect 87, 137
Diamond, Adele **23**
dictators 35–36, 82, 150–51
Dietz, Howard 27, 57, 61, 189–90
"Doing the Reactionary" 18, 21, 150
"Don Jose of Far Rockaway" 92
"Don't Wanna Write about the South" 75, 197
"Dost Thou" 77–78, 197–98
Douglas, Melvyn 57–58, 60, 70
Dowling, Eddie 35
Drake, Ervin 90, 190
Drama Desk Special Award 191
Draper, Paul 37
Dratch, Sam 17
Dreyfus, Max 98
Dubin, Al 32
Dubinsky, David 10–16, 20, **23**, 24, 133, 137, 161, 193
Duke, Vernon 15, 54–55, 65–66, 192
Dylan, Bob 190

"Eagle Soliloquy" 153
*Earl Carroll's Vanities* 59
"Eat a Little Something" 135, 139, 193
Ebb, Fred 55, 80, 95, 191, 193
Eben, Al 17
Edinburgh, Zitta 17
Einstein, Albert 24
Eisenberg, Emmanuel 15
Ellington, Duke 1, 2
El-Registan 40
*Encores!* 111
Engel, Lehman 3, 13, 19, 37, 70, 73, 78, 81, 98, 100–01, 106–07, 109, 115, 121–22, 133, 138, 146, 155–56, 158–59, 166, 168–72, 177, 182, 192, 196–97

Entertainment National Service Association (ENSA) 44–45
entertainment specialist 49
Epstein, Julius 191
Epstein, Philip 191
ethnic music 137
*An Evening of Harold Rome* 188
extravaganza 58

"The Face on the Dime" 67
Fain, Sammy 31, 52, 61, 67
"The Family Way" 133, 136, 193
*Fanny* 2, 3, 48, 71, 77, 84, 99–116, 123, 130, 137, 139–40, 166, 175–76, 183, 188, 196
"Fanny" 101, 109–10, 197
*Fanny* (movie) 113–16
Fazio, Anthony 17
Federal Arts Council of the Workers Alliance 34
Federal Bureau of Investigation (FBI) 3, 38–39, 92
Federal Theatre Project 11, 15
Feist, Gene 24
Fetter, Ted 66
Fielding, Harold 174–75, 180–81
Fieldman, Tillie 17
Fields, Dorothy 68, 192
Fields, Herbert 192
Fields, Joseph 96, 155–56
film music 94–95
Fine, Sylvia 12
First Amendment 84
"First Impression" 19
Fisher, Eddie 2, 90, **91**, 109–10
Fisher, Ian Marshall 108
Fitelson, H. William 75, 87, 102, 112, 114, 158
Fitzgerald, Ella 29
"Flippy, Floppy, Mopey, Dopey, Sloppy Joe" 46–47
folk play movement 87
Foote, Horton 174, 184
"For Charity, Sweet Charity" 8
Fort Hamilton 49, **50**, 51
"Forward" 40
Fosse, Bob 67
The Four Aces 123
"Four Little Angels of Peace" 18, 20, 23, 29, 150
Fox, Dorothy 30
Fox, Irene 17
Frankel, Julius 18
"Franklin D. Roosevelt Jones" ("Man of the Year") 29–30, 32, 39, 40, 150, 193, 197
"Franklin D.—Winston C.—Joseph V. Victory March" 40
Fraser, Ronald 156
Frederick Douglas Institute 152
"The French Have a Word for It" 33
"French with Tears" 72–73
Friedman, Charles 12, 15, 17–19, 26–30

Friml, Rudolph 2, 117
Fryer, Robert 105–06

Gabel, Martin 51
Gannon, Kim 7
Garland, Judy 29
garment district/trade 16, 21–22, 28, 31, 127–28, 130, 133–35, 137, 193
Garrett, Betty 46–47, 62–67, 145–46
Gascoine, Jill 126
Gaskill, Clarence 39
Gear, Louella 32
"Gee, but It's Cold in Russia" 46
Gelman, Sandra 18
*George White's Scandals* 59
Gershe, Leonard 117–19
Gershwin, George 1, 2, 12, 27, 28, 68, 72, 117, 139, 192
Gershwin, Ira 1, 12, 27, 28, 72, 98, 117, 192
G.I. 51, 58, 62, 63, 66, 67, 71
Gilbert, Billy 111
"A Gift Today" 193
"Gimme the Shimmy!" 75
gin rummy 172, 192
"Gin Rummy Rhapsody" 78
*Give a Viva!* 37
"Give a Viva!" 47
*Give My Regards to Broadway and Remember Me to Harold Rome* 187
"Goin' Home Train" 63, **64**, 67, 124
Goldberg, Martin **123**
Golden Globe 114
Goldman, Byron 120, 158
Goldman, William 194
Goldstein, Eugene 18
Goldstein, Hyman 18
*Gone with the Wind* (musical) 13, 140, 155, 162–166, 168, 172, 174–86
"Good Little Girls" 35
Good Neighbor Policy 65
"Goodbye, Love" 90
Goodier, Harry 179
Goodrich, Ace 51
Goodrich, Frances 100
Gordon, Mack 48, 67, 163
Gordon, Max 26–27, 60
Gordon, Robert 19, 22
Gorlinsky, Sandor 112
Goslar, Lotte 34
Gossett, Louis, Jr. 153–54, **154**
Gould, Bernie 21
Gould, Dave 29
Gould, Elliott 128, 131, 140–41
Grable, Betty 67, 69
Graham, Martha 34
Grassi, Enzo 18
Gray, Dolores 103, 121–25
*The Great Dictator* 35
Green, Adolph 192
Green, Bud 52

Green, Mitzi 47
Green Mansions 8, 12, 15, 23, 57, 85–86, 119
*Greenwich Village Follies* 59
Gregory, David 15
Griffith, Andy 120–22, 124
*La Grosse Valise* 125, 149, 155–57
*Guernica* 35
Guthrie, Woody 13, 39, 60

Hackett, Albert 100
*Hair* 69
Hale, Chester 37
Hambleton, John 29
"Hamburg Waltz" 156
Hammerstein, Oscar, II 1, 2, 7, 12, 28, 38, 42, 52, 61, 67–68, 71, 80–81, 88, 98–101, 117, 123, 139, 169, 192, 194
Hammond, John, Jr. 34
"Happily Ever After" 37
"Happy Song" 156
Harary, Nettie 18, **23**
Harbach, Otto 72, 117
Harburg, E.Y. 1, 12, 35, 39, 70, 98–100, 159, 192
Harnick, Sheldon 56, 95, 192, 194
Harold Rome Collection (Library of Congress) 160
Harold Rome Papers 6, 169, 177–78
*Harold Rome Sings Harold Rome* 148
*Harold Rome's Almanac* 160
*Harold Rome's Gallery* 142–47, 160
Harris, Julie 104
Harris, Mark 158–59
Hart, Kitty Carlisle 97
Hart, Lorenz 1, 12, 27, 32, 36, 61, 70, 99, 116, 119, 129, 163, 192, 194
Hart, Moss 12, 26–30, 37, 44–45, 57, 95–97, 187, 191–92
Hartford, Connecticut 5–7
Hartford High School 5
Hartley, Neil 158
Harvey, Laurence 130
Haskell, Jack 145–46
Hausdorf, Hattie 18
"Have I Told You Lately?" 134, 140, 197
*Having Wonderful Time* 12, **86**–89
Hawkes, Jacquetta 153
Hayford, Justin 1
Hayward, Susan 131, 134
Hayward, Leland 85–89, **86**
Heath, Tony 18
Hefti, Neal 56
Helburn, Theresa 38
Held, Anna 59
Heller, George 44
*Hellzapoppin'* 30–32, 157
Henderson, Florence 104, 109–11, 123
Henderson, Ray 48
Henie, Sonja 8
Herman, Jerry 190, 194

Herman, Woody 56
Herrmann, Bernard 95
"He's Not a Well Man" 132
Hightower, Louis 37
Hill, George Roy 95
Hirschfield, Al 147–48, 195
"History Eight to the Bar" 47
"History Is Made at Night" 32
Hitchcock, Alfred 94–95
Hitler, Adolf 20, 29, 31, 35, 39, 45, 49
hoarding 47
Hoffenstein, Samuel 54
Holiday, Billie 35
Hollander, Frederick 118
Hollywood 2, 9, 12, 44, 46, 59, 63, 68–69, 82–84, 94–95, 104, 113, 116, 127–28, 163, 175, 192
Holt, Thaddeus 176–77
Homer, Ben 52
*Hooray for What!* 16, 24, 35
Hoover, J. Edgar 38–39, 82, 92
"Horror Boys of Hollywood" 8
Horwitt, Arnold 15, 57, 63
House Un-American Activities Committee (HUAC) 3, 38, 82–84, 149
*How to Succeed in Business Without Really Trying* 128–29
*Howe and Hummel* 146
Hudson-Delange Orchestra 21
Hughes, Langston 83, 195
Hughes, Tom 184–86
Humphrey, Hubert 161
Hunt, Dan **123**
Hylton, Jack 96

*I Can Get It for You Wholesale* 106–07, 125–41, **132**, 160, 193–94
"I Did It for Defense" 47
"I Hate a Parade" 75
"I Have to Tell You" 104, 109, 197
"I Knew You Well" 55
"I Say Hello" 123, 197
"I Shouldn't Love You" 77–78
"I Want Romance" 37
*I'd Rather Be Right* 16, 24
*In the Pink* 96–98, 187
Ingram, Rex 29–30, 76, 171
integration of songs 90, 108, 110, 175
International Ladies' Garment Workers' Union (ILGWU) 2, 7, 9, 10–16, 20, 22, **23**, 24, 28, 57, 128, 150, 161, 196
"International Mountain Climbers" 29, 31
"Internationale" 39
interpolations 42, 59, 71–72
investing in shows 119–20, 153
Irving S. Gilmore Music Library 3, 6, 54, 98, 146, 169, 177, 189
Irwin, Bill 29
isolationism 42, 49
"It's Better with a Union Man" 193

"It's Fun to Be Free" 47
"It's Good to Be Alive (Lebe Is Gut)" 153
"I've Got the Nerve to Be in Love" 18

Jacobson, Dan 149–50
Jaffee, Lynne 18, **23**
Jaffe, Sam 34
Japan 3, 163–67, 169, 172, 176, 178, 184–86
jazz 5–6, 35, 95
"Je T'aime — I Love You" 55
Jenkins, Gordon 190
Jews 5, 7, 12, 28, 82, 85–87, 127, 131–33, 135–38, 150, 153, 155, 192–94
jingles 55–56
Jinguji, Sakura 167
"Johnny Is a Hoarder" 47
*Johnny Johnson* 13, 24
Johnson, Chic 30, 32
Johnson, Lyndon 160–61
Jordan, Glenn 51
"Jumping to the Jukebox" 53
Jun, Rose Marie 145–46
"Just a Little White House" 76

Kadison, Harry 18
Kahal, Irving 52
Kander, John 55, 80, 95, 191, 193–94
Kaplan, Hyman 18
Karpilovsky, Murray 50
Kaufman, George S. 8, 26–30, 45, 64, 73–74, 95, 157, 192
Kaufman, Rose 17
Kaye, Danny 12
Kean, Betty 67
Kelly, Gene 128–29
Kelly, Grace 94
Kern, Eva 98
Kern, Jerome 1, 12, 26, 39, 52, 61, 68, 72, 117, 192, 194
Kidd, Michael 95, 121–22, 124–25
Kikuta, Kazuo 164–68, 174
Kinburn, Bella 17
Kipness, Joseph 77, 155
Knipper, Lev 40
Kober, Arthur 8, 12, **86**–87, 89, 93, 172, 191, 193
Koehler, Ted 27
Korda, Alexander 96
Korngold, Erich Wolfgang 95
Kosakoff, Reuven 13
*Kraft Music Hall* 160
Krasny, Diane 146
Kruschen, Jack 131
Kupferman, Meyer 13, 155, 166, 184

labor movement 10, 11, 15–16, 25
Labor Stage 11–16, 17–18, 24, 28, 60, 149
"The Lady Is" 185
"The Lady Is a WAAC" 47
"The Lady's On the Job" 46

La Guardia, Fiorello 44
Lane, Burton 1, 99
Lane, Ziggy 51
Lang, Harold 131
Lang, Philip 106–08
Lansbury, Edgar 158–59
Lardner, Ring, Jr. 158
Latouche, John 15, 28, 32, 65–66
Laurents, Arthur 95, 125, 129, 132, 135–37, 140
Lawrence, Steve 128–29
Layton, Joe 95, 146, 166–69, 174–75, 178–79, 181–86
Lee, Gypsy Rose 8
Lee, Peggy 91
Lee, Tom 53
left-wing 8, 12, 13, 28, 30, 34, 36, 42
Lehac, Ned 32
Leigh, Carolyn 55
*The Leningrad Symphony* 40
Lenya, Lotte 98
Leon, Felix 149–50, 153
Lerner, Alan Jay 1, 2, 38, 96, 99, 101, 117, 138–39, 192
LeRoy, Ken 131, 134
Lescaze, William 7
Leslie, Lew 59
Lesser, Arthur 155
Lester, Edwin 55, 96, 183
*Let Freedom Sing* 46–48
"Let Freedom Swing" 35, 151
"Let's Talk about a Woman" 103
Levin, Herman 57–58, 60, 62, 70
Levine, Elias 17
Levy, Al 17
*Lew Leslie's Blackbirds* 59
Lewis, Jerry 78
Lewis, John L. 20
Lewis, Sam 52
liberal 3, 15–16, 28–29, 34–35, 39, 41, 82–84, 150, 159–61
Lieberson, Goddard 98, 133
Lillie, Beatrice 20, 133
"Lisa" ("Theme from *Rear Window*") 94–95
"The Little Brown Suit My Uncle Gave Me" 52, 53
*The Little Dog Laughed* 35–38, 171
"Little Miss Liberty Jones" 40
"Little Miss Victory Jones" 47
"Little Surplus Me" 187
"Little Things Meant So Much to Me" 76
"Little Wonders" 177
Lloyd, Arthur 13
Locke, Sam 47
Loeb, Philip 30, 37
Loesser, Frank 1, 2, 36, 52–53, 55–57, 95, 98, 118, 138–39, 192, 194
Loewe, Frederic 1, 2, 37, 96–97, 99, 117, 124, 138–39, 192
Logan, Joshua 48, 84, 85–93, **86**, 100–04, 106, 109, 113–16, 191–92, 198

Logan, Nedda 104
"Lonely Stranger" 175, 178
Lonergan, Lenore 72–73
"Looking for a Candidate" 151
Los Angeles Light Civic Opera 183
"Love Is a Very Light Thing" 105, 197
"Love Is Still Love" 78, 197–98
"Love It Hurts So Good" 72
"Love Sometimes Has to Wait" 52
"Love That Man" 76
"Love You" 94
*Lunchtime Follies* 45–47, 57, 62, 130, 187
Lynn, Bambi 131, 134
*Lyrical and Satirical: The Music of Harold Rome* 188
*Lyrics and Lyricists* 187

Mackenburg, Charles 50
*Man and Wife* 160
"Man of the Year" 29
Manilow, Barry 56
Mann, Theodore 155
Marand, Patricia 92
Marble Arch Gallery **144**–48
Marcovici, Andrea 1, 52
*Marseilles Trilogy* 99–101, 104
Martin, Dean 78
Martin, Hugh 32–33, 68, 178, 191
Martin, Mary 104
Martin, May 17
Mason, Karen 1
Mason, Melissa 37
Mathis, Sherry 184–85
Mauldin, Bill 69
"May Your Heart Stay Young" ("L'Chayim!") 153
McCarthy, Eugene 161
McCarthyism 38, 78
McCarty, Mary 76
McHugh, Jimmy 2, 32, 43, 68, **113**
McHugh, Mary 21
McMahon, Aline 44–45
"Meadowland" 40
Meany, George 20
Meeropol, Abel 35
Melachrino, George 105
"Mene, Mene, Tekel" 20–21, 23, 35, 151, 197
Mercer, Johnny 38, 48
Meredith, Burgess 96
Merrick, David 96, 99–101, 104, 108, 110–11, 117–21, 125–26, 129–33, 137, 140, 157–58
Merrill, Bob 95, 125–26, 194
Meth, Max 29
*Michael Todd's Peep Show* 72–75
"The Micromaniac" 48–49
Mielziner, Jo 29–30, 36, 87–88, 103
Mihalkov, Sergei 40
"Military Life" ("The Jerk Song") 64, 67, 187
Milken, Michael 135

Miller, Glenn 29
Miller, Mel 78
minstrel shows 58, 180
Miranda, Carmen 32–33
"Miss Marmelstein" 132, 139, 193, 197
Mitchell, Margaret 163, 168, 184
"The Model Hasn't Changed" 75
Modick, Murray 17
Molina, Alfred 126
Moll, Elick 194
"Momma, Momma, Momma" 134, 136, 193
"The Money Song" 78, 197
Monti, Mili 37
Morley, Robert 112
Moross, Jerome 11, 15
Morrison, Bettie 1
Morrison, Miriam 17
Morse, Robert 128–29
Mostel, Zero 38
Moussorgsky, Modest 143
Munich Agreement 31
Munsel, Patrice 104
Munshin, Jules 12, 66, 76
Murray, Jack 12
The Museum of African Art 148, 152
*Music at Work* 41
*Music Box Revues* 59
*Musicals Tonight!* 78
*My Fair Lady* 37, 96–97
"My Heart Decided" 55
"My Heart Is Unemployed" 29
"My Pinup Girl" 52, 53

*Nantucket* 54–55
Nash, Ogden 55
National Academy of Popular Music 189
National Museum of African Art 152
national tours 67, 88, 111
Nazism 35
"Never Too Late for Love" 105
*New Faces* 59
New Haven, Connecticut 6, 7, 66–67, 75, 78–79, 88, 162
*New Pins and Needles* 21, 22
New York Port of Embarkation 49
Newman, Alfred 95
Newman, Jean 17
Newman, Randy 56
Newmark, Rose 17, *23*
"Nobody Makes a Pass at Me" 18, 21, 23, 133, 197
North, Sheree 131, 141
Norton, Elliott 89
"Not Cricket to Picket" 18, 20, 21, 133

"Of the People Stomp" 47, 151
Officer, Philip 1
"O'Hara" 185
O'Hara, Maureen 104
"Oistgetzaichnet" ("Out of This World") 153

Olsen, Ole 30, 32
*On Borrowed Time* 160
"On That Old Production Line" 46
"On Time" 46–47
"Once Knew a Fella" 138
"One Big Union for Two" 18, 20, 22, 29, 34
*Oops Sorry or They Never Saw the Light of Day* 160
operetta 2, 42, 58, 111
Osborn, Paul 161, 172, 192
"Oysters, Cockles, and Mussels" 137–38

pacifism 35, 49
Pagnol, Marcel 99, 100, 102, 104, 108, 114
painting 3, 142–48, **143**, 195
*Pal Joey* 61, 128–29, 134
"Panisse and Son" 105, 109
pantomime 58
"Papa's Got a Job" 32
*Parade* 11, 15, 24
*The Passing Show* 58–59, 71, 74
Pavek, Janet 112
Pearl Harbor 44, 49
Pearman, Olive 17
period writing 137–38, 176
Peters, Paul 11
Petricoff, Elaine 24
Pevney, Joseph 46
piano playing 5, 6, 12
piano teaching 7
Picasso, Pablo 35
Pierce, Burton 30
"Pink" 187
*Pins and Needles* 2, 7, 10–16, 17–25, 26–32, 35–36, 38–39, 48–49, 57, 60, 69, 70, 73, 86, 92, 128–29, 133, 136, 138, 142, 149–51, 160–61, 171, 196, 198
*Pins and Needles 1939* 22
Pinza, Ezio 103–05, 109
Pippin, Donald 108
play with music 106, 149, 155
playing cards **143**, 148
"Pocketful of Dreams" 73–75, 197
Pocono Mountains 12, 85
Pokrass, Dan 40
Pokrass, Dimitri 40
political 8, 10–11, 13–16, 20, 23–26, 34–41, 45, 47, 61, 67, 77, 82–84, 91, 110, 150–55, 160–61
popular culture 45
Porter, Cole 1, 7, 9, 12, 27, 43, 48, 55, 61, 64, 68, 98, 119, 139, 178, 191, 194
Portnoff, Mischa 79
Portnoff, Wesley 79
prejudice 7, 150–53, 155
Presnell, Harve 175, 182
*Pretty Penny* 73–74
Previn, André 163
Prince, Harold 193
Princess Theatre 16, 61

*Providence Island* 153
psychotherapy 115
Puccini, Giacomo 117
Pulitzer Prize 27, 69, 127, 129, 139

Quakers 54
Quatropani, Grace 18

racial discrimination 35, 63, 66, 150, 152, 155
radical theater 18
radio 6, 21
Raimu 100
Rainger, Ralph 7
Razaf, Andy 39
RCA-Victor 45
*Rear Window* 94–95
"The Red Ball Express" 66–67, 151
*Red Channels* 82–84, 110
Reeder, George 124
rehearsal pianist 14
Reiner, Carl 67
Reinhardt, Gottfried 54
"Respectability" 123
"Restless Heart" 107, 109, 197
Revel, Harry 163
revivals 19, 24, 116, 126, 133
revue 2, 8, 10–15, 18–19, 21, 24, 26–27, 30, 42, 44, 47–49, 57–69, 70–81, 85–86, 90, 91, 101, 149
right-wing 3, 82–84, 150
"Rinso White Song" 56
Ritchie, June 178–79
Rittman, Trude 166, 169, 182
Ritz Brothers 8
"Roaring 20's Strike Back" 76
Robbins, Jerome 12, 77, 193
Robbins, Sascha 147
Roberts, Loma 13
Roberts, Pernell 182–84
Robertson, Dale 69
Robin, Leo 194–95
Robinson, Earl 14, 32
Rodgers, Dorothy *190*–191
Rodgers, Richard 1, 2, 12, 27, 32, 36, 38, 42, 61, 67, 68, 71, 80–81, 95, 98–101, 108, 116–18, 123, 129, 139, *144*–45, 163, 172, 176, 178, 192, 194–95
Roger Sherman Theatre *6*
*Romanoff and Juliet* 157
Romberg, Sigmund 1, 2, 30
Rome, Florence 3, 21, 26, 114, 116, 140, 152, 159, 164–65, 169, 171–72, 177, 192
Rome, Joshua 3, 34, 115, 133, 149, 152, 177–178, 192–93
Rome, Louis 3
Rome, Milton 5
Rome, Rachel 177, 192
Rome, Ruth 5
Rome, Sidney 5
Ronell, Ann 1, 2, 48, 178

Roosevelt, Eleanor 23–24
Roosevelt, Franklin D. 10, *23*, 29, 39, 44, 65
Rose, Billy 18, 131
Ross, Herbert 106–07
Ross, Jerry 99, 192
Roth, Joseph 17
Roth, Lillian 131, *132*, 135, 140
Roundabout Theater 24
Royal, John 21
royalties 19, 48, 56, 75, 78–79, 120, 147
Rozsa, Miklos 95
Rubinstein, Ruth 14–15, 18, 21, *23*
"Run Up the Curtain" 47
Russell, Robert 158
Russia 5, 13, 39–41, 151, 193
Russian War Relief 41
Ryskind, Morrie 27–28

*Saints and Sinners* 96
Sandor, Gluck 18
"Sandwich for Two" 156
Sanka Coffee 56
Saroyan, William 52
Sartre, Jean-Paul 35
satire 2, 3, 8, 10, 11, 13, 15–16, 20–21, 24–31, 34–36, 38, 42, 47, 49, 63, 65, 76–77, 92, 97, 123, 146–47, 150, 157, 188, 189
*Scarlett* 3, 13, 162–173, *170*, 174, 176, 181, 184
*Scarlett Letters* 3, 165
Schaffer, Louis 9, 10–16, 17–25, 60
Schary, Dore 155
Scheintoub, Emanuel 18
Schillinger, Joseph 13
Schlissel, Jack 158
Schmidt, Fred 18
Schomburg Center for Research in Black Culture 152
Schrank, Joseph 15, 35–36
Schreier, Moe 18
Schuller, Gunther 143
Schwartz, Arthur 1, 7, 27, 57, 61, *113*
Schwartz, Stephen 96
Scott, Hazel 29, 35
Scott, Raymond 55–56
sea chanties 54
Seelen, Jerry 67
Selznick, David O. 162–63
Seventh Avenue 134, 136, 137
Seymour, Paul 18
Shaw, George Bernard 96–97
"She Rolled Up Her Sleeves—She Hitched Up Her Hose" 46
sheet music 29, 156, 180–81
Sherin, Edwin 95
Shock Troupe 18
Shore, Dinah 109
Short, Bobby 1, 67
Short, Hassard 42, 59
Shostakovich, Dmitri 40–41
showstoppers 21, 63, 64, 136, 169–71, 178

Shubert, J.J. 48, 59, 74
Shubert, Lee 32, 48, 59, 74
Shurtleff, Michael 158
Sides, Isaac 18
Sillman, Leon 59
Silver Medal award 66
Simon, Dick 128
Simon, Paul 190
*Sing for Your Supper* 24, 31–32
"Sing Me a Song with Social Significance" 17–21, 23, 60, 151, 171, 197
*Sing Out the News* 2, 26–31, 37, 48, 60, 95–96, 129, 150, 188, 192
singing 37–38, 188
sketch writer 8, 15, 25
*Skirts!* 52–53
Sklar, George 11
Sklar, Sidney 18
Skulnik, Menasha 153–55, *154*
Slezak, Walter 103–05
"Slippy Sloppy Shoes" 156
Smith, Oliver 70
social significance 2, 8, 9, 12, 25, 28, 36, 60, 70, 78, 91, 99, 101, 129, 136, 149–50
"Solid, Solid, Suzabelle" 46
Sondheim, Stephen 1, 95, 192, 194
song integration 90, 108, 110, 136
"The Song of Meeting" 40
"Song of Our Love" 55
"Song of the Red Army Tank Parade" 40
song patter 77–78
song plugger 2, 12
Songwriters' Hall of Fame (SHOF) 189–90
songwriting 5, 8, 48, 71, 85, 95, 140, 142, 151, 164, 190–91, 195, 197
Sorel, Felicia 22
Sothern, Georgia 43
"The Sound of Money" 134, 136
Sour, Robert 32
"Souse American Way" 33
South Africa 149–50
"South America, Take It Away" 47, 65, 92, 146, 171, 197
*The Southpaw* 158–59
Soviet Union 39–40, 82, 84
Special Services 44, 49, 52–53, 57–58
Spialek, Hans 29, 37
Spiegel, Mae 18
Spingold, Nate 127–28
Spivakovsky, Michael 155
*Spring Frolic* 34
Stage Door Canteen 44
*Stage Door Canteen: Broadway Responds to World War II* 187
Stalin, Joseph 20, 29, 35, 39
*Star and Garter* 42–44
star vehicle 48
Starbuck, James 105
*Stars and Gripes* 49–53
"Status Quo" 18

"Stay Out, Sammy!" 49, 151, 168
*Steel* 11
Stein, Joseph 96
Steiner, Max 95, 190
Stewart, James 94
Stewart, John *123*
Stoloff, Morris 114
*Stop, Look and Listen!* 142
Stothart, Herbert 95
"Strange and Wonderful" 140
"Strange Fruit" 35
Straus, Oscar 97
*Streets of Paris* 32
Streisand, Barbra 131–33, 139–41, 171
Strouse, Charles 55, 86, 96
Styne, Jule 1, 52, 178, 191, 194–95
subconscious 8, 115, 142
Sugarman, Dave 51
Sukman, Harry 114
Sullivan, Ed 84, 109–10
Sullivan, K.T. 1
summer camps 2, 85–87, 101
"Sunday in the Park" 18, 21, 23, 26, 36, 60, 197
"Surplus Blues" 65
Swenson, Swen 124
Swift, Kay 98
swimming pool 85, 88, 162
synergy 90–91
Syrjala, Sointu 18, 23

Tabbert, William 103–04, 109–10, 123
Takarada, Akira 169
"Take Off the Coat" 77–78, 197–98
*Talk of the Town* 109–10
Tamiris, Helen 83, 106
tardiness 45–46
Tau Epsilon Phi 7
Taylor-Dunn, Corliss 24
television 48, 69, 80–82, 84, 87, 110, 120, 117–18, 160, 184, 188
*Ten O'clock Scholar* 127
"That Ring on the Finger" 123
*That Was the Week That Was* 187
"That's My Pop" 46
*That's the Ticket* 75, 77–78, 151, 188, 197–98
Theater Guild 38, 89, 101, 158
Theater Hall of Fame 191
Theatre Arts Council (TAC) 34, 35
Theatre Committee to Aid Spanish Democracy 34
Theatre Union 11, 18
"There You Are Again" 55
"There's Nothing Nicer Than People" 90
"They Never Told Me" 55
"They Won't Know Me" 92
"This Is Our War" 49
*This Is the Army* 61
Thomas, Danny 69
throat wobble 167, 169

Tibbett, Lawrence 111
"A Time for Healing" 185
"A Time for Love" 177
Timothy, Tim 13
Tin Pan Alley 1, 2, 3, 6, 8–9, 12–13, 34, 44, 49, 60, 66, 86
*Tin Pan Alley Girl* 1, 3
Tkambuza" ("Zulu Hunting Song") 153
"To My Wife" 105, 109, 114, 140, 197
*Toast of the Town* 84
"Tobacco — The Redman's Revenge" 151, 187
Tobias, Charles 31, 61
"Today's the Day" 178–79
Todd, Michael 42–44, 74–75
Togawa, Mariko 169, **170**
Toho Company 163–67
Tomasini, George 94
"Tomorrow Is Another Day" 178–79
Tony awards 92, 124
topical 13, 21–24, 34, 36, 47, 52, 60, 65, 70, 80, 150
Toye, Wendy 53
Traube, Sheppard 52
Trinity College 6
Troy, Hector 32
trunk songs 78, 118
Twentieth Century–Fox 67
"Two of a Kind" 175

Uchinoe, Noboru 167
underrated 37, 187, 198
union members 14, 19–22
"United Nations on the March" 40–41, 151
United States Service Organization (USO) 44
Unity House 12
Uretsky, Beatty 18
Ustinov, Peter 157

Vale, Jerry 91
vaudeville 18, 32, 35, 42, 48, 58–60, 71, 76
Verdon, Gwen 73, 120–21
vernacular 87, 136
"Victory Symphony Eight to the Bar" 46, 187
*Viva O'Brien* 88
vocal coaching 7, 15, 169
Von Zell, Harry 69
"Voting Blues" 76

Wainer, Lee 32
Walker, Don 79
Wallace, Ian 112
Walsh, Mary Jane 29–30
*Waltz of Love* 189
War Bonds 44, 66
Warfield, William 67
Waring, Fred 110
Warner, Jack 113–15
Warren, Harry 1, 2, 48
Warren, Lesley Ann 184
Watts, Richard 9

Waxman, Franz 94–95
"The Way Things Are" 134
Wayburn, Ned 29
"We Sing America" 38
Webb, Chick 29
Weidman, Jerome 125–37, 140–41, 146, 192, 194
Weill, Kurt 1, 13, 15, 44, 98, 107, 192, 195
Weiss, Ed **173**
Weissberger, Arnold 55
Weitz, Millie 18, 19, 21, 133
"Welcome Home" 105, 109
Western 117–24, 126
"We've Just Begun" 19
Wexler, John 11
"What Are They Doing to Us Now? 132–33, 136, 151
"What Good Is Love?" 18
*What Makes Sammy Run?* 128–29
*What's in It for Me* 127
"When" 77
"When Gemini Meets Capricorn" 134
"When I Grow Up" ("The G-Man Song") 18, 21, 38, 92
"When It's Love" 55
"Where Did the Night Go?" 92
"Which Way Is Home?" 142, 179
"The Whip Dance" 121, 124–25
White, George 59
White House 23–24
"Who's Gonna Investigate the Man Who Investigates Me?" 38, 151
"Why Be Afraid to Dance?" 105, 138
Willson, Meredith 39, 190
Wilson, Julie 1
Wilson, Teddy 35, 41
Winchell, Walter 92
Winston, Bruce F. 140, 186, 195
Winters, Lawrence 63, **64**, 66–67
*Wish You Were Here* 2, 3, 8, 12, 48, 71, 85–93, **86**, 101, 106, 115–16, 123, 139, 160, 162, 166, 188, 193
"Wish You Were Here" 90, **91**, 101, 109, 197
Wittstein, Eddie 6
Wodehouse, P.G. 72
*The Wonderful Door* 160
work habits 118–19
Workers' Laboratory Theatre 11, 18
working class 19
Works Progress Administration (W.P.A.) 7
World War II 42–53
WPA Federal Theatre 31–32
WPA Theater Project 12
wrecking crew 88–89
writing words and music 14, 32, 39, 71, 102, 114, 118–19, 142, 168, 187, 190–91, 194–95, 198

Yale Collection of Historical Sound Recordings 98

Yale Collegians 7
Yale Law School 7
Yale Orchestra 7
Yale School of Architecture 7
Yale University 6, 7, 85, 98
Yale University Band *123*
"The Yanks Aren't Coming" 35, 49, 151, 168
Yellen, Jack 48
Yiddish 11, 137, 150, 152–53
"You After All These Years" 55
"You Never Know What Hits You" 77–78, 197
Youmans, Vincent 61, 117
*The Young Dem Bandwagon* 160–61

*Your Hit Parade* 21, 53, 65, 90, 92, 139
Youth Theatre 46

zayda 150, 153, *154*
Zemach, Benjamin 18
Ziegfeld, Billie Burke 48
Ziegfeld, Florenz 58–59, 74, 75
*Ziegfeld Follies* 18, 59, 74
*Ziegfeld Follies of 1943* 48–49
Zulu 150, 152–55, *154*
*The Zulu and the Zayda* 3, 149–155, *154*, 160
"Zulu Love Song" ("Wait for Me") 153

www.ingramcontent.com/pod-product-compliance
Lightning Source LLC
Chambersburg PA
CBHW051214300426
44116CB00006B/571